TO DWELL IN PEACE

TO DWELL IN PEACE

An Autobiography

DANIEL BERRIGAN

1817

HARPER & ROW, PUBLISHERS, SAN FRANCISCO

Cambridge, Hagerstown, New York, Philadelphia, Washington
London, Mexico City, São Paulo, Singapore, Sydney

Grateful acknowledgment is made for permission to reprint an excerpt from "No Immunity: One Artist's Nightmare Confronts Us All" by Douglas Fuchs from the April/May/June 1986 issue of *Craft International*, copyright © 1986 by *Craft International*.

Library of Congress Cataloging-in-Publication Data

Berrigan, Daniel.
  To dwell in peace.

Bibliography: p.
  Includes index.
  1. Berrigan, Daniel. 2. Catholics—United States—
Biography. I. Title.
BX4705.B3845A3 1987   282'.092'4   [B]   87-45164
ISBN 0-06-250057-0

88   89   90   91   RRD   10 9 8 7 6 5 4 3

IN LOVING MEMORY

Freda Berrigan
Thomas Berrigan

Vita Mutatur
Non Tollitur

Contents

Introduction   1

1. The Wolf and the Child   5

2. Moving East   21

3. The Father   40

4. The Workhouse   45

5. The Jesuits, for Life   79

6. Priesthood: Year One of My Life   116

7. Brothers in Exile   175

8. Cornell: Poison in the Ivy   186

9. Catonsville: The Fires of Pentecost   215

10. Unless the Seed Falls: Underground   241

11. Prison: Lights on in the House of the Dead   259

12. Harrisburg: Trial and Error   267

13. The Healer   272

14. Israel: Ground of Contention   280

15. Swords into Plowshares   290

16. The Foundering of Academe   294

17. AIDS: The Dream, the Awakening   308

18. Another Way: Toward Life   331

Epilogue   344

Introduction

On the wall of my elderly apartment on West 98th Street, there hangs a painting; the artist is a New York friend recently deceased. The work portrays St. Francis, his lengthened arm embracing a thoughtful, wary-eyed wolf. The figures are drawn in an eerie, thick carmine with heavy black outlines, the work of a sculptor bringing her skills to bear on canvas.

The wolf in the painting seems a nearly preternatural being. He appears to be pondering with considerable care a proposal offered by Francis. The beast is by no means convinced that a change of heart is in order. Nor does he especially welcome the embrace of this master of ecology. Francis, according to delicious legend, has sought out the beast, attempting to bring a halt to wolfish carnage against sheep and lambs, in field and forest.

So, all unexpectedly, because of a kind of foolhardy courage, a wolf and a saint have met.

Francis looks within, gathering strength for the contest of wills.

What indeed can he offer his adversary, except a naked glimpse of his own soul, and the consequence of that glance, not only to the wolf, but to himself? So he makes his proffer: no sermon; more like a bargain struck, a kind of Pascalian wager. "If you will consent to live in a new way, to make a new start, I will be your friend. Cease ravening, no one will dare hunt you down. I pledge to be your protector, the bondsman of a bargain. My bond being not only my word, but this arm which embraces you—an embrace which places me in your power."

The painting is an emblem; it strikes deep. Not merely because the dying artist crossed my path for a number of years, a light in the encompassing New York gloom. But also because in making a gift of the painting, which was the last of her store, she said a kind of farewell to this world and her own work. She also pressed the image against my life.

I ponder her work, not as art only, but as a dramatic image, urgently to the point, here and now.

Inwardness conquering the beasts. Not so much conquering them, but drawing them, their anger and fear and heartlessness, into the human circle, where affection, compassion, might prevail in spite of all. Might work miracles.

Deliberately, the eyes of the wolf are painted as human eyes. They are lit with a kind of last-ditch intelligence. They weigh their chances against this untoward interruption, this interloping human who dares cross a forbidden line, not with sword and lance, but with the more dreadful proffer of love.

The story, and its telling, cut deep. The story is by no means to be restricted, as the artist knew so well, to a charming encounter between a naïf and his opposite number, the stuff of folklore.

The wolf is wolfish. The tag, be it understood, is applied to him by wolfish humans. He is hunted, feared, hated. There is a price on his pelt; he is condemned to live bestially and die in blood.

Thus ironically, the artist places on the beast the burden of human likeness. The hunted has come to resemble the hunters. The worst news, once promulgated, is verified. The animal is among the earliest "most wanted," an untameable prey, a savage self-fulfilled prophecy; wolf eat wolf.

Nevertheless, Francis starts afresh; he seeks out the hunted one, befriends, protects, even as he reproves and exacts. The wolf is summoned to mend his ways; presumably, so are the humans.

I have no evidence that holiness conquers the wolves of the world. I see no magical outcomes today; evil crushes the lives of countless humans; there are few to intervene, let alone call a halt.

Still, there is hope. Goodness, holiness, inventive imagination, in the painting as in life, intervene. Sublimely indifferent to the counsel of the world (complicity, numbness), here and there a Francis places himself in the breach.

What happens then is in even better hands than those of Francis. It is the act that entrances, not the outcome. I am told that the wolf in the story underwent a change of heart. And this is edifying. But the pious conclusion seems to me a later accretion to the story, a rather flamboyant tail on a kite already flying.

Perhaps Francis prevailed. But the eye of my artist friend rested elsewhere. The heart of the matter was brute force and moral beauty in contention. No victory, no concentration on merit, virtue, ego, God on someone's side. The valor of Francis, the valor (though of another order, surely taken seriously) of the beast. The sublime trust, flickering in the winds of violence, trust as yet unverified, either in Francis or his painter; or indeed in the beast, who edges toward a bargain, warily, filled with somber thoughts concerning the betraying and sanguinary human pack.

Art is emblematic. Indeed, so-called sacred art, drawing upon the Gospel or hallowed legend, both borrows and passes on, a vision renewed. For myself, many years had to pass before I could approach the painting with a measure of understanding. Mine was a pilgrim's progress, through a landscape fiercely antihuman and depressingly allegorical. But the progress toward Francis and his friend could be summed up in a rather simpleminded statement: the pilgrim had to be taught to see.

It was not that he was blind in a literal sense or even in a symbolic sense useful to present reflection. He looked at the painting, and he saw what his life up to that moment allowed for: he saw something charming. But only later, something tragic. There was no overlay of pentimento on the canvas (it was not old enough), but there was a film on the viewer's eyes (he had not lived enough).

There came eventually a sense of the painting, as though a shaft of sunlight struck. Then he saw. He saw the human, transfigured. He saw someone who moved, seized, apprehended a moment; and so offered an ideal, albeit a modest one, for those in search.

Therefore he grew hopeful, in the midst of his own cross-purposes, meanderings, enticements, glances backward. He saw the wrongness of this, the waste. And he saw another waste as well: the waste implied in wrongly looking forward—for proof, vindication, success, the verdict of history (whatever that might be thought to mean).

Would the wolf devour one or would the wolf transmogrify into a very lamb? One did not know. More in the nature of truth, the nature of faith, one could not know. To hanker after knowing, to lust after foreknowledge, to clutch at past victories—this was the forbidden quest that brought not joy, but all our woe.

It came to something like this, as he learned; a kind of Buddhist truth. The good was to be done because it was good. For no other reason, however plausible or weighty. The good was not subject to efficiency or worthiness or benefit or merit, in meager or ample measure. These were lesser goods; indeed, once they displaced the good, won that ground, they were revealed as lesser evils.

So there was the rightness and attractiveness of this, a concentration on the heart of things, what one might call a hunger for the source. It seemed to me there was also a psychological point worth attending to. The health of the mind lay in dealing cards truthfully, with attentiveness, without cheating. Play the game according to the rules of the game, for love of the game. Win, lose, draw, the game is the thing.

So conducting oneself, one might be beckoned into the game of creation, the dance of creation, of the holy ones.

CHAPTER 1

The Wolf and the Child

My brothers and I stand like the fences
of abandoned farms, changed times,
too loosely webbed against
deicide, homicide.
A really powerful blow, a cataclysm
would bring us down like scarecrows.
Nature, knowing this, finding us mildly useful
indulging also
her backhanded love of freaks
allows us to stand.

The implication
both serious and comic;
wit, courage,
a cry in the loveless waste

something
than miracle
both more and less

I am no Francis, it goes without saying. But there were wolves aplenty in the world of my childhood. We heard them across the Minnesota lake on whose shore we eked out for a time our parlous existence, in a town named Winton.

Each autumn we banked the house with a perimeter of packed leaves, held in place with a two-foot plank barricade. Thus our home, and its occupants, might survive until the tardy, grudging spring.

Winter wore on, the wolves tried the ice of the lake, edged closer under the moon. They could be heard whining and baying; their menacing chorus mingled with the wakefulness of a child, bundled like a papoose against the night rigors.

There is more to tell of the saga, how the wolves arose in the mind of the boy, a baleful shadow. One day in bright winter sunlight, an older brother was urged to take the boy outdoors for a trudge in the snow. The child was bundled up and hefted to shoulder. Then it occurred to the older; the occasion might be improved by a touch of macabre humor.

The child was borne into the brilliant and blinding sunlight. And suddenly he was indoors again; this time into the stygian dark of a shed. And he felt against his blind face something furry, stiff, menacing.

The child screamed and screamed, in terror beyond words. In an act of misbegotten humor, his face had been thrust into the muzzle of a timber wolf. The corpse, stiffened and frozen, was hung by its rear legs from a rafter, its mouth and eyes wide open.

It was the child's first death head. His face was pushed into death, death swung at him its hundredweight. Death in midair, green eyes and stiff fur. Death the hunter and hunted.

It was not wonderful that in later years, death should be a theme of his poetry, a theme more constantly invoked than was fitting, in the opinion of some. But had his critics, he was led to reflect ruefully, met their death head at the timorous age of two years?

In time, the child would long to be a Francis in the world, as he came to know the world and its wolfish ways. He dreamed of following the hunter's trail, that he like Francis might seek out the killer, making of him his own peaceful prey. And so might undo, with the chancy power of love, death's scurvy tactic.

The child throve, in a manner of speaking, though he was thin as a post, and never brawny; "a poor feeder," one brother averred with country humor: "He eats like a starved horse, but where it goes is anyone's guess."

The family was poor, but poverty, whether in Minnesota or later in New York state, was a strictly relative term, and mitigated in many ways. There was pride, and life on the land, and food, homegrown and sensibly prepared. The clothing was imaginative: hand-me-downs for the younger fry; the older ones making do with gifts from adult relatives, cut and sewn more or less to size.

My mother was past mistress of the art of improvisation. If our Sunday lineup resembled that of the Victorian Cratchetts, an unmatched sock here and sleeves to spare, why, the result was artful and decent and clean, and she was content, if the children were not.

And my father. One had best begin here, a fretful topic, and to the present day by no means satisfactory.

He compounded in one life the ironies and contradictions that are said to compose the Irish character. There was something Dickensian about him, if it be understood that his rightful image can by no means be reduced to humbug or caricature.

Poverty, he was wont to declare histrionically, was his plain choice in life. But the choice was in the way of default of choice. He went from job to job and performed a variety of work honorably and well. But the years passed, and the jobs went nowhere. He was railroad engineer and fireman, "bached it" in the woods of northern Canada, worked in the Ford auto factory in Detroit, grew wheat in Saskatchewan. In later years he would labor for the electrical corporation in upstate New York, and farm a patch of land in the small way of a renter. All, or nearly all, to no avail; or to as little avail as, with the patient collusion of my mother, would be euphemistically referred to as a living.

In the Minnesota years and later, he was absent from the household for long periods, seeking work on the railroad. Sometimes he found it, sometimes not. Actually he was part of a vulnerable labor force, at the mercy of the economy. He was master of several skills, but none of them, in a time of "recession," was considered "marketable."

We were born into a nest woven of a skein of contradictions, contrived by his workman's hands. Of all his convoluted ways, perhaps this was most remarkable: his ability to live a life that was an enigma to those closest to him. This way and that he wove his life, and ours around him. His character would make of that life, by neglect and industry, by violence and tenderness, by virtuous word and singularly unvirtuous conduct, by yelling and weeping and pieties and cruelties and inexplicable uxorious moods, by anger and obscenity and embraces and tears—an extraordinary conglomerate of passion and illusion. A world he constructed despite all evidence of the real world.

And then the shovings about, the commands to walk that world of his!

I am convinced he was an enigma to himself. His soul, a lake of unpredictable storm, was a darkness before his own eyes. Confronted with the bleak sanity of my mother, he reacted in a fury: she was offensive, she walked another planet, of whose terrain he was utterly ignorant. Were other families making do or prospering or going under, raising children in ways at variance with his own? And might such families provide clues? He blazed up, furious, dangerous. It was a fury of incomprehension and pride.

Early on, we grew inured, as the price of survival, to violence as a norm of existence. I remember, as my eyes opened to the lives of neighbors, my astonishment at seeing that wives and husbands were not natural enemies. What a puzzlement, novelty, it was, that affection might be though to exist between spouses and parents. . . .

He was willful and innocent and self-centered; an incendiary without a cause. He knew nothing of the world and its ways; and he fancied he knew them through and through. Hence his and our vertiginous lives, teetering on the edge of America. His hands remained empty, even as his restlessness kept him on the move.

He kept at nothing. And then the desperate crash of '29 occurred, and he was reduced to a "welfare" job, at a slave's wage.

He ground his teeth and vented his anger on his family. Our slightest peccadillo, and all hell broke out.

But we are still in Minnesota, and I no more than a wintry midge, white on white, in the frozen landscape.

I am the fifth of six sons and was born on May 9, 1921. I see in the mind's eye our little house, of no distinction, put together cursorily of wood and tar paper; one of several we inhabited in those years on the Iron Range, as we trekked after my father in his migrations: Winton, Ely, Chisholm, Hibbing, Virginia. . . .

I sit blinking in sunlight on the back stoop of the house. The washtub of tin, the emblem of household stoop labor, hangs on the outer wall. Memory is a curtain raiser, I am being presented to the world. And to myself.

I feel much like saluting that little boy, or taking him in my arms. At age two, three, four, he is already a survivor. His malfunctioning feet stubbornly refuse to bear him about the world.

Four years old, and still not walking? My mother was heartbroken.

But her mother, Louise, who dwelt with us, by no means despaired. She was stout of soul, a German immigrant, a survivor of note. The child would walk, of course he would. She believed it; and she knew how to bring it to pass.

I must be outfitted in special shoes, high-button shoes, the ankles of which would be reinforced, like a ship's hull, with struts of whalebone.

The shoes were inordinately expensive, specially made. Where would the money come from? The women were undaunted; and the shoes, by my grandmother's gift, were procured.

Moreover, children of the northern rigors required supplements to their diet, given the meager sunlight and interminable winters. They must have infusions of cod liver oil.

Exposed to the sunlight and warmth of summer, even those faulty ankles of mine were strengthened. My grandmother carried me, day after day, to a place in the yard where the sun briefly flourished; there she massaged my feet for an hour or more.

And I began to walk. I would hobble about at first, like a landlubber on a ship's deck, decked out as I was in my diminutive sailor suit and cap. . . .

My grandmother Fromhart! Everyone's childhood should be favored with so wonderful a presence. Born in the Black Forest of southern Germany, she had made the punishing sea passage to America, then undertaken the daunting land journey, New York to Minnesota.

My mother, a child of five years at their arrival in the New World, was the only one of the children born in Germany. Ten children were born in that bleak northern frontier, under conditions that can only be imagined today.

At some point, my grandmother was deserted by her husband, for reasons never revealed. We of the following generation never encountered him, or any sense of who he was. There was, as far as I know, no photo of him extant.

My grandmother coped through hardship, poverty, the death of two children. Through a government grant, she came into possession of some forty acres of land. She and her sons erected a log cabin adjacent to a stream; and it was there that my mother and brothers and I passed some portion of the summer.

Each autumn we would go blueberrying in the surrounding forest. We were thus occupied one sunny day, the rich berries thumping in our tin pails. And there came to our ears a low threshing of the underbrush, as of a giant presence nearing. Presently, some yards ahead, appeared a great languid black bear, pompously rolling along. She took no more note of us than of the flora of the place. She swayed along, a disgruntled nose and a bag of flab, followed by two roly-poly diminutives. The trio were, like ourselves, on the track of the succulent berries.

My mother was unmoved. She murmured to us, "Don't disturb them, they won't harm us." The bear and cubs lumbered on their way like harmless interlopers in a children's tale. And we on ours.

We were six offspring, all, unaccountably, male. My mother was heard to murmur now and then her gratitude that no girl had been born. "It would have been too much for her" was her laconic footnote. That "it" embraced our gypsy existence, the rigors and poverty and, most of all (though she pointed no finger), himself, the father.

Thomas was the eldest child, blonde and blue-eyed, straight as a reed in speech and conduct. He departed our circle, too young by far, to work as a farm laborer; to break his back, dawn to dark, at some awful croft or other. In thankless winters and torrid summers, a "hired man"—and this before he was an adult at all.

He would return home for the holidays, spruce, handsome, overworked, thin and wiry and uncomplaining. A great raconteur, a lover of land and animals, an inveterate reader, a mind both fine and wide-ranging. I look on him as one of the true originals; one of the fast-disappearing species of those who put hand to a task, almost any task, and perform it with brilliance and dispatch. And never wear out or burn out or give up; whether in the work of the mind or the hands.

Snatched from schooling, tossed into a world of scant return and labors lost, where lesser minds were swamped, he lost nothing of his mind's edge, to this day.

Work was second nature to him, as to my father. He went off to war as a medical aide, and in England met the first love of his life. And married her, Honor Pape, a wondrous, cheerful, self-sufficient woman. (She would have to be all of that, my mother commented; he was a Berrigan and she must survive.)

The couple returned to northern Minnesota after the war and produced a nest of children. Honor eventually died, he remarried happily, his good luck not deserting him. And presently, the couple muster their courage to see him through a crippling stroke, which befell him in 1985.

We younger fry adored him; in our brash years, he handed out dimes and affection into young hands, a very windfall. The adoration continues.

John came next. From the start he was the shy, reserved one. Dark-eyed, slow to speak, he became the target of my father's unaccountable fits of anger and derision. The first son had been all affection and spontaneity, the halo of his hair shone like a morning sun. But what was Dado to make of this second arrival, this dark, brooding changeling? Even as a child, he bore a leveling look, and veiled his intelligence. He regarded the world and its phenomena from the stronghold of silence, the power of summing up; a quick casting aside, a slow embrace. If touched awry or clumsily (my father was clumsy in gesture, even gesture kindly meant), the boy shrank back into himself like a sensitive plant. He refused all proffers but the genuine and gentle. In such refusal, know it or not, he sought others in his own lovely image. The others might go their own way; but not his.

Besides, he was frail; in Superman's frosty eye, a mark against him. Early on, he showed disturbing symptoms of what was to be a lifelong affliction: a terrible, wracking asthma.

Illness, physical incapacity of any kind, always brought my mother swifly on the scene and kept her there. With my father, it was exactly opposite. He wanted nothing short of perfection. It was as though in his mind's eye the world and the upper air should be populated only with Michelangelesque demigods, workhorses and their works, fit for a Greek frieze.

Alas, John did not qualify. Besides, he disapproved of my father's "goings on," and dared, from his youth, to say so; at times with scorching and shouts; and even more devastatingly, with silence.

Thus the stage was set for a rural tragedy, a lifelong friction. A no win.

I saw something more; in John I saw myself. A character too fine or weak; or simply ill-attuned to the sawing and whine of that great seething Instrument and his dance. John first, I later, refused to join the dance; or we tried to join, and fell out of step. And after that, we could not, or would not, so much as hum along.

This was not well received, and marked John (and later myself) for trouble.

James; and what to say of him? A bonny, chubby boy with an

infectious grin. He seemed a perfect country type. One could easily miss in his apple-cheeked, cheerful ease the fine mind that was developing, the skills that lay latent.

Considering the brute fact of survival (and we were well advised to take it in account), Jim had much going for him. He was, first of all, a brown-haired version of Thomas; a winner, and apt to win all comers. He restored the beat of the dance, where John had become only a shadowy presence, a silent onlooker. Jim could work alongside the Master of Fate, quick and flowing as quicksilver. He learned carpentry and plumbing and crops and the mysteries of electrical engineering; some from the Master, some on the job.

In the worst days of the Depression, when fingers scraped on the bottom of the family coffer, Jim signed up for the Civilian Conservation Corps and departed for the northern woods; and through him our fortunes grew less dire.

He married an Irish beauty, they produced four astonishing comets that still ricochet about our heavens. Jim and family would wander the Earth, electrifying in several senses, dark corners of the globe. He has kept his great heart and sweetness intact; I venture because he was forced to absorb less of the scorched lightning charges emanating from our Jupiter.

Then Jerome, together with Philip and myself, forming the troika of the youngers. There will be occasion later to speak in detail of this friend and kindred spirit. He was another of the unpredictables; a beautiful flaxen child, one of those who enter the world trailing a pure light. Easy to get on with, easy to love. And as he grew, a very demon for work, the father's skills renewed, a mind to reckon with, a short fuse, an adversary such as to scatter and confound the wreckers.

He grew, and the light grew round him. Spiffy, a very lion among cubs, a ladies' man. He would dance to his own tune; and let that Caller of Tunes be—not exactly damned, but just as certainly forewarned.

Jerry also went off to the war. And then to seminary; and thence out again. And into a marriage that is his joy, and beyond our deserving. But more of this later.

And of Philip, the youngest, much will be said later.

We played in winter a game known as Fox and Geese. It required our pacing off a great circle in untrodden snow, then treading the circle, cutting radii. One brother would stand at center, the fox. He had to risk a run to the circumference and tag one or another of the geese standing in place. The geese acted in concert, each standing at a segment; all had to move rapidly and as one, toward a new juncture, to avoid capture.

So we ran and yelled and argued and fell laughing, were captured or escaped. But in any case, raced about more or less in unison, center to periphery, or around the rim of that gelid world.

I see the game now; and more than the game. It becomes a kind of image of our lives. Foxy we are at times; and at others more goose than fox. We must take our turn, and did for years, standing now at center, now at periphery of events. And taking our chances on one another, at times against one another. Mocking and enjoying and in rant and conflict, racing about the world in all seasons (but perhaps mostly in the winter of the world, our lifetime's fierce weathers). And falling and impeding; and then pulling the other upright after a fall. And keeping a weather eye out for the next move. And arguing the rules of the game. And colliding angrily; and mostly, laughing it off.

All the years, all the winters! That mutuality and wit, those gifts and lacks, the distancing—and then, and always at the end, the fact deep as existence—the charge laid on us, the *bruderhof*. And our breaths wreathing about and marrying in the frosty air.

My grandmother lived with us, intermittently, for years. She and my mother had devised a kind of conspiracy of survival. Busy about some task, they would converse for hours together, always in German, a language that served them, to all intents, as both comfort and cover.

Against whom? Against almost everything that, in such times and locales, made up the lives of women. Against my father; against myself and my brothers and the weather and the killing labor and the loneliness and the routine. And most of all, against the sense one read in their eyes of entrapment.

My heart aches in the telling. My mother and her mother, beside bearing large families, washed and ironed clothing by hand, with water drawn from wells or springs or, when we were at the cabin, from a stream nearby. The water was heated over fires that had to be built and stoked. And because often as not, the clothing of the men had grit and filth ground into the fabric by their hard labor, clothing had to be boiled in a copper cauldron, for hours.

Washed by hand, wrung by hand, rinsed, hung out to dry, sometimes in cold or storm. Then gathered in, sometimes half dried; then sorted, ironed. So went the cycle.

As though that were all! But there were meals to be prepared, dishes washed, bread baked, floors scrubbed, shopping, mending, children to be cared for and cosseted and counseled. Too few hours to the day, too little sleep, too frequent illnesses.

And little prospect, except for more of the same. These were frontier women, and the frontiers were drawn, as though by the blade of a knife, through their bodies. They were inarticulate in the world, and proud; and though they had stories to tell—and what stories!—for the most part, they had only one another to tell them to.

The men meantime trumpeted their stories to the four winds. And the world listened, fascinated, and, often as not, fooled. The male stories of frontier days became part of the diffused, absurd, violent folklore of America. Warring males, bigger than life, overcame, championed virtue, defended "their" women, subdued brute creation, walked tall, drank deep, shot from the hip. A law unto themselves, and let none provoke them; whether savages, buffalo, the terrain, weather, horses, cattle, children, or women.

Thus the men became supermen: ineluctable heroes of films, plays, poetry, frontier novels and diaries and travel accounts.

But most of the women were speechless; they may as well have been born without tongues. They were faceless images of strength and silence. They seemed designed by an implacable nature only to fit and befit their men. They were the clothiers and servants of males, the producers of males (if they were blessed among women), bedwarmers and cooks and washerwomen and cleaners. They melded with the furniture and henyard and stable and pasture and kitchen garden; possessions, so much a head.

I look for a clue, both of my mother's fate (as enacted by her mother also) and the unassailable dignity and self-possession of both. What sustained them? I see my grandmother trudging ahead of her daughters, along a path of life that seemed at the time absolute, frozen. A matter of fate; worse even, a matter of faith.

Which is to say, the men had a loud trumpet. The church said what the men said. No wonder, it was a church of men; the clerics and husbands were as one. The one spoke God's will, as from Olympus or Sinai; the other exacted that will, jot and tittle. What an arrangement it was, how admirably simple; could not the simplest of women understand? "Women, obey your husbands. . . ." The church spoke loud, the husbands commanded their wives.

Loudly, learnedly, a divine drumbeat in the ear. Obey. It was the price exacted from the powerless for privileges of bed, board, stability. Obedience was a church matter, it was merit and sacrifice and the guerdon of a better life; something grandly referred to, with a quelling dominical look, as eternal life or the hereafter.

Thus did the finely attuned gears mesh, of church and culture. If my mother were to renege on her "duties," if she were to doubt that wisdom and truth lay like an ambrosia on the lips of her husband—why in such dire case, she was resisting not him alone, an individual, an equal, whose opinions and judgments must confront her own. No such thing. My father had at disposal a phalanx of priests, confessors, moralists, pastors—and further off, in mists of power and might, bishops, popes.

Males all. To shore up and verify and bless his version of the world, of marriage and family, of obligation and default.

The macho culture and the acculturated church; he was indeed in good hands.

Did my mother rebel? The answer all depends.

Were she to walk out of the marriage (as very few Catholic women did), the practical question arose, Where was the rebel to land? The question was unanswerable, complicated by the lives of young children, rendered grievous by economic plight.

And yet, and yet. My mother rebelled. She rebelled in her own sweet way and place and time. Not a leap into the void, but calculated, the results and risks weighed to a farthing.

It was a slave rebellion. She created, within the strait limits set by husband and church (she, being a believer, clung to both), a kind of slave culture; within it she breathed free; to its secret place she, on occasion, escaped.

She was neither eloquent nor educated in any conventional sense. She spoke seldom of herself; life had wrung her of the power of confiding her feelings or griefs. (Except to a few, except later.)

To our great loss, she kept no diary of her life, though a few women of her generation did, like the shipwrecked who thrust notes in bottles and cast them to the tides.

I have an image of her; it consoles and restores me. She is a heliotrope, facing the sun, turning with the sun. She spurns all lesser lights, with a discerning, proud, almost cellular skill. Her sun, her planet, is compounded of mighty sources and resources, a furnace, the heart of things—her children, her faith in God, the few friends admitted to her confidence. And her husband, of course; but in small degree of heat and light. He is a lesser fuel in the conflagration, in which she turns and burns like a Van Gogh flower.

The image is useful, to a point. I mention it, having so little to guide me, as I ponder the ways and means and subtle interstices of that world she created, within the unpromising shell of her life.

A matter of evenings after the day's toil and storms, of solitude snatched from labor, of Sunday worship and daily prayer, of songs hummed to herself or the children in her sweet, true voice, of the occasional (grudged) relief of a film, of her years of friendship (and conflict) with her mother. She loved music and the opera and, in better days, had attended concerts and stage shows, and was familiar with the names of divas and stars. But time dimmed the glory, it vanished into the pit of our family's penury and the indifference of my father.

Still she was unvictimized, either by childish nostalgia or bitterness. She accepted her life, not as fate, but as vocation. So her children and friends could take soundings from her, a woman to be counted on, a figure of nonbetrayal.

Early in her marriage, as I learned later, something untoward and terrifying occurred. It was like a wrecker in a house; it pulled down her hope. This is a painful thing to hear at second or third hand, to have in large part to speculate about. Something occurred, both of terror and reappraisal, after the birth of her first child.

The following might offer a clue. She was occupied one day in the kitchen, ironing a favorite gown; her poor best. My father was also in the house. By mishap, the fabric ripped under her hands. And he, noting it, burst into a guffaw; and she dissolved in tears.

Could ill come of so small an episode? But it was one among many that followed.

I think that at that time, she underwent a kind of second birth, an event matching the birth of her son. She reached the end of romantic love. Her childhood was ended. She became a woman, she was someone whom fate had laid a heavy hand on; someone vowed to fight against her fate. This is how I remember her; someone caught, someone fighting capture.

There is nothing of the slavey or drudge in her youthful photos. (Nor in any photo after, including those of her old age.) Before marriage, the gowns are almost excessively beautiful—and so is she.

But she was no conventional beauty, at least for long. There was that sea change. What I cherish most of all, a quality that stayed and stayed, is the level look she casts on life. In the photos her eyes glance never quite straight ahead, but a little to one side; as though weighing things, then weighing them again. Not calculating loss and gain, merely weighing her chances against that world.

Self-possession, I think; not pride, but taking the measure of things, this way and that, strengths and weaknesses, herself and others; when to make a move, when to hold firm.

A dance named life. She had been, we were told, an extraordinary dancer in her youth.

It was a spartan regimen in that home of ours, that miniscule Department of Health, Education, and Welfare.

My father was wonderfully indifferent to events that did not inhibit his well-being or encroach on his routine. Let misfortune or malfunction or illness strike; I might have made my sorry way, on all fours, as a lifetime cripple, for all my plight touched him.

I see him, the original Olympian, treading his own path, a way cleared by his labor, for his benefit. Others, including the family, might walk along in his wake; but the trek would be at his speed, in his direction. What lay to right hand or left, what seemed worthy of attention, pause, succor—this was of no moment. He strode on. The devil take the hindmost.

Strangely enough, for all the magnetism, the ferment he created, the ruin and chagrin, like the spin of a descending cyclone—for all that, I think of him as stalemated, powerless. More was less. Call it incapacity, disinterest, acedia, he never grasped the uses of power humanely exercised. His soul never grew its proper tegument. Persuasion was beyond him, tenderness, a cherishing of the helpless or young—except for momentary spasms that succeeded only in baffling and undermining.

He substituted force for true authority. I think of it with dismay; he could so easily have won our hearts, our respect and devotion!

He was alarmingly free and easy with money, to my mother's anger, charged as she was with keeping the enterprise solvent.

He loved to be known for largesse, a man of the world, superior to the pennypinching of the locals.

It was all a game, and a cruel one. The fact was that whether in Minnesota or on the clay farm near Syracuse, our finances were precarious.

Still, his selfishness was wonderfully innocent. It went without question that a grandiose wave of the hand would produce, out of thin air, an adequate meal. So also with the heating of the house, payment of bills, cleaning and laundry, repair of clothing—all magically easy. Jupiter had spoken.

He was by no means unique for those days. He was a male. Therefore cozened, paid tribute to, kept silent before, venerated as to opinion or whim.

Thus the game he lost in the world, he won with us. We, not his peers, were the pawns in his game of power and dominion. The public failure, the humiliating disregard of his mental prowess and personal charm, his good looks and bombast, his keen mind and forensic tongue, his withering ridicule and braying laughter (invariably in someone's despite); the deep-seated Irish envy (others of lesser gifts made it, he did not); the shame of it all mounted in his guts like a lake of bile. It overflowed; on us.

I linger, perhaps inordinately, over such painful matters; they are of moment to the fate of at least one of his sons.

Power, rightly, sanely used—this was an enigma to my father. Those gray-green hawk's eyes took his measure against the world, weighed lack and loss. This is how I judge the matter; at some time, before I appeared on the scene, he simply let the reins drop. From then on, his public role, his vaulting ambition, were reduced to humiliating stoop labor. And always, of course, despite public rejection, the tribute, obedience, humiliation he could exact from his wife and family.

Did he fail as drover of wild horses? Had the chargers broken loose? He would fasten the reins and blinkers on us, drive us hard.

But for my mother's opposition, now fierce, now simply a wordless balking, he would have broken our spirits, in somewhat the way his had been broken.

He was a failure in the eyes of others; and inevitably, in his own. He would never write the Irishman's version of the American dream. Farmer, plumber, electrician, railroad engineer, woodworker, romantic poet, mimic—was there ever such a jack of all trades?

But the skills lacked soul, compassion, consistency. He was helpless before larger issues—authority, moral choice, responsibility, the making of decisions that would require discernment and moral courage. He sought to compensate, to fill the void with his uncontrolled emotion, mood, perfervid imagination. It worked for no one under his roof.

So in a mechanical and merciless time, whose symbol was the indomitable chugger known as the Ford Model T, he careened about and went nowhere—as America would define and direct and chart life's achievement. No movement upward, no financial security, no goods and services unlimited.

His sons also, be it noted, went precisely nowhere as the world would judge. Not one of us has made a name for himself, or amassed money, or won pride of place. I am not aware, moreover, that any of us desired such things. We are, in this as in many other matters, strangely cut to his bias.

To speak more nearly of myself—so father, like son. As the world and its ways were enigmatic to him, so they remain (perhaps for different reasons) to me.

I was to enter the Jesuits in late adolescence. Rumor has it that the sway of power and authority and the credit of a great name are closely identified with the ethos of the order. Alas, I confess after nearly half a century, that world too is utterly closed to me. Not only closed—a matter of indifference. There are, after all, ways and ways of being a Jesuit. There are mansions and shanties, and their occupants. There are mandarins and day laborers, bureaucrats and mystics. Somewhere in this mythic mix, there was a place of sorts for the likes of me.

I admit such matters, and I taste no sour grapes on my tongue. Nor have I ever sensed bitterness among my brothers. Our talents, as well as our moral and intellectual limits, simply have moved us in other directions. As shall appear afterward.

The person under scrutiny is still a little boy.

In Minnesota we were surrounded by Finns, Norwegians, and Swedes. No Irish, my father lamented. (Few, if any, Germans, it must be added; but their lack, if my mother felt it, went unmentioned.) The offspring of the Finns were unwarrantedly fierce, and a source of considerable travail. I remember small, blue-eyed demons, with touseled blonde pelts, invariably roving in packs.

Grinning or snarling, they were uniformly lacking in front teeth. (The cause of this was laid to their addictive love of coffee, a semisolid brew boiling away at all hours on the stoves, the solace of winter days and nights. The coffee was taken boiling hot, seived through a chunk of sugar clenched in the teeth. Hence the early decay of the sprites' ivories.)

But whether this lethal sludge also served to fuel their bellicosity, I am at loss to say. It remains that there were frequent incursions against our clan. And my inability to advance or retreat with celerity made me peculiarly useless to the defending forces.

As far as domestic history went, we could hardly be classed as ethnicly isolated. Both in Minnesota and in our later move to the East, there hung prominently on our wall (and presently hangs on my wall) a sepia photo of a venerable Slovenian priest. Monsignor Joseph Buh officiated at the wedding of my parents in Ely; at the time he was a renowned missioner among the Chippewa Indians and Slovak immigrants of northern Minnesota. An aura of holiness and sacrifice surrounds his memory. He lived to a grand age, dwelt in bark shelters like the Indians did, spoke their tongue, partook of their diet.

I have often reflected on the blessing thus conferred on our generation, long before a tumultuous century enveloped us. My father revered the priest (no great or unique tribute, because he clung to all and any clerics without distinction). But my mother loved Monsignor Buh; another matter, and a credential of note.

CHAPTER 2

Moving East

Who told me I was entering
the kingdom of very sorrow? who said it?

Who chose the way, chose me?
Blank eventuality
makes nothing of it. Pursue the shadow!
wall to corner, blind men collide.

Yet somewhere
a bone reverberant
bangs. Raises the dead.

In the third month, mother earth
whispered; heart
beats. death
henceforth
never

Our lot in Minnesota was cast among the nations. There lurked in my father's breast a hankering after the "blue remembered hills" of the East. More exactly, he was homesick for the Tipperary Irish, a prosperous farm clan outside Syracuse, and for the Berrigan clan, his mother, sisters, and brothers.

Thus in 1927, he proposed a move. Reversing the national tide westward (he was a great one for going counterwise), we would remove our meager chattels and persons, fleeing inclement weathers and uncertain fortunes and (chief gripe) the non-Irish populace of the Iron Range. And repair east, where, to his romantic inner eye, Irish beatitude flourished.

I was, of course, too young to gauge my mother's feelings. A considerable uprooting was being asked of her, across a third of the continent, to settle among comparative strangers. As a German immigrant, she could have had small hopes of a warm reception from the clan.

How would she be received? She had visited her husband's family some years before, when the two oldest children were infants. Photos are extant; she sits among them like a stranger. I had the impression that the visit was an unhappy one, that she felt, if not ill-used, at least unwanted.

Accompanied by the older boys, my father traveled east, purportedly to seek out lodging and work, and take the lay of the land. Toward autumn, Philip and I accompanied my mother by railroad. We stopped for a visit with my grandmother Fromhart in Detroit, arriving in Syracuse in September.

My memories of the hegira are dim, I presume because the trip was uneventful. My grandmother's flat was hardly adequate for three additional birds of passage. One day, as I accompanied my mother to the neighborhood grocer, she remarked sadly that we were "wearing out our welcome," and would cut short our stay.

She was soon to taste that bitter status in plenary degree, and for years.

I can summon no clear image of the little boy who arrives to take his place on a far different stage.

I find him pleasing and puzzling at once, an errant leaf floating with the current. He is intrigued with his new home, which is in process of refurbishment by painters and plasterers, as to minimal shelter—walls, windows, and roof.

The leaf pauses here and there. The boy ventures out, exploring the acres around his home. He is intrigued by the vast red barn at the foot of the yard. He climbs about on his spindly legs into the hay mow, agleam with dusty shafts of autumn light.

In the house, he climbs to the mysterious attic, and holds his breath in a crepuscular light. The attic is unfinished, and through some hidden aperture, the birds and bats of the air find entrance. There lies a musty dead sense on the air of something expired and gone to dust. And wonderful in the exact middle of the enormous loft, another stairway rises. It leads upward in the gloom to a four-sided airy space, a cupola.

He climbs and stands there; magical! It is as though he stood within a great insect eye. He sees in all directions: Lake Onondaga below; the farther shore, Solvay; swamp and pasture; all in their autumn beauty.

The boy lingers. Over the years, his glance will fall on large portions of the world's beauty and horror. But for the childish present, those eyes of his are orbs of pure spectation. They are not seats of judgment, but of absorption; they are seeing sponges.

Still, however circumscribed and parochial their present world, they will, in the strange course of the years, cease at some point merely to look. The eyes will come to their mature task of judgment, conclusion, responsibility.

Was the boy happy? I think that in his unquestioning way, which his older brothers found both naive and winning, he was. With those sad, unspoken reservations, which no adult can finally make sense of, even as the adults create and heap them up, and lob them carelessly at the young: incomprehension, strait discipline, internecine conflict.

He hears bitter conflicts raging; their lightnings fall on him. Does no one take him in account? Worse, does no one think him capable of sorrow, fear, stalemate, at sight of adult ways that chill the blood?

Slowly, by hook and crook, gift and borrowing, the family assembles a ménage. Furniture, barrels of dishes arrive in stages from Minnesota to the house on the hill. They prove embarrassingly meager for the big, yawning cave of a house, and are austerely augmented by contributions from my aunts. A bed here, a dresser, a chest of drawers. So we make do.

Some fifty years later, I move in my mind through that house. I see the shape of each room, the placing of windows and doors, the colors and furnishings. Is this a mere trick of nostalgia? It proceeds in any case, from no romantic or thoughtless love. Along with my mother and brothers, I grow in time to hate the house; its creaking discomfort, its spiritless, immense rooms. And then, with more time, I come to love it, or at least am reconciled to it, as a captive long inured to his keep.

The worst times of all are synonymous with my mother's absence. The taste of those hours lies like aloes on the tongue. Child or adolescent, it makes little difference; deprived of her, the house is an empty vessel, a tomb.

For one-half day each week, she sought relief from her indentured servanthood by venturing into town and joining a circle of women, a sewing group who made and repaired clothing for orphans. One or another of us was delegated to keep the house and to serve the evening meal, prepared beforehand.

I braced myself for a bad time of it, in that creaking dwelling of ghosts. Alone, alone. The sounds, the very atmosphere of the place underwent a change that brought the heart to one's throat. Brought also dread of the father's return from the day's work, his face unsoftened and his temper unmediated.

Empty, empty. To say the word is not the half of it. A pure and painful absence, as of health in illness, life in death. The hours were tedious, they stretched before me, a daunting boredom.

He comes in toward evening; he is out of sorts because my mother is "away again." It is not that he rejoices in her presence; he is irked that she has found a respite, she has flown the coop.

Present or absent, she offers occasion for complaint. Something that should have been done (always relative to his own comfort) he finds left undone; something that was done in the same department was badly done. It is all the same, harping and carping. . . .

To every house, there is appointed an antihouse; a gnostic or platonic view, no doubt; and having to do with more than architecture or taste. Something about light and darkness, and their wrestling, and who might be thought to prevail.

There stood, some seven miles to the south of us, not as the crow flew, but as a trolley car meandered, the house of my uncles and aunts, once the dwelling of my grandmother Berrigan. This was our antihouse, the focus of my father's continental trek.

Here my father repaired, from the time of our arrival, and week after week, and year after year thereafter, in a strange, dominical pilgrimage.

Did he not already make his home with us? And if so, why this determined lifelong devotion to the clan? Were there not words in the marriage service to the effect that he was to "abandon father and mother" and all else?

It was something we never understood—or perhaps came to understand too well. As in many tardy Irish marriages (he was thirty-four at the time of the event), my father's loyalties were divided from the start; between the new, largely unassimilated burdens and obligations (children and spouse invariably took this stony form in his mind)—and the old safe nest, warmed and watched by vigilant females, otherwise unattached.

Thus the antihouse exerted for a lifetime, and in spite of the marital bond, a strong umbilical pull. A twitch brought the boyo running "homeward." "Home" being the nest never in truth flown from, the siren call of Tipperary and Galway Bay and Danny Boy and Father Ned the priest and Our Holy Father the Pope, all that fond hokum that serves to brim the Irish eyes while smiling.

And could he weep and weep! The merest gesture or word of Holy Mother Church, of his mothering sisters, of Father Ned or Sister Josephine, those family emblems of assured salvation—how these would set the kerchief to nose!

The world, its sharp angles, the ingratitude and irreverence of "the gang" (the term unfondly conferred on us six), the unsatisfactory, refractory wife, the decline and fall of practically everything public or political—so the dirge went on, this strange local variation of Sunday rest.

His eyes ran like the river Lee in flood. Now and again, was the bad state of things relieved? The tears flowed none the less. Ireland, church, clan, catechism, nuns, priests, along with Victorian poetry and Shakespearean effusions—there existed a universal solvent, an aqueous cosmology: all is water.

So Sundays came and went, the day of the holy flowing in the vale of tears. They wept together, "cups and cups," as one of the sisters reverently described their dampening sessions.

But this by no means exhausted their occupations, in those Sunday sittings. From inklings and hints that he let drop for our confounding, my father made mention of other items on the agenda. A critique there was: one by one, the males were held to accounting; the priest of his ministry; bachelor John of his alcoholic fallings from grace; my father of his work, his marriage, the family ups and downs, including the peccadilloes of my mother, the backslidings of the progeny, all of it.

Their attitude toward my mother was hardly ambiguous. She was the outsider, pure and simple. Alas, it was hardly her fault, but she had not been born Irish. She might think to recoup the fault by years of travail, poverty, the hauling of water and hewing of wood— to no avail. She carried her loss like a stigma.

A scene sticks in the boy's mind. We are assembled, the clan whole and entire, first and second class, for one of the periodic "celebrations" of the year. The occasion commanded smiles, geniality, unity, religiosity. We were to forget on such occasions my mother's year-long exclusion from the weekly examinations of conscience. Here she sits, is not all well?

I summon up the scene. It is the New Year, "the gang" are rounded up and transported to the mansion, on our best and falsest behavior.

We sit about in discomfort in the comfortless parlor. The rectangular space, malevolently gleaming with wax, is rendered more angular still by the quadrant of uneasy guests, in-laws and cousins, uncles and aunts, facing each other in the highly geometric sense of the term. The wintriness of the scene is remarkable.

Corners and shadows, shadows and corners. The four corners of that room, the angular faces and lives of the dwellers, their four square rectitude. Such a contradiction and denial and distaste for round faces, round suns and moons, song and ribaldry and the bounciness of the young!

It was the New Year, no bells sounded, no wine of life was uncorked and passed. They saw in the gift of time, the turning of the year, only a summons to endurance and merit and the working out of sinfulness. It was a house of the dour and the doers of good, of damp celibates and bachelor souls. My father put off his marriage like an impeding greatcoat at the door. He entered the ancestral tomb wrapped in his wintry spirit, chaste and angular as the dead— or the living.

The New Year is, so to speak, the other side of the other side of life in this house; the presence of the habitually absent, the excluded. And among these latter, my mother.

The boy remembers. How his mother endured hour after hour, as we waited out the hiatus between lunch and dinner, chatting desultorily.

To say that the young fry counted for little says nothing of the atmosphere. We were, after all, part of the decor of the occasion. But to say that my mother was ignored and passed over, and yet remained tranquil and self-possessed: this is something nearly unbearable. The conversation went on—politics, church, family, current events, economics. It would pass muster for fairly intelligent talk, lacking surely in ease and frivolity; sonorous, dead serious, self-consciously Catholic. And it all passed my mother by, utterly and deliberately.

She might have been a chance debris along the banks of their stream, something carried along, lodged for a time by an impediment, unable of its own momentum to flow onward. She sat there, in her scarce finery, head erect. No pride of place, no tension or anger. Conquest by grace.

She rode them out. Hers was the revenge possible only to a clear-sighted compassion. Her loneliness, the isolation they laid on her—she saw them clearly, took their measure, even as she took her own. And what she saw served only to steady her.

I see the faces of my aunts. One, Elizabeth, is a bird of passage, home from Washington for the holiday. She is secretary to someone in the maze of the Congress. She wears a pince-nez on her distinguished beak, is fashionably thin under her nest of plumage. She seems, in a tony, cosmopolitan way, the least unbearable of the quintet; possibly because she is seldom at home.

Elizabeth died suddenly in 1936 of a stroke. My mother, unwelcomed among the living, was invariably summoned on occasion of death. She helped lay out Elizabeth's corpse, washing and composing the poor frame in preparation for the wake. She was, as usual, noncommittal; but she later admitted that "it was among the hardest things I've been asked to do."

Agnes was a teacher, one of several in the family line. She was also the drudge, housekeeper and maid, cook and washerwoman. In summertime, she concocted great chunks of vile soap in the rear yard; the essence, we were told, of wood ash, shoveled from the furnace, and lye.

Agnes was the best mind in the family. She was also the one that most nearly won the respect of my mother.

She died of cancer. During her last illness, my mother and I visited her several times, as her craggy features received the stamp of Claimant Death. At the last visit, my aunt's face stirred with an unwonted grief and loss. She murmured to my mother something to the effect that when she recovered, they "must have a good talk." It was the nearest any of them came to repentance or regret.

Then there was Aunt Margaret, the nurse. Vestiges of former grandeur served, like a diet of silver filings, to sharpen her features and temper. Of all the parsimonious shrifts dispensed in that house, hers was the shortest. A strange compatibility of spirit drew her to my father's side. Rumor had it that when votes were cast at a family pow wow, she stood four square with him.

As she aged, her complexion turned an indescribable saffron hue. Her visage joined what we called the Nutcracker Suite—chin to nose. Thus was conferred on her the face she had labored to create, for she was a great one for smelling out default and telling the world of it.

A mustardy outlook. Her view of us in particular was laid heavily with that sharp condiment. We were to be regarded askance, as apt to disrupt the bland taste of life; our kind could bring tears to the eye and disruption to Christian entrails.

To her view, nothing in the six merited distinguishing one from the other. We were announced on arrival to all and sundry, in parroty tones, as the gang. "Here comes the gang!" she would cry, as we dismounted from the Model T. It was a greeting apt to lower the most mettlesome spirit.

At her cry, Patrick the parrot would stir angrily in his parlor cage, as though for battle. He was in perpetual moult, an aged and dangerous patriarch of that house. In his eye lay congealed the anger and dissembling of the tribe. From time to time, as other fauna might drop a turd for very contempt of the world, Patrick would let float on the air a single feather. Defeat, default? The relic was gathered with reverence.

If I linger over the character of Margaret, it is because she, of all the aunts, would exert the deepest imprint on our family, as events will show.

At some point, in a flash of hostility and respect, she and my mother knew that in the other, each had met the adversary. Indeed, each had. It was Margaret who, with connivance of my father, decided that Matson Avenue, that principality and power, would oversee, judge, hover above, heavily shadow, the family of Old Clay Acres. As if this were not enough, and more! No, she would actually for a time, rule that unruly and unpromising roost of ours.

The manse was hot to the point of spontaneous combustion with religion.

There was the priest, my uncle Ned, lately ordained.

In matters of family feuding and feinting, I see in retrospect how little he counted, how easily his mildness and humanity were overridden by the women.

But this was hardly to the point, in the view of the protagonists. His presence cast a fine mist, a sacred fog, over the strife-laden

scene. His function, as they saw it (and it mattered not at all how
he saw it), was to invoke the divine, that events might proceed in
outward seemliness.

Also present from time to time, and more formidable by far than
the male cleric, was Josephine the nun. She was in many respects
a remarkable woman, who had entered the Sisters of Charity in New
York, at age thirty-four. Her vocation was delayed while she supported the fatherless family, teaching country children in upstate
New York. She was to survive into her ninth decade, remarkable
also in old age, as teacher, mistress of novices, comforter of immigrants, principal of the schools of her order, superior of various
convents.

A formidable woman. No youthful rebellion or backsliding but
would find itself sternly called to accounts. She would appear at
our home each summer, swathed in enveloping black robes. On her
head was a long cone bonnet like a strangled cornucopia, tied with
an uncompromising black ribbon beneath her chin. Her clipped,
elegant tones spoke of sacrifice and duty and scholarship; and each
year she exacted a rigorous report as to our progress, domestic and
academic.

Accoutred head to toe in black, she seemed a sacred witch trac-
ing with her graceful black-clad hands the runes and forms of ideal
life. Of all the Berrigans, she lived the Gospel of a salvation straight,
narrow, and singleminded.

And then the contrast. Uncle John, who might be thought to
offer relief from too much salvation, was rendered hors de combat
by the others. He had no vote. His affection for us was reduced to
backstage whispers and the passing into our palms of surreptitious
coins.

Uncle John was the classic black sheep of the Irish, the object
of a Christian solicitude designed to reduce him to a zero. His relatives, in reality his implacable adversaries (all but his brother the
priest), offered him grudging board and room in the manse. As occasion required, he was plucked from his alcoholic delicts, even
delivered once or twice from the local jail. This latter was effected,
as can be imagined, amid great hush-hush and click and clack. John
was shamed and subdued. In his last years, he was taken into a
country rectory by Father Ned, cared for and shown a love long
denied.

My mother's sympathies were with the underdog. She had small patience with the winners. Her acid comments concerning the "goings on" at Matson Avenue spoke of her grief and her exclusion, and the retention of her good sense. They were "off base," she would declare.

I am now, if the fiction is bearable, a child of six years, a sprout transplanted to a far different soil and climate. The year is 1927; the times are bleak, the future is to become more so. We are situated, kindness of an order of nuns, rent-free on some eight acres of scanty yield, overlooking Onondaga Lake, some two miles north of Syracuse.

Our house was purportedly readied for our arrival; but the shape-up by no means included such amenities as interior plumbing or central heat. Ancient walls and floors have been decently painted. But in the New York winters, the house offers only a vast space in which to be iced over; high ceilings, windows rattling in the storms off the lake, drifts of snow to hem us in. My mother breathes deep, looks about her, reads her fate in a glance. We settle in.

From age six to eighteen, it is the only home I am to know, a nearly total environment. We are, in large part, self-sustaining as to essentials of diet: milk, butter and cream, meat on occasion, pigs, chickens and ducks, a large corn field, hay for horse and cow, produce from the kitchen garden, ample for winter preserving. And flowers for the table, a touch of grace insinuated by my mother.

Twelve years of school and working the land and caring for animals and climbing trees and gathering fruit and reading and studying through the winter nights; trudging the two miles to school; being conveyed, in a series of ancient, sturdy chariots, to Sunday mass; "making" first Communion and confirmation; being honored, on occasion, for a good turn at studies and far more frequently reproved for backsliding; forming friendships; fighting (and usually taking the worst of it) with brothers and schoolmates.

School, and more school. I am age six; Philip and I are too tender, even in my father's austere eyes, to be launched on the two-mile road between our home and the nearest Catholic school. Especially because the twin neighborhood wonders, the Red School and the White, lie in conjunction and near at hand.

So we are duly enrolled in the lower school, a property contiguous to our own, a brick creation dating from the Civil War.

A superannuated gorgon, a Miss Howlett, presided for a time over our destiny. Miss Howlett's view of her vocation might be characterized as bony. Her view of her charges was cut to the bone; the bone of discipline and good order. We were considered miniature uncompleted forms, to be nudged bonily forward, with all speed, into the community of bony adults.

The world according to Miss Howlett was not a place to be small in, or young in, or ourselves in. Harden those bones, grow fast, grow like me! In her presence, young jellies set, habits hardened. Shortly we became to all outward appearance stilted versions of Miss H. Something known as school comportment seized on us. We learned perforce to bow and scrape and talk like automatons. And all this charade at age six!

I hear it yet, the school bell sounds from across the fields, the wild dash out the kitchen door, schoolbooks under arm, across the meadow northward along the locust hedgerow. Then an open field and fence to be navigated. And the bell clamoring away, Miss Howlett's genie of brass.

It is early October, there is a bite in the air. I have all but disappeared into an uncle's olive green First World War overcoat, brave with brass buttons; the coat has been cut down to perhaps one third of its bulk. The warning bell sounds, I am pummeled into this wonder, with haste. I run and run, reach the slender aperture in the fence. And to dismay beyond telling, wild-eyed as Peter Rabbit, am stuck there! I tear free at last, but one of the great buttons is irretrievably lost in the long grasses. . . .

An interminable year passes somehow. Then I am liberated along with my peers from bone-stiffening influences. And am shuffled on to the next arena of testing, the so-called White School, which contained the next higher grades, a quarter-mile north of our home.

Red School and White: like the queens of the Alice story, the appellations are to be set down in capitals. The schools are named for no district or hamlet or city; nor are they connected in public understanding with popular heroes or founding fathers.

Who were our heroes to be? Localized impressions are new and indistinct; we are a mixed populace of Italians and WASPs and a scattering of Irish Catholics; poor, new to the American scene. Many families dwell in small, miserable clots, making do on the land or at odd jobs in neighboring Syracuse.

The White School seemed entirely normal, acceptable. It was, all said, the only school we knew. And what, in any case, would a better one have looked like?

It is as though I enter it once more. Up the rickety wooden front steps; then into the first of two vast rooms. These compose all the space, dusty, utterly cheerless; one on the first floor, the other lying up a battered wooden stairs. The architecture, like the instruction, is worthy of a Dickensian workhouse.

For a generation, the medium included the message, conveyed to the district by a pinchpenny school board. To wit: this weather-beaten shack, creaking in the winds and baking in the sun, this setting of contempt, befits the contemptible poor. Come, be instructed in your status and destiny.

The lower room houses the lower four grades. Each is assigned to a corner of the place; all four are presided over by one teacher. Condemned to this galley was Marcella Gaffney, aged nineteen at the time of my entrance on the scene of enchantment. Her counterpart, Miss Dixon, held the even less defensible Fort Apache on the second story.

Each of these young women, recently graduated from a normal school, was responsible for the mental development of some ninety youngsters; Miss Gaffney, grades one to four, inclusive, Miss Dixon, five through eight.

The situation, whatever its appeal to frontier romanticism, was desperate from the start. The teacher, in a desperate improvising, divided her burden in four more or less adjacent parts, assigning work to each. She passed among the groups throughout the day, doing her best to attend to the wants of an undernourished and ignorant mass of youngsters.

She was also responsible, in the bitter winter weather, for the heating of the vast open shed of a room. Arriving at dawn on Monday, Miss Gaffney lit and stoked and maintained the classroom fire.

The situation was not only absurd; it was cruel. No wonder that, come Friday, and the hubbub beyond control, Miss Gaffney tossed in the gauntlet, and could be seen, head in arms at her desk, nursing a violent headache.

A seven-year-old, no hardiness in his nature, is moved to compassion or curiosity or some emotion between the two. He approaches the desk and inquires in childish tones whether something is awry, if something may perhaps be done. The young woman raises her head, her eyes filled with tears of pain and frustration. But she manages a smile of fondness for the solicitous youngster, assures him that thank you, everything is quite all right.

A friendship is struck up between the two. It spreads like a benign healing, until it includes the families Berrigan and Gaffney; includes also the relatives of the latter, the redoubtable and affluent O'Briens.

A year passes. The White School is by no means fulfilling its function with regard to us.

The indictment, filed by my father, is a grave one: we have learned next to nothing.

My father and his sisters form a solid phalanx. We must be transferred to the parochial school, two miles distant; and that without delay.

Our religious development was unremarkable. Throughout the year we were part of a catechism class, conducted for neighboring children by my mother, in our living room, in preparation for first Communion. We also, of course, attended Sunday mass in the parish church, and joined in family prayer in the evenings.

My father, as usual, prevailed. In my eighth year, together with brothers Jerry and Phil, I started anew. In foul weather and fair, we undertook the trek to our new citadel, St. John the Baptist Grammar School, on Park Street, Syracuse. For a decade, the parish school was to be our guarantor of place in church and state, the seedbed of our vocations, the scene of blood and tears and dust cast up by our hooves, against a redoubtable system.

We trod corridors and gymnasium and adjacent church; we coped with priests and nuns and report cards and fear and trembling; all the welter and pain and loathing of adolescent development, retardation, refusal and consent, awakening and despair.

I have a sense that the gods were brooding and keeping watch as, at the tremendous age of eight years, I gird my soul for the trudge schoolward. It is a scene straight out of apocrypha: the idols governing the entrenched scene flex their muscles at the approach of this puny warrior. Schooling! Serious business!

Alas for all that. It should be stated at the outset that the Berrigan fry were inclined, with the laziness endemic to our kind, to resist tooth and nail any effort to inject us with the serum of facts, figures, and forms. The needle descended, in the hands of one or another nun. Alas, often as not, they missed the vein.

Appropriate schooling. We were bunched together, cheek to jowl, like herds of restive animals rounded up for flesh and pelt. Writing, reading, geography, religion, numbers, all more or less indiscriminately enjoined, inevitably by an overworked and harassed nun. In season and out, year after year. The times took on the iron quality of fate. Ours was an education decreed from on high by iron-browed idols, determined to produce a race of sycophants.

I write of the years from age eight to eighteen. Mitigated catastrophe is the phrase that fits. The mitigation was strictly by the way. It was extracurricular to the main event, which sought, in a prosaic, flat-footed way, to create in our minds a version of a future presented as desirable—or in any case, inevitable. We were small fish in a small tank; we would never, horrors! tumble forth as troublemaking adults, alarming or outrageous or colorful.

Dun, dun, and it was done. Mitigation. I cling to the word with what humor I can summon. I search out, like someone unaccountably sprung from incarceration, moments of goodness or laughter or sports or dancing or companionship, moments that might serve to whisper, It couldn't have been so bad! Doesn't something cling in the mind, helping a ruinous season make sense?

The school was like an elaborate vise in an old medical illustration; an instrument in which the skull was held firm, in order that ("for your own good") the skull might be sawed open and some horrid remedy against this or that ill be applied.

Memory and rote. It was of no import whether the subject was mathematics or catechism. One plus one plus one undoubtedly equaled three; this was akin to the fact that the Father, Son, and Holy Spirit constituted a Trinity. One could reach a rather simple and obvious solution in the one instance; in the other, an indescribable mystery was totted up.

But the distinction was useless in practice. We were to memorize the one and the other, conquer them; twin Everests or twin molehills, as the case might be. The one might help us tot up a grocery bill and the other enchant us for an eternity, but we were left to ourselves to puzzle out the rather considerable difference.

Thus for better or worse, my schooling got underway, at the far end of our road—in itself a symbol of the sweat and tears and in-

herent anxiety of the enterprise. In all weathers and seasons and
times of year, that long march into purported wisdom went on.

We brothers made it together, like ambulatory beads on a loose
cord, strung out along a buzzing highway. The cars sped by. We
shouldered our book bags, heavy with the freight of the centuries'
images, minds, morals, lowered our heads, and pulled along. It was
not a bad image of the way life would go.

The indelible lesson of my first year at St. John's had little to do
with books or marks. I was eight years old, assigned to the fourth
grade. Thirty of us were placed in the hands of a young nun, a
woman barely finished her novitiate and whatever spasmodic preparation for teaching.

It would be nearer the truth of the case to say, She was delivered
in our hands. Her incapacity, panic even, shortly surfaced in episodes of cruelty. What indeed was she to do, but raise a smoke-
screen or a cry or "make an example" against the potential chaos;
all those warty, snotty faces, their plots and ploys, those snifflers
and shufflers, those latecomers, whisperers, snickerers. . . .

She was fair and wan of mein, remote and virginal. A child
somewhat older, hardly more experienced, than the children she
stood before; so slender, so set of jaw, so trembling of voice; bound
about, chin to heel, in the suffocating linen and serge of her con-
secration. A victim bound to victimize.

She knew what she would do. These children must be taught a
lesson, and quickly, lest life turn to nightmare.

One morning, the weather being adverse, a few of us arrived
late and bedraggled from our long haul. She worked herself into a
fury: how dare we enter her classroom, bedraggled and tardy and
with no excuses or explanations, beyond a burst of weather?

She stood to announce the penalty. We miscreants had lost our
right to desk and chair. We were, then and there, to take up our
books and pencils and pens and notebooks, all chattels and paraphernalia, and position ourselves standing along the walls of the
room. Indefinitely. We were, moreover, declared responsible for
whatever notes might be required, or assignments, or parsing, or
whatever.

It was a theater of cruelty. The books were insufferably heavy,
our limbs slight. We could scarcely keep in one defined bundle
notes and tomes, all of different size, all madly shifting and sliding

about, unbalancing and falling with a thump to floor. The sound, like a second crack of doom, merited yet another threatening look from under her brows.

Torture or education? No useful purpose is served in inflating the espisode, wrought by a childish inexperience and panic. Indeed. Except that in one life the terror of that punishment, exacted for crimes unknown, abides.

The episode was deepened in memory rather than dissolved, because there was no recourse at hand, no wiser head to interpret, perhaps even render humorous, the occurrence. One was well advised never to carry home in those days the story of the day's mischance. The law was in the hands of the lawgivers, come what may; presumption of guilt lay heavy on the third estate.

No recourse. Thus the abnormal attained a kind of spurious normalcy. This was the way the world went; large dog eat small. Too bad for it, one was small. There might come a time when one grew large enough to dispense the law himself. But that time was unimaginable, to conjure it up was asking a galley slave to play slave-master. One might someday taste a kind of glee at cracking a whip over others. But the dream corrected nothing, by day or night; neither the dreamer's moral condition nor the folly of human arrangement.

The child resolved matters as best he might, in his own mind, secretly, as children do. He settled into a kind of low-voltage despond. He functioned, at times even well, in all that was required by his mentors. But he grew to expect less of himself, that less behind which one hides out, disguises his gifts, rebukes his own dreams.

With regard to his elders, which is to say, his betters, judges, prosecutors, dispensers of a justice that simply made no sense—he concluded their conduct was none of his affair. It became clear that he could never uncover the rhyme or reason of what went on among them, above his head, out of his ken. Their judgments were a foreign language, like the German tongue of his mother.

He was one species, adults another. He might one day transmogrify into one of their kind; but such an outcome held no attraction and, in any case, was unimaginably remote. Meantime, he must arrange things as best he could.

Indeed, the event in the classroom cast its shadow ahead. A suspicion grew in the boy's mind, almost a claim. Something about

catastrophe, awfulness, inevitability, an interfering presence that
would not let him be.

He began to expect that life would go badly for him. He was
luckless; the shadow had substance. What else was a shadow, except the portent of something or someone who spilled out an ink
of darkness? It was a warning: the light of his day would be interrupted, rudely and repeatably.

The foregoing was no more than a diffused sense; even if encouraged to do so, he could not have understood it at the time it
settled on him. But like many early impressions invading the immature spirit, such foreboding concentrated a charge of enormous
power. Time and again, the impression returned of an illness in
things; more properly, it never left him. It laid on him the shadow
of a hand, and eventually a hand. In due time; in its own time.

I do not know if he could have borne at the time to speak of
such things. And even supposing the occasion, what was one to
say? Supposing he could pour out his spate of dread—what was a
teacher, a parent, to do? Taking the temperature of an ill child does
not easily render up the fact that the temperature of his soul has
plummeted, that cold has settled in on a life.

His terror took shape now and then in a curious sort of dream.
It was not so danger-filled or dreadful as to qualify as a nightmare.
Still its malignancy roused the child in tears; his mother must enter
and bear him away, into her orbit of light.

The image was ominous; it was his nighttime version of his days.
It came together in a kind of floating, shimmering lozenge, a five-
sided figure connected to no palpable structure. It hung in the black
air before the child's mind, all aglow, illumining the dark with a
malign stillness. He cried out, his mother appeared. And when, after
a time, she questioned him as to what had shaken his sleep, he was
dumb to tell.

He sensed in later life that the form of night was the reverse of
the shadow that lay upon the days, the pentagonal shape of things
to come. He would banish it, it would recur. And with an outcome
of some moment.

Still there were mitigations, and even minor pleasures; taken all
in all, life was bearable, and sometimes even more.

Our family rode an uneasy saddle, between city and farm. We
dwelt on the land, among such misfits and characters as the urban

homogenizing machine had not yet pushed off the earth. A ribbon of highway passed our acres, joining town and country; alongside it, the trolley cars rolled, meandering and swaying like dromedaries.

If our holdings were at all remarkable, it was for the variety of domestic fauna that, along with the sons, formed our ecosphere. There were no parental objections to our assembling a menagerie, as long as (my mother's sole insistence) the animals "know their place and keep to it"; in this case, the areas outside her domain, the house. She had a sharp sense that humans and beasts were in best conjunction when the latter were kept to their territory.

Thus the bestiary: dog, cats, goat, ducks, chickens, geese, cows, horses, even white mice and turtles. It was a quite remarkable ecumenical spread, democratic and, for the most part, in unison of temper. When winter arrived and snow fell in protracted episodes, the whole menagerie crept closer, for warmth and companionship, in stable or haymow.

There is little reason to consider our life idyllic or to wax Wordsworthian in its regard. There were quotidian tasks without number, feeding and milking cows, hauling manure; and in season, plowing, harrowing, cultivating the earth; and then harvesting, haying. We grew in knowledge of "country matters"; both crude and taken for granted.

My brothers were my father's constant co-workers, whether in field or barn. From time to time, attempts were made to induct me also. I resisted; and grew in time to be considered either inept or physically unfit for such rigors. So I became a species of house boy. I cleaned floors, washed dishes, learned a bit of rudimentary cooking. In such wise, I took the long path around my father.

My older brothers plugged along and took the heat. As for Philip, he showed such physical prowess and handiness as made him quite the equal of the others.

I admired my brothers from afar, for their ability to fend off my father's volcanic and unpredictable moods. Toe to heel, they stood to him. Scenes were recorded that all but brought down the heaven in shards.

Indeed his theory of governance, as far as anyone could judge, never landed in the twentieth century, or took in account the mettle of his sons, or showed pride in them. Perhaps, I thought, his arrogance would not allow the admission that they were fast becoming his equal. He gloried in prowess, but only in his own. In others he saw only adversaries, challengers.

It would have brought us a weird sort of relief had he been predictably unbearable or autocratic. But there was no telling. Morning red and evening gray, or vice versa, his weather offered few sky or sea marks.

What will he be like this evening? we would wonder as we came in from school. And what will he be like this morning? was a first question on rising. But who could know?

I was by now, age eight or nine, set on a path of no distinction and considerable misery, along with some thirty city sprats, at the Catholic school. Rattling about us each day were the dry bones of discipline and instruction.

CHAPTER 3

The Father

Sanity; your face, dropping its mask
    asleep over a book;
Irish intellect; now and again
a piercing stab of virtue; a boy
kneeling beside you at Mass, a 6-year-old
rocking horse Catholic.

Thank you, old bones, old pirate
old mocker and weeper.

At home, spring and summer, we ran wild, in denims and bare feet, subject, more or less, to assigned work in field or barn or pasture; finding in my father's absences a parole from servitude; and in his presence, especially on weekends, pure misery.

Indoors or out, holiday, work day, winter or summer, he was a presence to be reckoned with. Two occurrences particularly enraged him. He had no comprehension or patience with the games of children, or with their illnesses. Indeed, the second was treated as a personal affront, and the first a vagrant waste of time, squandering hours that might better be spent in proving one's self useful. With what dread we awaited his evening arrival from work. As the sun declined, a thick atmosphere mounted on itself, like a fog from damp ground.

Suppose an illness. One was abed with fever or other indisposition. Heavy footsteps mounted the stair, his image flared up before he stood in the room. His footsteps, the sound of judgment. Along the corridor, the quasi-military stride, indomitable. To the child his father's arrival is enormous, overpowering.

For his part, the father is out of sorts; there is a hiatus in his routine. He conveys bewilderment in the only face he can summon; set purpose, sternness.

Well, what's this all about, boy?

No auspicious beginning. The father advances to the bed. His eyes rest on the child, and he is touched. But sternness is habitual to him, and tenderness a lost art; his next move is jarring, inept. He lays a great hand on the child, roughly strokes his brow. It is by no means a healing touch; it passes over the face like sandpaper.

He mutters a phrase or two of commiseration and shortly leaves the room. A vague cloud of relief follows in his wake.

It must be understood that the scene is as painful for the father as for the son. The father's capacities and strengths are all for the strong; for those who resemble himself. As for those others, the unfortunates, the weak, they are beyond the pale. To open his heart, he must let go those heavy tools of his, let his hands hang helpless. For such as an ill son, he can do nothing.

What slight clues I command in attempting to decipher such episodes! In my father, strength and weakness were alike opaque. In his presence, I had neither capacity nor will—to respond, to show spontaneous affection—let alone to grow angry or resist. Between us for years, there existed only an emotional stalemate; it had roots in ground too deep for me to penetrate.

He would declare from time to time, in a phrase that stung me to speechless anger, that I was "the son he never knew." There was a grain of truth in the statement; but he meant it only as a reproof. He knew the other sons, or so he thought. He worked with them, verbally abused them, in their younger years battered them about. But with me, there was no contest. And this, given his version of the world as a pit for bear baiting, was intolerable. Of what use was a no contest in a world whose entire meaning was conflict?

The fact was, of course, that he knew precious little of any of us. A superficial camaraderie arose from time to time among men working together in hard physical ways. He and my brothers could discuss, in apparent equality, matters of farm and the land, machines, animals, tools, repairs. But it all stopped there; their aspirations, their uphill struggles and small triumphs, their affections, their rages—these escaped him entirely.

And when their time of achievement began (especially my own), there wakened in him only a base jealousy. Every event touching on us, sour or glorious, must ricochet off his ego. Were we disgraced in some minor imbroglio at school? He gloried and fumed at sight of our squirming. Had we won a round, with studies or sports (or

later, in my case, with writing and publication)? He would begin to
incant his own "lost chances," as though in some incomprehensible
way we had cheated him of distinction and fame.

What indeed were these lost and wasted talents, this neglected
genius? He preserved in his room a trunkful of manuscripts, poetry
written over the years. A few verses had been published in local
newspapers. As to fame, that was all. As to worth, the work could
only be judged indifferent: lengthy effusions, much in line with his
temperament, an overripe romanticism.

His literary rejection over the years soured his heart, and intensified his sense of being a neglected genius. There was no correcting
or countering this. My mother, who had the clearest sense of his
limits and strengths, was dismissed out of hand: she was considered,
by him and his family, "limited." It was his sisters who knew him,
only they. Tom's talents were such that the world, beginning with
his own wife and children, could never be expected to honor, etcetera.

It touched them all, that infection of the mind: clannishness had
built an immune system against reality.

I wish I were capable of stating, at some fifty years' remove,
what he meant to his sons, what his influence was. I summon his
ghost, and question him. Did you love us, despite all? Did we love
you, despite all? Where did things go wrong, for you, for us? I drop
my hands in frustration and grief.

As he was. This is how he stands before me, not a whit changed
in the crucible of death. He grew older and faded like an oak leaf,
and wavered, awaiting the November blast that would set him spinning. But young as he was in my childhood, then older, and then
simply old, in important respects he did not change at all, or come
to new vision, to reconciliation or regret—or learning. And this is
the impasse, the despair that stops my mind cold.

He survived to the ninth decade. And he stood where he had
stood; as he was buried, after his immense wandering, where he
had been born. It was as though we were lowering the corpse of a
newborn, or a child, or a young man: time had stopped where life
began. The law that says we change, we learn, we submit, we bow
beneath burdens, we take on the burdens of others, we grow compassionate or wise or heartily generous—the law was suspended.
He was immovable, willful, stuck. His old age was a powerful ex-

ample of the petrifaction of the moral sense. Age seized him, put its lamprey mouth against his body. It left the shell, and the soul rattling feebly within, seeking release.

He was the same, always the same. No Jekyll to Hyde, more a story of Dorian Gray. He grew old, he did not grow. The alterations wrought by time were, in the final analysis, cosmetic. What had been bellicose and dangerous was now merely pitiful: death was drawing his fangs. That religion of his, compounded of tears and platitudes and rote—it sustained him not at all. Where he had been a fighter, and lashed out, for ego, for pride of place, for vindication—he caved in.

Toward the end we saw only a withdrawn despair; he turned and turned, a husk in purgatorial fires; turned finally to the wall, against us, and time, and the rogue world. Died as he had lived.

That his influence on us, his sons, was enormous, penetrating, enduring, there can be no doubt. He shadows us, who knew him best; we advert to his ways, mannerisms, attitudes; sometimes we laugh, at times a wave of anger or melancholy washes over. Others note how he lives on in us; it is not invariably a compliment.

Peculiar, and so mixed. One could console himself in an easy homiletic way—he gave us our faith. That would put things simply—and uselessly. The statement would be true, and just as clearly untrue; for what he gave with one hand, he took back with the other.

His influence was so equivocal that any attempt to sweeten, flatten out, indulge in pieties, serves only to yield before his own method, his own faith even. And our faith, as we came to know, had another source than him; it came from our mother. Strangely; for with regard to things religious, she was reticence personified. But in the midst of all, and stuck as she (and we) seemed in a cul-de-sac, her example could not but be noted, even by the blind.

It counted for nearly everything, the patience, plain goodness, long-sufferance; and now and then, the right word filling the space, and the religious piety that was never once overbearing or showy, but that carried its burdens, carried others along, and finally carried the day. Oh (as the Irish never conceded), she had a way with her!

I have a hunch with regard to my father. He offered something other than faith or a viable or attractive religious sense. Something of persistence, stubbornness, skepticism, a queer kind of gnarled integrity, a sixth sense for the right order of things, thrashing out in all directions. If only this could have been disciplined and directed, what a strength!

Something lurked behind the eyes, an extraordinary capacity: to look closely at the fabric of life; to weigh and touch and lay one's hand along its length and breadth. Not to be taken in. And then, when much has been discarded, and with what overt contempt—then, now and again, the genuine article comes to hand. That is it! One hastens and buys; and pays up, at great sacrifice, if required. And then, one wears the garment like a second skin. Or a first.

As indeed he did.

Life grew somewhat more tolerable if one survived adolescence. The hard part was to be small and helpless. Or, as in the case of my mother, to be a woman.

She declared, What a blessing we never had a girl. She would never have survived.

CHAPTER 4

The Workhouse

Come, said the flower,
race me to evening!
                    Time is a way
no one knows.
                    Who
goes there?
                    Who went there?
answer our tears, our sighs,
our flower's ghost.
                    Growth is a death
on my youth laid.

But as to schooling.

Fifth grade, age nine; no improvement in my plight. Some thirty of us were delivered over, body and soul, to the hands of another Sister. This estimable woman was short in stature, ruddy of complexion, abrupt of temper. She was also afflicted with chronic dislike of the young.

It was clear from the first day: we were congenitally condemned; we could do nothing to please her. There were only degrees of displeasure; from slightly nauseating to outright heinous. This was the range of her classroom moods; she aired her distemper (it was like a sorting of soiled linen that turned her face crimson with distaste) with a kind of sour eloquence, under little or no provocation.

One might think that a bad situation was at least clear, that visible lines were drawn. But such would be of advantage only if we had been of an age to rebut her conduct. Alas, we were a knot of terrorized, disoriented youngsters, instructed to show unfailing reverence for this mysterious hooded figure. What recourse could be ours against the crucifix and rosary, those twin swords of the Spirit? And what means were at hand to suggest that the assault was not heavenly at all, but monstrously cruel by any standard?

No standard was available. Justice was not for the young; the very idea was off base.

The method was terror. One must leave it to others, experts in such matters, to fathom the motives that boiled away, or turned the nun, on less awful days, merely sullen toward her charges.

Indeed, life weighed heavily on all the nuns of St. John's, some fourteen of them crowded into the drafty barracks of a convent. Deprived of privacy and breathing space, condemned to musty classrooms, imprisoned in a code of manners both rigid and eso-teric. It could not be wondered at that such as ourselves, the clods, drudges, and indistinguishables of the fifth grade, appeared to this poor woman as a fifth degree of torture, plaguing her days and haunting her nights.

It could be argued that we did no more than illumine a situation already in place. Quite independent of us, and lodged like a stone in the sandal, was the suspicion that she was the wrong person for the task. Or that, though she might be the right person, the task was wrongly presented, ill prepared for. That so undertaken, it could only end badly.

She was intelligent, she knew her plight: this was the crown of the curse.

She would dart about like a dervish under force of her theory— a general roundup to avenge individual delicts. Or on a theological level, she put in practice her belief in the total corruption of the human lot. Justice restored, ourselves smarting from her blows, she would retire to her desk, all hot and bothered and yet somewhat assuaged, tossing her veil, disarranged by her exertions. Then she would improve the occasion, announcing yet once more her ex-treme dislike for the teacher's lot, her desire for a different setting than (with an indescribable curl of disdain)—this one.

We were not even capable of hating her. We cowered there, waiting for the storm to pass. She was a fact of nature, we dwelt in a tornado belt.

More; hatred was forbidden, rebellion unthinkable. The very no-tions invited retribution from on high; like a blow of the keys of the kingdom against our powdery souls. Who were we, after all, to hate anyone; let alone a nun, a consecrated being? One who, over and above the code of Irish chivalry, had been swept from our low estate, once and for all, by sacred and scarifying vows?

Hate? It was beyond our ken. It was an outlaw emotion, outside the laws of existence. We could only cower on our benches, shamefaced, benighted souls that we were.

One day she went too far.

A girl in the class was disabled due to polio. Her disability obliged her to project her foot somewhat from the area under her seat into the aisle. Our nun, passing on a tour of inspection, observed the projecting limb, and proceeded deliberately to grind her heel against the foot of the child.

It was an act of cruelty so gratuitous as to rattle the chain of command. The links rattled, a few fell apart. Could Sister do wrong? It seemed as though. There were forays at higher levels, between the parents of the girl and the superiors of the nun. The likelihood was raised of a legal process. And one day, as unthinkable as the Last Day of All, the mother of the child, accompanied by the principal of the school and our holy punisher, appeared together before the class. A public apology was issued by the teacher.

For an hour, chains fell in a great rattling heap, from thirty pairs of hands.

I do not know the impact on others. But for one child, suddenly grown thoughtful, the grip of authority could never again rub so cruelly. He had eaten of the forbidden tree, he possessed forbidden knowledge. They were fallible, those great ones, those Olympians. They could sin. But more wonderful by far, they could be held accountable for their sin.

He lifted his eyes, and breathed deep. How sweet was the air, and how sweet the revenge of breathing it! Stale air, stalemate of soul; for once they were lifted. It might even be that once was enough.

His sense of freedom came and went, arose and fell back. It was checked, warned, crushed, by a conflicting sense alluded to earlier: that sense of catastrophe or ill luck.

Toward the end of the year, under the tutelage of Sister Mary Amazon, it seemed to him, all in secret, that a pattern was established that would govern the future. The sad fatalism of a child! He came to believe, as others believe in a governing Providence, something far different. That there would occur at least one fall from grace, one public humiliation, one damnable mischance, each year of his life. He believed it; he set his bones to fend it off, as best he could. Such events were utterly out of his control; perhaps they escaped the control of God, he did not know. But obscure as they were, they would determine his faith or the lack thereof, would color bleakly everything, all of life.

I risk blowing things beyond their true size; but the risk is preferable to default. I was unable for many years to free myself from this malignant sense of failure, ill luck, blank destiny. It lowered my capacity for joy and verve; followed me through schooling and into the Jesuits; touched on friendship and family. And inevitably it was carried in secret, for who of humankind could be expected to understand so bizarre a sense, of life at the bottom?

It was a denial of freedom in myself; and of the freedom of a God who, I was taught, cared, manifested concern for mortals. And so He might; but in my regard, no matter how others were cosseted or cherished, God was blind as a bat and indifferent as a grave.

A child of contradictions! All the while, of course, this skinny agnostic was memorizing his catechism along with his peers, was preparing for his first Holy Communion, was expressing and implying, in all sorts of way, a fervent faith. And faith he did have, or faith had him, in its grip. But it was no consolation to be the creature of such a God as this; who beyond doubt existed, who showed a quite peculiar interest in this subject—an interest that could hardly be equated with Providence.

Did God not resemble his own father? Was that the rub? Certainly his father existed; and just as certainly God existed. To no great comfort, it must be added, in either case.

The question of resemblance was put in all seriousness.

One thing seemed certain. The God of school and nuns and priests and rules and commands and generalized misery—this God in no way could be imagined to bear the slightest resemblance to—his mother.

Still, in his crabbed and cowering way, the child believed. He even became known, to the derision of some, including his father, for his piety. And all the while, in desolation beyond telling, he bore that stone in his heart.

Could the two coexist, he wondered; a sense of being abandoned to the tides of fortune, and a faith in the God whose loving Providence was hourly proclaimed—was, in fact, the governing supposition of life, whether at home or in his schooling? Every teacher was a living proclamation (so it was said) of the goodness of God, an energizing line of life, an umbilical joining him to a divine source. Example and word; behold!

So the child was tossed about in the crosswinds. Earth and time made sense (it was said), only as these were breathed on by the winds of the Spirit. And heaven's will was manifest, pressingly so, in the somber clothing and deportment of the nuns, in rituals, singing and praying, the images of the saints, the crucifixes multiplied, room to room, like an unbearable echoing outcry, a chorus of redemptive suffering.

It all went together, or so it was said. Only, it did not all go together. At some angle, in a shadowy corner, a warp developed, two joints fell away. A child's mind knew sin. It was as though a worm crept out of the warp, and invaded him. It brought news, a vermicular whisper sliding into the soul.

Reality? Reality was not close fitting, reasonable, predictable, sound, impervious against all voices but One. Reality was a nun's distemper, his father's darkness of soul. The agents of the One and Only were themselves apt for the Fall. They could be gross caricatures of the perfection they purportedly embodied.

In somewhat such ways, a desolate presence entered the doorway of the child's soul. It lay there at the heart of things, this curled worm and its ambient darkness; ineluctable, consequential.

I ponder these notes, I wonder if I do not lay too heavy a portent on a rather conventional child. Am I missing the mark in thus pursuing the child's moods into his tenth year? Let me recount something, before passing to happier topics and days.

The time is September of 1932. Our usual complement of survivors sits in place, row upon row, awaiting a new teacher. An elderly nun appears; her countenance is framed in white, as though disembodied in the doorway. The face is of such pallor as to seem carven from alabaster. Her expression is utterly immobile.

The Sister entered the room, and took command, as usual. And, as usual, we were in for it.

On occasion of some plenary malfeasance, one of two dicta shook her frame and impelled her eyes aloft, in the manner of a Teresa of Avila, racked by Earth and winging for heaven.

The first cry was, "May the angels be praised!" And the second, rather more secular in tone, but nonetheless fervent, "And to think they shot Lincoln!"

She was in ill health, and wrung the dregs of a bitter joy dwelling on her frequent foiling of death. Her movements were restricted by bodily weakness, but ominous. When required, she moved about the room slowly, with immense dignity, striking out as she went. Pursuing a course down the aisle, she would remind one of an immense draped funereal ferry, entering among quaking reeds, bent backward in her wake.

The question may arise whether the capacities of ten year olds were benefited by so marmoreal a presence. It was as though there were placed before us, in view of our Christian improvement, and for an entire year, one of the more flamboyant images of Grief Rampant, from a Tuscan cemetery. An image that from time to time stirred to life, implying in word and tone the subterranean existence of the dead.

The nun's appearance, her aura, her monotone, her blanched features, the words that varied between minatory and accusative— all these coming together induced in young spirits a tendency to reduce life to the famous Four Last Things: Death, Judgment, Heaven, Hell.

She concentrated reality into one hard, bitter pill; style and message were one.

The message, in my case, was clear. It was also being verified before my eyes. By now it had the force of a law: when things are bad, they can only worsen.

One day I was summoned to her desk, before the full class, which, an arraignment being in the air, had the inconsolable look of a criminal court.

Yet once more, O ye gods. It appeared that a classmate who was also a neighbor and crony had been delinquent from school for a matter of months. He held in our neighborhood a route for newspaper deliveries and was particularly adept, not only at playing hooky, but at covering his tracks. A number of us, including myself, had been bribed with dietary benefits, hot dogs and ice cream and similar delights, to keep us mum as to his delinquencies.

Quite a number of us were, as I recall, the tainted beneficiaries of the Artful Dodger. How the awful truth reached the ears of our teacher, or why I was singled out, remains, to this day, obscure. What was clear beyond doubt was that I was on the griddle, about to be tossed in the fire.

She was a great one for "making an example." I was summoned forward, in a silence that portended but one outcome: the estate of the powerless was to be demonstrated once more.

She had prepared beforehand a letter, to be delivered by myself into the hands of my father. The note requested, in tones acerbic and imperative, an explanation. How could it be that such crimes as to be hereafter described, could proceed under his roof, for a considerable time, without his intervention?

The crimes were recounted: shielding of a criminal (our Enterprising Dodger) from his just desserts and sharing in the fruits of crime, by frequent conspiratorial imbibing of hamburgers, iced delights, et al. The note concluded with calculated insult: in a Christian household, were children actually being instructed to lie and cheat?

I was commanded to deliver the note that evening to my father. Kill the messenger.

In spite of my terror, I kept my wits. In fear and trembling, with a glimmer of hope, I handed the note to my mother.

She knew the outcome as well as I, were she to refuse to intervene. My father was bound to raise very hell. A nun could do no wrong!

My mother's mind was practical and nuanced, and endowed with a courage I can never forget. More to my advantage, the nun had overplayed her hand. All unknowing, she had penned a message that roused my mother's fury. Taught to lie and cheat indeed! Who might this woman think herself, to write such noxious follies, quote them to youngsters, order them delivered by a child's hand? My mother girded herself; in her eyes, the nun had become the true delinquent.

We two walked into the convent parlor. The nun, primed for a scene of self-justified triumph, was met with the unexpected, indeed the unimaginable. My mother, known for her mildness, stood eye to eye with her adversary. She demanded abruptly how it could be stated, by a religious no less, that Berrigan children were being taught to etcetera, etcetera.

It was a wonderful turnabout, a Greek reversal of fortunes. The nun calculated her chances, swallowed hard, and recanted on the spot. No offense was meant, she hoped none was taken. Could not the matter rest there? It could, and we retired.

Not that I was guiltless, my mother was at pains to point out to me. I had indeed enjoyed the fruits of pilfering: my cohort had altered his financial accounts and doled out ill-gotten gains among his friends, buying their silence. And I must rightly be ashamed for my squalid complicity.

How admirable was my mother's moral clarity; and how, in consequence, her authority flourished in my mind!

And on the other hand, how difficult to unravel the intent of my teacher throughout the imbroglio. By implication, I had sinned in not playing informer against a friend. I could hardly pull a virtuous face in the matter; at the same time, I am puzzled at the code held up for emulation.

It was the midthirties. My family was yet to know the trauma of the Second World War, and the plucking of four sons by the military.

If we were poor and parochial of mind, we were also blessed to live on the land, among interesting, even bizarre, neighbors, with whom we were generally on free and easy terms.

Among the six sons, the oldest, Thomas, bore the brunt, both of my father's vagrant temper, and of our poverty. He and the two nearest him in age, John and James, became, all too early, drawers of water and hewers of wood, their schooling incomplete, their future already taking shape, as it seemed at the time, bleak and inevitable.

We three younger ones were shielded, at least in degree. Our lives were less harassed, we were in less danger of being pushed, out of due time, into the rude world.

Thus in spite of formidable obstacles, we knew a measure of happiness. At times, life and love and even joy seemed to overflow as we made our cursive way around my father, around schooling. Homeward from incarceration at the end of day, taking the longest laggard route, savoring the intoxicating springtime, beneath the budding chestnuts of the road; sparring, fooling, trotting, malingering, tormenting one another or a hapless companion, munching the remains of lunch, stopping to gaff with a neighbor, stoning a snarling dog, detouring at the railroad tracks to challenge one another to "walk the rail.". . .

. And eventually, jumping the ditch onto our turf, to be greeted ecstatically by our beloved spaniel, Pal. Home safe, the unloved day dropped from our shoulders, a sack of galling boulders. Home free!

And if weather were mild, and the mother amenable—into summer garb, the denims. And off with shoes and socks, and the breathing earth against our feet.

The slight and fragile round of a child's happiness! Slight not merely in the chancy nature of happiness itself, as our teachers were at pains to remind us. But in its small orbit too, our small patch of earth. And in the time granted, so fleeting and quick to pass. And finally, in the threats that hemmed it round, when evening would bring the hated hour of homework; and on the morrow the trudge schoolward, the clamor of bells, the long single lines, the hours and days that belonged in no wise to us, but to the overseers and beadles. Fate, like the Eumenides, descended bodily on freedom, its easy prey.

In due course, all six of us underwent our Christian initiation: we received first Communion, and were confirmed sacramentally by the local bishop. I am not aware, nor were our parents, that such occasions of grace brought notable improvement in our conduct. The holy wafer on the tongue, the bishop's reminding blow on the cheek, left us improved only for the hour. We remained remarkably bellicose among ourselves, prone to laziness, imaginative in avoiding duties, lightminded in reading habits. We procrastinated, some of us stole, others lied, all at one time or another concocted smoking materials and grew dizzy, smoking them in secret. And as confessed, we coveted with zeal such small moneys as crossed our palm, from whatever source.

In sum, we were children of darkness and light; and the two were in contest in our souls. If our vices seem puny, and fit only to awaken humor or pity, it must be recalled that they were the only ones to hand. In regard to sin, as contrasted with duty or study, we did our level best.

My own development slogged along, counter to that of my brothers. It could hardly be otherwise, given my temperament and theirs, and the driving will of my father. Where my brothers were dexterous of hand and strong of arm, I was both puny and clumsy. I well remember the shame when called on to seek out a tool from the workbench; how often I returned, the correct genus in hand, and the wrong species. I could not, for the life of me, learn the difference between an object referred to as a monkey wrench and its numerous cousins.

The ill luck principle applied here with a vengeance. And if a brother were in the mood for a spell of fun at my expense, he had only to refuse the signal (or offer a wrong one) that, at my father's back, would call my choice of tools: right—or wrong again.

Not to make overmuch of small potatoes. If I grew along different lines than my peers, there were, as well, points of deep convergence and more: an affection that has overcome the divisions wrought by war, politics, the church. The affection, in spite of all, flourishes to this day.

And yet, and yet. In those years our fighting and wrestling and internecine rages were beyond limit in frequency and intensity. Oppressed as we were, we worked out on one another the pain of life with Father. And as in all families, those in the top echelon of age and strength dealt ambiguously with the young. Sometimes they mimed the father and played harsh tyrant. At times they could also be unexpectedly tender and careful. And as might be expected, the intramural warfare came to an abrupt halt whenever one of us was threatened from outside.

Jerry, above all, I remember as a great fighter. Despite his limited stature, he was brawny as a northern oak. In a number of school-yard forays, I was held hostage in an enclosure guarded by underlings of one stripe or another, a camp of contempt. Known as Four Eyes, with my granny spectacles, spindly form, and general air of hebetude, I fairly invited insolence. A battle would develop, the spectacles would go flying in the air, an arc of ruination. A dusty, clamorous mob would form in a flash, to cheer on the mayhem. And suddenly, the oppressor would feel the hammer blow (one would suffice), as my termagant brother came to the rescue in the nick of time.

Word got around: I was not to be worked over. I had reprisal at beck and call.

The wonder is that we did not hate school, or my father, or the nuns who daily broke the seventh seal of our fate and let loose the day. We accepted such and, as best we could, made our way around them. We created piecemeal, like a child's secret shack in a wood, a world to flee to, a world that made a modicum of sense; whether by fantasy, reading, daydreaming, friendship, evasions, untruths on occasion, or simple love of the day and season and countryside.

Time was kind to us. The summers stretched far and wide as a meadow that met the horizon—and beyond. Those dewy mornings, all the world made new: one's bones fairly ached with the splendor of it. The child wandered out of the old house, into the dawn, blinking with awe at the unbearable beauty.

A monumental St. Bernard dog, all but equine in stature, arrived to replace the deceased spaniel. On torrid summer days, this portent lay panting in the shadow of the stone house. He was an angelic guardian, weal to us, woe to any passing canine. We could wrestle and fool with him to hearts' content, climbing and falling, hanging from his imperial limbs, without danger—though he could have swallowed the largest of us at a gulp.

There was also an extensive sandbox built by my father. There one could explore and build and pull down, dig hands and feet deliciously into the damp and cool. Adjacent, a wire enclosure was filled with crawling turtles of every size. Another amenity—a cage of white mice, with their mousy smell and cunning hands and feet; and at times, and all unexpected, a nest constructed overnight, and the mysterious blind newborn.

Farther down the yard, between barn and chicken house, a magnificent rooster lorded it over his hens, a flamenco magnifico shaking out his comb, daring us to venture onto his turf.

In the barn, Ursus the billy goat awaited us, wicked eyes agleam, the wary glance of the born con artist. He was original sin on the hoof, and obscenely proud of it: he wandered the yard, his mean little lips positively itching for trouble. On wash days, Ursus rose to his hind legs and, until chased off, began to make his noon meal of the clothing drying in the sun.

The goat was no respecter of age, beauty, sex. If one were so thoughtless as to turn his or her back on Ursus, the unfortunate bade fair to be sent sprawling before those lowered horns, that festering eye. Thus the mailman and his sack of letters sailed one day through the air; and on another occasion, Mamie Powell, an ubiquitous and incurably nosy neighbor. Semiblind, she mistook Ursus for a friendly dog, patted him on his wicked pate, turned about toward the house. Then she and her ample skirts and her untidy string bags were altogether upended.

And in the stalls to the north of the barn, a spavined horse or two dwelt, and two or three cows, warm and odoriferous; and in season, calves lowing in their pens.

Then above, the hay mow, a region of rustling and mystery. The golden harvest was heaped, as though summer sun and meadows were gathered and trapped there, not merely for winter feeding of the beasts; but for us. The vast, shadowy loft was transformed into refuge and circum maximus. There the world's toil and trouble, discipline and tasks, receded to a minim; a mere hum. We swung like living pendula on frayed ropes, above the fragrant void.

Or we dug tunnels, deep, deep; and, once or twice, uncovered a nest of kittens, blind as bats, their muffled mewing betraying them. Sensing their fate, the mother had borne them in secret and hidden them cunningly. All in vain. Our parents' sentence was peremptory. Closer to birth the better, they must be placed in a sack together with a large stone, all but one or two spared by our intercession; then drowned in the watering trough and buried in a field. Thus in humble fashion, death entered our garden of innocence.

I almost forgot to pay tribute to our swine, a lamentable neglect of worthy creatures. This mulling, drooling, amatory pair dwelt in porcine solitude, at some distance from house and barn. Their shelter and trough were placed strategically, to waft off on prevailing breezes the overmastering piggish effluence and emanation.

My father was particularly strong on classical names, inaccurately applied. He insisted that no barnyard beast of ours should be dishonored by merely common or local appellation. In consequence, in a burst of mischance the goat was yclept Ursus (which is to say, "the bear"). The uxorious hog became known as Antony, his spouse, Cleopatra. Thus were the beasts to manifest, in a prosaic world, the benefits of classical savvy.

One autumn, it was apparent that the swine had attained the limits of porcine inflation. Day after day in autumnal heat, they swayed about laboriously, stuffed to pink snouts with corn and mash, barely able to move from table to couch. They fed with enormous gusto, then made for the shadow of the locust trees, to collapse in grunting ease.

All unknown to them, their hour was at hand. Vast preparations were underway for the apotheosis. Doors were laid on trestles under the fruit trees. Great vats of water were scalded, an array of gleaming knives laid out. Finally a signal passed from my father to his aides. The men laid to, a heave of shoulders was set against a harness of ropes. The first of the victims, some five hundred pounds of terror and inertia, amid thunderous grunts and piercing screams, was dragged by the trotters out of the pen.

The butcher approached. The hog was flung, flailing and thrashing, first to its side, then its back. Each of four men held a trotter, kicking its tattoo for dear life. Like the throat of a monstrous pink baby, the great hog received the knife. The blood geysered in the sun.

It was terrible for a child to behold. Before him was no drowned kitten, dumped moist and flaccid into a hole in the ground; nor a chicken or two, necks swiftly wrung for Sunday dinner. This was bloody death, blood drenching the grass and ground and the aprons of the executioners. The cries of the victims pierced the ears, lingering in dream.

The child never forgot that morning, when an innocent orchard of plum and cherry rang with the screams of an abattoir. And until snow fell, and even through snow, the grasses flourished, wild and green for the blood that drenched their roots.

Let the fiction continue. I am to be thought of now as advancing to the seventh grade. It is the eleventh year of my age, I am roughly of size and weight equal to my younger brother, Philip.

A nascent sense is taking hold: a sense of being someone; of rising from passivity and vegetation. Could it be that I am more than a stone in the road, over which fate treads roughshod? I test things in a feeble way, even venture a thought or an opinion, at table, in class; something of myself. Traits break through the soil, traits that set me off from flora and fauna. I have, if not a mind of my own, at least a mind that is not totally someone else's. As the summer of '32 drew toward autumn, I pondered with an altogether new edginess what the school year might bring.

What it brought was momentous.

Mirabile dictu, a teacher, Sister Mary Lua. An advocate, friend, someone of discernment and skill and instinctive kindness. One for whom the presence of children was a joy. Not a haul, not a burden, not a revenge, not a purgation. Not an occasion to work off taedium vitae, or to exercise contrary virtue, or to please a pastor, or to stroke the superego.

Someone who had chosen to work in the classroom, because that was a vocation indeed, and a noble one. Among children. Querying them, beckoning, reproving, praising, prodding, laughing. Nothing to dissemble, nothing to "work out." A teacher who was not a workhorse, or a drone, or a tyrant, or a drover. A woman who cherished, and revealed, something of Socrates and Jesus and Mother Jones and the Virgin Mary.

Something else too. Something of the high and mighty brought low, and the hungry filled with good things. The vagrant at the back door of the convent asking for food; and being fed. All of which she told about, all of which, she insisted to us in her upstate patois, constituted the heart of the matter. Indeed, if it didn't, what did?

Therefore stories, examples, her life, our lives. Everything made sense. She spoke of convent life, its loneliness, its consolations, why she undertook it, what she found there. And for the first time, the nuns and their lives made common sense; almost common cause.

We were to love the Eucharist, she insisted, and vows, and baptism, and one another, and the Holy Trinity, and Mary. Yes, and sports and dancing; and even now and then, our studies. It was all one, wasn't it, and all good? And if so, was God also not good?

Her tone, in the classroom or out, was simple, conversational, direct. What she had to say came, not from "the cloth," cut to the occasion, dead platitude on a platter. It was herself speaking; someone who lived her words; and then a bracing sense of take it or leave.

Formerly, when a student touched the life of a nun at any point outside the classroom—on an outing, in the convent parlor, on the street—he or she was struck by the double life imposed or adopted. There was the starchy disciplinarian, the "official" person, the one who smiled or frowned from a great height. And only rarely, so rarely as to seem unreal, a flash of the human.

But our new teacher brought the dawning of a great hope.

It says much of the times, and our expectation, that her image stays in the mind, momentous, all but miraculous. And yet she was a simple country woman, afflicted with ill health, neither brilliant nor sophisticated nor politically aware. As far as one could tell, she had no great objection to the convent regime; with one exception.

In such days as those, when the forms of church life seemed set in concrete, this woman spoke scathingly of the subjection of women to the almighty male clergy. On which subject, I recall with gratitude, she could deliver herself of splendid polemics, whether to us, or directly to their Eminences.

At long last, a teacher.

I sit in slack harness, at sixty-six years. A smile breaks on a phiz the child would hardly know for his own. Wrinkles and ruts aplenty, the plowing of the garden of experience.

—Do you remember, I ask the child, the year you started to breathe?

He is puzzled momentarily, but he takes my meaning: I do, he answers. And his grin matches my own.

—Do you recall the face of that nun?

Of course. She was beautiful, not in the way of convention; but of suffering, dignity, self-possession.

—Why this talk of a "great light"?

Because it was the first time, in my cursed desert, the first time I encountered a teacher who was also a human being. Remember how long those years, and how deadly?

—I think I do. I think you know that I do. I think you recall, moreover, that those were by no means the last time someone fastened on a mask of cruelty and terror and boredom and ego and threat and rote—and then, straightfaced, announced that EDUCA-TION was underway.

Indeed. But we were talking about one month in a child's autumn. I knew in my mother a woman of grace and evenhanded love. But I had known no other like her. And the question rises in me whether one such as she is sufficient. Especially when one's life is delivered over, for months and years, into the hands of drones, wasps, jellyfish—and now and then, a certified scorpion. To each and all of whom, if it can be credited, someone, something, has unaccountably conferred a name of moment and dignity and responsibility: teacher.

—It took no time at all, that apotheosis; there was no warning.

On that first day she came briskly into the room. She had piercing black eyes that held nothing but kindness in their depths. A largeness, a scope. She stood there, and surveyed us, and a smile broke; on her face, and ours. We knew at that moment that we were well received, that the year ahead would be a good one.

She would take us at our word, at our conduct, beginning from

that hour. And her expectation was a simple one: that her knowl-
edgeable good sense would draw the best from us. (Would also draw
the worst from us, like a healing purge.)

It came to this: I wanted to learn, after all. That was the light
she kindled. I had not known how desperately I wanted to learn.
The hunger was buried deep, under layers of frustration and contempt. I had become used to half a life, a life of little account. I
was reputed a nonentity in the official ledgers, where jot and tittle
were the rule, and the juices of life ran in a ditch.

—What a darkness I was to myself!

There was the odious blue monthly report card; it laid my fail-
ures open to the four winds, left me cowering and indifferent and
sullen, as the judgment passed from hand to hand.

It was not that I was failing to, as they say, "do well." I did
moderately well, according to the absurd criteria of the report. That
was the curse, that pallid, half-dead moderation in a youthful being.
It was mere fawning in place of achievement; I would please them,
and get out from under.

There was no one to race against, or indeed to announce that
a race was underway, and we the runners. It was life in the doldrums, scrounge and scrape by—and die where you were born.

—But what did the fabled nun do for you, that your memory of
her is so vivid?

She did so much that bears telling, and marks me as lucky at
last. I see her, like a musician, drawing on the wayward strings;
strings that in the wrong hands had soured the music of the spheres
to a hideous cacophony.

—And yet she was no patsy, she held us accountable.

Of course. Before her stood a prime specimen of the omnivorous
reader, a sharp eye—but also an untidy mind, and neglected. He's
running wild and foolish amid *The Rover Boys* and *Tom the Inventor
Sawyer* and the penny dreadfuls. For want of help and direction,
he's being inducted into America. And then—like the Hound in the
ode, she plucked me from it by the hair.

And I ask my soul, What greater benefit could she have granted
me? She dealt the cards fairly, and hearts were trumps.

The dead, or near dead, was coming alive. Here were a few of
the vital signs.

I no longer hid out from life. I came out of my hole and blinked
in the sun, like the animal that announces the coming of spring.

I read books that were something more than fillers for the mind, soporific, unterrific.

Started also taking my measure against my brothers and father. Not in opposition necessarily (though as to my father, one never quite let down the guard). But as an opposite number—who could, for a change, see himself as something more than a cipher.

I was still afflicted with partial blindness, off to the corner of the eye. A cloud of fear and indecision lay on me; it invited trouble.

Under the cloud lay a void: it was that part of me left unfinished, or prevented from being finished; inertia and the forbidding hand of authority.

With delicacy and care, that part might have developed by itself, as the soft spot of a child's skull will close in time.

It did not close. I was tempted to do nothing toward closing the space. To allow others to move in, order me about, control things that (as I was told paternally) were best left in adult hands, experienced hands—never my own.

An element of delightful irony here. After some years, I would pass from the shadow of my father, not into sunlight certainly; but into the shadow of another paternity, a Jupiterian low-riding, lightning-bearing cloud: the Jesuits.

Talk about the paternal hand! Direction, control, contretemps, commandeering of life! But this is another subject, for another time. . . .

We were becoming, each in his own way, and by many a meandering path, great readers. My mother hauled home from the city library, week after week, novels listed and ordered by my father. There were Hardy and Dickens and Scott and Trollope and many another Victorian.

It was notable how much was missing. No moderns, no hint that the twentieth century had affected any writer, poet, novelist, essayist, biographer, priest, or pope. No hint that our own century had been, or was in process of becoming, a matter of self-invention, of hope and horror, and the celebrating and mourning of these. A matter, in sum, to be taken seriously.

Curious indeed. Here we sat reading through the long winter evenings, after the day's debts settled; hard labor in my father's case, school in ours. Willy nilly, we were in this world and time; we were the children of the thirties, its votaries, wage earners, even, to a limited degree, its mental spelunkers.

Our fate lay within the times; the animated round of its clock. We must tinker with it, await its summons, obey its rhythms.

And despite all this, we were ignorant as the unborn of the times, of the world of imagination seething and boiling around us. Playwrights and poets and novelists and chroniclers and filmmakers. We set our watches and obeyed the bells, and concluded that these alone were required. But in all matters that touched the world to the quick and drew blood, revolutions and inventions and explorations, economic and political and religious turmoil, we might have been tending the graves of long gone Victorians; or been buried with them.

In the strange, self-immunized, monkish life we led, the influence of my father was paramount and, for a time, overbearing.

He detested movies beyond measure, and aimed his largest discharge of spleen at Hollywood in the thirties, as the filmmakers dared bring his beloved classics to the screen. He contended that all such distortions, whether announced as *David Copperfield*, *Captains Courageous*, or *Vanity Fair*, were detestable amputations of the originals. As such, they were not worth a rag, let alone three hours of rapt attention. They betrayed the plain intent of their origins; they cut and spliced and distorted events and characters, which the printed word had left to one's imagining.

Who indeed, he stormed, were Metro-Goldwyn-Mayer, to tell us, through their overpaid stars, through snips of dialogue cut bodily from context, who the great human models and villains were, what they looked like, what their motives were? By what right was inspired dialogue excised from the page, and worse and worse, other banal converse substituted? What criteria were at work, except a prosperous pocketbook and a shrinking span of attention? What species of taste would abridge seven or eight hundred pages of dense material into so squalid a span of time? And by what right did they tag this botchwork with the splendid title of its original, debased beyond all recognition?

Endless. His veins would swell and redden as he declaimed. It was clear that deeper matters were at stake than those under discussion.

A similar ballyhoo roiled away in matters of poetry. My father was a poet. The title must immediately be modified. He was a poet manqué. And this, as the poet has said, made all the difference.

I concluded at the time, with the perverse logic of the young, a logic drawn from no experience, but from a pressing fact, close to home, that all poets were defeated poets. I had met one such, and generalized to all. God forbid, they must all be like him, defrocked, defeated, debunked.

The fact that my father was a singer unsung, and likely to remain so, made his song all the more strident. If he was deprived of the large audience that was his plain due, he would be tyrannically lyrical at home.

He was a caged bird (the image is outlandish, and his own); he would split our ears with his urgent dissonances. For lack of public, he would create a few victims.

The Victorian and Romantic poets of the nineteenth century were, with the sole exception of Shakespeare, his passion. We, his audience perforce, had at hand no standard by which to judge. We simply knew nothing of such matters.

Talk about revisionist history! According to his infallibility, there had occurred in England, around the time of his young manhood, a splendid eruption of poetic genius. The coterie lived and wrote, then disappeared, and was not replaced. A volcano had erupted, shot to the skies its lavic genius, and grown cold. It protruded there on his landscape, all was dead around it. And here we were; thus the twentieth century. But he was the recorder of that hour when all had been lurid and alive.

The governing images were awry and put him permanently at disadvantage. We, being uninstructed, were subject to the worst kind of instruction: his ranting. What should have been a discussion, became instead a passionate argument—with whom, was never clear. The ungrateful present, its media hounds, its unintelligible poets? His passion ricocheted off four walls.

My mother bore all this with a weary submission. And his sisters and brothers, in varying degrees, cheered him on. He was the neglected genius; an ignorant and foolish and benighted public (and his own children!) were blithely ignorant of the greatness in their midst.

It was all the veriest hogwash. He was, alas, no better or worse a poet than a thousand kitchen scriveners of the time. Some earned a precarious living designing verses for occasional cards and calendars and the title pages of ladies' diaries or the "commonplace books" in vogue. And this, of course, was understandable, and even charming.

But his lack of serious talent, and his efforts to make much of little, this was another matter. Even in failure he must breathe deep and double his stature. His poetic ambitions, like his ego, were Napoleonic; he tended in style not to the brief, modest lyric, but the Pindaric, the ode, the epic. He spent himself hour after hour behind closed doors, we being warned to keep our silence while he composed his reams of windy rhetoric.

It was all extremely sad; it looks uncharitable in the setting down. Do I trace an unrelievedly dark picture with few nuances?

Let me summon to mind that other side, the moments of rare charm and warmth, that wit and style and verve. If his morbid ambition fell short, he had other, less torridly pursued, talents, of great moment and surpassing modesty. They were gifts that were, in a sense, afterthoughts; they leaked from his person like gold or grain from a faulty pocket. He neither gathered nor coveted; the living grain lay there, to our benefit and delight.

In my boyhood he was in the vigor of manhood, well set up, handsome, strong, lively. Now and then he shook off his stiff public bones, fell to the rug, and wrestled and squirmed about with the younger children, rode them piggyback, pranced about the house or yard, to the accompaniment of the most delicious mimicking of the animal world.

Or of a summer evening, he would set the three youngest beside him. And reward our clamor of "Tell us a story!" with stories indeed; wild and improbable and altogether enchanting, like dreams stealing into the eyes of sleepy children.

Invariably, the stories dwelt on his railroading days in the Wild West; exploits never performed on land or sea; characters who ne'er walked the prosaic earth, until he conjured them up.

And what a conjurer he was! What turns of phrase, what tropes and mime and mockery he could beckon out of thin air. The Irish and Swedes and Yankees of his youth, the country adage, the phrase that capped an argument or crowned a character—all these, with no visible striving or strain, he was master of.

He is dead, years since. From time to time, his sons gather. Inevitably they set about recalling, even rejoicing in, his memory. And guffawing and marveling too, as they savor again the salt and spice, the unrepeatable flavor of the man. With a wince, or a silence, or a merciful passing over of the deep faults in his nature, as these took their toll on ourselves. It is as though we have reached an age of mercy; perhaps sensing in our bones the hope of receiving it. For we are of him; and the need of mercy will never pass.

His great, undoubted virtues lay beyond self-understanding. He paid them no heed. But his faults were another matter: they lay at the center of his being; he claimed them. And they him.

This is the pity and the loss.

He passed those best years of his life, years which coincided with my youth, at slavish and ill-paid work. He never complained that the work galled him. He was, in fact, a clever and valued workman, a member of a gang of groundmen that dug holes for electric poles, maintained and repaired equipment, was on emergency call during storms. The work exacted all his strength, and next to nothing of his talent. Fair weather or foul, it left the better part of him unchallenged.

The Depression of the early thirties struck us a body blow.

The National Recovery Act and a panoply of Roosevelt measures attempted to deal with the financial plight of the poor, unemployed, and dispossessed. I remember taking part in a great parade in downtown Syracuse, celebrating the purported end of our stagnant submission. Schoolchildren, along with workers and professionals, marched down Salina Street in holiday mood. There were brave banners and flags numberless; we were supplied with paper stickers to be applied to our clothing, marking us as red, white, and blue enthusiasts for the new order.

There was, alas, suffering and unrest aplenty in our neighborhood, which took on an increasingly dour look. Those who existed with heads barely above the line of survival began to go under.

We, having a spot of land, a barn, farm animals, crops, and the prestige accruing to rarae aves, those slightly mysterious Catholic churchgoers, became an unlikely focus. The underdogs came to us. Into my mother's kitchen arrived many of the women to disburden themselves. And my father's wide range of acquaintances and admirers gave him access also. Indeed, in such days he came into his own; an audience of more or less stupefied neighbors, and he declaiming spiritedly on the decline and fall of "the days of God."

He prided himself on a political acuity which one was permitted, only at the back of the hand, to doubt. He conveyed even the most dubious truths with such vigor and such passion and such an onrush of vocabulary (much of the usage imperfectly mastered, if truth were told)—as to quite confound local skulls.

Thus the various gifts and connections of my parents responded to a time of travail; and mysteriously crossed the path of a political savior. The reverberations were to shake to its foundations our heretofore tranquil front parlor.

The first faint rumor reached us through the oracles of Matson Avenue. There were other reports too; my grandmother Fromhart had heard the voice, a golden enchanter, broadcast locally into her home in Detroit. Father Coughlin had started in a rather conventional way; a young priest offering pastoral consolations to the housebound and elderly of the city.

He caught on, made wave upon wave, leapt radio station to station; until his thunder, weighted now with oracular certitudes of an undoubted political character, shattered the dominical somnolence, East Coast to West. He set the ears tingling; the Catholics, especially, bolted upright.

There had never been his like in America. Religious charmers aplenty had risen, had their day, and fallen: evangelists and doomsayers and quacks and revivalists and abolitionists and pacifists, crisscrossing the continent; setting up their tents; trumpeting judgment; excoriating social evil, war, slavery; denouncing sinners and backsliders.

But these, the Catholics said smugly, were the grotesqueries spawned by Protestants, who owned the nation's subcultures, and must be granted their freaks and saints.

Such had little or nothing to do with the one, holy, Catholic and apostolic church. The Catholics were occupied in producing, generation upon generation, priests and nuns and bishops cut from single whole cloth. These were something else: builders and maintainers of a vast unitary structure, complete, weathertight, and fully furnished. Planted securely on American soil were classrooms for children and nascent universities and hospitals; convents and priests' dwellings, and here and there a bookstore or publishing house.

As for those entrusted with the care of souls, as well as the souls being cared for, they were advised to obey, hold their tongues, and await orders. There was, in fine, neither tradition nor welcome for the freakish, the uninhibited—let alone for challengers of the political status quo. The (divinely appointed) guardians of the Edifice were convinced that it (and they) owed too much to the American arrangement to undertake even a mild critique. Catholics minded their business and said their prayers; their business in consequence, flourished.

Then into the stale sacristy air thundered the Voice, its owner an altogether unexceptionable cleric. Beyond doubt, he was "in good standing" with his bishop. He began to take on the national establishment, his tones leaning heavily toward the insinuating. Thence he became declarative; and thereafter and permanently, declamatory. The message was deceptively simple, with the simplicity of the sainted or perverse. Week after week, he touched the raw nerve of poverty and disaffection and wholesale suffering of the Depression years. He gave voice to the voiceless: the jobless and evicted and desperate.

At long last, someone cared! The voice stroked, soothed, lashed out; a touch of gold, a touch of God, a promise of healing, the flick of a whip. And then the sinister undertones: anger, factionalism, and in time, anti-Semitism.

A volatile mix, pouring out, week upon week, for years. It was by turns syrup and brimstone: it promised and threatened and cajoled, whispered and boomed like a bell of summoning.

It reached us. Whether at Matson Avenue, where the minor Fates raveled and spun, or in our rustic demesne, the Sunday calm was shattered. About the radio gathered the votaries of "The Hour of Saint Therese."

It was inevitable that Coughlin, having offered his analysis of the American ills, should set out to correct them. There were millions at his side by now, his indignation was their own. His mail was enormous; a squad of volunteers read every letter; somehow, it was said, he supervised an answer. I remember the jubilation in the poorest homes, where the aged and impoverished huddled at their stoves through the brutal winter. The gruel was thin, the outlook unimaginably bleak. But a letter from Father Coughlin flared in the dark and cold. It was produced proudly, to be read to the visitor. The message was reassuring and vague, in the manner of a guru: all would yet be well.

Eventually Coughlin announced a political program that embraced the economic theories of one Dr. Townsend. The proposals touched on weak spots in the Roosevelt recovery program: retirement benefits and a guaranteed income for the aged.

The Voice grew more assured. Something was wrong in the land, someone was responsible. Scapegoats were sought out. Surely, behind this economic and moral disarray, an evil power lurked! Jews, in particular the Raskob empire; and then the good friend of capitalists and millionaires, Al Smith. And even the president.

It was a gnostic universe indeed, battle lines neatly drawn, good and evil contending, victim and victimizer.

After a political program, a political party; and a newspaper, and local organization.

The neighbors began to assemble with regularity in our home. The inarticulate began to speak up. We youngsters were excluded from the assemblies; my understanding of their content is, in consequence, arrived at thirdhand, and somewhat hazy.

Nothing hazy, however, in the singleminded poor who gathered, week after week, to discuss the latest pronunciamento of their oracle, to discuss among themselves the subjects he raised. Issues that were matters of life and death to themselves: jobs, income, welfare, employment, the cost of food and fuel.

Into our kitchen they marched. It was winter, men and women stomped the snow from their feet, small jobbers, farm laborers, factory workers, those whose grubstake was vanishing before their eyes.

Coughlin had announced the formation of a national political party, and a candidate for president. A weekly paper, *Social Justice*, made its appearance, extolling the program and puffing the leadership.

It came to this, our locals exulted: with the exception of President Roosevelt, no one on the scene could hold a candle to Father Coughlin in brains, eloquence, charisma.

That autumn the presidential election was held. The candidates put forward by Coughlin trailed badly; the party folded. A wave had passed. It left a shore strewn with the battered and bewildered.

Rome was stirred by Coughlin's bold moves. At the behest of the pope, the redoubtable Cardinal Pacelli insinuated his elegant self into America. He made a courtesy call on the president and stopped in Detroit for an exchange with Coughlin's bishop. The cleric was thereupon called in and cooled down.

Effectively, Coughlin was no more: a frontal assault on the American system had folded. But the issues he raised, in tones vicious, tainted, passionate, persuasive, and self-serving, had not gone away. Neither, to be sure, had riches, or poverty, or war, or slums, or bread lines—or conventional politics, that wondrous false front behind which the true drama of power is played out. Money, deprivation; false hope, real despair.

At the time of Coughlin's triumph and fall, another Catholic was also championing the poor. She was armed with great gifts and fueled with a like indignation. But with a difference.

Dorothy Day was, in some respects, similar to Coughlin. She was witheringly contemptuous of the political game as it played in the national arena. Converted to Catholicism, she dug deep into her faith, into the quest for justice, and the spirit and tactic of nonviolence. She lodged her roots in rock. They endured there for a lifetime, and bore fruit.

Presidents, she knew, might come and go, right, left, center. The poor were still poor, the homeless, homeless. Slums festered, lives were wasted. The "filthy rotten system," in her pungent phrase, cast up generations of victims whose lot the system was either helpless to, or indifferent to, relieve.

In her view, solutions were not to be sought in the terms proposed. War and poverty, poverty and war; the cycle would never be broken by shoring up the existing arrangements and their savage ideology of dog eat dog.

What was required was a renewal of the imagination, stalemated by two centuries of business as usual, war as usual, poverty as usual. Not only the poor, but the rich also, were stuck where they were born. The church as well, because to all intents, it took poverty and war for granted, rhetoric to the contrary notwithstanding.

Was this indeed the church she had joined, after her tumultuous voyage through despair and disillusion? The church, another system both benefiting from, and beneficial to, the economic and political system? She heard the preachers announce a kind of debased fatalism: "the poor always with you." And the same church she saw stretching its theory of just war to embrace any and all horrors. The church had become the great moral adjuster, soother, conspirator, jingoistic and complacent.

She loved the church nonetheless. The church of saints and sinners, in places high and low. The church of the poor, of Francis of Assisi and Teresa of Avila and the Cure d'Ars. Like them, she sought a fulcrum, an instrument that in the right hands, and with however slight a leverage, might turn things on their head.

She came on the tool: the right hands were her own. The tool was neither politics as practiced, nor public acclaim or opprobrium, nor the enlistment of the masses in vast movements. She had seen all that, and seen it fall. The simple task, the one practically everyone boggled at, or bowed out of, or commended to others; this she would do. And if required, would do it alone. She would live and work among the urban poor; she would commend the Gospel by living it; the first change of all would be exacted of herself.

Thus she would declare peace, as others declared war.

Dorothy Day embraced this design, be it noted, not in order to bring political or economic changes (though these were desperately important, and respected as such). Not in the first place. The first place was sacrosanct, and existed independent of political gain or loss. She would live in such a way, and speak and write from the bottom, not because it made sense in the world to do so (it made no sense, she would be vilified and despised for it), or because it converted the world (it converted very few), or made human tragedy somewhat less likely.

None of these. Her politics stemmed from a command that she heard proclaimed from Someone of no time or place, of every time and place. Blessed are the peacemakers, blessed are the poor in spirit, what you do for the least of these, you do for Me.

She would not become a media personality, she would offer no political or academic alternative, as such were commonly understood, to things as they were. She had an impetuous dislike for "alternatives" that accepted things as they were as a given, a point of departure for political action—and so never ventured far from things as they were.

Coughlin rose and fell, the wild icon of a mad time. The icon was revered for awhile, as is the way with American worshipers. Then it was pulled down, and seen no more. His image compelled and fired the imagination; but the fire was fitful, the vivid image quickly faded.

He was, as a more thoughtful time revealed, the perfect cleric for the time and culture; he fitted it hand to glove, blessing and curse. Unbalanced by ambition and ego, he ended by worsening the ills and discontents he set out to cure.

Dorothy Day, Charles Coughlin. Each had a presence in our home. Coughlin with his beguiling voice, the fierce homilist of our once tranquil Sabbath. He was our Luther, our Zwingli, our Savonarola, our fierce fundamentalist restorer of justice and thy kingdom come.

Dorothy's paper, the *Catholic Worker*, also found a place of honor in our home; from the start, as I recall. I cannot, at this remove, assess her influence on our offering of hospitality to the homeless and food to the hungry. Such things developed at their own pace, it seemed. But Coughlin's paper, *Social Justice*, and Day's *Catholic Worker*, in addition to the *Commonweal* and *America* (the latter two loaned by my aunts), were, beyond doubt, influential, then and for the future.

The years of Depression were dreadful and punishing. The poor were at our door, at our table—and on our hands, so to speak. Thus, as the theologians would have it, we passed from orthodoxy to orthopraxis; words that would have brought a frown to my mother's brow, a pursing of the lips. Theory being, in her view, at one with practice; and what might be the problem, why should they be separated?

I dredge the image of Coughlin from memory, a rather sinister figure, a voluble ghost.

But Dorothy Day, if I may indulge in understatement, is someone else. No phantom she, no curiosity. Alive, resonant, a decade after her death she is a presence that exacts and invites. She became my friend and the friend of my family; and the friendship was to spur our moral and political development.

The child tasted, and has not forgotten to this day, the malice of anti-Catholicism; as in 1928, Al Smith ran for the prize, and was smartly tripped as he ran. No Catholic in the White House!

Even in so unlikely an arena as the miserable dust bowl of our schoolyard, anticipation of his defeat (and by implication our own) was celebrated. Older yokels than myself (this occurred, of course, in the White School of the neighborhood) gathered about the few young "Catliks" to chortle their delight and afflict our ears with odious slogans.

Coughlin struck back hard, and mitigated the ugliness. Dorothy Day, on the other hand, was simply not interested in instructing such minds as took seriously "Rum, Romanism, and Rebellion." To a surface view, in the matter of American bigotry, as in other areas, she changed little or nothing. And yet, over the long savannahs of eighty years, what changes she brought; and to my family also.

Through gentle osmosis and less gentle nudges, she introduced us to a sane and perennial Catholicism: a circle of prayer and compassion and service. Hand to hand, hand to mouth, she served. The warmakers, the believers in war, she answered by a simple, unanswerable expedient: she went to jail and said her no from there.

Her example would last and outlast. Her faith met every fierce, nationalistic, moody, chic, polluted current with her own countercurrent, her drive and eloquence and insight, deep and strong and ultimately prevailing.

And this same current she set moving in us.

Up against it as we were, politically naive and isolated, we might have become hard-core Coughlinites and, in one way or another, have gone down with our mentor. We did not.

We could also have been induced, then or at some later time, to enlist in one or another group of crazies; and thereupon have perished. We might have become the Luddites of our century, the Weathermen of the seventies, the Falwellians or Reaganites of the eighties. There are many ways of going mad in America, a specific insanity for every decade; each offering its own bizarre form of "definitive solution." None of these ways seized upon us.

This is by no means meant to claim that my brothers and I have not been guilty of absurdities, foibles, fallings from grace. These occurred, to our shame, and are confessed here. (If indeed such confession is not redundant, our sins being a matter of public record, subject to frequent review and denunciation.)

I bring up such matters as occasion of tribute. We could hardly have known in our childhood that such deep pilings were being laid in earth and time, or that landmarks were even then being set out. And all for our sakes.

I had never met a Jesuit, we knew little of Dorothy Day. And yet there were Jesuits in the world, and I would become one. And Dorothy Day, and her houses of hospitality, and her grasp of the Sermon on the Mount—she was waiting too. It is an ecstatic reflection: a world of moral splendor, a very banquet of creation, was being spread for us.

In regard to our parents, our attitudes were complex. Beyond doubt, we took our mother for granted. I am not sure that in this we differed greatly from children of any time. That she was there for us, in season and out, was a matter of fact; the one who, we presumed, would always be there; the one who was there in the nature of things.

To put the gift thus dispassionately is one way of expressing the awesome, all but biological, selfishness of the young. Perhaps in extenuation, one could speak of a ploy of nature not to open doors of understanding and regret too quickly, for risk of spinning the young soul off center.

As to a fact. It was only later, perhaps too late for repair, that so peerless a survivor and stylist as my mother appears in her true grandeur, surrounded by the lesser lights who lent foil to her radiance.

In my case, delayed gratitude, like delayed justice, is indeed a puny thing, all but contemptible. The tardiness galls the memory and cries for pardon. Gratitude delayed for years and years—what sort of gratitude is that? And how, in any case, does one repair ingratitude and indifference toward the dead?

The reparation includes tears and humiliation, and more. Perhaps the sorry best one can attain is the resolve to live, as best one can muster, that sublime humaneness and constancy tried, long ago, so sorely.

And there was my father (whose ashes these pages perhaps rake too fine). With him, my game was survival, my trick, hideaway. Life was a hide-and-seek: I wanted only to be off his retina. Let him summon me peremptorily, let him grow attentive, and all was lost. Or so it seemed.

I was a child fast transmogrifying into a different specimen entirely. One who was beginning to live by ideas, to love reading and study—who would shortly begin putting reflective powers to the test.

And yet, and yet. In the presence of the one who could be of most help, I was struck dumb. The admission is offered as stark fact; it stems from no pride, only a deep humiliation. My father was like a merciless brand cast into a dark place; the glare struck one blind.

The mother knew that the boy must be offered protection from that light and heat.

Something fortunate had transpired. A teacher at the White School, Miss Marcella Gaffney, had befriended the boy. And long before he departed for St. John's, a warm bond was in place. She and her parents, her brother and sisters, made him welcome in their home.

It became a Saturday ritual after a time. The seven-year-old would be hefted aboard a trolley car wending its clanging voyage northward in the direction of the outlying village, Liverpool. By prior arrangement, he would be met on arrival, and lifted down. And there, a pet indeed, he would pass the day, at play and meals in the old frame house of his friends, overlooking the northern reaches of the lake.

In the afternoon, a Packard motor car would purr into the yard. In it were ensconsed, under furs and rugs, relatives of considerable substance. Unheard of style, luxury even! A country ride was in store.

In we bundled, seven of us. Such grandeur! The boy was placed on a folding stool and swathed in an auto blanket, like the scion of a pharaoh. And off we went grandly, through a ten- or fifteen-mile circuit of countryside.

The likes of this chariot had seldom crossed his sight, and had never welcomed his limbs. The glory of it rendered him intermittently speechless and feverishly talkative, to the wonderment of the adults.

And finally at dusk, he would be deposited at his own door, the invariable gift of a dime in his hand, or a quarter on special holidays. Warm farewells, urgings that he return a week from the day.

The Gaffneys, the O'Briens, such friends! With what ready tact and unspoken understanding they helped my family steer its child into calm waters!

It is perhaps unnecessary to add that the arrangement described here was unpleasing to my father. One citizen of his domain had slipped the leash. But my mother chose her ground, and stood there, come hell or high water. She was adamant: I would continue to visit my friends as long as I wished.

We were growing apace, and we hardly knew it. For one thing, there were few markers along the road against which to measure our passage. For some ten years of my boyhood, neither wedding, baptism, nor funeral occurred within the family circle. It seemed indeed a closed circle, untouched by event of note or notoriety.

We went with the seasons, and returned at their bidding; to

school, to work in field or barn, to church, to an occasional dance or sporting event or outing. We traveled not at all, if by travel one understands the passing of a day and night elsewhere. I remark the wonderment when one of us, an older brother, actually voyaged to New York City; and, O marvel!—attended a play on Broadway.

There came a time of serious illness, my mother's. Expenses increased; it was required that the oldest son abandon his schooling and take on a man's burden. In this case, farm work, contracted with a friend at some distance.

The scheme, alas, lengthened out, and lasted for years. What started as an emergency became a form of fate for my brother, brilliant and promising as he was.

My mother was hospitalized with tuberculosis. The story of her displacement by a maiden aunt, of the unhappiness that marred our life, and indeed awakened the worst and darkest in each of us—of this I have written, and it requires no detailed recalling here. Those of the children still living at home became subject to a strange experiment, to the background applause of my father.

In a modest way, the children had thriven under my mother's culinary art. But my aunt found our living too fat by far. She began applying a practice immortalized in her own meager frame: the Thinning of the Soup. Having no experience of children, she nonetheless felt qualified to apply the salutary Dickensian method. Let them give thanks; and let no poorhouse boy ask for more!

Thus while we thinned down under a regime of Slim Pickings, family fortunes brightened. My aunt was able to display, week after week, to my father's delighted gaze, the shrinking of the red ledger and the bulking of the black. He was quite beside himself with admiration. We heard such sounds of high-minded mutuality as almost to compensate for our growling bellies. Almost, but not quite.

Autumn arrived, but no season of mellow fruitfulness for us. Thanksgiving that year stands in memory as a kind of bleak domestic *Beggars' Opera*. Turkey and trimmings were declared unsuitable for growing boys. My aunt sniffed categorically: soup and bread made more sense; the diet would serve, moreover, to curb our fractiousness. Pumpkin pie? Mincemeat pie? Horrors. Too rich for young bones. The infamous molasses cookies, familiar and disgusting, dry as steerage biscuits, must suffice.

It was a glum era, it went on interminably.

My father exulted. The paling of my mother's moon was the rising of his sun.

And pale my mother was, with the dread spotted lung that condemned her first to bed, then to hospital.

But she was by no means defeated; the usurpation of her kitchen and keys burned within her. Only give her time and patience; indignation, like a larger fire, would consume the lesser one of illness. There came a day when, in her judgment, if not that of her doctors, she was to return home.

Enough patience. It required a mere twenty-four hours, once she was within our walls, to effect the permanent eviction of the Artisan of Stone Soup. The feat was accomplished, as I recall, in an icy calm. In level tones, my mother expressed gratitude for the labors of the Meager Manager, adding simply that because she, Freda, was now all but recovered and, in any case, resident in her premises, there could be no point in a further sojourn of so kind and capable etcetera, etcetera.

It was not advisable to take my mother for granted. My father, according to her, had concluded in the darkness of his mind that her illness was fatal, that nothing stood in the way of a replacement more to his taste. And once again he tripped over that unconquerable will of hers.

"He was hoping, of course, that I would die," she recalled later, in her laconic way.

Though he lived long, she survived him for a decade.

I grew to high school age. There was no change of venue: St. John the Baptist, the same order of nuns in charge.

During these years the die of my future was cast, with regard to habit of mind and vocation.

I was to be a student and reader of books for the rest of my mortal days. My reading habits, however, then and now, hardly evoke the name or nature of scholarship. At age thirteen, I was voracious and persistent, in the image of those bookworms that purportedly do their work silently, in the dark. I read in four years everything that chance, occasion, the school library, our own bookcases, hands careless or careful, cast at me: from Shakespeare (to recall the gamut) through the jejune novels of a Jesuit, Francis Finn;

stories that bore such improbable titles as *Tom Playfair* and *Percy Winn*.

Literature, and its sedulous apes, imitations, and second cousins—this was the passion. I was an indifferent student of Latin, better at French, and abominable in math and science. The latter two, and our consistent unsuccess in their regard, probably mark a defect in the genetic construction of the clan. Not one of us mastered the rudiments, not to mention fine points, of geometry, statistics, or even algebra. Philip did least shamefully; and he was no great champion. For the rest of us, we sidled by those great roadblocks.

A few teachers stand out in memory. Not because any was unusually endowed. But each in her own way had a generous sense of the human, a measure of simpatico for youthful flagrancies and foibles. And each was able to give a nudge at the right moment to a glimmer of ambition or talent.

And of one it can be said in all simplicity that but for her I would never have dreamed of knocking at the portals of the Mighty Fortress of Jesuitry.

She was a teacher of French, which she spoke and wrote elegantly. Holiness dwelt in the sweetness of her smile, her radiance, the patience with which, in spite of ill health, she shepherded her recusant flock into pastures new. Among the saints she loved Joan of Arc, whom perhaps she resembled.

For reasons that remain obscure to this day, she spotted me for a priest. Me? I squirmed and dodged, she played the line with patience; and one day the bait was taken.

She was mistress of an old method, and in those days an honored one; and I am not at all certain that it is dead today, or dishonored by later experience. It went this way: "promising candidates" were regularly hailed into the convent parlor, there to be interrogated as to their works and pomps, their prayer and social habits. The first of such interviews might open with a question: whether one had seriously considered the priesthood or convent. If so, he or she was enjoined to continue, by hallowed means, to seek out further light on the "will of God." If not, why not? Serious counsel was given to ponder whether this awesome step might not represent the sovereign will.

To be so summoned was momentous: it marked one as part of

a select company. We were enjoined to receive Communion frequently, to open the question of our future to a trusted confessor, and to report with regularity as to progress or pitfalls.

CHAPTER 5

The Jesuits, for Life

I sit like a dunce in the incandescent noon
stool, cap, notes,
a liberated blind man
whose eyes bear him like wings
out of night's stinking nest, into the world.
Intellectual vision, reality by definition?
No. The Jesuit mind, a Homer
assembles fleets, sails for its continent
across seas tamed by the ordering governing glance.
But to light on and finger the world, bit by bit
an old woman in a flea market—
junk, onions, ordure. Ingredients and parts.
The old fingers, wise as eyes, come on something. A yes.

My closest friend, a classmate, was singled out for this practical attention. Thus matters deepened: from now, two would be in quest of the Grail, side by side. I watched and waited, and was touched by an obscure sense, sometimes disturbing, of being blessed in a way I had hardly chosen.

I have seldom dwelt in these notes on the theme of friendship; perhaps because I had yet, at that time, to feel to the quick its impact. My brothers and I could count a whole squad of knockabout pirates and neighborhood urchins. We romped and played and worked the fields together, swam the old Salt Pond; and, against orders, dared Lake Onondaga in an unseaworthy scow that should not have been launched in a bathtub. But for all that, those closest to me were my family.

But now something of note, this impeccable gent, this Jesuit to be! He surely merits a pause in the beat, a lengthy and grateful word.

He was the scion of a European-style middle-class family that dwelt in all but solitary spendor (by our bug-eyed standards) on the suburban edge of the parish. His father was a highly seeded official of a corporation known to my family, and generally among working people, for its harsh dealings with employees.

The family was convoluted as a shell, and close as an ear to its own murmur. What the shell murmured, what the ear heard, was known to few. Day after day, the Packard chariot would deposit them at school: sister and brother, she a splendid redhead, he all dignity and elegance.

In school and out, the two navigated strictly on their own. No horseplay or antics, never a citation for breach of discipline. The clothing matched the demeanor: it was correct, correct. Life is serious business! Family first and last! If there was a family escutcheon (there probably was, somewhere) surely such as these mottoes were blazoned on it.

By a process both mysterious and simple, I was admitted to their castle keep. It was a friendship fated to endure weathers and age, illness and separation, diverse interest and works. It was to prevail— even in the Jesuits, who perhaps do not offer the ideal nest for such dovetailing.

He was a fascinator. Even today, despite the onset of creeping decrepitude, we make a good pair, by "trine and opposition." He is as he was, collected and intellectual, all buried fires. He of the mandarin vocal qualities and stance. And I, in common estimate, a species of Irish dilly, ready for the road and its chances and mischances; often beckoning trouble to my side without reckoning consequences.

At the time of our Great Decision, he was strictly a mother-and-daddy boy, the apple of doting eyes, the self-conscious bearer of the banner. I might well have come into existence in the gang of six at a chance roll of the dice, lucky or unlucky. I happened to be set down there and, like my brothers, was taken for granted. He was adored and cozened and played piper to, in school and out. I dwelt uneasy in the pull and undertow of a war, now hot, now cold, somewhere in no-man's-land—brothers in one trench, Dado in the other. And the mediating mother running medical aid between.

The litany of contrasts! He had money in pocket, mine was empty as last year's nest.

From age eight, we sat and suffered in the same classroom;

though by common estimate, His Imperturbability suffered far less than most. Or so it was judged, and enviously.

I kept a weather eye out in his direction. Something about him was immensely intriguing: a discipline and nobility rare indeed in our undisciplined crew. More, his self-confidence shook me. Who was this character, so spiffy, so sure of himself? The rumor had all the force of prophecy: cursed or blessed, he was bound for the priesthood, and had been for years. He seemed a modern version of the quaint martyrological tribute we were to hear so often in the seminary, that so-and-so "never knew the world rather than left it."

He would probably dispute the preceding as too simple by far. I set it down with due apologies. Thus he appeared to a friend.

And this must be said, affectionately and with a full heart. But for him, I would be sporting a far different cap and gown today; or none at all. My half-century in the Jesuits is due, under God, to him. A conviction that, given the world and its mad hammers and anvils, is no mean tribute, and promises no sorry outcome.

That is how I sort things out in the mind: I became a priest and, more specifically, a Jesuit, because of him. The estimate bespeaks modesty of mind, conferred, I would suppose, by life itself—a stripping away of heat and rhetoric.

God was in the picture, indeed enthroned there, in the manner of a Solomon or a Pontifex Maximus, solemn-faced and formal, a splendid potentate under a canopy. And disposing all things, and us as well.

But this is an image drawn by an innocent's hand, by no means my aging one. It summons another time, a time byzantine, lucid, childlike; the firing of a splendid cup, and then its breaking. The heat rose, the cup broke, the image dissolves.

What remains is—what remains. The Jesuit cup lies broken on the altar. The imperial Christ looming above, blazing there, ordering all things strongly and sweetly—He is shaken. The radiant stones that compose his face fall to pavement, a storm of diamond and gold. What remains is impoverished, diminished, a mere breath on a glass. What remains, the One we name or misname, or in fear refuse to name; the One beyond all images, the exhalation of the holy; the Spirit.

Come Holy Spirit. Perhaps that Breath and Hint and Pulse comes in order to correct the images we coveted and concocted, all wrong.

Were we not deceived, self-deluded, inflated with our quasi emperor worship, love of pomp, lust after "riches, honors, the credit of a great name"? Perhaps in such worship, in such churches, surrounded by such a Christ, mirroring back on us our own appetite and ego, we were worshiping—ourselves?

At least the illusions are gone, or perhaps they exercise less dominion. My friend has endured illness, loss of fame, denigration of his great talents. He has been shifted from pillar to post by hands less disposed to integrity, and more itchy after ego and institution, than might be admired. Indeed the splendid cup has been broken.

And what of the friend of my friend?

In the summer of '86, I was invited to England to baptize the newborn son of Sinead and Jeremy Irons. The ceremony was held on a faultless day, on a splendid promontory overlooking the Avon. The focus of our gathering was a carven font, dating from Reformation times, come upon by Jeremy, and set up laboriously for the occasion.

The font had been broken by Reformation vandals. The pieces had been reassembled and cemented, in view of our ceremony. But when the waters were lifted and poured over the child, we saw how the font leaked, the waters seeped through and ran down the splendid carven sides. One imagined them making their secret way underground to the river, and thence to the sea.

Broken indeed; but then, the rush and release!

My friend was gifted with a native modesty. He knew a stone from a slice of bread, and this world from a better.

If I offered the friendship something, it was a slight zig and zag to his straight and narrow. His danger was dwelling in Dullsville; as mine was Life as Circus. He needed a slight punching up, a prod to the anatomy here and there; as I must, from time to time, be consigned to the town stocks, for a space of thinking things through.

We spent hours together reading, quieting down, small or large talk, speculation on that most delicious and fearsome topic. What indeed were we to make of our lives, where to invest that golden egg?

And then he visited our farm. My mother sized him up, and liked what she saw.

His family was by no means reconciled to the idea of his entering a religious order. The diocesan priesthood, of course. But the Jesuits, those vows, that isolation, being shipped off, hither and yon, perhaps to another end of the world, at someone's nod! It was intolerable, it was inhuman.

His mother was a vivid Irish beauty of considerable musical talent. She aired her objections loudly to my parents. If her son persisted on his course, she would fall to the ground and lie prone in the doorway of their home, she averred; he must pass over her form in order to enter on his foolish will.

The father was an introverted, silent type, a closed book whose title was—*Me*. Handsome, successful, unalterably conservative, unto himself, he was all suavity and buried fire.

He also took much for granted. His son would be reasonable. Under that basilisk gaze, a seventeen-year-old son would presumably come to heel.

Fathers before and since, have mistaken the fiber of sons.

My parents welcomed these distinguished guests into our parlor, listened and observed. What my mother saw was an essentially lonely boy. He needed, first of all, to rid himself of "being old before he's young." She made him welcome in our rough and tumble existence, its loony informality, a seat at the boardinghouse table and first come, first served. A bit of country air, she observed, a bit of time in the open, someone to take him for granted.

He bent a little, I straightened a tic. We went about together, to films, to the lake for a swim. We traded ambitions and hopes; and fears—his mother and father nudging him in unwanted directions, his own inclination and longing, his unease, working through such thorny questions.

Questions aplenty were crowding me also. But in the fog of uncertainty, my mother was at pains to remind me that "at least you don't have your family at your throat." And she was right.

Slowly, a preliminary why was yielding to another phase; a why not?

The most awful presentment of that question, like a phantom dagger in midair, came to me, of all places, in a film house.

I had stolen away one afternoon, seeking an hour or two of distraction. I sat there in the anonymous dark, some long forgotten film rolling its eyes. And then it was as though the eye of the universe blinked; and darkness fell. A sky of adamant, the element of time itself, the vault of the future—fell on me. A lifetime, my own! It was wrested from my grasp, falling away: one choice, and I was tumbled out of the world.

There was no question of trial and error, this or that temporary go at things. If I went, it would be for good; and if it were for ill—

Such a moment is not easily forgotten; not for half a century. It was ironic and terrible; the place, the occasion. He went to see a film, and the sky fell in. Was it an obituary or a birth notice?

Why, in all the weal and woe since that day, the known and the (mercifully) unknowable, does the memory persist? Something happened, something struck home. Making no sense, making the only sense. It was not the vows, perhaps it was the God of the vows. In any case, something never quite absorbed or done with, a tease, a lodestar, a blow. As though from on high it was decreed: it were better that the weight of years and years fall to him all at once. Let him know what this entails, from the start.

There is a Jewish tradition of the Shekinah, the cloud of unknowing that followed the exiles in their desert wanderings. Maybe that cloud, as is implied in the book of Exodus, was also a crushing weight—vocation, choice and consequence, bearing down on the wanderers. Maybe too out of the cloud came a voice like a scarcely distinguishable mutter of thunder. "This way and no other. This way, though the goal is obscure as the landscape of the moon. This way and no other, though the way is without track or precedent."

Easily seen how clouds, especially when they lower and mutter mysterious messages, realizations, codes, become symbols of the sacred. My cloud seemed, at the time, not sacred—only the bearer of news as unwelcome as it was crucial. Perhaps the two are the same, and that is the rub, and the relief.

In due time, my friend and I knew beyond doubt that our paths were concurrent. A matter of simple logistics remained. We had passed through the furnace, and come out on scorched feet. Now, even though we would limp for a while, we could be canny and cool, and pick and choose. Among the many orders of priests, which ones?

Which orders would take us? (Presuming, of course, that we were considered worth the taking.) Or, better still, in our magnificent insouciance, which orders would we choose? (Presuming, of course, that any order in its right mind would fairly leap at his or my proffer.)

We went round and round, abetted by our nun, that believer in unicorns.

The truth must be told of this holy conniver. She presented herself in the guise of a simple adjutant, a meek surveyor of the Lord's harvest field.

Meek as a Valkyrie! She had determined on an outcome. The Jesuits alone would do.

We suspected nothing of this, how the game was loaded. We wrote letters, each of us choosing four seminaries, requesting information.

And then received our answers. From several there arrived a rather intense come on: snazzy illustrated booklets, full colors, photos of premises splendid and forbidding, seaside property, lake property, country property, tennis courts, swimming pools: come, be sanctified, be all-American with us!

Everything was easy, natural, miles of smiles, the ecclesiastical escalator to—Utopia? In any case, to tasks in foreign missions or classrooms or laboratories or hospitals or prisons or the military. In retrospect, whether the garb to be donned was black or brown or white, how unabashed and American it all seemed.

We exchanged the packets as they arrived, we pondered and kept each to his counsel. Like the shepherds in the Auden poem, we were simply waiting; and for we knew not what.

Then there arrived, tardily as I recall, yet another response; whether addressed to my friend or myself.

It was an envelope so plain as to qualify as possibly containing obscene material. The material was sent by the Jesuits.

Neither of us had laid mortal eyes on a Jesuit. My father's bookcase included a formidable set of five livid green bound volumes entitled *Pioneer Priests of North America*. The author was a Jesuit historian, Campbell by name. I had labored through the series; they recounted in some detail the lives and exploits of Fathers Isaac Jogues, Jean de Breboeuf, Jean de la Lande, de Smet, Marquette, and other explorers and missioners of the continent. I was awed and set to thinking.

Then arrived this booklet in the mail. No hype, no photos, no come on. Its chastening paragraphs turned, so to speak, an impassive, cultivated face—not in our direction precisely; more in profile, as though an ear were attentive, but the concentration were else-where.

The tone of the writing was as fascinating and warm of heart as, say, a railway timetable. We could take this train or that, or none at all; it was all the same to the conductor. While we were deciding, there were other passengers to be attended to. We could, if so minded, apply for a ticket, which would be processed in due time.

The booklet outlined the course of Jesuit training, year by year. You were sent here or there, you studied, you were taught, you taught others, you prayed, you studied some more; and then some more. In matter of longevity, if you proposed finishing the course, you had best be a direct descendant of Methuselah. At approxi-mately double your present age, and presuming you survived the run, you would be ready. Whether for death or the labors assigned, was left unstated.

Behold the pertinacity of the young: we were fascinated. In our hands lay a far different proposal; a nonproposal. A message dropped with studied carelessness, by the way; and in its chanciness perhaps even a summons. Mysterious, impersonal as a blank check. The message: a scrutiny that spared nothing, excellence with no holds barred; Don't phone us, we'll (perhaps) phone you.

We had agreed on a ground rule. We were each to come to a decision separately, and only then to confide it to the other. So we passed a week or two absorbing the small gray print of the half-penny screed, gray on gray, an intractable tract for the times.

It was to be the Jesuits. For both. Separately as to the search, then corporately, for a lifetime. Understatement had won, and in-direction, and the slightest tug on the line.

We graduated in '38, my friend first in academic rank, I third, no great distinction for either in a class of some thirty-five. We were cleared for the run. Or so we thought.

But we had yet to encounter our first Jesuit, and they us. And what, we wondered (and perhaps they too), might that bring to pass?

We were instructed to appear on a spring day in May of 1938 at the Shrine of the North American Martyrs in Auriesville, New York, to be interviewed.

And so, with some trepidation, we obeyed, I with queasiness writ large, my friend, as usual, self-contained and at least outwardly composed.

Without effort, I summon up the four "examiners." The seventeen-year-old, untried and immature, would retain a memory of presences grave, weighty, kindly, altogether winning. He had never met the like; and he went home at the end of the day, chugging along the Mohawk River on the New York Central Railroad, he and his friend utterly snared.

One of the Jesuits was an old man of authority, bulky and benign. He took snuff between his great fingers as he spoke, his mild blue eyes regarding the world and me as though from a great height, his face like a full moon. Intermittently, as though signaling a change of topic, he blew his nose, with a great honk, into a workman's handkerchief.

Another wore a mask of sorrow, as though traced by Van Gogh. He was a noted master of things spiritual, and breathed heavily through his nostrils, like a thoroughbred to whom God had assigned every course uphill.

Another, just for balance, was a plump trotter, and a species of jollificator. He queried me in solemn jest as to which of the vows, poverty, chastity, or obedience, I judged as presenting most difficulty. He answered for me: it was "a great trouble, keeping this within bounds"; and he patted his paunch portentously.

The fourth was emaciated and inward looking. He had a homely phiz assembled, one might think, haphazardly, from spare parts. By a coherence laboriously achieved, the face had come together, as handmade things do, by being lived with, honed down. It was he who spoke concretely of what might lie ahead for us in a place referred to as St. Andrew, or the novitiate.

Possibly, or even probably, but not yet. We were bade farewell by hands cool to warm; as though in the handclasp, the flesh of the Company had touched but not yet adhered. They would notify us in due time; that was all.

Letters subsequently arrived. We were not accepted, neither were we finally rejected. We were instructed to pursue our studies further, concentrating on Latin, in which we had been found wanting.

To make a long year into a short matter, my friend set out for Holy Cross College in the autumn; and I, being of penurious means, was enrolled for a "postgraduate course" in Latin at my old high school. And was employed for after-school work, as a species of maintenance clerk, by the state of New York, for the princely sum of six dollars per month.

Thus separated by distance and contrasting circumstances, each of us, in his oxymoronic way, busily hibernated. We met at the holidays, and found our purpose unweakened. And the following spring, were accepted as candidates to the order.

On August 14, 1939, we traveled together from Syracuse to Poughkeepsie. My family took the separation in stride; my friend's mother spared us any baroque outburst.

We were welcomed at the portal of a granite and brick pile lording grandly over the Hudson Valley. And shortly were melded in a group of some thirty-five young males, most from the New York area, each in background, class, education, undoubtedly my superior. "Old boys," in the Jesuit sense, graduates of schools of the order, at ease with its members, ethos, spirit. Connections, from the start.

The greetings were hearty. Then the doors closed on us in a silence that seemed, at the time, both horrific and final. We arrived, we vanished into a new world. We would shortly be inducted into a new code almost without prelude, into a life as different from the old as the world differs from the womb.

The transition was based on the principle of the sudden, scalding plunge as preferable to any gradual immersion.

A plunge into silence; penance; disciplined comportment; stereotyped, coarse, lookalike clothing; meditation and manual labor and regulated hours. The days were disposed of as though by a relentless metronome: go when told, come when bade, follow the bell, join the long black line. Kneel until your knees ache and swell with pockets of fluid like an abused camel's. Eat when allowed, fast when instructed, write letters when permitted.

Let the world fall away. Own nothing, want nothing, complain of nothing. Be instructed, be rebuked, be next to nothing. Be homesick, be lonely, be glad, believe. Your reward, which is not yet, shall be.

We were an endangered tribe, and we did not know it; the last of the Mohicans. We were being pressed, molded (the words are instructively passive, they speak of an era done with), into a form that had perdured, without fault or crack, for some four centuries. Europe to Asia to Africa to America, the long line had marched, forced march, portage, exhaustion and renewal, sweat, tears and blood, studies and books and fame and misfortune and myth and muddle. Across time and distance; intact, in step.

To this hour, this place, this beat. St. Andrew on Hudson. I looked about me, and exulted. I was home free.

We dwelt in an ecosphere, a self-justifying, self-sufficient world. The heaven above our heads! Newman had said it, the Jesuits quoted it to us: "a Jesuit novitiate is a foretaste of heaven." The world of ours, flawlessly transparent, so nicely fitted as to stand surrogate for the crystal heavens of Aristotle. Our world; it would endure.

Or so we thought. And so were assured.

And who indeed could have thought, or told, otherwise?

A horrid war was about to break on the world; but it would reach us only as a distant rumor. What concern could it be to us?

And, by implication, what concern of ours were the events that would follow the war? Hiroshima, the Cold War, Korea; or, for that matter, Vatican II, Pope John, or Vietnam, the shuffling and re-shuffling of the cards of faith and fate? Were our own faces engraved on those cards—kings or knaves or jokers, winners or losers or both?

Of such things to come, of such images of ourselves, we were innocent by decree, innocent as the unborn.

Meantime, life as usual. We were to undergo that autumn one of the chief tests and scrutinies of our training, the famous long retreat of thirty days.

Our mentor and Master, who would conduct the meditations of the retreat, deserves the tribute of a long held breath. In this man, cannily, the Jesuits had put their best foot forward. That foot of his! It could kick out, could crush; it could also dance and feint and prod. It could pause in compassion above a novice's misery, or pass by fastidiously, with a feigned indifference and a weather eye out; but, in any case, a conviction that this or that trial of soul must be borne, as vere dignum et justum.

We were to see, at shrine and altar, the soles of those shoes, as he knelt in Spanish supplication. His transfigured face in such moments recalled Father Ignatius and the images that hung, dark and minatory about the house.

His best foot was forward, no doubting it. The foot could land with a metaphoric thump upon the rear of the recalcitrant or cow-ardly. It could also pump the pedals of the old piano in the grand hall, striking up those domestic songs, many of them composed by himself, all of conquest and armies and the taking of unlikely distant shores. Thumping, rousing themes, all; calculated to set young hearts aglow. We bellowed them out, it was a wave that carried itself, carried us along.

No one of us had ever seen the like of Father Master. Few of us, I venture, would claim, a half century later, that his equal crossed our path twice in a lifetime.

Almost without effort I summon his shade; so deep is the imprint of that face. A most untypical face: tormented, preternaturally blanched, compressed, lined and scored as though with an acid tool. A face all made of eyes, like a being from Apocalypse, to inspire terror or ardor, or both.

He was the lion at the gate, named Leo.

For some twelve years he guarded the gate known as the novitiate, granted entrance to some, turned others away. By the year we arrived, his twelfth class of novices, his gaze was seignorial, his power all but absolute. He was king of that ordered and humming cosmos, in which some survived, and many went under.

We could hardly know it at the time, but his was the last leonine roar of an era. The niceties of conduct he imposed, the piety he embodied, the loyalty he exacted, the juices of life he forced from the open vein (both his own and others')—these have long fled the Earth, or drained from the Earth, along with his own ecstatic spirit.

So controversial he was, so exotic and superannuated the version of Jesuit life he conveyed, the most charitable verdict of the brethren has been—let his ghost rest in peace. Of all the renowned Jesuits of my lifetime, he is one of very few whose life and work have merited no attention, no obituary. The peace he rests in is little short of extinction.

Yet renowned he was, by any civilized appraisal, a man of gifts and an evoker of the gifts of others. He glided noiselessly about the drafty corridors of the house, rapt in the Spirit; and yet, in his Jesuit way, missing not a whit. Missing neither jot nor tittle of the slightest deviance, right or left, from the holy rule. And calling to account; the memory of a scrupulous pachyderm. Merciless on himself with fastings and night prayer and disciplines and chains worn about his body.

He had studied theology in Spain, and the stories he told of the rigors and penances of Spanish Jesuits made us cringe like sybarites in our supple leather and linen.

Truly he was a baroque visitant, a tormented mystic, all primary glare and shadow, come to life before our eyes.

What to do, how react? We were young, the choices were not large. We fell in step, we obeyed, hewed a line. He was, for some of us, a second dose of biology and family. For me he was a second father, wild and willful as the first.

We were brands for the burning. You loved him, you feared him. He was confessor, prod, spur, consoler, clown, hellraiser, discerner of spirits, flaming sword, wrecker and inventor of lives. His moods were quicksilver; and beyond moods lay, or hung suspended, that soul of his, a knot of fiery purpose. He would form others to his image and likeness; which was, as he trusted mightily, the icon and oracle, though minor and marred, of the Lord Christ.

He would wrestle the neophytes. The prize was their future, their very souls.

If they yielded, they were dismissed out of hand, for the world to rescue and play Good Samaritan to. If the conflict ended in a draw (and that was the point of the conflict)—a robust nature would come through, dawn would break, that irresistible charm of his would enfold you like Jacob's angel. You were One of Ours! This side of beatific vision, nothing of equal moment could be imagined.

That October, thirty of us, first-year novices, embarked on the Spiritual Exercises, under his tutelage. The order of the day was Spartan, for him as for us. He led us in four hour-long sessions, points for meditation. Each of these was followed by an hour's period of silent meditation. There was a fifth session in midmorning, a conference on the various rules and apocrypha surrounding the Spiritual Exercises. In between, we attended Mass, said communal prayers, walked about the grounds.

And always that eye of his, the eye of a storm or a providence, kept watch.

To this day it is hard to credit. He held an interview with each retreatant, almost every day. The session might be quick, in and out; he touched the soul uncannily, sensed what play the spirits were exerting, gauged the mood, the danger, the light dawning.

October descended on the Hudson Valley, remote, magnificent, savage in hue; then, as October waned, the fires banked to a bronze. The splendid hills lay in a kind of Advent haze, waiting.

We walked the woods, we pondered the life, death, rising, of Christ. We passed dark hours considering other, less consoling, facts of life and death: sin, hell, the fate of the pusillanimous and betraying.

October and the peerless air: a suspended sword, all danger and opportunity. Or the time was like a baton, signaling an orchestration, a gathering of forces temporal, holy, darkly ominous, demonic. Majesty, depth, splendor; a month of our lives that, come what might, would never come again; and, in the most claimant sense, would never end.

My memory retains nothing of the grind, and few of the groans of the spirit, which are supposed classically to accompany the treading of fire. I had, after all, only just passed my eighteenth birthday. And the retreat, that momentous threshing ground, had been designed for mature spirits: men of the world, men of quality and stature, great sinners perhaps, brought to knee by a cunning interweaving of grace and psychology.

And here I was, here we were, hardly hatched, knowing as little of the world's works and pomps as did the moths of morning.

In consequence, the retreat was both inordinately fervent and undoubtedly abstract. Fearful and awful its God, and the Christianly revealed facts of life. But we could hardly bring to such truths the weight and wisdom of years, or professional scope, or wide reading, or the love of women, or the begetting of children, or heavy losses borne.

An example will suffice. There was great matter made, toward the end of the second week of retreat, of something known as a plan of life. We were to outline it in considerable detail, as the Spirit might be thought to move us. What were our dominant virtues and weaknesses? How might we deepen the one and outlaw the other? What light had been granted, what resolutions would fuel the light?

The plan was to be scrutinized and approved by Father Master, as the fine point of that intense month. And thereupon, so theory went, compass would be set and future course assured.

Alas for all that; for the good intention, the rational citing and setting down of means and end, principle and foundation, right resolve and follow through! How mercilessly life moves against the fervent and untried! I would be hard put to recall, whether in detail or main outline, the plan then so grandly adopted and approved. I venture further that those of my companions who survive would admit to like lapse of memory.

Half regret, half chagrin. Was it all loss, then, that convoy of words and silences and images and resolves, of rosaries, Masses, fasts, droughts, and delights? Like a tornado they raced through our minds, claiming right of way, discharging their burden of biblical and cultural images, of art and resolve, of rules and fidelity and discipline and steadiness of will.

A foreign burden and cargo; so the tempter memory, at once enticing and deceiving, whispers. Alien as to time and place; accepted without question or scrutiny, a spurt of fervor camouflaging the pain of the long haul. . . .

Another question. Were our majestic Hudson acres no more than an immigrant outpost, and we inducted into an impossible language, a wooden style and rote?

The temptation, for all its base metal, had an authentic ring. Our master was, all unknowing, an immigrant of the spirit. He knew a great deal more of Europe than of America; and what little of America he learned through his infrequent forays outside St. Andrew, he viewed with disdain. Europe, more precisely Hispanic Europe, the post-Reformation Europe of Ignatius, was his home ground. He loved the baroque Jesuit churches, their extravaganza, their trappings and statuary. These were the images that swirled through his brain. The pavement of such temples was as near a true ground as he knew; their trompe l'oeil ceilings the nearest equivalent to heaven. Here he abode, in awe.

He contracted with a Roman studio, copies of late baroque paintings arrived to cover the novitiate walls: saints in combat, saints in ecstasy, saints dying, the apotheosis of saints. They swam and hovered in the air, they whispered their supernal choices, they enticed and drew and repulsed and reproved. Talk about a cloud of witnesses!

When, in due time, we departed the novitiate to pursue our studies, we would carry with us, as the displaced of the Earth carry portions of holy soil, those outrageous, savagely hued images of divine combat and conquest.

The suave October air grew chill, the retreat came to its close. We fell to Earth with a thump.

The Earth we landed on was arguably not America at all. It was Europe; or some seven hundred acres of merely purported America. Or perhaps somewhere between; and we to all intents dwelling on a kind of transported, rustic Ellis Island.

I risk belaboring a point which, even at this remove, remains bewildering. Our Master was surely at odds with his time and place. Still, such a predicament is by no means to be considered bizarre. It is common to serious Christians that they exist in the world as in a conscientious limbo, out of their element, walking uneasily.

More sorrowfully to the point, our Master was at odds with fellow Jesuits, peers, faculty members, the rector; and with that larger, obscure pool of Jesuits laboring in public life. He was like a ranting version of the early chapters of Paul's letter to the Romans, a flash point of the dangerous, disaffected vocation, the reformer.

In his image, we were to become very paragons of observance, walking instances of the holy rule. There crept into our souls a kind of siege mentality. Not against the world as such, a properly Christian unease; more dangerous by far, against other members of the order, our brothers, teachers, mentors. According to him, these were to be judged (as we were) against a rule of immense complexity, a midrash of minutiae. Placed against the conduct of any of us, without benefit of mercy, that rule, cold as iron, pressed hard against the stoutest resolve.

Many of us in consequence became night riders, a species of stick men; ironbound, we kept the iron rule. More to our discredit; we judged others, and found them wanting, to our shame. They were not European enough to suit us; which is to say, they were too American to be Christian. Letter of the law, letter of the law! We became the obsessed guardians—of a baroque folly, all but abandoned to the weather of time.

What was lost, what gained, in those two years, as we trod the vast, angular warehouse of the spirit, learning, unlearning, getting born?

I speak for myself: I was, on the one hand, quite seriously displaced, even before I had won what might be called my own place. I did not know what it meant to be an American Christian; and how was I to become (and make sense of it) a European one? My head was filled with pneumatic ideals and resolves, minute, forensic as the rules of the Good Young Pharisee; all untested, and all rigidly held. I was, in sum, a kind of wooden Indian Jesuit, a caricature of the real thing; carved out boldly by someone who specialized in such artifacts. I kept the rule woodenly, was difficult to live with, all elbows and opinions, jottling and tittling as I went; and much wanting in the quality of mercy, whether toward myself or others.

And yet, and yet. I must have a measure of mercy on myself. There exists an old photo of my parents and myself, taken around the time of my vows, in 1941. My mother is all smiles, her face radiant under the brim of a dark fedora. My father exudes the dour satisfaction ("now didn't I tell you so") that, among the Irish, accompanies death, weddings, or the descent of the Bolsheviki.

Between them, cassocked neck to ankle, stand I. On my youthful head perches something known to Romans as a biretta; a black quadricorned creation of cardboard and serge, of no ostensible use in the world. It looks something like a nest abandoned by geometric crows. We were taught a holy lust in its regard; it signified status. According to the photo, I am now a card-carrying, biretta-wearing, certified Jesuit.

I look on the scene, my heart is touched by a modest glory. The boy is scarcely out of short trousers, the mother and father so fond and proud. The exalted and unimaginable has come to pass: a Jesuit in the family!

The parents are long dead, the glory is brought low; by cruelty of time and opposed wills. They lived long and paid to the farthing the cost of this day, this photo.

The cost is not easily reckoned, and continues to draw interest. It is one thing to be a cleric, for them to have a son a cleric; and quite another, for him and them, to combat the infection of clericalism. One thing to have a Jesuit in the family; and quite another to have a prisoner in the family, a felon; and he still a Jesuit. In the inelegant and telling phrase of Camus, the parents paid up.

And so, in measure, did the novice. But not yet.

He pursued his studies, according to the time-worn, time-tested formula. During the two subsequent years, there were doses of Greek and Latin to be taken, whole and piecemeal, according to mood or style of the professor. He performed passably well in Latin, abominably in Greek. In literary studies in his own language, rhetoric was a total loss, and poetry a glory, his home ground.

He came on a world lying beyond the fevers and lesions of his father; a world that included Hopkins and Eliot and Pound and Frost and others who, as he came to understand, had formed the sensibility of his generation. Tardily it might be, but he saw that they had also formed his.

Such poets might be despised, as his father had despised them, in the name of romanticism or nostalgia. But they could hardly be ignored with impunity; unless one was ready to wash hands of human imagination as it created wondrous images, images to conjure with and live by, images that illumined an otherwise impenetrable time.

If you hated your world, you probably ended hating the people of that world and, ultimately, yourself. The permitted form of that hatred, the one that could be reconciled with a Christianity of sorts, was an ill-tempered distrust. You fitted ill; nothing befitted you. You were infinitely superior to the raucous, obscene, flat-toned poets who believed, actually believed, they were writing poetry!

How much better to wrap oneself in a cloak of untouchability and summon the ghosts and language of the dead.

That language, those ghosts, might indeed be dead; and have little or no power to mediate the rhythms, faces, mores, seasons of woe, urban life (especially), all the tics and travails of contemporary life. But after all, was there any reason to celebrate such a world, such times? The times were evil, and those who celebrated the times, partook of the evil. . . . And so on, and so on.

The poets who celebrated the times helped the neophyte Jesuit rid himself of the clinging ghost of his father; and of his father's ghosts. Let the dead bury the dead! He was fortunate in at least one teacher of poetry; that one lifted a shroud from his back. With encouragement, he gathered to his heart the noble interpreters and celebrators, read, committed to memory, began to write.

Still, all this granted, a mystery met him; it was never satisfactorily explained. Why the humanistic studies, so touted and insisted on, failed to produce a more human clutch of teachers. With one or two exceptions, the Jesuits who taught the humanities appeared to be grubbers of footnotes, grammarians. They parroted with gloomy finality opinions of long dead Oxonians, also dated and narrow; quoted them as a veritable scripture. As for us, our task, it appeared, was to parrot the same opinions from our lower perches.

The professors were, for the most part, exceedingly caustic, and curmudgeonly. Their credentials, in their opinion, made a virtue out of sour spirits. They took a gloomy species of glory in making the students miserable, as we ground out our themes and groveled where we sat.

They kept, in fact, a nineteenth-century British public school, steeped in humiliation. And all the while, outrageous claims were laid out, claims denied in daily practice. We were informed that we were privileged to attend the workshop of the immortals. We worked the bellows, we held the hot tongs, as it were, in the creation of the new being (albeit the pre-Christian one) by Aristotle and Homer and Sophocles and Cicero and Horace and Juvenal.

Who this new being might be, and how he might conduct himself, was rendered obscure rather than lucid. We observed, covertly, as do the oppressed, and formed our conclusions—and kept them, of necessity, to ourselves. If these were the new men, we stood with the old.

Still, all contradictions, fussings, taxidermics aside, those were not bad years. There was a sound library at hand, and the volumes of the poets were available, for consolation, surprise, beckoning. If the classes were sand in the mouth, one bore with that; there was also the solid nourishment of community, friendships forming, a sense of being on one's way.

Classical studies were, all said, what one made of them, with the slender help of one's peers; and here and there, rarely, a helping hand from a teacher. Unless one was to make a career of paper, print, glue, and someone's footnotes contesting someone else's footnotes, one was well advised to make his education a matter of secret ideal and discipline, put in his time, read, discuss—survive and move on.

Other ways of teaching I was to learn later, by dint of trial and error.

Not everyone in our classes objected or suffered. Sensing their time had come, the achievers among us, a rather narrowly endowed group, began to sniff the wind and press ahead. They worked like drayhorses; parsed away like mad. They could compose elegantly in dead tongues. On special occasions, one or another was chosen to play sedulous ape to the faculty and further befuddle us. A Greek or Latin oration was proffered, droning and groaning along incomprehensibly for some forty minutes in the refectory. A harmless exercise to be sure; like Johnson's dog on its hind legs.

Achievement, competition, winners, losers. Those who fell behind merit some passing notice. It must take the form of a near epitaph: many of them never pulled abreast again. For every thoroughbred winner, how many losers!

Thus, so quick and self-contradictory, did the spirit of the world enter, without challenge or exorcism, into our esprit de corps. We were embracing, in more subtle form, the spirit we had so recently, and with such pain, renounced. Out the front door, change of costume, in through the back.

Which is to say, we played our academic game according to the niceties and rules and ethos and damaging cruelties of the world: winners and losers. It was a war game, our sanctified version of public strife. Our war, the war of competing talent, was like every other war in history. It was, by supposition, a just war; its morality was judged entirely an internal affair, of no one's concern beyond those who declared it and conducted it. More, it had produced winners for the order; tested and approved and whipped to the front line of scholarship many a peerless mind. . . .

And then there was the Great War. But we scarcely knew that in those years, beginning with 1941, the world was plunged, to its head and beyond, in a sea of blood. World War defined and defamed the times. And in the Hudson Valley, the Jesuit minihumanists walked their sylvan retreat, lisping their numbers, winning and losing.

We were denied access to news, with one or two concessions. The front page of the *New York Times* was posted, two days after its dateline, on a common board. And each week, a professor volunteered to inform us as to the state of the war.

In such wise we were exposed, week after week, to a monstrous body count; lost planes and ships and troops on either side; the submarine war of the Atlantic shipping lanes, the air war over Britain and the continent, the grinding Pacific carnage. The professorial tone was one of glee and chortling when, on occasion, he could report good news from "our side." His statistics of the living and dead were abstract as an Olympian weather report. He might have been moving about the room with a long pole in hand, above a floor map of the world, toppling toy figures as he went, scattering toy ships and planes; so many here, so many there.

It came to this: we ourselves, willy-nilly, were becoming war casualties. And we did not know it, as the dead are declared not to know.

My companions and I entered the Jesuits in the midst of a maelstrom. We lived on in a species of normalcy, which Cassandra herself could not have penetrated, exempted as we were from military service, neither dislocated nor bombed nor incommoded as to food or lodging. For us there was no loss, nothing to endure, no dislocation, no wounds, no death, "for the duration." And worst of all, no impulse to enter on moral judgment. The war was just: it was our war, wasn't it?

"Your country needs you." The saying, and the pointed finger of the old Uncle of Undoing—for all our exemptions and immunities, the finger came to rest on us also. America needed us and got us with a vengeance: got our silence, got our cardinals and bishops, got our people, got our sons and brothers. Got our taxes, and our tax freedoms. Got our blessing, the biggest get of all. We younger Jesuits lived like the enchanting piglets in the tale, in their cozy dwelling of bricks and mortar—and the great huff and puff, the hovering horror, was just outside the door.

Ancient humanism as main issue, modern inhumanism, war, religious exemptions from the guts and blood and terror—thus were we paying, in that most terrible of payments, the deferred one, the usurious one, the unconscious one—to be collected on The Day. This was the first disservice done by the order to its young members; a body blow dealt against itself. The Body of Christ would bear the scar, it lies on us still.

And more. How many of the talented among us gave up! How many gifts of the spirit were painlessly put to death, how many writers and scientists and confessors and men of compassion were hardly heard from again—dwelling as we did, during those years, in a crypt, sealed in jars like Dead Sea Scrolls.

How retarded our moral development was, as it touched on the first moral question of our lifetime, that of war and the war-making state! Indeed, in regard to this question, it was implied, and even stated on occasion, that such questions simply lay beyond our concern. Jesuits were teachers and writers and missioners and chaplains of hospitals and prisons and the military. Our work lay in the future, we were told. And for the present, our forte, as well as our tradition, placed us exclusively in the life of the mind.

So we were instructed. And so we came to see ourselves; and so our future took shape, or misshape.

It is perhaps unnecessary to suggest, some fifty years later, that there was a grievous imbalance here, or that the imbalance still awaits correction. The works of mercy at odds with the works of justice. The "life of the mind"; which is to say, conscience quite decanted and set aside.

The consequences, to note in passing, are present, though hardly accounted for. Jesuit campuses, peopled by apolitical refugees from the heat of the times, Jesuits and others, are a seedbed of reaction and militarization. There the ROTC marches, government research is lusted after; and theology bows in shame.

Thus, in the phrase of Neibuhr, and according to a process he scarcely understood, do moral men clot and form an immoral society; even one named so nobly, Jesuit.

At St. Andrew I blossomed into a postadolescent poet of sorts, with a Marian effusion published in the Jesuit magazine *America*. I also imbibed, come what might, a fanatical dislike and dread of a certain mode of teaching: the bullying presence heretofore referred to, in the china closet of the mind.

I would be humiliated later to learn that I had not quite unlearned a like conduct. Indeed, that on occasion, and more than occasion, I was quite capable of a bullish snort and rush of my own. It was not easy, it would not be easy, to allow the callow human its mistakes and detours, to allow others what had been disallowed in my own life. So went life; and how damnably difficult not to reproduce precisely what one fervently despised: the oppressive Big Boy!

The next phase of our training transported us to the Maryland countryside, to the oldest American Jesuit seminary, and indeed the most respected, Woodstock.

Rustication, whether at Poughkeepsie or in the Maryland hills, was considered in those days by eminent heads as beneficial to youthful spirits. Indeed, one Jesuit senior gave classic expression to what could only be called a kind of beefeater's myth. He declared that the objective of the order, with regard to the formation of its young members, was to ensure them "an acre a man"; quite as though we were a herd of Hereford steers put out to graze.

So, assigned to Maryland, we grazed freely; and much against our wills.

The studies, mainly of classical philosophy, with minors in everything from anthropology to literature, were demanding in the extreme and incomprehensible in dispensation. We were required to "take it on faith" (it could hardly be demonstrated) that from such elements, mixed with the driest dust ever to settle around the spirit of the ages, would be compounded a miraculous nostrum for the mind, ourselves, the age—a healing for every ill.

If we studied, we would prevail; not because the studies were inherently fascinating or soundly presented. They were, in the main, neither. We were under bond: that was the point. We were to study because at this stage of life, philosophy was the divine will. It was as though God were attending uneasily to our attempts to prove, from unaided reason, that He exists.

Then logic, metaphysic, something curiously known as natural theology, cosmology, classical psychology, ethics. Behold Woodstock and weep. Three years of the divine will, impenetrably disguised, signed, sealed, and delivered.

The arrangement might be judged somewhat failing in the divine part. In less stressed circumstance, inferior teachers might be called to account for beating hollow drums, whether in ennui of spirit or declamatory fervor, determined that their drumbeat become the cadence of captive hearts and heads. Or something such. The will of God, in any case, proved a poor surrogate for breadth of mind or command of language or empathy or the ability or will to give out with one's passionate faith. In the main, the tongue that conveyed the major studies was a Latin dead as the jawbone of Aristotle.

I thought at the time, The insistence on Latin is a perfect cover. If one is speaking a foreign tongue (and a dead one at that) to equivalent foreigners (ourselves, non-Latins), ineptitudes, disdainings, indifferences, sour spirits, contempt—these are harder to discern. Away, then, with the vulgar, revealing vernacular!

The time, place, atmosphere, all conspired toward disaster. Our instructors and spiritual advisors insisted that all works of imagination, all pursuit of drama or poetry or painting, wherever these meager weeds might push through, be laid aside. The most promising among us scarcely survived. The hacks, gifted prodigally with rote memories and inflamed with combustible motives, flourished. Three dreadful years! Transformed, despite all goodwill, into the turba hominum proscribed by our Father General, a drifting mass of weedy minds; some of us retained the capacity for unalleviated misery.

It was the time of the honing of Occam's razor; which instrument seemed designed only to be laid against our own throats.

The long black line snaked along, like time itself, through corridors and chapel and classrooms and dining hall. Long and black the line, officially anonymous, passionless. Cassock and cincture, old and young, birettas on hoary pates and youthful, learned and eminent, inquiring and bewildered.

At the head of this sinuous, lengthy being was someone who gave orders and took them, being himself subject and surrogate, in command only for a time. The superior gave and received commands; he was the instrument not of innovation or vital images or untrodden ways. He existed only as a needle rests, with infinite lightness, on a lodestar: to tell true north.

Or he was there as the human expression of the law of the universe, and the Lawgiver; to pass the law along, that the body might move in unison with the stars in their course, and all together sing the glory of God.

For everyone, therefore, high and low and intermediate, obedience. It was a virtue endowed with majesty by Ignatius, it implied an elite humanism that kept Jesuit heads on high for centuries, sent them to distant places (even to Woodstock, Maryland). The ventures were whetted like a blade; they frequently promised, and kept the promise to the letter, only failure, loneliness, demise of high enterprise, violent death.

We knew all this. It flowed like an unguent from our history, our martyrology, the shrines of our saints; the aura of the prideful Company. And yet, and yet. Incarcerated as we were in Woodstock, far from macadam, bright lights, crowds, jazz, films, human variety, and funk, it was difficult indeed to trim and shield the lamp of glory.

Difficult to remember, and be comforted with the thought that others had borne the same yoke, dragged the same burden of des-

ultory time: classes, Latin texts, examinations written and oral, syl-
logisms. And the gray, indeterminate Maryland weather, soggy and
sullen by turn.

Yet we had only to fasten gaze on our altars to know again, and
to accept anew; how such unpromising hours and seasons had
cracked like a stone egg, incubated by the spirit of God—into what
glory.

Or we could lift eyes to the ceiling of the old Sestini library to
see verified in paint a cosmic order of things, a visual act of faith
traced there by a lonely old Tuscan scholar and astronomer, one of
the nineteenth-century heroes of our line.

We stood beneath such a firmament; the order of our days, the
refining and enlarging of intellect were both its mirror and vindication.

Or so we were told; and so a few of us believed, at least numbly.
And yet fretful, even rebellious, thoughts intruded, like worms with
a will of their own. What sense indeed was this manner of life
making, here and now? Could we justly be required to abandon our
sense of here and now, in favor of some eventual good, or some
larger good, a good that seemed always receding from our grasp?
A good that, all promises aside, seemed weirdly like the good promised to real toads in hypothetical gardens?

Obedience was a tight rein. The obedience of the Jesuits, grand,
encompassing, overriding as it is, includes as well elements of the
inhuman. The defeated know this, as do those who ride high. A
submission all too human and, inevitably, on occasion, inhuman.

The ironies are awesome. The complexities would go something
like this: a consuming passion for the perfect, embraced by the
newly converted Ignatius (himself plucked from a very pit of im-
perfection)—and then, the vision of perfection transposed to a rule
of life, on the all too imperfect!

So we were subject to a visionary rule. The understanding being
that at the end of the process we might have become its skilled
practitioners, even keepers of the flame. There was to be no crack
in the incubation process: if an egg split, the egg must be discarded,
as spoiled or infertile.

We were, to put matters in a light struck only later, a long way
from the freedom of the Gospel. Human freedom, announced and
embodied by Christ, was held up to us, but only as a good to be

attained "under the rule," to a measure allowed and approved by a local superior. He, in turn, was allowed to allow others their proper measure, by someone placed above; and so on, even unto the august papal throne, whence presumably all freedoms flowed— or stopped short.

To speak of those like myself, still in formation: questions of personal freedom or initiative never, in any practical way, came up. We merited the blessing promised to children. Others were in charge, and knew better than we, what was good and what harmful—also what (more to the point) was beside the point.

The images of Christ, and the implications of those images, were crucial. During times of retreat, the images were carefully filtered through the Spiritual Exercises; which is to say, the images were internally chosen, colored, heightened, by the ethos of the order. Who indeed was this Christ, who was He to us, to our generation? Who was He to technology and superpower politics and world wars? What did He have to say, to deny, to excoriate, to rejoice in, given such a world as ours? Did Christ, to the point, if point there was, curse or rejoice in the carnage of the war? And if he rejoiced, what of us? And if he cursed, what then?

Something of substance, something infinitely precious, was lost in the Woodstock years. Or so I judge. Life for most of us was reduced to mere endurance: distinction of mind, impulse and out-reach, passion and vision, these grew contained and cautious. We began to resemble our elders—gray matters, like a universal dye, turned us gray.

It seems by no means to be wondered at that at the close of our training, many of my classmates settled in Jesuit institutions and campuses, as did their Fathers before them. There, like organisms to a reef, they clung, and there were mortised.

I cannot, for the life of me, summon a single redeeming feature of those three years, at pain of being dishonest or trifling. I wish it were possible to praise this or that: it seems terrible to review so long a period, at such a fork of youth, and draw a blank; to recall that one's spirit, instead of volatilizing under a flame, grew slavish and sluggish, a drudge of time.

The World War meantime widened and worsened, as is the way with wars. A tablet of honor appeared at the Woodstock chapel door, inscribed with names of relatives in the armed forces. And here and there, a gold star appeared preceding a name: someone's relative had perished.

There came eventually D day. My brother Philip, who had been decorated in Europe, returned from battle and paid a visit to Woodstock. His return was received with an audible sigh of relief—not only from me, but the entire community. One phase of the horror was ended; the joy overflowed.

Philip quickly became the impromptu leader of a ragtag parade around the seminary grounds. It was a scene both bizarre and dear: my brother, spotless and spiffy in his uniform, bearing a huge flagstaff, I at his side, a chorus of cheering, singing seminarians following.

In August of that year, I was a patient at Mercy Hospital in Baltimore, ill and exhausted. And one morning, a sister nurse placed on my bed the daily newspaper, rolled up, a trumpet of doom. Doomsday, Hiroshima day: the Bomb had fallen.

I read, turned to ice or stone.

Neither stone nor ice. I was getting born; and I was ignorant as the unborn. I read of the obscene triumph of the president, the estimated casualties. And my eyes were illiterate as the unborn. What had happened, what did the future hold?

A sense would come to me later with the force of a thunderbolt scoring its message on a wall, a sense of before and after: before Hiroshima, after Hiroshima. All unconscious as I was, hardly born, I had no sense that we had crossed a line, all of us. And what that might mean, what pit yawned at our feet, when we awakened from our stupor—or did not.

Far in the future, inconceivable to the mind, was any foreboding—of what that news, on the day of Christ's Transfiguration and our degradation, would exact of me, how its heat would cast my existence in a new form.

All this was hidden, and mercifully so. I returned to the intellectual sweatshop, to work the treadles for another year.

Among other salutary projects, we were to grind out the "quinque viae" of Aquinas, proving, in our landlocked void, and through unaided reason, the existence of God. Without respect, need it be added, to the new existence of another god, the Bomb. Our fond and errant abstractions were toppled, and we heard nothing. It was as though an undersea temple had fallen, the temple of Atlantis, and all unheard.

In May of 1946, figuratively holding my nose and closing my eyes, I took the final philosophical examinations; as one might take a dollop of brimstone and treacle. And passed, as an organism might be thought to pass a bad matter, with only minor distress. And so departed Woodstock, without a vagrant tear, and forever.

A more hopeful setting by far: St. Peter's Prep, in a Jersey City slum. There I was assigned to be a teacher of boys, unwilling and intractable and altogether delightful, for the following three years.

Good times would succeed ill, I had been assured in the bad times; and believed not a word of it.

I became, as I was shortly informed by the headmaster, a fairly capable mentor. Which meant simply that I was demanding, driven, and driving; a disciplinarian who could "keep order" from the start.

And found, before many months passed, the emergence of various gifts long suppressed: instincts, simpatico, love of the young, skill at twitching the line and moving the dullards along.

Indeed it seemed at times as though a dam were bursting in slow motion in my brain. The dam buckled and fell; the waters gushed out. Was I human; and a gifted human after all? How I rejoiced to find my own way as I went!—having fled, at least for a time, that detested black line—of which I had been only a slightest, most expendable point of articulation. Could it be that life was a celebration, and not a virtuous, set-jawed act of endurance? I smiled, even in my sleep.

Waking hours were hectic indeed; the drovers were themselves driven. In the pecking order of the school, younger teachers were assigned the onerous tasks, the most impenetrable skulls, the longest hours. It was we who were charged with monitoring the sodalities, debating teams, sports, newspaper and yearbook committees, language clubs. These, in addition, of course, to preparing classes, spurring delinquents, correcting papers.

I loved it all. And throve under it, with my companions, despite all. Forming, as twelve of us younger Jesuits did, the coterie of the oppressed ("religious" but not "clerics"), we were, by supposition, endowed with the endurance of water buffaloes.

In those days the Jesuits were blessed with numbers of vocations exceeding anything seen before or since. So it was by no means unheard of that a young priest of considerable promise passed vigorous years of his life pounding the rudiments of Latin grammar into the heads of adolescents; assured that in so doing, God was his collaborator. As usual, plenty begat waste. And as usual, God was invoked and praised, even as the sacks of grain leaked life.

It was an exhausting time, dawn to midnight; but following on Woodstock and the lean years, it was a poor man's paradise. We dwelt in attic rooms, consumed plain food, said our prayers in a fog of exhaustion, touched the skies or hit bottom emotionally, dependent on the performance of our students—their performance being, as authorities judged things, our own, writ large and public.

I added my own projects to official responsibilities. I had a hunch, later explored brilliantly by Paul Goodman, that the city itself was our first field of education. Now and then, squads of students and I took the "tubes" to New York, visited museums and points of interest. There were excursions into the countryside also, an annual boat ride up the Hudson, a class retreat. All in all, a heady time, and a good one.

My guardian spirits in those days were Ronald Knox and George Orwell. I also began corresponding with Thomas Merton around the time of his ordination in 1947. Our exchange was aborted; he was being kept under wraps. But the friendship would resume later, and be interrupted only by his death.

In light (or darkness) of nuclear developments, one episode stands out. I had read a little book by Knox, *God and the Atom*. Uninstructed as I was, I thought the proposal he offered deserved a hearing. He urged that the Americans in possession of the new weapon would have been vastly better advised to drop the doomsday package on some uninhabited Pacific isle as a visible threat and show of force; one that would have spared so atrocious a toll of life as Hiroshima and Nagasaki exacted.

I presented Knox's alternative to my adolescent friends. And was shortly subjected to a barrage of my own. I was learning ever so slowly, the assaults that lurk in the sky or sea or bunker of the mind, for a specimen such as I, the perpetual naïf.

That classroom of fifteen-year-olds! They suddenly became an aroused chorus, savage and loud. No moral doubts clouded these Americanettes. With considerable heat I was informed that I scarcely knew my arse from my elbow, a bomb from a berry. We did good! We saved lives, didn't we! It was them or us, wasn't it!

I was to hear such sentiments from older and purportedly wiser heads, time and again in years ahead. Even so slow a learner as I might come to confusion, perhaps even to enlightenment, my innocence confronted with something known as the facts of life.

Might come to know the ways of the world, and how those ways intrude and claim the church for their own. Ways that lead even to the altar, to the baptismal font, to the place of confession, to the throne of the celebrant of mysteries. The sacred and the hideously profane, the beatitudes of Christ and the accursed Bomb. The claim and symbol of the One (forgiveness, cleansing, "My body given for you," the anointing and strengthening and healing). And then the hanging image of the God the world has dealt with (and the church has all but dealt with), "once and for all," as presumed.

What had I learned from the mouths of vociferous babes?

It came to something like this, a bitter pill indeed. One could undergo, as they had undergone, and their parents before them, the entire Christian induction, the seasonal rhythms of Christian worship, could receive the Christian sacraments; could be exposed year after year to elite Christian education. And still one would go off to war, in apparent good conscience.

In the course of the war, any war, vast numbers of the enemy, whether combatants or bystanders or the ill or aged or newly born, would be disposed of by slaughterhouse technique. There would occur also vast numbers of casualties on one's own side.

And all this would be wrought and undergone in truly awesome good faith; a faith shored up and accompanied by the church's blessing.

Further; this increasingly lax conscience with regard to mass murder—this could be expanded until it encompassed all the living. There would be no limits established, no end in sight. The nature of state violence was illimitable; persuasive reasons would be adduced for ending the human venture.

Nor would any limit be set by the church.

All this was a possibility since Hiroshima. Indeed, as time went on, and the normalizing of mass murder proceeded, the possible edged over into the probable.

There would always exist an excuse for the next round of war. That war would include its own justification; not in its wake, but before the fact. The combatants, whoever, whenever, were prepared by the previous round and its concomitant ideology, for the round to follow. Thus would the dominoes, and the bombs, fall: war would prepare for war, in aeternum. And no war, actual or imaginable, would ever prepare for peace.

Meantime, people like myself had best take warning. History did not favor the likes of us. And in war, history was everything: not merely a bulging catalogue of nation against nation; but an inbred sense, in people and policy, that war was the indispensable ingredient of the good life. It guaranteed "us" something known as identity.

It was as though war were injected, as the substance of the human gene, into the genetic bank. We, whoever, knew who we were, humans, in the act of war. Ancestors were, first of all, warriors; in that degree only, they merited honor.

Ancestor to child; it was presumed that violence needed no teaching, it took care of itself. It was nonviolence, civility, that required discipline and instruction, and was under perennial assault.

If the past exerted a contrary pressure, the future would be no less hostile. Those with a contrasting or resisting or differing vision of church or state, a version that included peacemaking as essential ingredient, would be caught in a veritable riptide.

That vortex might well be named peace by those interested in the durability of war. The deviants such as myself might object. But the vortex won; a furious justification of past follies and crimes and, for the present, a cool war, not quite icy, not quite declared, not yet bloodletting—an uneasy nightmare between the war ended and a war looming.

Thus my students became my instructor. I smarted under a lesson that fell like a lash. I limped home, in no wise converted, but ever so slightly the wiser.

The superior of our community held sway over a high school, a parish, and a college. He was, in the main, typical of the superiors of those days; like his peers, he ruled by divine ordinance. The conviction indeed cut across all boundaries and traditions, whether the sovereignties were Jesuit, Trappist, monks, nuns, priests, or Brothers. Those in charge were oracles of the divine will, absolute monarchs, with all the powers and privileges accruing thereto.

If truth were told, and it seldom was, this amounted to something uncomfortably like a secular arrangement, rather than a sacred one. It owed a greater debt to the politics and economics of the Middle Ages than to the primitive ethos of the Gospel—which dismayingly appeared to favor the underdog and call the mighty to accounts.

The superior held in his jurisdiction awesomely broad areas, the disposition of talent and lives, even control of conscience. He (or she) could exact a rigorous account of motive, of sacramental life and professional conduct. The superior said go, and he goeth; come and he came. One might remain at an unpromising work for a lifetime, under orders. Another would pack his bags under like orders, and take off for distant or near parts. Such removes, moreover, often occurred after one had sunk roots and affections deep in a given community and work.

There might or might not occur prior consultation with the one affected. (There was, of course, regular consultation among the authorities themselves as to the good estate of institutions, places to be filled or vacated by this or that Jesuit.)

Entire generations, indeed centuries, of the sons of Ignatius had lived, worked, died under such arrangements, understood simply as the will of God. There was no deception here: one knew from the earliest days in the order that such was the Jesuit way. Indeed, the novice had only to look around him to see his own future taking shape in the lives of elders.

The trainee could accept the arrangement or leave it. The novitiate, and the long course of studies, trial and error, scrutinies, changes of locale, and assignment of work—these were designed to help all concerned, subject and superior, arrive at a sensible decision: whether this youth, of this temperament, these gifts, these limitations, might be thought fitted for "our way of life."

The superior, for the duration of his office, was vested in the mantle of the Jesuit "charism" of government. The gift was first mentioned by St. Paul; it guaranteed that a decision reached, with or without the concurrence of the subject, was the temporal form of the divine will.

To go on command conferred a blessing; to come also. So, in the primitive imagery, did the watering of a dry stick; on command. So did the placing of one's self before the superior, detached as a corpse before the diggers. In the inelegant phrase, there was about the imagery, and occasionally about the uses it was put to, no fooling around.

Over the excesses, even the tragedies, which from time to time rent this seamless arrangement, I have no heart to linger. Such threnodies are the burden of memoirs of the rejected and wounded, the quondam religious who return to the world, burdened by their grievances. And live with them; and, in some cases, live to tell of them.

There were, of course, superiors who were humane and humble, who hearkened to those in their charge, who preferred community to institutional prospering. But these were exceptions, as was Pope John and many another of lesser notoriety.

For the most part, women and men in the orders (those who remained) lived out their years, peaceable, silent, respectful, having found their niche and settled into it. Few questions were raised, fewer answered. Indeed, it was commonly considered that raising questions about governance was tantamount to raising a red flag. One might be professionally competent, even eminent in her or his field; but the gifts stopped short at a portal; beyond, the dynastic and vatic came together, an oracle, a destiny.

In 1949, everything on schedule, my teaching record cleared at headquarters, my moral probity and religious discipline approved, I was instructed to appear with some thirty others, to begin theological studies in Weston, Massachusetts.

My mates and I were then in our late twenties, veterans of nine or ten years in the order. Several had finished graduate studies, others had tested their mettle, as had I, in the classrooms of the East Coast. We were older, and presumably harder driven and more closely tested, than our peers in the seminaries of the American dioceses.

Few of us, if truth be told, arrived in bucolic New England content in spirit, our hopes high for the immediate future. Studies again, the grind again; and our hearts, so to speak, in the macadam highlands of New York, Buffalo, Boston.

Those years have the air of a predawn: a darkness with, here and there, a shaft of light breaking through. And ghosts abroad.

Theology as presented was a strange exercise indeed, an omniumgatherum culled from times primitive, medieval, eras of reform and postreform. And then a heavy infusion of the safe and sterile nineteenth century, with its loyalty oaths and rounding on the heads of modernists, Americanists, et al.

A hatful of watch parts, someone described it. We were to undertake study of canon law, ministry, sacrament, discipline, morals, Scripture old and new. Also of the clerical state and its peculiar rules. Also liturgical regulations, equally peculiar; and the niceties and nuances clinging to our post-Reformation order. And all this, be it understood, cudgeled into our pates in the Latin tongue, in accord with Roman regulations.

The schemata, sequence, and subjects were inviolate. There was no least hint that the "beast from the earth" was stirring in sleep. No warning of detours ahead, dead ends, queries, shaken foundations; the nearly fatal burst of vitality, vulgarity, falling away, social eruption—not to mention war and rumor and alarm—all the terror of awakening that was so shortly to gather momentum, about and within the church and, inevitably, in the Jesuits.

The long black line once more. We moved about our baroque barracks in a befitting silence and inwardness. But under the relentless hands of time, the clock of events, we did not move at all: we were immobilized. We were, in fact, very nearly the last of the Stonehenge men.

We had been shaped and set in place; like standing stones, we were to stand where placed. Our deployment and its rationale were both mysterious and clear; with a clarity that a tradition confers— but confers only now and then, precariously; when function and form, for the space of a heartbeat, are one.

Who was to tell us that in reality we stood on a pivot, and the pivot would shortly begin to wobble? We were the stone figures, and would abide. We defined the sacred enclosure, even as we cried out our Procul Este! to the uninitiated. Guardians of the portal, faces turned two ways, we would keep the enclosure intact, the mysteries, the hovering Cloud of our Numen.

We could hardly know (and the ignorance was pure mercy), that in the savage weathers to come, some of us would be ground to dust, others would topple. And still others, despite all stony intractability, would turn about face and walk away.

Meantime, everything and everyone stayed put. This defined our universe. Everything in its place: ourselves, our professors, dogma, texts, law, history, adversaries, proofs, loyalties, the stars in their course. Everything stood because everything had withstood.

It might be (as some of us even then suspected) that every thesis of ours, proof against age and gambit, might yet, like the moon, have its shadowy antithesis. Alas, *antithesis*, the very notion, had a Protestant ring, brought with it the muffled pounding of rebellious Luther. And was, in consequence, anathema.

That shadow of antithesis! It was judged, in effect, secular: it lay outside the quasi-sacred form in which theological history was presented. And the secular stood condemned, nineteenth-century popes had pushed it beyond the pale. And the Jesuit theologians had gone with the push, had declared the world an enemy, and its works and pomps. The secular (and its carriers, the Protestant theologians) we could have no part in, nor could the structure or method of the searching mind of faith.

As presented. Faith as presented; and the mind, and the limits of the search. The antithesis was disposed of by the relentless thesis. The other side was not precisely irrelevant; neither could it be granted anything approaching equal time, or sympathy, or a hearing. It was reduced in scope to a minor adversarial position. To be swept aside in the grand, irresistible sweep of orthodoxy. As presented. As defined—by the orthodox.

Lucky for us (or otherwise), we knew little of the signs of the times. Indeed, what soundings were taken, what warnings issued or directions charted, were announced by servants of the structure. In whose readings, all signs pointed one way—and all wrong.

We were like the crew of a ship of fools: we were reassured by our captain. All, we were told, with a trimmed sail here and a good wind there, was well. And we were bound, straight as an Iroquois arrow, toward disaster.

There existed on the seminary grounds a seismographic center. It was capably managed, and registered night and day, the tremors of earth. But the seminary itself was no sort of seismograph, though theological earthquakes were then and there brewing away in Europe. de Lubac, Congar, Danielou, the Rahners, Catholic as these undeniably were, movers and shakers of earth and time—they, through one decree or another, were pushed beyond the pale.

When they and their work came up for scrutiny, it was either

as adversaries or in a dispositive style that signaled only danger and
the locked shelf. In sum, they were deviants; or, at best, of little
account in comparison with the conventional giants.

The notes of a Jesuit named de Chardin, so a story had it, were
being distributed among seminarians in France, clandestinely. Purportedly, this visionary paleontologist was seeking a synthesis between revelation and science. He had been forbidden to publish;
hence the notes. But even these, if they existed, were, as the jargon
went, "inaccessible" to us. And perhaps the whole thing was no
more than a rumor. It was a measure of our bondage that even a
rumor would appear so delicious.

Indeed, the question arises, as it did then, and without resolution: for what were we being prepared? It could be adduced (and
was implicitly held) that we were being fitted and joined to stand
immemorially in the Stonehenge circle. To stand there, while the
Vandals wreaked their worst, and all in vain; until the Parousia,
when all things would be ground to dust or toppled.

Or in secular, and necessarily partial, terms: we were being prepared to work as loyal, unquestioning civil servants; in whatever
capacity might be determined, by others, in light of talent and temperament. We would die where we had been twice born, clothed
in the cassock, crowned with the biretta. Or so it was thought; and
so thought I.

I was indeed a late and scant bloom. It was not until the last
year of four at Weston that it became clear to anyone that I might
offer something substantial in matters theological.

I a theologian? As a requirement for the degree, I had prepared
a paper on the church. A young professor waxed enthusiastic over
the piece. In some trepidation, I had drawn on leads offered by the
great work of de Lubac; tentatively, and in full anonymity as to my
inspiration, because in official quarters, his name brought no delight.

Astonishing: the paper caused a minor stir in our still pond. My
mentor insisted that on the strength of this essay, I must apply for
European studies. The praise and attention were a balm; the paper
was published in a seminary manual, a kind of trial run, and published a few years later in my book entitled *The Bride; Essays in the
Church*.

In a minor way, I was launched. No full-masted vessel, no tall ship; rather in the nature of a rower's skiff, fit for inland waters. But still, something.

In the midst of the long and level days, there were diversions, innocent and sylvan, as befitted our state. A golf course, swimming pool, in season. On holidays, we picnicked in cabins in the wood. There were day-long walks through country lanes; and each summer, like orphans on holiday, we assembled in busloads to be transported to the seaside at South Norwalk, Connecticut. Once arrived we were housed in a series of old barracks by the shore, free to take the sea air, swim, and otherwise modestly disport ourselves, unwinding the theological knots that had tightened in our heads.

In the course of the school year, some were unable, despite strenuous efforts of law and order, to shed their urban skins. They were covertly drawn to populated areas and verboten pleasures. One duet, venturing, horrors! into a shopping mall and its crowds, were unwittingly photographed in the background of a celebration mysteriously announced as the crowning of Miss Market Basket. The photo appeared in a local paper; the pilgrims were subsequently hauled on the carpet and issued a stern warning.

CHAPTER 6

Priesthood: Year One of My Life

I wanted to be useless
as life itself. So
I told the president so
and told the pope so
and told the police so;

and one and all chorused
like furies, like my friends;
And who told you so?

The dead told me so,
the near dead; prisoners
all who press faces
against a pall of ice
against a wall of glass
a grave, a womb's thrall.

I read their lips, alas.
I told the poem. So.

Finally, in June of 1952, amid considerable wonderment and rejoicing, I was ordained. The event was accounted at the time as a
grace, and still is. Numerous photos were taken on that day of days,
whose high drama time both caught and caught up with—and eventually rendered both quaint and inviolate.

For all that was to follow, and threaten and undermine, the
anointing of ordination was a momentous healing and enlightenment. It justified the long haul and its sweat and tears, it struck a
light that has never been extinguished.

The healer and lighter of lamps was the then Archbishop of Boston, Richard Cushing. He performed the ordination at a tornado
pace and pitch. Each of us was caught up. When his great bassoon
sounded, announcing this or that stage of the proceeding, one could

entertain no least doubt that the gift offered was in fact being conferred. The chariot swung low, and swept one up. And I had at last
become what I was called to be.

The Archbishop was, in all respects, the ideal agent of a transfigured moment. He brought dignity and coherence and validity on
the day—a day awaited and worked toward for thirteen years, and
with what trepidation! Cushing stiffened our wavering spines and
watery knees by the fierce thrust of his own resolve. At the altar,
he conveyed a relentless, rugged faith; the faith of a medieval
bishop, perhaps, not only a spiritual shepherd, but the ruler of some
vast, untamed fiefdom. As indeed Cushing was, in the Boston of
the Curleys and the Irish tribes.

I was a priest at last. It was Year One of my life or the first day
of a new creation, I knew not which, nor cared greatly. I went out
into the sunshine, blinking with the wonder of it all, to greet and
bless my family.

Another year of studies followed.

Infrequently, we newly ordained were released on weekends to
help in local parishes. But these ventures into the active life were
strictly limited: the main issue was our books and classes, leading
to a final comprehensive examination.

This latter is a horror peculiar to our order. Its scope includes
vast material drawn, at the pleasure of four examiners, from four
years of theology and three of philosophy. Besides the unmanage-
able enormity of the material, a further, fiendish obstacle lurked.
Practically no one of us who were eligible for the bruising had had
opportunity or will to consult a philosophy text for a matter of six
or seven years. Spit and sweat and polish: it must all be reviewed.
The examination, conducted totally in Latin, was a breaker of health
and spirits.

The New Year of 1953 arrived. Classes were finished: we were
on our own for the last push toward May, and Cerberus at the gate.
Meantime, emoluments were offered the sacrificial victims, such as
to set the head spinning. They fed us like steers bound for the abattoir; we were granted privileges and variations from routine. One
ventures that a meeting, even a prearranged one, with Miss Market
Basket would scarcely have been frowned on.

January to May, as the northern winter held firm and then
yielded its grip, we wore our britches thin and staggered about the

house in a blur, our skulls like cauldrons brimming with (foreign) alphabet soup.

The horrid day arrived, as such days will. One way or another, I passed muster: perhaps Cerberus was drugged or my theology was less frayed than feared.

And that summer, to my dumbfounded delight, word arrived that I was to pass the following year in France.

Who could have imagined it: France! I was to pass ten months in a remote Burgundy town, Paray le Monial, in ascetical study and practice. There, under the tutelage of a renowned master of things spiritual, and in company with an international group of priests, I would peruse the constitutions of the order, engage in a thirty-day retreat, minister in parishes and convents.

At a stroke, fourteen years of academic burdens lifted, new horizons beckoned.

Yet not altogether new. A number of us, appalled by the doldrums of backbroken domestic theology, had heard other voices reverberating in our bones. By one means or another, we had gained possession of the works of the European scholars, mainly Jesuits and Dominicans, who were even then preparing the ground for the Second Vatican Council. (But this happy outcome was all in the future. At the time, the fifties, a purge was on. They were suspect and surveilled by Rome; shortly, several of them would be removed from teaching positions, silenced, forbidden to write.)

At Weston, more or less on our own, we read the forbidden Europeans, met for discussion, pondered, opened our casements, and breathed the fresh air.

It is difficult to convey the delight that lifted in me that summer, as I prepared to weigh anchor. Landlocked, and for so long! I had been child and youth and seminarian and priest, always in America, among Americans, living out a cruel age between upheavals and wars, knowing little or nothing of other ways of conducting life, other views of the world. Worst of all, perhaps, having never known peace (as I came to realize), but only its spurious great power counterfeits, its fevers and chills, cold wars and hot. Not having tasted minority status for years, clothed as I was in academic smarts, Jesuit bile and honey. Never having been poor, never surviving on my own. Nor anonymous, my clothing giving me away. And along with the clothing, habits of mind and discipline that created a sense of myself as strong and adamant.

All untested in the world of the faceless, the day laborers, the gleaners and drayhorses.

Berrigan: Jesuit. Indeed, the cassock did not make it happen, nor the vestments of Mass, nor the university degrees. What indeed was a Jesuit, this elusive bird, this changeling, this purportedly charismatic being, this myth? The subject of tracts and novels and films, and much overspill of rhetoric and parti pris, loved, hated, and feared. . . .

What was all this to me, did it lie within me? The priesthood, membership in the Society had been conferred; but was I a Jesuit in a modest, workable sense, as one who dwelt in the guts and heart of the human, whether at prayer, or in public fret and conflict?

From outside, the Jesuit thing was like the mythic engine construed by Henry Adams. It drew its energy from its own mass and molten heart. It followed, then, that Jesuits must exist en masse. The Jesuit fuel was strangely akin to the Masonic—a glance, a handclasp, a liturgy, a day of vows, the clink of a glass, a joke. They were themselves, among themselves.

But in the world, something else occurred: their élan was often dissipated in the spending of that concentrate of life.

Sometimes the energy gave out altogether, they became mere ornaments of a culture, of the media, the arts. *Jésuites de salon* was the phrase. The tension they generated leaked away, they faded into servility and social clamor. A few became known, here and there, as patsies of power, a revolting game.

In "Ours," as one among them knew, the best and worst tended to commingle, in ways not always acknowledged, even to one another. And yet, for one Jesuit's part, this was the first, indispensable confession—the darkness and light that existed within himself, opposites, yet twins, in conflict, yet conniving.

Now and again, rarely, the drama played itself out in public, became a matter of notoriety or even scandal. It was a sign, he knew, of the mysterious wrestling match that proceeded, desperate and unresolved, in darkness of soul.

If he had learned anything, as he departed for Europe after some fourteen years treading the fires and being warmed (and occasionally scorched) by them, he had gained at least an inkling: the yin and yang, the correspondence, the conflict.

It was the glory of the order, as well as its shame: Jesuits walked the world, and took their chances there. He thought, renouncing any romantic formula, this was the least unsure way of putting a puzzling matter.

The chances were difficult, the stakes high. They did not invariably walk away with the swag, whose image was nothing of glory or gain, but might more properly be named the cross. From time to time, the horrible opposite occurred. The world walked away with them, having prevailed over the spirit of the cross with one or another spurious proffer, which their founder knowledgeably named: "honors, riches, the credit of a great name."

There was one renouncement they were forbidden to make, under any circumstance: the community. Indeed, they had the reputation of standing by one another, through hell and high water. (He wished with all his heart that event matched rumor, especially when one or another Jesuit risked heavily, staking his repute on a work that met with official thunders.)

Was this not simply what a Jesuit was called to, supposing the worth of a task and the competence and conscience of the doer? They had a great saying, often repeated: Jesuits belonged "at the cutting edge, not the soft center."

Alas, the saying, so to speak, cut both ways: lofty words were celebrated; honorable acts somewhat less so. Disapproval from Rome (or worse, demands for someone's removal from the order) often went unchallenged. And yet another Jesuit was sacrificed: "for good order," it was said, or "for the common good," or "for the greater good." So it was said.

By Caiphas, also, regarding another troublesome Spirit.

On such occasions, he believed, the Jesuits became a mere conduit for special interests. A word was passed along to one or another deviant. "Cease or perish."

That cutting edge again, and its application. It was Abraham with a knife to the throat of Isaac, "under orders." Or the Heavenly Father, weighing out on the scales of justice the sacrifice to be exacted of his Son.

This Jesuit would never comprehend such theology: perhaps he

The Early Years

"Jerry was a beautiful child," someone said. But for years, Dan (right) looked like the tiny lion monkey in the movie "The Mission." Babbitt, Minnesota, 1922.

The mother as patience on a monument. Jerry (left) contemplative, Dan stymied. Babbitt, Minnesota, 1922.

"Who's boss around here?" was a hot question, often raised, requiring no answer. Father's phiz allowed for no doubt. Front (left to right): Dan, Phil, Jerry. Rear: Jim, Dado. Liverpool, New York, 1926.

Age seven, disaster. I am yclept "four eyes" by the rabble of the White School. Liverpool, New York, 1928.

Dado's silk suit. He proclaimed often that he wanted to be buried in it. He outlasted the suit by some fifty years. Mother, Dan, himself gazing imperially into the middle distance. Liverpool, New York, 1929.

Briefly Dan (middle front) grew taller than Phil (to Dan's right). The three youngest are decked out in grandmother's knitted sweaters. Others, rear: Jim, John, Tom; front: Jerry. Liverpool, New York, 1930.

Under the old pear tree and its hospitable perches.
Knickers and sweaters and little joy in sight. Dan,
Phil, Jerry, Mother. Liverpool, New York, 1930.

"When I had them all under my wing" was
mother's caption. Front (from left): Phil, Dan,
Jerry; rear: Tom, John, Jim. Liverpool, New
York, 1936.

Mother advances to a fur collared cloth coat.
Dado has laid a heavy (though profitless) hand
on the author, whose tendency is, from the start,
toward the freewheeling. Liverpool, New York,
1936.

Mother and sons, Jim (left) and Dan. Gloves,
purse de rigueur; the paralytic Sunday look. Liverpool, New York, 1938.

By now rather portly, mother scans the future for a sign—or the past for solace. John (left) and Dan, do neither. Liverpool, New York, 1939.

The author, fattened on eggnogs for the long haul, and boyhood chum, John St. George. Both planted, for a time only, in the Promised Land. St. Andrew on Hudson, Poughkeepsie, New York, 1941.

Clerically irreproachable, Dan (left) pays a visit to Jerry at Epiphany College. The visitor appears becalmed, the host bemused. Newburgh, New York, 1948.

Year of first Jesuit vows. A long, long trek ahead, but O the pride! St. Andrew on Hudson, Poughkeepsie, New York, 1941.

Sr. Mary Marcella, a long-suffering high school teacher, visits Dan and discovers a once distempered pupil converted to godly ways. LeMoyne College, New York, 1963.

did not want to. Even Kierkegaard, for all his broody genius, made a less than good case of the worst, as did Anselm.

The mind at its least unhealthy tended to move among human realities in searching out the divine. This at least described his method, and the method and source of his passion for justice; that justice that defends and succors and cherishes the brethren.

At all cost, he whispered to his soul; at any and all cost. At the cost of institutions, of good repute among the powerful, of investments, connections, the smooth sailing promised by the world (and worldly popes and bishops), as the winds of the world huffed and puffed into well-trimmed sails.

At their best, the Jesuits survived the world. They survived as well, the worst in themselves. Or better than mere survival, they came forward now and again (and often) with something to offer: something of Christ, something of presence and word, the word that stood for the deed. Their offering was subtle and unmistakable at once—the gift of conscience alive; of life lived to the hilt.

When this happened, and a Jesuit so lived, the immemorial conflict and duality lifted. What emerged visibly (visible perhaps only to a few, for the best Jesuits were often shy as moles) was a unity of the human. Everything came together. Someone was available: someone variously known as Brother, advocate, friend, stand-in, repairer of wrongs. Someone to lean on, to be counted on. Someone who did not betray.

An old priest, not of the order, once said to him: There are Jesuits and Jesuits, good and bad.

He remembers being offended by the sentence. At the same time, he was given pause by its source, a good priest, outside envy or advantage. And for all the Jesuit could tell, the judgment was offered in a good spirit.

How much he had to learn!

Forty years later, he has not learned much. Especially in regard to what is known as the Jesuit thing. And even when he thinks to come close, he knows he has described nothing more remarkable than the common calling of Christians.

An ex-member of the order, a scholar of some renown, even of dark renown, referred to the Jesuits as an enigma—a word that implies a taint, as of secrets artful and even duplicitous.

There are indeed enigmas in the world, and enigmatic persons. And closed doors, and power broking, and contempt for others, and recourse to violence. No one endowed with even a primitive sense of the century needs instructions in such matters.

The world appears to me as morally enigmatic. Its secrecy, lying, violence, and lust for power render hearts and institutions opaque, resistant against scrutiny and confession and accountability. This is the world as enigma. It does not know itself. Generation after generation, it clones its own methods. It resists that change we name change of heart or conversion; whether in leadership or institutions.

But the believing community is another matter entirely. Its image and ideal is Christ: crystalline clarity, forthrightness, direct speech, moral leverage, sacrifice, cohesion of word and act. So, it seems to me, is our calling.

It comes to this, I believe: the Jesuits are an enigma only in the degree that we fall victim to worldly ways; that we allow ourselves to be pelted with that filth that goes by the name of "riches, honors, the credit of a great name." As indeed our founding saint solemnly warned, he having been cleansed by the might and mercy of God, of the miasma.

The temptation remains, if not always accountably.

It takes the form, I believe, of pride of place, that siren of the celibate and professional.

The old priest was right. There are Jesuits good and bad.

At some point, it seems to me, each of us makes a wager, in the manner of Pascal. The terms of the wager matter greatly: whether the honor of Christ is to weigh heavy in the scales, or the high tide of ego. If the latter, our methods come to resemble (even as we dissemble), the methods of the world. We conduct our business in secrecy, moral opaqueness. We become part of that larger enigma known to Christ and his disciples simply as the world: the blind leading the blind.

Now and again, this has been our shame. Jesuits have woven the Byzantine toils and mazes of Roman politics, have laid out little and paid up nothing. We have sought institutional propspering, and whored after the rich; and so built up a kingdom of twilight.

Whether, the kingdom battening, students and penitents and

friends and enemies witness a dawn—find in us something of the moral lucidity of Christ—this would seem to be quite another matter.

And then there are other Jesuits; and this is literally salvation.

Apart from these (among whom I presently live and work), I could come on no persuasive reasons for abiding in the order at all. I have found a reason, and am grateful.

So Europe beckoned, for the first time, and by no means the last.

First time was a love affair. Yet only a romantic afterimage would report that the year was an easy one. I summon the thirty days of silence and prayer in new and austere surroundings; the retreat conducted in what was, for me, strictly a second language.

The walls of the old house on the main street of Paray were of gray stone, sweating with perennial damp. The weather, as winter deepened, was a soul-chilling gloom; one's room, in consequence, was outfitted for a tomb. Toward dawn or dusk, a wisp of what might pass for heat huffed out of ancient iron pipes. But for the remainder of day and night, a deadly chill rode the air.

That ugly provincial town, its contrasts, the moribund ecclesiastical atmosphere, an ominous haze over all, the spendid Romanesque basilica beside a redundant nineteenth-century Sacre Coeur confection, the proliferation of convents and chapels and shrines and parish churches, all competing for the cramped soul of the place! And then the poor and unemployed, mostly railroad workers, haunting the bare cupboards of Indochina wartime, a war graceless, ugly, and seemingly beyond outcome.

The workers of the town were heavily Communist, we were informed. They were the first specimens of that species to cross our eyes, fresh as we Americans were from the domestic rasp and fury of the McCarthy years.

The scene was reminiscent of an inferior romantic novel. When we clerics passed down a street in our cassocks, mothers pulled their children away; or we heard from the windows above, a derisive cawing. A flock of church crows was winging by.

The church? People? Church of the people? We may as well have been exotics in saffron, chanting our om. The canon of the cathedral lived in a graceless bourgeois style, the nuns of the Visitation were mortised into their convent walls. And the people glowered darkly from their doorways: anticlerical all, and no wonder.

The rector of the Jesuit house, Père Charmot, was also assigned to lead us in the classic thirty-day retreat. He was a marvel, his reputation stood high in America as well as Europe. Young Jesuits from every continent came to Paray to pass a year under his tutelage.

He was a square little man, burdened with obscure infirmities. He poked his way painfully along the halls of the old house, a solid geometric figure from biretta to rectangular shoes. His face was luminous and large, a face of intelligence and tranquility; his voice was like a sonorous bass viol, gently and strongly drawn.

He was the author of some twenty books; one of them, a history of Jesuit humanism, had been crowned by the French Academy.

So we arrived from all points of the compass for our final year of the Jesuit course. It was one of the worst years in French history. The war was at a bloody impasse, the domestic government a shambles, Dien Bien Phu in the offing. One Frenchman put the tragedy: "After this abomination there will be nothing left of France; only French Canada."

The church was also in trouble. Pius XII had all but proscribed French theologians and cashiered its best minds. The worker priests were proscribed. At the nearby Jesuit seminary in Lyon, prestigious chairs of theology were vacated, their professors removed and silenced. The Dominicans had fared even worse than the Jesuits. A Roman edict ordered the superiors of the order to evict from France those who were promulgating the "new doctrines" and aiding and abetting the worker priests. Either that, or the French province of the order would be suppressed.

It was a bizarre, even a desperate, time. It touched us all, from every nation, indebted as we were to the convergence of minds and methods that made of France the glory of the church universal.

It was also a time too painfully resembling events of the middle eighties. One American bishop, all but alone in the new wasteland of Roman orthodoxy, has put matters well; matters then and now: "There is a need to avoid the fanaticism and small-mindedness that has characterized so many periods of the church in its history—tendencies that lead to much cruelty, suppression of theological creativity and lack of growth." Exactly.

The pope was dying. He was favored, so the stories went, with visions of the Blessed Virgin. He was also cutting a swath of destruction against the innovators. There were denunciations of Scripture scholars. Superiors were summoned peremptorily to Rome, to answer for the unattended misdeeds of those in their ranks.

In January of '54, came the final blow: the worker priests of France were given an ultimatum. They were ordered to abandon their work in factories, fishing fleets, agricultural areas, and return to traditional parish work—or face excommunication. Large numbers, the bravest and best, simply walked away.

The fortunes of war! One victim of the purge was the eminent theolgian Henri de Lubac. He had held a chair at the famous Fourvière Seminary. Generations of Jesuits had sat in his classes, favored with the scope and breadth of his scholarship. Now he was silenced and sent off, like a recalcitrant child, to some corner or other; forbidden to lecture or write. A close friend of Charmot, he would appear at our house, a distinguished ghost.

His rehabilitation would occur a decade later, at the Vatican council. In his extreme old age, another pope would honor him with the Cardinalate. Fortunes of war, fortunes of the intellect, and chancy indeed.

As the American bishop continues: "In the 'fifties (many eminent), theologians were silenced. Then they were rehabilitated by the Second Vatican Council. . . . A better way of proceeding." The bishop speaks of Pope John, quoting, "The church prefers to make use of the medicine of mercy rather than that of severity. . . . She prefers to show the validity of her teaching rather than by condemnations."

In such an atmosphere, dangerous, beyond prediction, we dwelt in our shabby estate, behind a high wall topped with broken glass.

Charmot himself was under fire. Summoned to Rome for an accounting, he developed a fortunate malaise of the spine, took promptly to his bed, and shot off a telegram of regret.

His style was the sticking point. Young priests of his community had been exposed to the suspect worker priests. During the Christmas holidays, Charmot had closed the Paray house, sent young Jesuits to the Paris or Lyon regions, to live in the factories or mines with the priests, and taste the lot of the working poor.

Worse even: certain of the proscribed scholars were welcomed at the house, and there, it was reported, questionable doctrines were aired.

All such ventures must cease.

And did, to a point.

Charmot was a master of improvisation. Where good sense was at risk, he was a great one for quietly drawing the fang of the law. If the theologians could no longer be welcomed, their books were at hand. And if we could no longer venture among the worker priests, they could visit us: that, at least, had not been forbidden.

It was in such atmosphere that our retreat got underway in October. Four lengthy meditations each day. Four weeks of prayer, silence, and more silence. And when speech was allowed, in French only.

There were consolations of the meekest sort. I was summoned to the rector's room at the start. It was decreed that I, being American, and therefore accustomed to a substantial breakfast, must be allowed an egg for the morning repast; "so that your mind may remain clear." The connection between albumin and lucidity being best left to Gallic logic.

The Europeans among us had endured the Second World War. A few of the French had survived the front. All had known bombings and dislocation, one or two had been transported to Germany as slave laborers in the factories. One of the priests, a medical doctor, had served the Algerians in dangerous times; he was pallid and weak, and died in the course of that year.

Charmot himself had been a refugee, in and out of occupied zones. A delicious story was told; how at a particularly perilous juncture, he was borne to safety in a curious, three-wheeled bike-and-basket contraption. Hidden under a load of bread loaves, he was cycled safely past the checkpoint.

War or no, we were all veterans of sorts. We were nationals from Germany, Africa, India, Brazil, Malta, Italy, Venezuela, England, Belgium, Spain, Argentina. We had survived scrutinies and checkpoints of our own, and a succession of superiors, good, abominable, and indifferent. We had tumbled about for years in various communities, testing and tested alike. Some were competent teachers, some were scholars, others fitted more nearly for pastoral work.

The future of more than a few of us, as matters turned, was—speculative.

I would venture this, as I recall the faces of my compatriots of that year. If any group could be thought prepared, by chance and mischance, by long marches, by loss, catastrophe, and simple endurance, by ego and talent—prepared to tread the fires of the Spiritual Exercises—then it was ourselves. If not now, never. We breathed deep, and dove.

We were in the hands of the best and tenderest of masters. Père Charmot knew beyond doubt that he had not assembled a clutch of phoenixes about his circle of fire. He was dealing with mortals, brothers in the Company. Which is to say, we had broken the bread and passed the cup, for years; first at the hands of others, then ourselves pronouncing the words: "Do this for a memory of me."

We sat at his feet, if not literally, still in profound quiet and content. We were by no means his peers in wisdom or experience or the deep dredging of the Scripture, in which he bore the title of master. We were disciples; and that said much.

Images of fire, images of water. We dove, and surfaced again, sputtering, at sea. And trod the waters somehow, and eventually found our landmarks, and made our way ashore. Each, according to grace and gifts, speedily or slow. We meditated on the old-fashioned truths; truths the new theology had by no means held in contempt. Sin, death, heaven and hell, the judgment of God, the mercy of God.

All these, and that curious "principle and foundation" of Father Ignatius, a statement so dry as to cast dust in worldly eyes. It states dispassionately that we were created "to the praise and service of God," surely a truth any child could memorize. And then the rub: that all things created were to be scrutinized, embraced or set aside, as they were useful or destructive to one's vocation.

It was heavy going, that first week: heads had broken between those rocks and hard places. We moved in a kind of pre-Christian void, a strenuous continuum of prayer and conference and meals and silent walks in the garden. Something about "natural truths consonant with our faith"; natural theology, anti-Barthian. And hardly a One in sight to lodge our faith in.

It was a classic Burgundian fog, welling up from the river, slow-ing the bloodstream. Père Charmot shuffled through the corridors, knocking at each door, inquiring after the occupant.

Ignatius could be understood only as a child of his times; the week concluded with a meditation on The Kingdom. Christ the grandee appeared briefly on the horizon. We dwelt on his meek manifesto, the Sermon on the Mount, and were refreshed at last.

It had taken Charmot ten days to shake our world, persistent as he was, and vigilant, and no more disposed than Ignatius to let us off lightly.

We were freed finally, chastened, shy of palaver, to pass a day in the countryside, shaking the chills from our pates.

And so it went, a difficult month. The aspens along the canal shed their gold. It was a wearisome passage demanded of us. Beyond it stood the beckoning Figure, and a full welcome into the order as well.

The Charmot mystique! He was not a Scripture scholar in the classic tradition, he broke no new ground. He was in the line of masters of ascetical life. He was solid and sensible, a peasant from the mountain country of his patron saint, François de Sales.

He would appear in the shabby conference room in his dusty shoes and faded cassock, recite the opening prayer, mount the platform laboriously, seat himself, large hands shuffling his handwritten notes.

Then that voice! The Gallic tongue admits of a certain mesmeric quality. De Gaulle was to exploit it to the full, the Napoleonic thunder.

Charmot was free of distemper and pride. His voice was equal to the language. He exploited it, artfully. It was a tone native to the sensibility of John's Gospel, which he loved, quoting texts from memory, or commenting from meticulous notes. He lit a fire.

Said to me one day: "Your face is so alive during the conferences, all attention!"

And I, "No wonder! For the first time, I hear Scripture spoken in a living way."

The retreat was over, we resumed our modest local ministries: Mass in some convent or chapel, the worshipers invariably a few women, nuns, old men.

The town, like a moribund shell cast ashore, was resonant with history. It was here in the seventeenth century that a nun of the Order of Visitation was favored with visions of Christ. He appeared as a vulnerable Surrogate of God, suffering the crimes of the world, pleading in most ungodlike tones for love of humankind, their conversion, a response from "special souls" like herself.

It was a strange humanism from on high. Sister Margaret Mary was pilloried for proclaiming it, along with her Jesuit confessor, Claude de la Colombiere. The priest, a reed in the ecclesiastical gales, consumptive and scholarly, was already sinking to an early grave.

She and he were at length rehabilitated, and the teaching they inspired became part of the Catholic revival in France: the "devotion to the Sacred Heart of Christ." In the chapel of the Jesuit house stood a gold and crystal reliquary containing the skull of Claude, brown and smooth as old ivory. And down the street, the relics of Margaret Mary were similarly and disconcertingly ensconced. It is a measure of the grasp of the devotion of the faithful that by the eighteenth century, every order of the church had put roots down in Paray. Communities proliferated in the sleepy provincial backwater, pilgrimages swelled.

Two communities emerged, in uneasy conjunction. There were the barely baptized, the nonpracticants, the men in blue denim, the women in seedy black, dwelling in side streets and hovels. And then the official church, the canons and nuns and priests, the buildings and walled properties, the conferences, retreats and Masses, evening and morning devotions, bells and bell towers.

On the one hand the families of the poor, their squalor and contempt. On the other, the religious and their holy indifference and secure livings and noses on high.

Ironies, contrasts. Each June the Feast of the Sacred Heart was celebrated in our town of revelation and stasis. The limousine of the papal delegate, festooned with papal flags, prowled like a hearse through the narrow streets, under the smoldering eyes of the poor. His eminence came in splendor, worshiped with the crowds of pilgrims, and departed. And he saw nothing. And who was served, and who disserved, by such a spectacle, no one could say.

I had never seen the like: two planets whizzing by, different orbits, danger, disdain, muttering. Incompatibilities, injustice. Two walls set one against the other.

The retreat was over. I was summoned by Charmot. He noted from my dossier that I had a measure of experience in caring for the ill and aged. I was therefore to undertake the care of an ancient Father shortly to arrive in the house; a formerly distinguished superior. He would be entitled to "the best we can offer."

The Father arrived in due time and was installed in a room on the top floor. There was no infirmary, no special equipment, no water available in the room. Plank floors, dead gray walls, a single bulb dangling disconsolate. What a hole, I thought, to pass one's last days in.

Luckily the patient, though testy of temper, and vaguely retentive of the glories of his estate, was quite unconscious of the absence of amenities. He lay there, malevolent or comatose, peering out from under his skullcap. He was rudderless, at the mercy of the moon.

There were, however, a few stable factors. One was his love of great bowls of chocolate and milk; the other and consequent one, the working of his bowels. These were unpredictable on the instant, but constant in the larger span of hours. I would think, as he placidly overflowed, that he was dramatizing, in a way perculiar to his condition, his lost psyche. He had been known as a superior who, from his catbird seat, often vented spleen on the hapless.

Hapless I was, and continued to be. A typical night would find me composing him for sleep: clean sheets, clean night clothing, clean nightcap. He retained by his bedside a display of devotional objects, a statuette or two, a medallion, his crucifix. Whatever affection his soul allowed was expended on these artifacts: before turning to sleep, he would kiss each of them. Then he would dismiss me querulously.

Lights out. And before I had cleared the room, I would hear the dreaded rumblings of intestinal catastrophe. On with the light. A gleam of perverse rationality, even of satisfaction, on the old phiz. Kisses indeed for the icons, something else for me. . . .

Another incident, involving a local character, stands out. A disabled Jesuit dwelt with us, a veteran of the First World War. He humped about the corridors on a wooden leg, a relic of the days when priests and seminarians, along with all other males, were sent to fight and die in the savage trenches.

Our priest was mobile: he putt-putted about the town, to the terror of chickens and piglets, in a wondrous creation of French whimsy, a three-wheeled motorized vehicle fitted out with a steering pole like a bishop's crook. This celestial chariot was conferred on him by the government, in payment for his war wounds.

He grew ill, the chariot lay idle in the rear garden. The Père was transported to the neighboring hospital and the care of nursing nuns. And we began to mount the traditional death watch.

I was included in the sacred chore. First I was instructed, in some detail, as to the Père's peculiarities. He retained a horror of dying, it was explained, had repeatedly refused the anointing of the ill, and could be anointed and shriven only at the exact moment of expiration. Indeed, he retained his stout cudgel at his side, and threatened anyone who dared approach for salvational reasons with condign blows.

Even in decline, he bade fair to make good his threat, a beefy old man with a spud face, all bumps and humps, and the mighty torso of one who hauled himself through life. I was warned not to underestimate our patient: he might be thought able, even in extremis, to lay his stave about the head of the unwary.

I was assigned a night watch in late May. My instruction went as follows: at the moment of death, if it came during my tenure, approach the bed and minister a conditional anointing and shriving.

The quandary was evident. If zeal or panic took over and I swooped too soon, I would suffer for it. And if too late, his airborne soul might suffer lack of the holy benefice.

A night to remember. The impersonal room, the old priest whistling and snoring and tossing; and the open doors, giving on a garden in full moonlight. The nightingales were sounding their plaint from tree to tree, invisible, tormented. A night of death and rebirth, in the French manner, operatic, impeccably staged. I paced in and out of the sickroom, in and out of the garden, lightheaded with song and sleeplessness.

Then, toward dawn, a change occurred in the patient.

He began to cough dry, deep in his throat. He thrashed about in the bed, the stick lay useless at his side. I grabbed the holy oils, approached the bed; all atremble I said the words of healing and reconciling, dabbed the oil on his forehead—and got myself out of range. He laid not a finger on me. His jaw dropped, his soul fled.

The Sister entered, plangent, professional. She tied up his jaw

with a towel, murmuring her formula like the old stager she was:
O mon pauvre Père!

And I returned home, to recount the last hours. And to be re-
galed as well with a strange tale.

It appeared that many years before, le pauvre Père had been
enlisted as a foot soldier in the Battle of the Somme, that he had
been severely wounded, and was transported behind the lines, to
an improvised tent hospital. There, examination showed wounds of
such severity as to require the amputation of a leg.

The operation proceeded. And in the midst of it, another barrage
struck the tent. Poles, wires fell, lights failed, pandemonium ensued.
Hastily, the operation proceeded, in semidarkness. And in the panic
and speed, le Père suffered the amputation, not of the damaged
limb, but the perfectly sound other!

Whereupon the surgeons, appalled at their error, set themselves
an altogether unprecedented effort. And despite the wounds, salvaged the mangled limb.

Which explained the perpetual solicitude of the state, the putt-
putt machine, the free fuel, the Croix de Guerre that, along with
biretta and priestly stole, lay on the casket during his funeral service. . . .

He appeared suddenly one day in the spring of 1953, at the
door of the old Jesuit house in Saone-et-Loire. It was one of those
tepid evenings that seemed to rise from the dispirited canal nearby,
an evening fruitless and miasmic, transforming everything solid in
nature into an uneasy dream.

He was obviously an American and, judging from his comportment and bearing, a man of note. Elegant clothing, an assured,
seignorial manner: this one had made his mark somewhere. He was
looking for an English-speaking priest; I was referred to by the
Brother porter, who came lurching through the corridors on his gimp
leg, seeking me out.

Almost anything, you understand, would have been a relief in
that characterless provincial town where, on windy nights, the very
trees groaned aloud in boredom; where we Jesuits were thrice segregated—from New York, from Paris, even from the town plaza and
its plane trees with their military haircuts, standing at attention like
upright ghosts. Segregated, it goes without saying, from the Hotel

of the Great Pleasures, a dismal gray dome sitting ungainly next to the dreary railroad station, like a dunce hat discarded by a dunce.

It developed in the course of our first meeting that the American was lodged at the hotel in question. He was on pilgrimage to the shrines of Europe; these included, in a rather modest way, our town. The pilgrim would pass the next day or so performing his devotions at the chapel. And then came the grand gesture: I was invited to sup with him that evening, partaking the modest amenities of the pleasure dome.

Talk about delirious diversions! Some thirty-five of us Jesuit priests, ingathered from four continents, were nearing the end of a year known in the order as tertianship. The unwieldy term, to be found in no lexicon, signified that somewhere between the ages of thirty to thirty-five, Jesuits are detained under a species of mild house arrest, as often as not in a foreign land.

There, in invariably remote acres, behind singularly cheerless walls, we moved about the house in silence. We took our recreation sedately as octogenarians, in a rear garden notable for its arthritic dampness. According to rule, we departed the premises only to offer spiritual succor to a deprived and suspicious citizenry who, in the classic Gallic manner, had long since learned to dispense with us; or to nuns even more straitly enjoined than ourselves. Quite a year!

In such manner, toward the end of winter, as a grudging spring dragged the spirit down, the American appeared out of nowhere. In that month, one would have settled for far less: the diversion of a mouse in a corner or a bird at the windowsill, with whom to hold mournful communing.

More than a bird was in hand. Permission was granted for my evening out.

The American and I were greeted at the front door of the Pleasure Palace, by the redoubtable owner, Madame Defarge (so my mind named her, formidable dame, as a word or two chipped away from her stony mouth in the street on market day, or a nod of recognition was conceded in the aisle of the Jesuit chapel). She was a terror, her charms mitigated by mercantile cunning.

Madame walked the streets of Paray surrounded by a faintly brimstone aura. She had won her medals. If her fellow citizens bowed deeply to her in passing, if they spoke her name with awe and then clammed up, this reaction paid tribute neither to gentle birth nor beauty. Madame was no haute bourgeoise: she trod her beaten track between market and hotel kitchen; she was also given on occasion to blue, unsettling speech.

It was fate had set her apart: the memory of a virtuous crime.

The gesture, real or mythical (it was real enough, and therefore mythical) signified to the townsfolk, for whom the past was far more real than the postliberation plod—embattled as they had been, humiliated, occupied by Nazi swaggerers, divided disastrously among themselves (better a live collaborator than a dead lion)—her gesture signified the highest reaches of soul, the plucking of flowers of courage and imagination from the verge of the world. The laurels were hers: she had resisted, and survived.

To a stranger like myself, the woman and her story were no more than a morning mist of rumor. But not for long. Ten years after the German defeat, I moved like a sleepwalker among memories far more alive than the living. The place had been a stronghold of the occupying forces, there were executions and reprisals. Along the garden walls, a series of small, gloomy tablets like stations of the cross, festooned with rotting flowers, commemorated a bloodletting, grown impersonal with time, Nazi or partisan.

And then there was Madame: concerning her, it seemed, everyone knew something—or at least purported to, which in Paray came to the same thing. Mention of her name brought forth a Gallic rolling of the eye and pursing of the lips, signifying unutterable access to the unmentionable. No one breathed a word, everyone gave her away. There was cloud of rumors, a multitude of rumormongers, prepared to raise a hand and swear.

In sum, Madame was the true ornament of Paray. Neither monk nor nun nor patron saint could exhibit the *mysterium tremendum* that was her aura: a mélange of superstition, fear, and admiration. She was iconic; more honored than the metal tricolor in Miriam's arms in the town square. Madame held memories strong as death, memories both bitter and bracing.

The Nazi occupiers had suborned the Jesuit house to bunk their lesser fry. The officers had dragooned Madame's hotel: superior board and room. Little could they know what lurked in her smile. She served them equably, she offered satisfaction in all respects:

not quelled, exactly, as one might wish, or cheerful in her service, as one might command; merely laconic and satisfactory.

And then one day, the commanding officer was nowhere to be found. This eminence, under whom many a townsperson had disappeared without trace, and many a partisan had suffered capture and summary end—he was gone. Kaput. His suite was in order, so were his papers. No investigation, no seizing of suspects or hostages lent so much as a clue. He disappeared, he stayed disappeared. When I arrived in town, no one knew his name. No one cared to.

Was Madame involved in what came to be regarded as a daring, indeed life-risking, exploit? Rumor persisted, rumor fused into time itself.

The rumors were like numerals on the town clock: they told the hours but uttered not a word. But if they tolled the hour, it was an hour of judgment. And if rumor lettered a plaque, the words went something like; Vengeance is mine, said the woman.

Such a personage loomed up in the hotel doorway, bidding welcome, welcoming the Père first. A deep bow that left the dark gleam of her eyes hanging on the air like an afterimage. For all my foreigner's innocence, there was no missing the glance; or the bow. I was being sized up to the millimeter.

She led us to our place in the dining room, deserted in that season. Then she stood to take our orders: I remember ordering the omelette of the house. What an unheard of delicacy in those penurious times, when the nuns of Sacre Coeur were scrounging food about the town; and memories of those denied sustenance during the Nazi years were still vivid.

The American said his farewell a day later, and moved on; to Rome, as I recall. He also promised to visit my parents in upstate New York, and assure them of my well-being. Which he did, in due course; and, as they reported, he dwelt at our home a few days, and edified the family with his presence at daily Mass in the parish church.

Before leaving Paray, he also presented me with a book of devotions, as a memento of his visit. I opened the book in my room; the inscription was *Devotedly, to Père Daniel, from Ramon Navarro.*

Ten years later, I was teaching at LeMoyne College in Syracuse. I had initiated a student community off campus, with a view to service projects in Latin America. The students and I labored like stevedores to put our dwelling in shape. Included was a chapel where we might worship in a gentle, understated setting. Penurious as always, I proceeded to send out begging letters, seeking accoutrements for our chapel. Among others who responded was my distinguished friend of a decade previous. He sent a warm note and a check.

The year 1968 was The Year of the Inconceivable That Came True. It seemed at times that the end of the world would come as a positive relief from the tide of catastrophe and crisis.

Would the world ever again turn upside up? Few of us would bank on it.

This is how that calendar unfolded, like the book of doomsday in a demon's hand.

In February of that year, I was under American bombs in Hanoi, as I sought to repatriate three American Air Force pilots. Then in May nine of us went to Catonsville to burn draft files. In October we proceeded to trial and were convicted. And in December the dying year lashed us once more with its scorpion's tail: Merton perished in Bangkok.

And then, as in a Red Sea of torment, yet another bloody interjection.

In late October, a week or two after our trial, I returned to Cornell and picked up the pieces of my scattered life. We nine were free on appeal; prison was a sure bet. And then another blow.

Ramon Navarro had been murdered in his home in California, by two brothers, drifters. They had bludgeoned him to death; for no ostensible reason. He had been there, they had been there. In the region of the Manson slaughterhouse, that was perhaps enough: the boredom, the emptiness, the human desert that thirsts for an open vein, and opens it, and drinks the rain.

Our Paray community scattered during Lent. Part of the year's discipline was the undertaking of ministries in parishes and schools—and the military.

I was assigned to a military chaplaincy in West Germany.

It was a measure of my unawakening that I traveled for forty days through American camps and installations, exhorting soldiers and officers to shore up their observance of the faith. And not once did I refer to the fact that nuclear weapons studded the landscape. I met constantly with chaplains and military personnel and their families. And the question of war never once, according to my memory, surfaced as a moral question. One and all, we slept on, the military and I, in an enchanted cave: the workshop of Mars.

The highest-ranking officer in the chaplaincy, as it happened, was a New York Jesuit. He was like a sixteen-speed machine, fueled by coffee and cigarettes, burning up the roads and airways of Germany in his quest for the souls of GIs. He thought little of gathering a busload of soldiers, transporting them a great distance through the night, starting a retreat in early morning, putting them (and himself) through smart paces, then driving back to the casern, also through the night. To appear at his office the following morning, spit and polish and a day's work.

He died suddenly a year later, a Herculean heart giving out.

I recall him as a virtuous priest, zealous and faithful. And yet, and yet. A public conscience, one that questioned the existence of the American military on German soil, let alone a nuclearized military—such questions were far beyond him and me.

Our church existed in a kind of predawn obscurity. We, all of us, took Cold War lunacies, well underway, as inevitable as changes of the moon, even as God-given ingredients of our world. We were, after all, favored by being "on the right side"; Spellman at home, the Army in Germany. Who would question so mighty a fortress, the conjunction of holy church and mother state—and all in contravention of the godless?

It is small comfort to dredge up one's memories, and come on a moral blank screen. Thirty years ago! What an unfinished human I was, for all the years of Jesuit life, the study, asceticism, sacraments, choices and byways, teaching, exhortations and retreats, scrutinies and testing. I remember the words of Joan of Arc, in the poem of Péguy, her mourning how long it takes to create a human, how quickly a human is destroyed!

And how long, too, the clumsiness and groping, false starts and cowardice, the good, bad, and indifferent in the human meld.

I walked the earth blindly, no pondering the awesome fact: the earth was mined, prepared at the slightest touch to explode all the living. I was asked to accept this as normal; almost as though the earth, fully equipped to self-destruct, had thus left the creative hand. Or (no different aberration) as though human hands, planting disaster in every furrow, were enhancing the work of creation. God left off, technique took up: the method and morality were one. . . .

A three-year assignment followed, at Brooklyn Preparatory School in New York. I was back in the hustings, with a vengeance. With an enterprising team of laymen and Jesuits, we started honors courses in classics and English literature. I sojourned regularly with students to the Lower East Side of Manhattan; there we made ourselves useful at the Nativity Center, whose open doors were welcoming the great influx of Puerto Ricans.

The times were a heyday among Catholics. We were reading magazines such as *Integrity* and *Jubilee*, and the older standbys, *Commonweal* and *Catholic Worker*. Younger people had taken the bit in their teeth, less clericalism was befouling the air.

Some priests, appalled at the changes that were easing them from last year's nest, scuttled for cover. Others went along with events, partners or instigators, confident that a place remained for them, relying on friendship and mutuality. Such qualities were beginning to count for much: the temperament and humanity of the priest, rather than the dispensing of nostrums from on high.

Quality, verve, insight, standing with others: the priest was friend and brother. I began to see that the working people I dealt with (I was now a chaplain to the Young Christian Workers) were a seedbed of Christian community. The discovery was intoxicating; we met each week to study the Scriptures, draw conclusions, and decide on actions to be taken in the workplace, actions that would make work less demeaning. Together, we were setting out toward the Promise.

I dwelt on the fortunate side of the river, the one called Brooklyn. There, enterprising and thoughtful priests, of whom there were many, were emerging as chaplains to young workers and students. I was in excellent company from the start.

Nonetheless, invading my mind at that time, through osmosis, exposure, mischance, and improvising, was a parade of second thoughts worthy of Hamlet. How could it be that the work of teaching, and the communitarian life of the schools, so often narrowed the vision of teachers, dug a furrow that, in time, became a very grave? How explain the racism and anti-Semitism of several Jesuits I lived with? And at the far end of our efforts, how did it fare with our graduates, those darlings of our long belaboring? Were they notably superior in moral understanding for having been exposed to our ethos over the years? Had their imaginations taken fire from our own? Or were we, and they, merely sedulous instances of a cruel and wounding culture?

I did not know; I had little help with the questions. I am not certain even that I aired them at home. I knew the same doubts hung in the minds of others, but it was considered bad form to press them at common gatherings.

Thus I dwelt pretty much in my own compartment in limbo— so often the Jesuit fate, relieved, if one is lucky, by the presence of a friend or two.

I think my soul was moving in a contrary wind.

Or another image, I was dwelling at the eye of the urban hurricane. I would walk long distances in the city, invariably alone, usually late at night; then would return for a quiet hour in the chapel before sleep. I was communitarian by discipline, a loner by instinct. I cultivated my soul with a fierceness that could be understood only as a passion for survival.

I read widely, and wrote as I might. All untried, I already considered myself, naive or arrogant as I was, a professional in the making. But I took it for granted that someday I would be known as a poet, and a chronicler of the times.

So I wrote and read, uphill. My hopes, never high and seldom encouraged, were nonetheless secretly nurtured; they were light enough, airy enough, to give a kind of recoil to my step.

I wrote poems, and reviewed and mulled over poetry written years before: in seminary, as a young teacher. It seemed to me good poetry, better than much then being published.

Then something happened. Somehow or other, my path crossed that of a young editor; he heard that I was a poet of sorts, and inquired further. I was reluctant to pursue the question, but he insisted, and we resolved on a wager.

He would submit the manuscript to a scrupulous and demanding reader. If I could pass that exceedingly narrow gate, I would be home free.

He was as good as his word. Soon after, a phone call sent light-ings into my ears: the mysterious reader had taken the manuscript to heart and praised it beyond measure. The reader was Marianne Moore. I was, at long last, to be published.

I was like a vessel constructed for high seas, then condemned so long to dry dock that it forgot its element. Still, such a ship may be thought to hum like a shell with the rumor of winds. Which is to say, I had accepted my fate and I had not accepted it. I never gave up my discipline, never resigned myself to a creeping illiteracy of spirit. I had carefully assembled a manuscript, then judged the time inopportune and laid it aside. In a kind of Buddhist spirit charged with eventuality, I waited on a better time.

I may have been lucky, but my luck was hard bought, paid to the farthing.

The book was published: *Time Without Number*. It was sea-worthy, and felicitously launched; it went from glory to glory. It was praised and cozened and reprinted and won a prestigious prize. Its furrow left a wake for others to follow.

I set down this first minitriumph, conscious of an irony both delightful and fraught with pain. Some thirty-five books later, trans-lations in many languages, other prizes gained. And yet the pub-lishing of each book has been chancy in the extreme. Many have been long delayed, others remaindered, others, with dreadful ease, have passed out of print. And at least one, in the bear pit of cor-porate mindlessness, was tossed in the shredder without my being notified.

The world is such that one had best prepare the soul for night-mares. Here is a recurrent one. I am walking a road; underfoot a resplendent red rug unrolls ahead of me. I happen to glance behind. The rug is rolling up, mysteriously, almost at my heels. I must move at a smart trot, because the rug rolls up as quickly as it unrolls ahead. Otherwise, I may well be swept up and rolled along, a bag-gage of time on rampage.

Every new act is prelude, until the curtain goes down. I still wore the accustomed clothing, trod the usual round: classes, coun-seling, worship. I lived attentively, but with little thought to the cyclone in the dust: a tiny swirling that, up to that moment, would hardly have lifted a dog's hair.

In 1957 I was assigned to the theology department of a young Jesuit college in Syracuse, New York. My poetry was in the public

eye, a second book of essays on the way. I would have been regarded by colleagues as a promising gent, a bit to the left of perfect
balance, perhaps, but one who could be counted on not to rock
things seriously.

I was in home port, and took up my new work with a vengeance.
Syracuse was a heavily Catholic, Republican enclave. The old
WASP families were on the decline, their bleak pseudo-Norman
churches, vast and all but empty, tolled the glories going. The Irish,
German, and Italian Catholics were flexing their muscle: they had
a vigorous chain of parishes strung across the neighborhoods, the
parochial schools were crowded.

And then, after the Second World War, the Jesuits arrived in
town, naming their new foundation after an early missioner, Père
Simon LeMoyne, priest extraordinary among the Iroquois nations.

I was entering a vigorous theology department, heavy with talent
and savvy, dominating the school. LeMoyne had the look indeed
of a kind of seminary for laity. There was serious Scripture study
and, for those times, a remarkable liturgical spirit. The innovations
in the latter area were frowned and grumbled at downtown by the
chancery old guard and the bishop, an aged incendiary; but to little
avail.

The bishop was even led to entertain second thought about his
original invitation to the Jesuits. LeMoyne students were becoming
untowardly attached to priests, who also were professors, counse-
lors, confessors, friends. There was a rush to seminaries and novi-
tiates, especially to the Jesuits and Maryknoll.

The friction was petty indeed; but it charged the atmosphere of
my arrival. We were appraised of the way matters stood, and advised to be sensible: that was all.

Toward the next spring, I stumbled over a trip wire.

A friend had gotten out of prison after serving a term for refusal
to pay war taxes. He arrived in Syracuse for a visit, lodging at the
home of my parents. In the course of his stay, a project evolved.
Karl Meyer would become a key person in the establishment of a
Catholic Worker house, in the manner of Dorothy Day. He would
live on the premises, oversee volunteers, and be in charge of the
work: feeding the poor who came to the door.

It seemed fairly basic and simple and Christian. And it raised
holy hell.

I had been advised to put together a written plan to present to the Bishop. For safety's sake, it was implied. Because he, in a small company town, presumably oversaw not only the ecclesiastical factory, but the company store as well.

In my letter I ventured to describe Karl's pacifism, mentioning his recent prison sentence, and praised him for his courage. I commended him for an ideal volunteer: he was eager to undertake a difficult and thankless work. One much needed in a (snug and smug) town.

As was later revealed, the letter inflamed. His eminence fretted and fumed. And finally, out of the blue, one day I received a brimstone phone call. It was himself, venting the passions my letter had loosed.

How could such as I presume to bring to town (to his town) someone who, naming himself Catholic, could also be, and be approved by the likes of me, a "pacifist"? Was I so foolhardy as to presume that this person could be foisted on the Catholic diocese of Syracuse (his diocese)—to perform work, moreover, that was already, thank you, quite adequately performed by the parishes?

Moreover (the moreovers kept coming over the hill, squads and phalanxes of them) I had dared state that I was his spiritual director. He ranted, "It is is you, Father Berrigan, who are in need of a spiritual director, if you imagine such theories and practices can be legitimately etcetera, etcetera."

More and moreover! You, F. B., are presuming to teach theology to the young Catholics of Our Diocese. You are manifestly unfit for the work, and will be subject to removal.

By now he was raving. I was counseled "not to dare say a word, my secretary is listening on another phone. . . ." The true and Catholic doctrine regarding war, so cavalierly contravened by me, was taught and proclaimed by Pope Pius XII: it clearly blessed the defensive guns of the virtuous, together with their virtuous explosion in the flesh of the unvirtuous. Did I not know that the just war was, and would remain, a cornerstone of the Catholic edifice?

I was rendered speechless by the assault. After some twenty torrid minutes, he put down the receiver with a bang. Short of identifying myself, I had not uttered a word. It was lightning in the summer sky; there was thunder to follow.

Rudimentary wits did not abandon me. I must approach friends on the faculty, open the situation, enlist support. The storm might yet be turned aside.

And so it happened. It was, in my experience, one of the few times when professors stood by a colleague in trouble.

It was made clear to the president of the college, even before the bishop summoned him, that were I removed, he would have to deal with five or six other Jesuits, each of them indispensable to the flourishing campus.

The presidential vanity was also cultivated. The ruff rose on his neck when it was pointed out that "proper channels, and his own office, had been denigrated, in the attack on Berrigan."

This was the only knee-stiffener he required when the bishop requested his attendance. Matters stopped there. I remained at LeMoyne five more years.

I bring up the affair, trivial as it is, because it was a crucial event in my education; which, given events to follow, might be thought to have had its painful inception here. I was something like a child who, on his first day of class, undergoes a thorough birching at official hands. I was warned, but not quelled.

Disease of power is the phrase that occurs. Whether the malaise strikes in church or state, I am not at all certain that it takes a different form. In the ecclesiastical instance, there is a dread and double jeopardy implied: the sword is two-edged. The will of the authorities is presented as God's will. And that weapon of sovereign will removes limbs and heads so cleanly it becomes almost a privilege to perish at such hands—under the Excalibur that whispers as it kills: God's will! God's will!

I could see no great advantage in my perishing at anointed hands rather than secular. It seemed to me, moreover, that claims of embodying God's will in vexed cases must themselves be verified by the human conduct of the claimant. I was to be shunted about vigorously in the years that followed, by one authority after another. Each of the removers assured me, with all solemnity, that I was out of order, a truly divine order, one they stood well within. They were entitled, moreover, to define, from within, my status: a pertinacious outsider, addicted to troublemaking. In consequence of which, certain steps were required. In sum and to speak inelegantly, in accord with God's will—Would I please, and with all deliberate speed, get lost?

This was not well received, by me, by others similarly dealt with.

But in time, I also mastered another lesson. There are ways of receiving such treatment, ways that do not merely reproduce it.

When the offended party yields to contempt and counterviolence, I came to understand, both sides are demeaned, no light is shed, wounds are exacerbated. There must be another way.

I came on the other way, gradually and with clumsiness, through friends: Dorothy Day, Merton, my brother Philip, certain Jesuits. These in person. And Dr. King and Gandhi and others, my noble ancestral teachers.

It came to something like this. With no loss of dignity, I could acknowledge, even in the most inhuman authority, a coercive power—even when that power was unjustly wielded. I could obey—even a Herod. Obedience, time and again, in the most painful and unpromising circumstances, shed a momentary light on the way I must go. Something happened, over which the authority had no control: the crooked lines straightened.

Another image occurred. The wielders of big sticks could show me nothing of example or icon. They were wooden signposts: at a crossroads, they might point out the right road, without ever going there.

The images are not offered with contempt. When life has been "spiritualized" to the point that critique is declared off limits, it might be helpful to bring things to ground, even with a thump. In the Jesuits, as I presume in other communities, one heard at the time of my first thrashing, rigorous invocations of God's will speaking through church authorities. Granted; and yet not granted. Granted in principle, questioned when such terms are misused in order to stymie discussion, to "bring matters to a close."

In such instances, a capital point. One reads the words of Christ as they touch on authority—its right use and more than occasional misuse. Something about a stark contrast between the methods of authority in the world and in the community of faith. Something about "lording it over," as contrasted with "service one of another."

One summons the glance of Christ, as it rests on the seats of power, and those seated there. The look, as implied in His words, is both level and leveling. More, when the glance touches on misdemeaning authority, it becomes scornful, withering. He deflates those who ride high: he counsels authorities to dig deep in the human condition, to discover there the roots and resources of authority (his own roots and resources)—in service rather than domination.

In such discovery, it seems to me, authority itself is invigorated, even as it is questioned. Authority might even take fire. Might discover and imagine, for instance, the difference, often so troubling, between craziness and new turns of sanity, between coping and creating. And so become a partner, enabler, in the danger and exhiliration and fury that inevitably attend change.

This is the health of power.

I report, some thirty years after the event described, that the disease of power presently flourishes in the church, as in the state. The plague has become a pseudosacred form of the secular, cultural illness. Thus, sorrowful to witness, the burden of illness is doubled.

But it must be taken in account, and rejoiced in, that something else is occurring within the church; most surprisingly of all, in the American church. And this, to say the least, offers a great hope.

It was the late fifties. I was becoming known here and there through my books, was teaching, leading retreats, lecturing, offering poetry readings: working like a demon, and loving it.

I was accounted stern in the classroom, and not solely regarding points of Scripture. When assignments were due, I poked about in corners of grammar, punctuation, with a fine-pointed stick indeed. I sought literacy as well as imagination. My image in those days is of a devoted drayhorse in harness; students must arrive similarly geared for plow and furrow.

My peers and I had an influence that went beyond formalities. We were quasi gurus of the college: we walked in light. We also kept a weather eye out for the best students, and beckoned them into our light. So there developed around us a group known as the Sodality. The members underwent a spiritual discipline of sacrament, prayer, social action. They also regularly reported to a priest director, who was monitor, curb, spur; perhaps most important, a good listener.

Thus our influence grew. And so did the opposition, something, after all, to be expected. We were handling volatile materials, even inducing a flash point in young lives. Students graduated and were encouraged to continue in the communal discipline they had undertaken in college.

Young professionals, a wider horizon. Together we began to scrutinize urban structures, housing, banking, investments. What we found could be described as a species of unsavory chic—an old story, but new to us.

The local Catholic establishment, that is to say, had a large hand in the trough named real estate. They fed exceedingly well there. And in proportion as the arrangement worked well for them, outside scrutiny was discouraged.

Neat dovetailing was the well-kept secret, as we studied the city and its power brokers. Each of them owned a bit of everything. Each was rich, but no one was ostentatiously rich; a bit here (quite a large bit), a bit there: real estate shares, banking shares, manufacturing shares, media shares. The same faces appeared on corporate boards, a vote here, a vote there. It added up to enormous power judiciously parceled out: maximum benefits, concealed accountability. The gentlemen who owned Syracuse owned, one by one, only parts of Syracuse. Putting the parts together was our task; and it was devilishly hard.

Who was accountable, say, for an uninhabitable derelict dwelling, a crowded slum block? Who collected rents and refused to make repairs? Or who, after a disastrous fire following all manner of violations, was indictable for loss of life?

These were the questions we tackled. In the breach, as it happened, because Syracuse, like any city one might mention across the land, was pocked with shanties that on winter nights went up like torches.

We were on touchy ground. The monetary mandarins were influential not only in the political establishment, but in the church as well. They oiled the gears of the city; they were also conspicuous consumers of parish services. More, and for us, worse: they were among the founding geniuses of the Jesuit college.

So the question seethed away: should these venerables be subject to scrutiny, nay to legal challenge? And this, in face of their largesse to LeMoyne College? Talk about conflict of interest!

I felt, in my discouragement, that the conflict ran so deep as to be beyond resolution. Institution versus conscience, college versus public interest. Or, more precisely, the college versus the right of the poor to bare survival. And now, a professor at the college, and a Jesuit to boot, encouraging graduates, against the best (and vested) interests, to undermine, even to topple, its deep-set pillars.

The drama continues, the dilemma is unresolved. The Jesuits are not the first to undertake a sacred work with highly charged secular tactics. The old monasteries had been founded by kings and princes, openhanded with their often ill-gotten goods, an insurance against judgment. I was feeling the brutal force of the dilemma, even in the act of heightening it.

It occurred to me that I could continue such work only by separating out from the college community entirely, dwelling downtown among the poor.

I did not do so: another way opened before me.

Pope John was elected, he summoned the Vatican council. With a massive creaking and groaning, the old hinges of the church were swinging wide on the world. Even at LeMoyne, even in Syracuse, a perennial winter was breaking up. I stretched and blinked in the sunlight. An old dream, long put aside but never abandoned, might now gain a hearing.

I hoped to initiate a community of students, and live with them. My eye rested on a dwelling at the edge of campus; a dozen of us might alight there and improvise our style of worship and work. The members would pledge a summer or a year of service in Latin America. My idea was in accord with the Peace Corps: middle of the road, but still, given the times and the town, something daring and new.

We must have a chapel. It was a simple necessity, I thought, no more a luxury than a kitchen. The chapel must express something of our faith and hope, the work we were pledged to. The week we moved in, we came on an abandoned room in the basement, untidy, unfinished, the joists and two-by-fours exposed, baggage and trunks and trash piled ceiling high, raw concrete underfoot.

Just the place. We labored like motivated ants. Slowly, things took shape. Winter yielded to spring, we laid a floor of flagstone, installed lighting, enlisted an artist to paint a mural. Vestments and altar vessels were designed and donated. The jewel of the place was the altar and accoutrements.

I approached my father, that Tom of all trades. He was approaching his eightieth year, but he sat regally at the wheel of the jalopy known to the neighbors and family as the Green Beetle. His cronies, workers at local junkyards and lumberyards, could be counted on to help. More, his eye was gimlet, and his hand followed unerringly when he set a tool to its task.

Yes, he would build us an altar. He journeyed to a mill, and returned with a great, solid plank tied to the roof of the Beetle, a sight to behold. He already saw the table in his mind's eye: an unplaned surface of plank, treated and waxed, otherwise left untouched. Not a nail would be driven: the lengths of wood were to be pegged together, rough and true.

And what of the table legs? He thought and thought; and, as usual, came up with a solution esthetically brilliant and right. If the tabletop was to be massive and crude, the legs must complement this; and with a subtle contrast, in color and dimension.

He settled on black iron; slender, angled away from the top, rather than straight downward. His eye was true, the angle was reckoned, the holes bored, lengths calculated to the fraction of an inch without deviance. Legs dull black, planks pale gold. Wood thick, massive, weighty, legs slender, unobtrusive. It worked like a genie's charm.

In her quiet way, my mother came up with a contribution. It was her table linen, a gift at her wedding, damask linen, dazzling white after more than fifty years. It unrolled luxuriously, and fell to the floor like a snowfall.

The chapel was finished. Our worship was simple, direct, and elegant. How ready we were for the consequences of worship remained to be seen. . . .

My mother and father are dead these many years. The table is vanished, along with the linen; the house that was our pride is in other hands. The students of those days are scattered. No abiding place! The garage workshop on Matson Avenue where my father tended the potbellied stove on winter days, and spat into its glowing heart, and cut and planed wood, is sold. The house that sheltered three generations of Berrigans is presently occupied by an interracial family, the first in the old neighborhood. After some initial rumblings from the Irish oldtimers, things have settled down once more.

Not so my father's spirit. What is hereby described is the event closest to folklore that our family has ever occasioned.

The mother of the new family occupying our house tells the story. How my father's troubled spirit long walked the halls at night. How she would call out, to the effect that "It's all right, your family knows we're here. We're taking good care of your home." In time the ghostly walks ceased.

And then the new owners decided on a thorough renovation of the house. And the troubled presence resumed, the night walks commenced again. Only now he walked by day in the garage, which was being refurbished, and in the basement by night. And again, the woman called out reassurance, tranquil as she was, and in no wise troubled.

There was another related tale, of an older place and time.

The family of my oldest brother lived for many years in a mining town of northern Minnesota, in a hundred-year-old house. An upper room was troubling to those who entered. It seemed as though a spirit dwelt there, helpless and hidden, but palpable.

My father had recently died. And one day the youngest child, sent in the room on some errand, was heard to cry out. The mother found her fallen to the floor in a faint. On recovering, the child related that she had seen her grandfather and he spoke to her and asked for her prayers on the next day. On the day following, as it transpired, the child's first Communion was to be celebrated.

Our family would qualify, perhaps, on some learned psychological chart, as fairly sanguine with regard to life's harsher presentments; and, at the same time, as fairly skeptical of anything occult. All of which, it seemed to me, makes the preceding episodes all the more remarkable—not only in their purported occurrence, but in their matter-of-fact reception by members.

The Minnesota mother who told me the story of my niece and the supplicant ghost could be fairly described as a gentle belittler of fantasies, childish or adult. Yet ten years after the event, on her deathbed, she repeated the story with great seriousness; and the child, by then age seventeen, verified its details.

No such stories are extant concerning my mother, nor are they likely to be. In this world, her spirit was the opposite of vexatious or unresting. So it may be presumed that she rests in peace.

Vexed and vexing he remained, true to form, to the end of life. And a cause of chagrin to all who knew him, as he fought death, and its prelude of humiliations multiplied. When my brothers were no longer able to cope at home, they took the steps usual to a beleaguered family—steps no less regretted for being inevitable. Because my mother must go where he went, and because he must go, we placed both parents in a decent home nearby, conducted by nuns. But from the day he was led there, my father fought like an

aged lion. He thrashed about, sowed unhappiness and trouble indiscriminately. His desperate longing was to be amid his garden and
roses, his workshop, his own turf, "puttering about," as my mother
would put it.

She settled into her new home, made the best of things, long
practiced as she was in the difficult art. He, like the child he was
reverting to, took to disappearing, fleeing the premises, the mild
detention he so detested. He would try, in a confused way, to reach
his home once more; to what sensible end, because others were in
possession, remained unclear.

As we were to learn, his arrival on familiar ground was not the
point, or what he was to do on arrival. His confusion carried him
in a bolt, over hill and dale, in a direction he knew not. He would
be found in a ditch or field and brought back to the dovecote. It
was our humiliation as well as his own.

It came as no great shock to us that death brought little peace
to his bones.

Indeed, he had known little peace in his mortal life, and had
allowed even less to exist around him. He had a dubious faculty of
banishing peace from his presence; as though tranquility of spirit
were the enemy, and he God's own exorcist.

In any case, the students and I flourished, after our kind. We
named our new dwelling International House, in celebration of our
calling to the world. We lived in amity and planned our future. As
though the gods of thunder with their guns were not even then drawing a bead.

I departed the LeMoyne campus in 1963, purportedly to enjoy
a year's sabbatical in France. From some few among the faculty
there was an all but audible susurration of relief. And from myself,
a deep breath also; of gratitude for all that had been. What was
accomplished at the college was as permanent as anything could
claim in such times; it would bear fruit.

The fruit is long in coming: the season's chill endures.

Of the brightest and most promising who entered religious orders
in those halcyon years, most have long departed. It was so of those
who became Jesuits. Indeed, our Sodality, which in those days was
considered a seedbed of a flourishing future, is, for the most part,
disbanded. The members are scattered, the ethos not so much dis-
credited as laid aside. Problems of faith, broken marriages, disen-

chantment with the church, departed clergy—the common changes rung, the afflictions, the opened eyes.

High and dry we are left, an old guard with precious little to guard. And woe is me if I indulge in nostalgic obsession or become a necrophiliac of memory, hovering around the salad days, or making them a measure of the future, or of my future! It must all be let go, the precious and hopeful and persuasive: no abiding in that place.

All is preamble until death raises (or lowers) the curtain.

LeMoyne was preamble to much; more a preamble than a summing up. I had gained a precious grounding—in innovative worship, in community, in the joining of conscience to professional skill.

I summon those years with all grief and gratitude (I in the minor mode, surely) of a Newman departing Oxford. I had lost an honor won at some cost. Never again would I be, for any appreciable time, a member of a Jesuit faculty. Never again dwell fondly on the thought, as I did in those days, of "my college." The satisfaction, achievement, devotion to study, the communality of faith with the young, these were gone. I lost my aura; more grievously, I lost a home. Henceforth I would be a wanderer on the Earth; here and there, an overnight dwelling; and only of late years, folded in a Jesuit community at last.

But the aura, that was the point at the time; and its loss. The loss was, of course, joined to ego. It was a poor consolation prize indeed, to land a year later in New York, in totally different circumstances, my assignment amorphous and undistinguished, associate editor, *Jesuit Mission* magazine. No green acres, no panache or ceremony. Life was to be hectic and lonely and—dull. Dull as ditch water.

For a time only. God, I can report, is not to be thought of as mayor of a heavenly Dullsville. Beware. Interesting times have scarcely begun.

Meantime, the sabbatical was held out to me.

More than the LeMoyne years were ending. It came almost like the sounding of a knell; but the tolling was so deep and gentle as almost to merge with the murmur of life itself, and be lost there. Who could tell what changes were being rung, what death and birth? And by no means my own solely: beloved friends on the faculty, young women and men entering convents and seminaries.

And more: the tonality and travail of academic life, the near ecstasy of friendship and work and worship and life together; the fabric of things, so dear, so closely woven, and (as I was discovering) so easily raveled.

The sixties gathered momentum: whether we knew it or not (most of us did not), a way of life was drawing to a close. My own departure, painful as it was to me, and obscure as to outcome, heralded more terrible events by far. I would return, if not to a campus, certainly to a Jesuit community. But life was bearing friends away inexorably.

So I voyaged once more to my beloved France. This time to no obscure backwater town, but to Paris.

The financial benefits offered by my college, seemed, even for those times, austere. I was to receive five dollars a day, and make the best of it.

But by September, there occurred to me a way of making the petty stipend serve not only survival in Paris, but ambitious plans for the year. I must find work that would repay me with board and room.

I came on a house for students, 61 rue Madame, near the Luxembourg Gardens on the Left Bank. My duties as chaplain were minimal. I was to take meals with the students, offer Mass on Sundays, be available a few evenings of the week for counseling. My command of French was found acceptable, I moved in.

The Maison des Étudiants was an old gray warehouse of a place, its architecture, to dignify the reality, a nineteenth-century curiosity gone to dark and dust. There were priests in residence who worked as chaplains and professors in the city; they took meals apart from the students, in considerable style. A woman of commanding stature and impeccable deportment kept the house, sacristy, table; kept, moreover, a weather eye out for everyone's comings and goings.

The lady, christened Madame Générale by the students, was indeed formidable, on no account to be trifled with. If one arrived home after a designated hour, he would find the front doors bolted tight, Madame chastely abed. Our tardy scholar must somehow arouse her from a third-floor bower, she being in possession of the sole key of the keep. After considerable rattling about, and muttered apologies from the delinquent, Madame would be pleased to lower the key reluctantly on a rope. It was much like the ladder of salvation let down by the princess in the fairy tale.

For me, the true advantage of the year did not lie in Paris; or indeed in western Europe. I had had my fill of western Europe, which I sensed, even then, was drifting closer to our Atlantic coast. If the process continued, in another fifty years or so, one might reasonably think, the land masses would merge, and Paris become a kind of sixth New York borough.

I had little need of outposts of New York, or of European appendices of America. Nor was it a question on my part of something so vulgar as hatred of one's homeland. It was simply that I was determined to keep on the move, to make the most of limited time and travel, those fleeting resources.

I had come to Europe; and Europe was best understood, at that period of my life, as a landing stage and point of departure. I had a year, and only a year, to dispose of. I felt a fierce beckoning to go farther.

Eastern Europe, for a start.

Beckoning? To eastern Europe? Given everything, the gesture could only be ambiguous. In those days American Jesuits went, in some numbers, to Europe; but no one went to eastern Europe. No one, that is, Jesuit or no, who was in his or her right mind.

That mind, those politics, that president, that Pope, admonished them—as a matter of plain good sense (or Cold War sense), where they might be welcome, and where not. And in eastern Europe, welcome they were not. Or so the instruction went.

This was no news, it was rather an old story, one which had hardened into a kind of dogma. It was a belief that defied time and season, which ordained that every winter must yield to a thaw. But in 1963, the season, in America and western Europe, was not so much wintry as arctic.

One felt that the unnatural freeze could take only two possible directions. It might harden further, into a permafrost, a wintry pole; or it might hotten up in a moment, in a torrid nuclear blast.

I had trouble with all this. I thought, in an obscure way, that metaphors drawn from nature and applied willy-nilly to the life of nations ought not be regarded with insuperable reverence.

Indeed, there must be Christians in eastern Europe! Even the guardians of the coldest pole admitted, however grudgingly, to the existence of such. But the ignorance surrounding the lives of these obscure fauna was truly breathtaking. One might as profitably credit rumors concerning the Loch Ness monster or the Siberian snowman.

Such ignorance bred further and deeper ignorance. The ignorance was inhuman in the degree that it implied moral indifference. It came to something like this: the fate of Christians of eastern Europe mattered, throughout the western nations (and the western church), only insofar as their existence served to fuel the Cold War. Those mysterious hooded Christians! They appeared to us exotic as Laplanders, or prisoners keeping a vast icehouse, piling floe upon floe in a perpetual polar twilight.

Christians of those unknown regions, we were told, were hostages, martyrs, prisoners, internal exiles, nonpersons. What we were told nothing of, was the misuse to which their heroism and suffering were being put in the West. The Christians of the East, if truth were told, were instrumental to the crudest politics, the politics of war.

The icehouse glimmered there, in moonlight or sun, guarded, remote, arctic. It was worked by furclad slaves, we were informed. Their condition, we were told, was, at least for the present, beyond repair or relief. But a great benefit accrued, as long as the frozen infamy stood, indistinguishable and abstract, a matter of dark conjecture in the West. That is to say, we knew who its keepers were. We had in our nuclear sights that precious necessity of the century of terror: an enemy.

The fact that said Christians were seldom heard from as to their condition or fate, or what manner of faith sustained them—all this was immaterial. We did not want to hear from them. We wanted only, in the manner of the divinely sanctioned guardians of the world's fate—to hear about them. We had no desire for such intercourse as might imply a call to modify or soften our views—themselves gelid enough. We wanted a mythology that would certify our nightmares, justify us, validate our enmities.

To say that I dwelt uneasily with such national and religious obsessions is to put the case smartly. To be sure, my unease was obscurely felt, floating and ill defined. I had little evidence to support a sense that whispered within me; I must discover firsthand, for myself, something of great moment. A reality that, I was commonly informed, only academics and experts of church and state were in possession of.

But these, I knew, were often as not the quellers of such blithe spirits as were determined to set out and see something on their own.

I kept my distance from the experts. I needed no one to cool my purpose with a "go slow"; or worse, a "don't go at all!"

Yet it all but came to that, by a hairsbreadth.

It was another sign of the times: no Jesuit superior in France would grant permission for my venture. The authority at rue de Grenelle was sympathetic but firm. He would relay my request to the general of the order in Rome.

Christmas approached, I bit my nails and fretted, and not a word. And finally, on December 23, the day of proposed departure: permission granted. I ran for the plane at the last moment.

Into the cold, into the void, into a world shaped like a question mark.

Today, years removed, I wonder how such metaphors, at once silly and portentous, could occur to me as describing a simple voyage by air. And yet today such images, far from being dissolved are set, like ice blocks, all the more firmly in place.

The icehouse, the slaves, the pole! Ignorance, like ice stored layer on layer, has hardened. It is compressed in a state of mind, a hatred of the unknown. The icehouse and its occupants lie on our consciousness, more bizarre than the crudest concoctions of outer space fiction.

I landed in Prague toward midnight. The city was windless, still, dead cold. I was conducted to a hotel, unheated and dank. There was little fuel in the city, and less food. I slept in my clothes, and awakened to Christmas day, an exile in a minor key—and perhaps closer for that, to the original Event.

The original Event was, of course, officially ignored: Christmas was a work day like any other. I made contact with my host, a professor at the Comenius Seminary, and was conducted through the city, in the manner of any visitor. And marveled at its architectural glories, the cathedral, the palace, the charm of the old city— so like Paris, but so sorrowfully lacking in exuberance and élan. A city of human forms, indeterminate, bundled, issuing from cold dwellings and stores and workplaces, into colder streets, with little comfort between.

And of Christmas not a trace: not a ragtag decoration or hint of gift for sale or conveying. That was the first contrast, and it remains vivid to this day.

A confession is in order. Among the evidences of my maladroit progress in the world, I must make mention of an inability to distrust others. It seems to me a fairly sensible procedure to proceed with an act of trust. Like it or not, one inhabits the globe in company with other humans, presumably decent, greatly various in outlook, hue, political habit, accustomed to name their God variously, or not at all. Most are capable of great goodness, many of heroism. They are also (we also) capable of appalling degradation, outrage and crime, on a scale unimaginable to our ancestors.

I beg leave to set down such truisms, at risk of bathos. It is a kind of strength to traverse the world and cross borders on the assumption that a thread of humanity leads one along. On the assumption also that human differences, unattended to, become subject to a riot of special interest, and magnify monstrously. And as for the church, when we yield before the politics of the virtuous versus the "kingdom of evil," we become, willy-nilly, the spiritual arm of ever-renewed violence.

It could not be denied that the Christians of Czechoslovakia, among others in eastern Europe, were suffering. I was hardly in a position to deny the fact, mingling among them that first time, and many times since. Their schools are closed, their churchgoing is surveilled and penalized, they are forbidden access to professional and political life. Pressures are applied, some subtle, some overt, to conform to a party line that would, in effect, deny their faith.

On the other hand, many are angered, not with their own government, which they incline to accept as a harsh fact of life—and of faith. Angered rather, in face of a western church that insists on making them into Cold War pawns.

On the occasion of a later visit, one of them said: "Your Mr. Reagan has made us into the new disappeared people. As far as Americans are concerned, we are anonymous. It is as though we have fallen through the earth."

The point, I believe, was well taken, and bitterly so. In naming the enemy, we have succeeded also in misnaming the Czech Christians: victims, abstract, without style or hope or vision, nothing to teach us. A misnaming indeed so grievous as to ricochet on ourselves as alienated and overbearing.

I wanted to explore that other world, on its own terms and my own. This I thought was a postulate of sanity and integrity. I sensed that the creation of victims was a skill that flourished on both sides of the infamous "curtain," whose lowering was a feat of malign genius—on both sides. I too was a victim, in the measure that I allowed my fate to be defined by others; the curtain, they said, was of iron. The iron was edged; it cut me in two.

And who indeed, in the wake of the crimes of the Second World War, the Vietnam war, the invasion of Afghanistan, was fit to define, from a position of probity or innocence, the crimes of the "other side"? All were criminal: the judgment of the Letter of Paul to the Romans was never more bitterly or bloodily verified. If any were innocent, they had perished, either in the camps or under the knife or noose. And if, on the Allied side, some had been graced with another form of innocence (but the same), if they had objected against the brutish crimes of America or England, from Dresden to Hiroshima—they rode out the war in prison, subjected to official obloquy. It dawned on me: if one wished to remain innocent of war crimes in my lifetime, one was simply asking for trouble.

I reflected on the meaning of this in the months after my visit to eastern Europe. The hypocrisy of the West clung to me, haunted me. I had moved among Christians who lived their faith with steadfastness, under a shadow of disrepute and disenfranchisement. They refused the quick fix: to flee to the West and join their voices to the maculate free world and its choristers. Those socialist Christians were marked by a dogged sense of patience and resolve: they chose to live in circumstances, however harsh, which they believed permitted by God. They would make something less inhuman of their fate, and of the fate of others, through the freedom with which they embraced an edgy existence.

A generation has passed. I have returned to Czechoslovakia and Hungary several times. Admittedly, very little has changed, especially in Czechoslovakia. There is a restless ebb and flow of restriction and easement. The law is capricious, it is difficult to separate official malice from malaise. Christians are jailed at times, at others are let be. But whatever the circumstances of my friends, I take joy in their capacity for endurance. They are Christians; they are called to be where they are. To them it is all quite simple.

And at the same time, they cast a cold eye on the myths that flourish in western minds; and especially, it would seem, in the minds of church people. That America, beyond all criticism, is the ideal political, economic, and military arrangement; for Christians also. That the Kingdom of God is all but descended on "America the beautiful"; that all other realms and principalities must lie in shadow. That those in the Soviet orbit are "enslaved"—a word that allows free play to the most callous ignorance and prejudgment. That Americans, in contrast are—"free." Simply that. The simplest of worlds, manageable, gnostic.

One lingers over that freedom of ours; one all but weeps. Free to consume, free to vote in a moral void for vapid political clones, free to amass wealth, free to attend slack and superficial worship, free to build and pay for Armageddon weaponry. This is the judgment of our eastern European sisters and brothers, upon us and our dreadful clichés. The critique runs deep, and hurts.

Back in Paris for the winter term.

Easter was approaching, and I thought to turn southward. I was invited to Southern Africa for a number of weeks, through the good offices of Archbishop Hurley of Durban, and the women of the Grail, a Christain community in Johannesburg.

Irony, that harsh staple of life. As I set this down, the Archbishop has been indicted, tried, and finally set free by Pretoria. The Bantustans are aflame, the jails overflow. And in the same months of 1985, an extraordinary awakening has seized on Americans.

One day, in an event that has become typical across the nation, some twenty of us, black and white together, were arrested for vigiling before the South African consulate in New York. We were herded into wagons and driven off to the station house. An old story, a new occasion. The police are polite, almost apologetic. There is an easy, affectionate interplay among those arrested, gratitude for one another, a surge of hope. Something conscientious at long last, we are not defeated, we shall overcome.

It might have been the first dawn of creation, a lurid explosion of light over Africa. The cabin of the plane looked to be all afire, the heart of a furnace. The world turned abruptly on its axis fourteen hours out of Paris, from mild April to mild autumn, falling leaves, early twilight.

My hosts understood: I had not come for tourism. I mingled freely or covertly, according as my guides decided, in the black "reserves." I preached in white churches, passed Good Friday amid a black congregation, hearing, close to tears, a Zulu chant for Jesus, "the fallen warrior."

Then, at the Holy Saturday vigil, a harsher assignment: preaching to an affluent white congregation, segregated tight, portal to portal, birth to death, baptism to burial. I made bold (knowing this was my chance, there would be no second one) to suggest a biblical idea: the distinction between the mystery of that holy night and magic.

Silence in the face of crime implied the invasion of magic into our worship, I said. A manipulated god, created to our own image, a god in servitude to our fear, our ego, our instincts of cruelty and violence.

And mystery: something other. It implied our submission before a God whose name was Truth, who gave voice in Christ (and gave us voice), on behalf of the victimized and outcast.

The word *apartheid,* I was told, had not been heard in that pulpit for a generation. The cowardice and complicity implied in that ominous silence made me the more determined to speak. It was a debased magic, our presumption that God, the true and truthful One, could be invoked by a cowardly generation. The God of the Bible, the God of Christ, abhorred the crime of silence: the crime once committed, we Christians were left to our own devices, fantasies, untruths; Christ departed our midst, to stand with His despised sisters and brothers.

My reflections were not well received. I see even now those stony faces, above the Easter finery, like drapery on a hecatomb.

At another gathering, a more attentive one, I was asked the inevitable question. And if we are arrested for conscientious action, what is to become of our children? And I attempted a response, in effect another question. If we are not arrested in such circumstances, what then becomes of our children?

It is a question that the times have ironically raised at home in the years since. We used to hear, during the Vietnam years, objections raised by parents against their taking part in civil disobedience: We simply cannot do such things, there are the children to be taken in account. . . .

And then, only within a few years, the breakthrough: parents, grandparents, arrested in the Plowshares groups, spending years in prison. And they say, in a new tongue, governed by a different spirit: We must do such things; for the sake of the children. . . .

Archbishop Hurley invited the priests of the city to meet with me; I offered reflections drawn from our civil rights work. The question of jail hovered uneasily on the air; and I pounced. Clergy in the United States, black and white, were being arrested, some were risking their lives. Several had been murdered. And when would this example strike home in South Africa, where such witness was so desperately required?

As I recall, there was great hedging and bridling at this, and no little anger.

Off the record, there were meetings with black leaders. One or another of the exchanges was recorded on tape. On advice, before departing, I mailed the tapes to Europe, rather than risking South African customs. But the precaution, if such it was, proved useless: the tapes disappeared in transit. The event went beyond itself, ominously; my lost chance of returning to that country.

End of tour, northward to Europe once more. In Addis Ababa and Cairo, I paused for a few days' visit with the Jesuits. In Ethiopia, French-Canadians were being eased out of their college by the government. In Cairo I was guest of the French in their College of St. Joseph. And there one evening, I took a tape recorder to the great flat roof, to set down a few reflections on my extraordinary voyage. A muezzin called the hour of prayer from a minaret nearby. The tape was sent to Merton, he wrote in appreciation, evoking the strangeness of the background chant, and its mysterious tones, at once mournful and prayerful.

My reflection dwelt on the theme of Camus's novel *The Plague* as a useful ruling metaphor for South Africa. In the novel, someone inquires of the doctor, the antihero of the story: Why did the epidemic strike the city? He replies: They forgot to be modest, that is all.

I found the words disturbingly on the mark. The immodesty of the racist regime of South Africa was apparent. But the plague could by no means be isolated there, as matter either of principle or fact. Who could dwell in America and be ignorant of a like pretension, pride of place, intransigent racism infecting us also?

And there was the Vietnam war. The war was to become an all but permanent horror, a kind of great salt machine in the sea, churning out tears, bitter unrest, and death, turning national life to a welter of sorrow and division.

Meantime, another prelude. In June of 1964 I joined an ecumenical group of Americans traveling to western and eastern Europe and Russia. A friend and I, as Catholics, were a tiny minority in our little band of pilgrims.

The plan was to undertake discussions with Catholics in Paris and Rome, with Protestants in Prague and Budapest, and with the Orthodox and Baptists in Russia.

We also attended sessions of the Christian Peace Conference in Prague. There, in a immense, bare hall, several hundred delegates from mainline churches, East and West, talked interminably and debated resolutions, in the manner of their kind. Earnestness and political savvy and a measure of religious passion were in the air. Everyone, I had no doubt, knew the seriousness of the situation. The Cold War was sinking world temperature to a zero, the war in Vietnam was expanding more savagely. And by and large, the religious bodies of the world were stymied.

One could not but be struck by the costumes and conduct of the Orthodox during the conference. Even to me, who could claim a measure of international exposure, these churchmen seemed an ambiguous presence. It was as though they arrived on the scene with government instructions tucked in their valises. They gave every indication of a prior heavyhanded indoctrination; an exercise they were determined to inflict on us also. Expressionless, austere as to manner, bizarrely rich in costume, the ecclesiastics moved through the assembly like ambulatory icons, from podium to limousine to hotel; and in the manner of icons, never mingling or socializing with common mortals.

They were hardly reassuring, but they were warmly courted by the leadership of the conference.

Their political and religious clichés came down with a thump. Orthodox indeed! The root trouble of the world, they intoned, was western. Russia was innocent of wrongdoing, of nukes or invasions or controls or censorship or persecution or gulags.

Their message was the veriest nonsense; from a religious point of view, it was also profoundly disedifying. Flowing robes and jeweled pectoral crosses of gold—and then the party line, served up with immense solemnity. They took themselves so seriously! I could only pray: God of heterodoxy, have mercy!

The Protestants were calmer, more varied and tentative. In their sober broadcloth and cautious politics, they were a striking contrast to the birds of paradise. Those among them from the West spoke temperately; they were far from their turf. As for the Americans, the conduct of our country in Vietnam, which we were hardly disposed to defend, put us to silence and shame.

I could hardly fail to note that western Catholics were totally absent from the conference. The message offered by such aloofness, I thought, was hardly different from the ambiguous contribution of the Orthodox. To be present as government advocates, to be absent in a show of ideological disdain—each of the choices was wrongful, each was a useful tool for the peddlers of special interests or resentments.

The Orthodox showed one way: make peace with the oppressor; use him, even while you are being used by him. The Catholic decision: stay aloof from any assembly as might be apt, by its location or makeup, to compromise purity—of doctrine, as it seemed.

Still, one wondered: what precisely was the offended doctrine, and how did it differ from the ideology against which it stood, for years and years, in bitterest contention?

The Catholic position, as the Orthodox, implied a parti pris. Roman Catholic purity of means dictated a politics of abstention. The Orthodox, in a sense, took the greater chance: they appeared on the proving ground, armed formidably with their sacrosecular theses. But each, taken together, undoubtedly bent their considerable power in favor of the Cold War.

The western church stood planted on safe soil, its temples open, its properties secured, its priesthood flourishing, its faithful under no duress. What better arrangement could be imagined in this world, what more admirably apt for the flourishing of the faith? Could there be a more fortunate position from which to show an absolute opposition against the godless?

There would be the beginning of a thaw under Pope John; but the springtime was late in reaching Prague. The Catholics present at our first venture were easily dismissed; just as, East and West, the conference itself was ignored.

Little or nothing accomplished (we thought at the time), for all the grandiose air and solemn ceremony, the grave debates and resolutions, recorded word for word, as though the fate of the world hung on the outcome.

Yet this negative assessment was by no means the whole story.

For me, the conference was a delayed fuse, or a damp fuse, or perhaps something of each. But in any case, it would detonate at some time in the future, and my former life would be blown to pieces.

The trouble with the would-be peacemakers, I reflected, as these flocked together for such gatherings, was a grievous one. They had no true center. Many souls, a multitude of good souls; but no soul.

Warmaking, on the other hand, required no center: its reality was that of a machine, which we rightly called a war machine. And a machine had no center: it had parts, which were required only to mesh and move in gear.

And so with those who researched, constructed, tinkered with, the machine: they required no center. They needed only the machine, which proceeded from them and acted, from its inception and form, in place of soul or center.

The artificers evicted their soul, and the machine moved in on monstrous tracks, and took over. The phenomenon was called, in the biblical sense, possession; psychiatrically, obsession. And in the drug trade, a fast fix.

In any case, and again speaking biblically, those who made war must believe in war, as others believe in God.

The warmakers believed in god; the god of war. They marched to the common whip, in time with the military, and made a brave and colorful and glorious thing of sanctioned murder. The soul was in lockstep, for the machine and those in the image of the machine, had to ape one another; in efficiency and uniformity, within and without. For this was the soul of war, and no one could be exempt.

All this may have been realized by the peacemakers, the anatomy of war and the transformation of those who made war from the human to the machine. But the realization, if arrived at, failed to offer an alternative. And that was the real point, as peacemaking was the alternative to warmaking, and not merely its cozening, tolerant, or parasitic appendage.

The question for me, as peacemaking came to be a question, was one of soul, of center. Peacemaking did not require a charismatic leader or a resplendent public personality; though that might occur. The soul of peacemaking was simply the will to give one's life.

As war sanctioned the taking of life, peacemaking must sanction the giving of life. The gift might be a notorious, public act, as in the assassination of Dr. King. Or it might be a state execution of resisters, as in the White Rose group in Hitler's Germany. In the latter instance, the episode is hidden for a long time; at the time of occurrence, is received with contempt and indifference. The gift of one's life is simply unknown to all except one's immediate family, as the death of the Austrian resister Jaegerstaetter illustrates.

One can go further and consider the mass anonymity of the extermination camps, where, beyond doubt, multitudes of unknown heroes gave their lives, whether to salvage honor or save others or resist debasing conduct. The century offers a mad and bloody variety of human valor, of those who go under in possession of soul and wits and the unimpeded power of choice. Souls, wits, choices; all of which the machine, in its rampageous blindness, seeks to claim for its own.

I knew little of this at the time of the Peace Conference; and hardly know more now. But I suspected then that intellectual understanding was a far cry from the valorous deed. We had a measure of understanding at the conference; of a certain kind, even of what might be called a biblical kind. Everyone read from the Bible, whether the delegate arrived from Geneva or Moscow or Rome. But not everyone, it is safe to say, was willing to give his or her life for peace.

Many believed (many still believe) that peace will come through a certain nice adjustment of warmaking power, through diminished stockpiling, through a nuclear freeze. We still have not found our soul, or created a soul, or been granted a soul. We arrogate the metaphors and vocabulary of warmaking, and call it peacemaking. For the warmakers want peace too, and always have; which is to say, they seek a tolerable level of warmaking, one that will protect hegemonies and self-interest. And we too seek a certain level of peace: one that will protect our self-interest, modest as it may be— our ego, our good name in the world.

We are still unable to attend to the considerable and central question: that of soul. Or, more precisely, of the spiritual change required for peacemaking.

The machine is incapable of this because it is a machine; and the peacemakers are incapable because they are afraid. And each of these, the fear of consequence and the fearless machine, conspire in the end to the same thing; which is to say, war preparation and war. Or at best (in the case of the peacemakers), a pallid mitigation of the full-blown fury.

Twenty years were to pass before I could begin to see such matters with any degree of clarity. I am not certain even today that the measure of clarity granted to me is translatable into action. I keep trying and failing and trying again; and succeeding only in minor measure.

Not many of the living, I comfort myself, can claim to have taken such matters seriously, and brought them off. If some have done so, they are dead, and therefore speechless, and beyond stating claims. As for the rest of us, we are caught in the incomplete and hemming web called life, trying to weave a geometric sense above a void. The web sags or breaks utterly; only now and again does it hold; and only for a time.

I moved on, from eastern Europe into west Africa, and thence home. To war. I could in no sense qualify as a peacemaker, and my country was at war. More nearly to the point, I was assigned to work in New York; and there Catholics were led, to all intent, by a warmaking Cardinal. I planted my feet on the macadam of the city; but I was, in reality, stepping to the edge of a volcano. It was even then rumbling away; and its eruption would all but scuttle me.

Thus what might be called my real life, episodes that would set me, for good and ill, on a lifelong quest, were shortly underway.

Kennedy was dead. The new president had inherited the war, as in the old biblical story, one inherits original sin. The sin was war, a war altogether original in its blind, innocent course, its stampede of ruin, its mindlessness. The war was inherited, as sin is; the two coming to nearly the same thing.

The new president could claim, as he did when things went sour, that he had not committed the sin, he had only inherited it. But like the sin whose image it was, the war presupposed a disposition for war. One was American, and Americans did not walk away from a conflict—except, of course, when they walked away winners.

The war was to turn my life around. I recall the phrase of Chesterton: After his baptism, he said, it was as though he stood on his head in the world; everything rational and conclusive had gone upside down.

The war turned me upside down, my family also. Upside down, our pockets turned out, possessions and honors and the credit of a good name, routine, soutane, long black line, institutional life, all suppositions of geography and soul. All things normally to be thought of as up, or as down, tossed upside down.

Yet the war was normal in the common estimate of Catholics and Jesuits—as normal as any war in our past. And it tipped us up. What was thought of as normal—normal violence and normal killing and normal mitigations—these, once rejected by my brother and myself, became among Catholics an occasion of outcry and indignation. What right have they—? Those disgraceful priests! . . .

The courts and jails, off limits to decent folk like ourselves, mere phantasmagora at the back of the mind; or at most, places one visited from time to time as supporter or counselor of others—these turned about giddily in the whirlwind. Their doors swung wide. And we, turned about, were tumbled into their maw, to be judged, found guilty, locked up.

And repeatedly, there was a jostling of a much more venerable kind. We fell out of favor with the church. We were scrutinized and weighed, and found wanting; in respect for authority, or obedience to marching orders, or to silencing orders, or to orders about good order. In any case, convicted, invariably *in camera;* and summarily sent packing from one city to another.

It came to this, as far as one could judge in those tumultuous times. Violence was the norm, the war was the norm. The times, the bloodletting, these were normal. Their (always regrettable) "incidents" were the responsibility of no one in particular. What was one to do, what was a president to do, or a bishop, or any citizen? Alas, war was a very old story; and this one must be seen through, to the end.

Normal meant, morally acceptable.

What was abnormal, morally unacceptable, was—ourselves. Nonviolence. One superior in the Jesuits said: What you and your friends do is, of course, allowable and even laudable among Christians. But it has no place among Jesuits.

I speculate at times, or in idle moments, I pose the question to my family. What might have happened to us had there been no civil rights movement and no war in Vietnam?

It is a question apt to boggle the thoughtful. As though one were to ask, What if the sun were not to rise this morning, not to set this evening? Or something absurdly unanswerable in the nature of things, like, What if we had not been born at all?

I had been born; one began from that. And because of the war, I had been born again; and one must begin from that. Short of that event, and its befalling me, I could conjure up some ghostly mischance of a scenario. A cleric, professor, writer, strolls the acres of academe. He passes gracefully from sunlight to shadow. He is beloved of a coterie of readers of poetry and theology, is welcome at the tables of the wealthy, writes books diligently, teaches adequately. Each book published adds imperceptibly to his repute.

The ghost fades into the back of the mind. Then he is gone, and good riddance. A volcano rumbles, the lava runs like a river of light. I run before it, no ghost. A ghost might enter the stream of lava, and none the worse for it. But life is a different matter; a matter of combustible flesh, of blood that runs hot and cold.

My blood runs cold once more, summoning those years, after the marvelous intersession of Europe and Africa.

I was assigned, in 1964, to work as an editor of a Jesuit magazine in New York. The assignment I took to be a none too gentle nudge: the salad days of academe were over.

The time was early in the notorious sixties. No campus was looking for more trouble than was already brewing. Who needed to import trouble, in the form of the likes of me—given the bearish market, the millionaire trustees, the sanctities of property and investment?

From a sensible point of view (Jesuit officials are nothing if not sensible) I no longer belonged on a college campus. Where then?

I could do only the slightest harm, dwelling and working in the old shabby mansion on East 78th Street. The magazine issued there, *Jesuit Mission,* was not highly regarded, in the order or out. It was a broadsheet, keening away each month on the sufferings and needs of missioners and their people. Who could tell, instead of losing money for the Jesuits, I might even begin to make some!

My new community was a wondrous collection of odd fellows and creative misfits, a dozen or so. Our rector was a distinguished Jesuit of the old school who had matriculated with honors at Cambridge and had served as president of a large eastern university.

He arrived in our midst trailing a fading cloud of glory. He had hobnobbed with the great ones of the world, accumulated honorary degrees and conferred them. He retained, in consequence, a contempt for anything but a rather narrowly conceived excellence.

In him an old academic ideal, which was also a Jesuit ideal, of broad sympathy of mind, social passion, love of human variety, these had frozen stiff. Under a confected affability, there lurked the ire of a high executioner. His eyes gave him away, if one were at all alert: his glance flickered, like a cat-o'-nine-tails, over one's person, words, deeds, and omissions. He might seem, in the common room, only half attentive to this or that desultory conversation, sitting relaxed behind his newspaper. But his ears were up, he was an unblinking watchman on the ramparts.

One scene was instructive. I had appeared at his door to bid farewell, before departing for holiday with my family.

Noblesse oblige: he sat me down. There ensued a most remarkable monologue, the gist of which abides, a kind of prelude and parody of divine judgment.

Somehow, with infinite skill and subtlety, he insinuated into a simple exchange of courtesies a load of accumulated grievances against me and my kind. But always he was inchoative, oblique, feline. The grand seignorial manner never deserted him, his fury was under exquisite control.

The point was unmistakable as a dagger against one's throat. Always reflectively, eyes on high, he purred along sinuously. To this effect: the ongoing ruin of the order was in no wise due to the defaults of "subjects." In no wise. There were ways of "dealing with"—he paused—"such." The fault lay elsewhere. It lay with those "superiors, who refused"—he paused—"to take measures."

The self-control was unnerving. So was the abstract relish with which he invoked crime and punishment. It was as though a cat were licking lips at the prospect of a feast.

At one point an unwanted animation shook his frame. What was required, he arched forward in his chair—required, even at this late juncture, when the future of the order was so compromised, was this. Each year, each year, the "superior should turn the screw; just one turn a year." And here his fingers formed a fist, and the fist as though holding a driver, made an angry circle in the air.

"Then, in a short time, we should have things restored, the law enforced."

Our fierce quondam inquisitor has since departed this life; I am able to think of him without fear, even with a quirk of affection. How difficult to have the times pass one by! Especially when one's pride has created other, far different times.

He believed passionately that the will of God rested on institutional prospering, like a shekinah above a proud tower. He was ignorant as a child of the limits of accomplishment, the lurking temptation to pride of place. Thus he spawned, from his imperial brow, a generation of lesser bureaucrats. And in the flush of success, and all unknowingly, he sowed the seeds of a decline that speedily overtook the university, his own and others.

The beggars could hardly be choosers; or so it was reasoned. Money was in perennially short supply. The Catholic universities, like all others, lined up for government largesse. They were thereby drawn into the orbit of the military, through contracts, research, and the welcome accorded the ROTC on campuses.

Thus compromised, the Christian tradition of nonviolence, as well as the secular boast of disinterested pursuit of truth—these are reduced to bombast, hauled out for formal occasions, believed by no one, practiced by no one.

Such an outcome was undoubtedly far from the Most Reverend's intention when he sought to put Catholic higher education on an honorable and equal footing. Still, even in the days of his glory, politics of a disturbing hue intervened. He was wont, on great occasions, to honor one or another Latin American chief of state, and to inscribe their names on the stone esplanade of the campus. It seemed of little import to him that several among those personages were known to their suffering people as scoundrels and despots.

Thus this Jesuit luminary (to whom qualified honor for his stamina and intelligence) contributed to the rise and, all unwitting, to the fall of a great enterprise. Subsequent history of the university is no matter for rejoicing. Today the puffing of the *nouveaux riches* and of secular satraps is all the rage in academe, including Catholic academe. It is difficult to understand the logic or gauge the outcome of this. But a reasonable hunch would place the universities among those structures whose moral decline and political servitude signalize a larger falling away of the culture itself.

Shortly after my arrival, the staff of *Jesuit Mission* undertook to evaluate our writing and publishing efforts. It became clear to a few like-minded spirits that we must make an effort to transform the magazine. Our sense was that the publication was demeaning to our audience and ourselves: begging made knaves or beggars of us all. If we could rightly claim a tradition, our task was more exigent and enterprising; for we were not beggars, but educators; and the truth, if we claimed a truth, must out.

We set to work at the new vision. And the outcome was not long in arriving. It was stunningly final. After an exhilirating interlude of two years, we succeeded—in closing down the magazine. We lost subscribers by the thousands, and gained new ones only by the hundreds. And though the hundreds bought our publication for the right reasons, drawn by its serious articles and attractive layout, it became clear that one does not publish a monthly in New York by dint of serious intentions and skills.

Meantime, the war expanded. I remember saying to Philip, soon after my return from Europe in 1965, something to the effect that we had best be declaring our No loud and clear and soon, under pain of never saying it at all.

We started to say No. The word was tentative at first, hardly audible. It came from our mouths like the first word of an infant: No; a word simple in the extreme, but still wondrous, on lips such as ours; on the lips of Catholics, clerics to boot, the word of foreign tongue.

It must be recalled that others, highly placed in the church, were saying another word with all their might: a hearty, confident Yes. Their approval of the war could be heard around the world. Among

Catholics, the Yes swept all before it, or pretended to. In any case, it drowned out, for a time, all conflicting sounds and second thoughts—uttered as it was with sublime confidence, from on high, from highly placed friendships and White House connections—as though from the lips of a Moses, unaccountably echoing a pharaoh.

There were many others, bishops and famous clerics, who said nothing at all; and that, of course, came in the end to the same thing. It was the Yes of silence, which here and there has been named the crime of silence. A silent Yes; and so understood by those directly responsible for expanding the war.

And who were we, we unconscionable doomsayers, to dissent, softly (at first), with our few numbers (at first), and our limited knowledge, our limited access to power and its lofty secrets, its data, its insuperable confidence?

Everything was against the dissenters. The war carried its own momentum, created its headlong course, its justifying ideology. The death of our boys! Communism on the march! The falling dominoes!

And included in the ideology, like a leaven in dead dough, was the sanctioning approval of the church. The church, sooner or later, would bless the war. The blessing had invariably been granted in past wars; there was no reason to doubt its conferral now.

The confidence was admirably placed. Church and state were smoothly adjacent; as complementary, as soothing, as hand and glove. Indeed (the common reasoning went), the times being chill, the hand had best be in the glove, the glove warming the hand. Then in emergencies, the hand, clothed and armed, might kill, and bless the killing; and who in right mind would object to that?

Right mind or mind awry, we would. The "we" included, first of all, the indomitable Dorothy Day and her community.

I attempt in *Portraits* to recount the magnitude of the debt owed this woman by Catholics. Enough to say here: she accomplished what no pope, no bishop, no Jesuit scholar, and no combination of these, had ever brought to pass. One must summon the God of Ironies; what a stunning blow was dealt the oracles of morals by this woman and her unimpeded conscience!

Many years before Vietnam housebroke our souls, she said No to war—once for all, unequivocally. Once was enough perhaps. But she repeated it month after month in her paper, the *Catholic Worker*.

Her "saying" went beyond mere words; and that remained her secret, and her power. She was a very witch in the art of dramatic gesture—gestures extremely powerful, silent, confronting others in their clarity and silence.

She said No to war in ways that were a kind of choreographic genius, gentle, subtle, unnerving, primitive. By her life among the poor, by the sacrifice of her freedom, jailed as she often was. She said it with pen and tongue and heart and mind, with that incomparably beautiful face set into contrary winds—those winds of war that disclaimed and disowned and scattered the conscience of Catholics, our responsibility and honor blowing in the wind, our tradition a soiled debris.

She said No without contention or malice or dour judgment against tardy, commonplace minds like our own, as we ventured toward the truth—our own devious dance, two steps forward, two back—our second thoughts, our backward glances.

Through thick and thin, No to war. Mostly through thin; the life she had chosen implied the thin shank of the menu, the pick-me-ups and hand-me-downs at the end of the line. That No of hers embraced all related choices; renounced security, rip-off affluence, the deadly centrist conscience.

The church, eager to canonize the holy dead, is seriously embarrassed by the holiness of the living—especially when the living refuse to give way. Cardinal Spellman, equal to any passage of arms, decided early on to let the woman be; under the assumption that if left to herself and a few followers, the New York vortex would swallow them whole.

Spellman was seldom wrong concerning worldly matters. The trouble was, Dorothy Day was no worldly matter. The times worsened, as times will. She grew both more vocal and more publicly visible. Her communities grew, as though on a fruitful tree. The wars came and went, each justified, certified as just, regrettable, inevitable. They came and went and exacted their bloody subtraction: of life, of the goods of conscience, and the integrity of the church.

She saw them come and go. But, come war, come peace, one phenomenon never disappeared or diminished—the presence of the New York poor. They, according to Dorothy's logic, were the progeny, multiplied beyond all prediction, by the great wastrel, war.

She united in her person, in what I can only call her art, all that the culture serves to tear apart. Holiness and great practicality, life in the spirit, life in the world, responsibility and prayer, God and the neighbor. She healed, and stiffened spines, and taught us lessons as no seminary or retreat had taught.

It was a matter of a center, a core, a heart. The world, and the worldly church, infected us, the young, with what might be called a passion for orderly disorder. Everything in good shape, even the misshapen whole. The household humming along, virtue, industry, prayer—good housekeeping in a national morgue.

Whether this was a useful or evangelical image of the church, the shape of things according to the mind of Christ—this was possibly another matter (and remains so).

What is certain beyond doubt is that this was far from her vision of life in faith. Dorothy turned things around: her life spoke of a kind of disorderly order. That was it! Order at the heart of things; an order of truth, mindfulness, secure vision, follow-through. And this while around her, for the large part of her life, disorder reigned, all but supreme. There was the immediate disorder of street people, the mentally afflicted, the furious and defeated and violent. And then, hardly less trying, the insurgents who invaded the *Worker* with their own brand of Catholicism: The Way Things Should Be.

And then a wilder swath—the supreme disorder of public life, politics, war, greed, cultural mindlessness, the moral void. And then the church, which seemed partner in the disorder, its fomenter even, with that power it misused so willfully, its silence, its obsession with moral trivia, its blessing placed on the great disorder.

The *Catholic Worker* was not an image of a church given over to Good Housekeeping. It was an anti-image, it went quite deliberately counter. Order in the heart, disorder in the world. The well-ordered heart can sustain, penetrate, interpret, resist, minister to, even at times heal, or at least mitigate, the whirlwind. This she lived and, so living, taught.

After the ecstasy, the Buddhists say, go do the laundry.

One thing, Americans say, whether warmaking or peacemaking, leads to another. We were being drawn into peacemaking as the nation was drawn into warmaking. It was all but a law of nature. The law was total in principle: if not immediately (it took years for the war to "rev up," it took years for us to come to the point of life)—then inexorably.

War, even so-called conventional war, constantly blurred the moral sense, the sense of limits: inevitably, war became total war. More troops, more firepower, more bombings of civilians, more everything.

And at home, equally and inevitably, more lies, more disclaimers of guilt, a constantly shifting language of justification, shoddy politics, the corruption of once decent public conscience. A growing unease, in a public used only to its ease. The unease moved for a long time in a void. It was as though a sleepwalker wandered about, wringing hands in a darkened house, seeking, in inarticulate plaints, solace for the crimes of conscious life. What to do, O where to go? The implication, the guilt, were plain: there was a corpse in a house locked and empty and dark. But there was, as yet, nothing to do: so the sleeping one wept.

We found a few things to do. Something in us insisted: there were tasks, we must come on them. The process was largely improvisational. We tried something, it failed; no matter, try again.

Which is not to say that we had no guidelines. At our best (which we attained only now and then, by fits and starts) we saw this, and paid tribute to our stars or landmarks or titular gods. They had left us a good legacy, we knew right hand from left, we need not wander witless in a witless world.

Nonviolence first and foremost, with its fiery trail of implication: compassion for the adversary, care of one another, community discipline, prayer and sacrament and biblical literacy. Long-term carefulness and short; care of little matters and large, the short run and the long.

It was easy to set down a formula, and devilishly hard to live by it, even in minor matters.

We had to discover such things for ourselves; by reading the lives of the saints, pondering their secrets and spirit and tactic; what they had come on, what accomplished; the place of trial and error, that great winnower and humiliator. And by pondering the gospel. And by listening to one another, and talking. But listening more than talking, a rare proportion, and difficult to honor.

CHAPTER 7

Brothers in Exile

For us to make a choice
was always a wrong choice—
why not die in the world
you were born into? what was wrong?

They were patient almost as time.
their words ate like a tooth.

They looked into our eyes
wild by starts, like the times.
They saw
and marveled, and shook. We saw
out of the edge of the eye
hell;
out of the center eye
a command. And blinked
their *asperges* away; be blind!

Philip was teaching seminarians of his Josephite order in Newburgh,
New York. There he was kept busy putting together word and work,
so to speak. He and his students labored among the poor of the
town, especially the black poor, in housing and community orga-
nizing. The work was praised: it was, after all, consonant with the
aims of the order, north and south; and it was deemed a good thing
that seminarians practice early on the works of charity.

The works of charity—but what of the works of justice?

There came hard days and much turmoil, for Philip refused to
ignore the alliance of poverty and war. He refused to act as though
poverty were a natural phenomenon or moral disaster rooted in the
nature of things. Least of all could poverty be understood as a dark
disaster buried in some (human) grotesquerie known as the Will of
God—that great refuge of the deadly status quo.

His faith forbade such disclaimers and fatalism. The war, he thundered, had already come home: not only in the sealed boxes of the dead, but among the suffering living; in our urban stalemate and fix. Because there were limitless millions for the war, there was nothing for the victims of the war; here and now.

This was not pretty language; it was not even acceptable strong language. It was new language. He had forged a moral unity. Justice and charity, yes; but charity at the expense of justice? He would have none of it.

It was the autumn of 1965. Philip had completed the manuscript of a book, his first. To celebrate its publication, a party was planned in New York City, at a bookshop on Lexington Avenue. It was to be one of those gala occasions all of us needed so badly, marooned as we were in a church that preached an incomprehensible Gospel: go with what's going.

Then the war came home, in an altogether new way. That same afternoon, a phone message: Philip was being shoved abruptly out of the seminary. Objection of the city officials against his antiwar passion had reached a boiling point. He was assigned to a parish in the inner city of Baltimore.

It was the first such blow to strike either of us; and all the heavier for that. Philip had not been consulted, the decision was reached in secret; the word of minor political hacks was counting for more than his exemplary labors.

That night, friends gathered in New York for the celebration. I knew what was coming down, and bore my knowledge like a heavy sack of iron through the streets of the city. Little heart for rejoicing: I knew that on the following day, Philip and I would wend our way southward into his exile.

Nevertheless, we feted our new author. And the morning after, in a driving, dour rainfall, Philip's slender chattels aboard, we drove to Baltimore. My heart was raw with bitterness. I saw a rare Christian whom I loved, plucked summarily, in midyear, from his work. The work, it might be concluded from the deterrent overtones of the punishment, would be carried on by no one. A work whose import could be justly inferred from the fury it aroused, among Catholics and others.

We had much to learn; but our education was underway. Especially about the governance of our church: how peace of a certain

unsavory kind was bought, at almost any price, once certain misbegotten assumptions had been challenged.

Someone was to remark ironically at a later time: If the president
had announced, during the war, that all autos in America were to
be commandeered by the military, the war would have shortly become unwageable. But because he was only commandeering the
sons of citizens, the war went on.

The war had commandeered the church; and the war went on.
It had not seized church properties or investments, a fact of note.
The war had only claimed the consciences of believers, bishops,
laymen and laywomen, the lives of the young, one and all pledged
to abandon all things and follow the god of war: to kill and die and
maim and bomb. This was a small price, purportedly; it had been
paid before, and would be paid again. So the war went on, our
longest war, for more than a decade.

The decade was not half over; the Cardinal of New York rode
high. Riding a military jet, each Christmas he paid a highly publi-
cized visit to the war zone, accoutred in military uniform. In effect,
to bless the war. And no bishop spoke of the scandal.

The jargon that accompanied this pilgrimage to the Prince of
Peace was heavily self-justifying: he was "making a pastoral visit to
our troops." But his statements, on departure and return, grew each
year more bellicose and jingoistic. We were not far distant from the
words that on his lips were to become a kind of classique noir: "My
country, right or wrong."

So Philip went into domestic exile, a fate reserved elsewhere,
as we knew, for those who opposed governments; and in our country, as we were learning, reserved for those who resisted churches
that resembled governments.

We arrived in Baltimore, unloaded the car, were greeted by the
pastor, a hearty, sympathetic soul. Drinks were produced to help
dry throats swallow their bitter pill.

It merits recounting that Philip, as was his wont, wasted no time
attending his wounds. The parish was almost entirely black and
poor; there was need of his pastoral genius and deep humanity. He
set to work, and I returned to New York somewhat comforted.

To have no inkling of the future is a mercy. I could hardly know,
my bones being far from prophetic, that events were ensuring that
the fate of Philip would soon be my own.

By way of beginning, my delicts were being recorded with fervor.

In one bizarre incident, a group of clergy were picketing the board of education in Brooklyn. An affable police lieutenant passed up and down the row of clergy, pressing palms, inquiring, with his winning Irish brogue, as to name and status. It was all friendly, even jocular, and the picket, my first such, ended without incident of any kind.

My dismay may perhaps be imagined when, a few days later, a call from my superior informed me of a grave report, received from a police authority. I had been involved in an unseemly Brooklyn fracas, fisticuffs had been employed in the course of a scramble and melee.

I was dumbfounded, and could only insist on my version of the affair. There was no assurance that my story was credited. Why indeed should it be, when the implication lay heavy on the air: was it to be thought that a police official would lie—to a Jesuit superior, no less?

Whether it was thinkable that I, a Jesuit, should lie to a brother Jesuit—this also hung there.

Friendships, tested in the fire. Two friends who emerged, even as a cloud gathered about me, were the renowned biblical scholar Rabbi Abraham Heschel, and the Lutheran minister and theologian Richard Neuhaus.

Heschel had been an observer at the Vatican Council, and often expressed to me his growing affection and respect for the American Catholic community.

This was no ordinary exercise in parlor politesse. Heschel had been witness of the German and Polish atrocities against the Jews. He had also seen a weird commingling of crime and religion that marked the era: the mass destruction of a people, accompanied, in most cases, by an untroubled conscience. He told me how he had seen the guards at a notorious extermination camp in Poland lining up on Sundays to board buses, to attend Mass in the neighboring Catholic church.

Later, he visited Rome, conversed with Pope John, urged the ratification of the Declaration on the Jews. Such joys as the great man lived to witness: the church, which had been an abomination of his youth, renewing itself, renouncing its historic crimes.

Memory dwells on this extraordinary figure with an altogether unique affection. Heschel was a father to me, in more senses than one. His image endures, far deeper than a patriarchal beard, an Old World graciousness. The rabbi was an ancestor of the spirit.

Every Christian requires the shadow (or light) of a Jew upon life: a presence, a Shekinah, a friendship; something of the ancient blood mingling with his own, as blood of parent and child mingle. Blood which, as we celebrate in our worship, is the blood of the covenant, blood of the Savior.

Heschel was a solid little man, much given to elegant aphorisms, which he delivered in the softened consonants of his Polish English. He had mastered an English no less astonishingly resonant and varied than the second language of Joseph Conrad. His books are his testament, especially the seminal grandeur of *The Prophets*, whom he so uncannily resembled. He was a rare friend; the only one of many, I thought, whose obituary, when he suddenly died in December of 1972, could include no least critical tinge, no dark side. He could be trusted; he was a saint, before the judgment.

It was the proposal of Heschel that Neuhaus, himself, and I undertake to organize a response of the religious community against the war. To be named Clergy and Laity Concerned.

The announcement, among the Jesuits, was badly received. And with other events gathering their lightnings, our resolve would be part of the high drama of my departure.

Indeed, such troubles were brewing as would transform all former incidents, no matter how painful, into a species of child's play.

The sequence of disasters got underway one morning. A dreadful message arrived from the Catholic Worker house in lower Manhattan. A young member, Roger Laporte, a former seminarian, had torched himself in protest against the war, before the United Nations. He was hospitalized, his condition was desperate.

He died within a few days.

His death could not but touch my life with fire. Not because he was a close friend; but because his death was so terrible, such a homing of disaster in the youthful Catholic Worker community. I recalled Laporte only as an innocent face on the edge of the Worker community. He was known to be shy and withdrawn; as far as could be learned, he had reached his terrible decision on his own.

The next message, from my superior, arrived in tones of absolute panic. I was, under no circumstance, to issue a public statement regarding the young man's death. Such matters were presumably to be left to my betters; more exactly, to the authorities of the chancery.

The message of the Cardinal was delivered to the New York public in due time. It spoke of suicide; it reminded Catholics that our moral theology in no way countenanced such an act.

I thought that a series of nagging questions was by no means resolved by this pronunciamento. Was the death of Laporte, in fact, a suicide? And even if it was, did the official judgment on the matter reflect the compassion of Christ?

And more: what if the death reflected not despair, but a self-offering attuned (however naively or mistakenly) to the sacrifice of Christ? Would not such a presumption show mercy toward the dead, as well as honoring the grief of the living?

A Eucharist was held a few days later, at the Catholic Worker. I was urged to speak. I aired my reflections before the stricken community: the question of suicide and the possibility of sacrifice, suggesting that we leave the imponderables to God. It was the best I could do; it was also, I thought, the least.

Word of the liturgy got around, as was predictable. Garbled or accurately reported, my words served to hotten up the situation. I was accused of disobeying an order; although it seemed to me that a few words, offered at a religious ceremony, differed greatly from a statement delivered to the media.

In any case, the clouds were lowering. As to nature and particulars, the clouds were a kind of camouflage: whatever was underway proceeded in secret. Decisions were arrived at, I was kept in outer darkness, an object of obedience. I was, in fact, reduced to a zero, whose fate his unaccountable actions had placed in saner hands.

I walked into the cloud, which all but swallowed me. A cloud, in the classic sense, of unknowing. The cloud rumbled with undischarged lightnings. I sought a meeting to discover whose actions, decisions, were governing this murky state of affairs; a state that might be presumed to concern me. No meeting allowed; the cloud thickened.

At one point, at wits' end, I took my torment to a priest of my

community; and was told, laconically, that "the fat's in the fire."
What had kindled the fire, I knew; and whose fat, meager indeed,
was sputtering there, I also knew. But the knowledge brought little
comfort.

The abnormal was being normalized; and not only in public.
Abysmally abnormal, panicky, disorienting, the war brought to the
fore the worst in almost everyone. We Jesuits, willy-nilly, were becoming a sad microcosm of the war. We were at war within. Weapons were being drawn, mutuality was vanishing, our understanding
grew clouded, we abandoned the gentle uses commended by the
Gospel.

The war demanded that the highest decision proceed in secret.
Very well, then, we Christians would do likewise. The war demanded the crushing of dissent; likewise. The war pushed moral
and physical violence, dislocation, anomie, to absurdity; so with
us. The war canceled civility for the duration; among us also.

The damned war! It was a creeping miasma, an irresistible current: it swept along, in its filthy wake, nearly everyone and everything. Our community was put on a war footing. And because I was
objecting to the war, I must be treated like a deserter or an informer.
The form of punishment narrowed: there was silence, then ostra-
cism, scorn—and finally, exile.

The injustice wrought by the church is a matter of history. In
the world it is commonly received as part of that lightsome history
we name folklore. It is of no great interest, it is at one with that
darksome enigma Chesterton named The Thing. To the world, the
unjust church is simply a redundant term.

If I choose to dwell on one event, as touching on my life, it is
hardly from a worldly point of view. I write mainly out of compassion for those who acted, in so scandalous a manner, against me.
The main antagonists in this shoddy drama have long since departed, either from the Jesuits or from this life altogether. In either
case, their accounting is in other hands than mine.

One could rest easy with such reflections if the warlike powers
then invoked and exercised, in the Jesuits, in the church, had been,
in the meantime, renounced. Such, alas, is hardly the case. Indeed,
as I set down these reflections in the mideighties, similar tactics are
alive, and kicking out in all directions: denunciations, silencings,
threats, punishments arbitrarily and secretly arrived at. At the highest

levels of the church, an apparatus of control, surveillance, and censorship is once again in motion. It touches the integrity of theologians and bishops, faculties of seminaries and universities. And the heaviest hand of all is laid against women: to control, isolate, and demean.

The following are, for the record, a few elements of the decision regarding my fate, as this was signed, sealed, and delivered to me in the autumn of 1965.

—I must depart the country for Latin America, with all possible speed; as soon, in fact, as visas could be procured.

—I was forbidden to visit my family, though my parents were aged, and in ill health.

—No date of return was mentioned; presumably none was envisioned.

—Meantime, I must immediately leave New York, and await elsewhere the necessary travel documents; dwelling in whatever Jesuit house might be willing to receive me.

For days, no such house could be discovered. Finally, and with a notable lack of enthusiasm, Georgetown University offered temporary shelter. With the stipulation that I dwell apart from the Jesuit community, the room was provided in a Quonset shed, at a remote corner of the campus.

I had confided to a few friends whatever meager news I could glean as to events. Considerable indignation arose, questions began to surface.

And inevitably, a cover-up was arranged.

Exile? Of course not. I was sent on a "routine assignment" to Latin America, as editor of a Jesuit magazine, to file reports on the work of Latin Jesuits.

It was contemptible and saddening. For the first time, I had cause to be ashamed of my order, its honorable name, the history of holiness and probity I treasured.

I knew how awesome a thing it was to give over one's life to a community; once and for all. That had been my side of the covenant. I knew, as well as grace can be said to know, that the bargain would not be reneged on: it was a stigma on my soul.

But a bargain implies stipulation and fidelity, on both sides. What had gone wrong, that the agreement could be canceled, that a wounding machinery was massed against me?

I was ordered to distance myself from those I loved and worked with, transported, as by hair of head, to another planet.

But something more occurred. Violent dislocation went beyond the fact: it emerged as a symbol. I was becoming something crudely known as a standoff. I was morally placed at distance, by forces beyond accounting—from my order, from my church even. I could never again presume that scriptural words—compassion, truth telling, justice, integrity, peacemaking—that these were the engines and energies of a Christian community (my community)—words to be lived and honored, especially by those in authority.

Garden of innocence, garden of experience! I grew not cynical, but sad. My love for the Jesuits, for the church, underwent a sea change; more exactly, perhaps, a kind of continental shift. My love did not grow cold, but the decisions that all but destroyed me served also to distance me. I had eaten of the apple of Genesis; now I was capable of second thoughts; correcting, modifying; a language of "Yes, but. . . ."

Was this all to the good? Perhaps it was only inevitable, part of the process innocuously referred to as growing up.

One thing I knew. I must pack up, and go.

I am unable, even today, to say why. I saw how others, with far less provocation, have washed their hands of the Jesuits and walked away. It would have been far easier at the time to rid myself, once and for all, of a burden that had become an incubus.

I went; on my back, the incubus, both betrayal and burden.

And in four months across the length of the southern cone, I suffered the death of friends, unutterable loneliness, dread, even despair.

Ten Latin countries, a blur of weariness, astonishment, welcome, honor even. My story became grist for the international media. A coalition of American Catholics, outraged at my exile, took space in the *New York Times* to register their protest.

I kept a diary of those months, more like a fever chart, or a chill chart; or both.

Traveled too fast, saw too much.

And learned by everything I underwent, by reflection and prayer—the rightness of my conduct, the wrong of the punishment.

Encountered, in almost every country, a pre-Medellin church, a church either internally colonized or virulently imperial; the two being, perhaps, the same thing. In any case, a church for, of, and by the powerful and wealthy.

And here and there, like a radioactive capsule in a diseased body, were groups of biblically alert Christians: groups usually led by women, dwelling in barrios and favellas, passionately loving and beloved by the poor.

And I learned, and absorbed, and nodded assent in my deep soul. It was right to make peace, I would continue to make peace, here or elsewhere; the peace that does justice.

And I discovered, gradual as a dawn over the mind, the irony that is a most delicious form of knowledge. To wit: the act that was designed to break me in pieces was serving only to toughen my resolve. Who was it said, That which does not kill me only strengthens me?

And then word reached me from New York: in effect, Come home. All is forgiven.

Forgiven? What was there to forgive?

I acceded, under condition. To wit: no conditions imposed or accepted. The work that occasioned the trouble would continue.

Whether the aforesaid trouble might continue was in other hands than mine.

Thus was a large and vexing matter resolved, with small loss. Resolved, as far as I was concerned, with no loss at all, either to honor or vocation.

Indeed, the resolution came about as a considerable gain. I had gone forth in dubiety and dread. My mind grew clouded, under assault by the great guns of church and state. Then, through the force of public indignation, the guns were silenced. And in a frame of mind far different from the darkness in which I had departed, I returned. Having survived, through the prayers and compassion of my family and friends. Also, if truth be told, through my own resolve not to creep home on all fours, in effect abandoning my work.

Indeed, I questioned my soul, had authorities been so fond as to assume that exposure to the realities of Latin America would turn the offender from his offense? The assumption seems naive in the extreme. A far better plan would have seen me disposed of in mid-Sahara or some remote polar region, surrounded by ruminant camels or flocks of penguins.

The edict was thoughtless, the outcome almost hilarious. With neither dromedaries nor spiffy birds for company, but surrounded by the infection of misery and injustice, even a slow learner like myself found his learning speeded up wonderfully. I came home, worse than ever.

CHAPTER 8

Cornell: Poison in the Ivy

Left New York for Ithaca.
Fair traditing of cities? no,
but recalled during that flight
Pascal; "the heart has its reasons."

Yes. That organ
of inmost sight and surmise
commanded, and I came

a minor
humorously welcomed
species in the great think tank—

me
whom even,
crowned with his crown,
the incumbent whale
's regnant eye
rolls
sidewise to see

In the winter of 1967, two clerical gentlemen appeared at the door
of *Jesuit Mission*, armed with an altogether novel proposal. They
were staff members of the United Religious Work at Cornell University. In charge was a tall Texan, unimpeachably earnest; the
other, a sharp thinker-in-residence. The two were in search of a third
to complete the troika, someone whose responsibility was inscrut-
ably referred to as activism, off and on campus. Would I be
interested in such work?

I had no idea of what activism might mean; I suspected, moreover, that the more I learned of it, the less affection I would summon. But I heard my visitors out. Their mysterious neologism in-

cluded certain modest tasks I was well acquainted with: counseling, poetry and music and worship, the eternal war question.

Would I come to Cornell?

I would and would not. It was immensely difficult to consider leaving New York, a ground so precariously and recently won, for yet another unknown. The Catholic Peace Fellowship, a new reality, was launched at last. So was Clergy and Laity Concerned. This latter was in need of considerable nurturing, as is the way of the newborn. (Indeed, on one occasion, the rabbi was heard to say that an apter title for our group would be Clergy Unconcerned. Then, affirmed the great one, we should win unto ourselves a very stampede of new members!)

There were undoubted advantages to the proffer. Cornell was seething with antiwar Furies, most of them exploding around the religious community. There was need of cool heads to ensure that the blaze did not die out in a flare. . . .

My Jesuit superiors were amenable; I packed up for the Finger Lake country of New York state.

And was, of course, like a sailor in Lotusland, enchanted on the moment. That idyllic scene, the waterfalls teasing the ear from all points of compass, the Triphammer Bridge, a suspension slender as cobweb, swaying delightfully underfoot, fifty meters above the great gorges. An environment complete as God's own garden.

Cornell! It was as though, in a moment of whimsy, a mysterious hand had lowered a vast dome of glass over Cayuga Lake and shore, protecting these idealized humans and their culture and possessions and families and books and music and art and old-fashioned religion and new-fashioned science, their willfulness to have and hold, their febrile selfishness—all of which tweeds and pipe and verbal indirection rendered charming and harmless (for a while); a fiefdom, in sum, and seemingly unassailable (for a while).

It was as though (so the fantasy might be framed), the hand that lavished the very cream of creation granted also perpetual title. The pitcher of cream would never fail.

Faculty, authorities, students, they wanted for nothing. It all came free. Thus went the fiction that, after a time, held the force of fact. They owed no debt to the great, teeming cities and their endemic misery, or to Vietnam, or to the stricken world at large. Cornell would endure forever.

Religion was a minority item. It was welcome on campus, as long as, so to speak, its practitioners knew their place.

Another image occurred. Religion was conceived as a symbolic vehicle, beribboned and crowned with flowers. The celebratory cart moved along; its passage marked the cycle of seasons, rendered thanks to whatever god or gods (the spirit was old-time deist) might require a responsive gesture for such largesse of nature, income, like-mindedness.

Government connections, military research, the benignity of millionaire alumni and trustees—such were the predestinatory marks.

Why indeed make of such benefices, falling straight from the cloudless sky, unpleasant terrestrial issues? The literary and artistic claques were above all that: they turned away in disdain. The scientists held out their aprons, the manna fell from the gods. It was altogether an admirable symbiosis: appetite and arrogance.

The rhetoric, meantime, continued: Value free! Value free! Come to the enchanted garden, the queen of the realm will wine you and dine you and. . . .

Whether, in the slow enchantment, humans were being subtly and not so subtly degraded as the queen's wand touched them—whether, as the myth has it, one species was being transmogrified into another—the question was tasteless: it was never raised.

The year was 1967: an unpleasant time for sponsors of the good life. The atmosphere of Cornell could not but be affected. Like it or not, questions were being raised, as the cover on a secret place is raised, with shouldering effort, by someone who has dwelt too long in the dark, someone who longs to let in light, or to stand in the light, or both.

In this case, the raising of the questions was due to a whole phalanx of lifted shoulders, mainly young shoulders. They were aided and abetted, to be sure, by certain undeist religious folk. These latter, having abandoned the ribbons and flowers and the cart of plenty, could be found heaving away with the others, shoulder to shoulder: raising the questions, raising the manhole covers, raising very hell.

A printing press was established in a storefront on the edge of campus. It went clanking and humming away inkily, night and day, churning out a seemingly endless stream of indicting material. Such as, Who owned Cornell, anyway? And such as, What connections joined the Cornell trustees to the warmaking and war profiteering of the time?

The cover lifted. Young heads turned toward the light, away from whimsy and privilege, uncovering the sources of the very privileges that they, in the act of responsible research, were forfeiting. A storm of pamphlets, worthy of Tom Paine or Ben Franklin, poured out; such news as elsewhere, for reasons of privilege and status, was considered unfit to print. The works and pomps of trustees, professors, bureaucrats, bankers, investors, weapons tycoons.

The authors were students and ex-students and nonstudents, those who had arrived at the university not to study in any traditional sense (grab the goodies and run); but had come to sit in the harder school of scant survival and pamphleting and writing and demonstrating and resisting the war.

And then the faculty. Of some eight hundred, one could count on perhaps one-eighth of their number to support such work. The others went their sedate and measured way. The world was in turmoil, a measure of unpleasantness seemed to have invaded the campus. Still, they gossiped and cocktailed and took their constitutionals across Triphammer footbridge, noting with satisfaction that the foundations were firm, the bridge swayed not a fraction more than usual.

Let me pursue a kind of biblical mathematics. Of the hundred faculty who might be thought to hold a moral opinion with regard to the war, perhaps twenty-five would appear publicly at a meeting of the outraged young. And might, in the course of such a meeting, venture guidance or direction.

And of the twenty-five, perhaps five would lay something substantial on the line, given a crisis of career or conscience.

Those five paid: they did not survive at Cornell. A system alert to self-interest and riddled with jealousies found ways to dispose of such mettlesome spirits.

In somewhat such manner, the contention and yielding of Jehovah were verified in our midst: "Find me five just ones, and I shall spare the city."

Spared, fallen: the eye must follow the ironies; they were like the single edge of a double helix. Were the faculty, who in the vast majority considered themselves immune from matters of life and death—spared? On the other hand, I think of the fate of those who resisted, and so lost their faculty jobs. Of those others who refused induction and so were summoned to court and subsequently to jail, or fled the country—were they among the fallen?

There was a strange salvation in the ruin; a strange damnation lurking in the poison ivy.

Religion, religion, what was religion anyway? Cornell thought it knew; as it knew a great deal, and knew it with certainty, and went about with head high, a touch of immemorial smugness. In the university chapel, in mosaic and paint, the certainties were enshrined; such as they were. Spanning the semicircle of the sanctuary, portrayed in mosaic, a chorus of sexually amorphous figures, garlanded with flowers, hand in hand, celebrated the existence of a sexually inoffensive, amorphous god.

Conversely, to the rear of the chapel, another, perhaps more urgent, message was proclaimed. There, in marmoreal state, lay the effigy of the deist baron, Cornell. It was plain to see: the god his life conjured up, neither inoffensive nor amorphous, was four square American. One could all but see, in the marble fictions and folds of expensive broadcloth, an ineffable epiphany of the Great Sound Dollar.

And further, if one continued outdoors from this edifying diorama, the eye might range over the horizon, awed at the amplitude of the kingdom of the just. Property, money! The one god was two-faced. And what the god has joined, let no one sunder.

Mr. Cornell worshiped here. And the god he served, served him well.

The trustees worshiped at the same shrine, and flourished; even as they furbished and guarded the original shrine.

The faculty also had a stake in the shrine, a small stake, to be sure. But not so small as, in the breach, to make no difference. That difference might be called by an old-fashioned term: not the sin of silence, rather the state of silence. A state, nonetheless, of sin.

That the university might soon stand in the breach, few could doubt. The gods of property and money, domesticated at Cornell, and purring in content, were rampaging elsewhere; indeed, they had declared a war.

And the war came home. In a host of antiwar people, long of pelt and short of patience. They too declared war, a war on the gods of Mr. Cornell, on money and property. They put in question not the existence of such gods (there could be no denying their empery in such a place). But they denied that such deities held power over them; whether in the form of domestic wealth, or the form of foreign wars: two realities that they took for roughly the same thing.

In some such ways, the war came home; and was joined. It could hardly be thought that, in the conflict, the religious flock of Cornell would remain indifferent. What was wonderful, given sheepish history, was the side they chose.

They chose to stand with the students, against the war, against the majority of the faculty and virtually all the administration; against, it goes without saying, the board of trustees.

In consequence, the campus citadel where religion was purveyed in normal times, became transformed. Annabel Taylor Hall became a citadel and refuge and town meeting and sanctuary and an entirely new species of classroom. All in one.

It was awesome. Someone, or something, broke through the impregnable glass dome of academic heaven. Rude winds blew in. In the winds, flares were lighted. Two chaplains declined to carry draft cards, even such cards as signified their exemption from the war. They were shortly indicted. Many others, students and younger faculty, did the same. The fires took, as fire will.

I held forth in Annabel Taylor Hall. Next door, the masculine principle reigned: Myron Taylor Law School. The law school taught law and order, as befitted; and just as fitting, the United Religious Work taught disorder.

We were in it up to our tonsures, our somber Protestant stocks, our yarmulkes: the disorder of a new creation, battling toward birth. Chaplains and teachers, we made a new profession. We were determined passionately that the war become a moral issue on campus; that the university be held accountable for its military—economic ties, whether in weapons industries, investments, the corporate ringaround of the trustees.

In those days secret data was hauled into the light, much against the will of those in command. It appeared, from the evidence, that the gods of property and money bore a kind of octopus form. Their tentacles stretched across the land, grasped lives and institutions and, in the manner of such deities, grew bloated.

Much was thus revealed, evaluated, judged.

That "much," alas, was shortly to be forgotten. And this too was

in the American grain, which includes a marvelous facility in both
directions: remembrance and amnesia.

Still, for a time, memory had its heyday, and called the order
of the day: accountability. And that was not at all bad in a bad time.
It may well have been an honorable translation of the old Christian
summons to reconciliation.

In retrospect, I date from this time the decline of the university;
and not only Cornell. I mean as an alternative structure, an honorable critic of conventional politics, governmental chicanery, wars
and war preparation.

Others would possibly place the date far earlier. Indeed, it might
be argued that the university had never been other than a nest for
the darlings who one day would harness themselves in the gear of
public power. But for me this was the time of awakening; helped
beyond doubt by the suave bumbling of Cornell's President Perkins.

Too clever by half, too naive by half! Troubled by alumni rumblings as to my presence on campus, he requested my attendance
in his office. I was urged to help him compose a pacific note to the
critics, stating my "objectives" in accepting the Cornell position.

He shortly got down to business. What were those objectives of
mine, anyway?

I was moved to admit that I was fueled by no perceptible objectives at all. That I was perennially interested in community, in
teaching. I hoped that, in some obscure way, my presence on campus would encourage humane developments, specifically a community opposed to the war.

He fidgeted. It was clear that anyone so deprived as I of his
precious objectives was quite off the map.

As I bowed out, objectives unstated, he presented me with a
copy of his book, recently published. It was one of those perennial
efforts of prexies of America to flog the dead tissues of "university
nature and objectives."

I perused the tome with a mounting sense of disbelief. His thesis,
stated without cavil, indeed without style or elegance, was a simple
one. The university was definable as an organ of national governance. Research, teaching, ideology, dovetailed nicely with whatever political ethos was in the national interest. This mutuality, in
Perkins's view, was a given: it was true in fact and principle. Government and university looked, each to the other, for benefit and

service, research and resource. Included in the cozy arrangement presumably, was military research in any department.

The case could not have been made more clearly. Indeed, it was uncertain whether Perkins and his shabby utilitarianism followed upon or preceded the fact. The fact being that Cornell, along with the other Ivy League strongholds, was long gone in indebtedness to the national military. In celebration of Cornell's debt, plaques were attached to immense, ugly research centers on campus.

Thus, within my lifetime, a breach had opened; wider and more grievous by far than the earlier presumption: that Cornell aimed to prepare future leaders of government. The congruence of the two powers was widened, fused, in the sixties. The university was inducted: its function followed on, supplied, theorized, formulated, government policy.

In so buckling under, a tradition of university dissent from the vagaries and violence of government had received a body blow. Not one blow, but two.

Historically, campus dissent may have been an easily managed affair, a matter of a few students or teachers, now and then raising a storm against this or that national folly. Emerson, Thoreau, Henry Adams, none of these had been naive about the degree of dissent allowable on campuses. The center took power to itself. At the center, not the edge, the scions of the establishment gathered breath for a (sort of) outcry, against slavery, against the Spanish war.

Each of these Famous Men of the nineteenth century had ventured a second look and a loud cry against the university, its deceitful cohesion, its virtuous duplicity, the realities masked by its flowery rhetoric. A number of notables had simply washed their hands of the campuses, and gone their own way. But if the ghost of any of these gentlemen had descended on Cornell in the sixties, he would have noted with dismay something terrible and new. The fragile balance of the previous century had been set off kilter: science now ruled the roost; and the government ruled science.

It was a new kind of Science: it was all but claiming a capital letter for itself, in the manner of a new god. It made no pretension to being "value free"; it sprang from Jove's forehead rattling its saber, and shortly began forging a more deadly blade.

This Science was brutally direct, existential, a one-eyed giant. It was born to take charge; and it did so. And what a pallid face the university presented against the onslaught of this newborn nuclear Mars, his arrogance, his plans for human destiny!

It would not even hit the mark to say that Mr. Perkins shortly buckled under. Where there was no struggle, there was, properly speaking, no capitulation. Perkins, like others of his kind, was canny and ambitious. His sights were set beyond the local empery. He was, as well, untroubled by the peculiar intellectual and moral restraints of the previous century; restraints which, up to a point, had been the proudful legacy of such campuses.

Hence his bizarre little book. The giant named Science had invaded the campus; government had sponsored the invasion. The Cornell president hastened to justify the new arrangement. His function, if truth were told, was something vulgarly known as public relations.

In the nineteenth century, a cry could still be raised, and gain a certain hearing, against the betrayal of university ideas and ideals by its own. University presidents were still distinguishable as a class. They represented a tradition, however feebly, with whatever double minds. But one could still cry Shame, and make sense; certainly to the public, and perhaps even to the shameful.

At the time of my sojourn at Cornell, the tradition was broken. Perkins and his like stood within no tradition. They were corporate recruits, hired temporary hands, to serve at the pleasure (which is to say, in the interests) of the corporate society; which is to say, of the military-industrial complex. Their eyes held an uneasy look: they had ceded the mastery of their own house. In face of crisis, they presented a false front of hangdog bravado and jargon.

Deprived of a tradition, they were also without loyalty, even to a class. They leapt, light as water bugs, from campus to government service. They were appointed ambassadors after serving in the university; or they came from the military to head the university. It was all one in the pantheon of power, where gods could be created overnight, at need; and just as easily robbed of their thunderbolts, or exiled, or transferred to some harmless distant outpost.

I have taught and tarried at too many universities to be shocked any longer by the infection of the campuses.

The infection has been alive and well at Jesuit campuses as well. As to individual Jesuits, a certain levelheaded sense of honor is alive in many. They are devoted to their students, they convey a powerful moral sense. Thus they survive their own authorities, and cast a cold eye on the vagaries of the institutions.

At Cornell, I had, in this regard, two things to learn. The first was the boring sterility of bureaucracies, once their decor was penetrated. The second was the infinite variety of pretense, self-justification, myth, inaccessibility, bumptiousness, pomp and circumstance, with which the emptiness was concealed.

The front office sums it up. Rugs underfoot, discreet paintings on walls, subdued colors, the hum and clack of machines. It is as though immortal thoughts are being recorded, deals beyond imagining consummated, manifestos sent winging to the corners of the universe. It is all quite empty. To complete the decor, a knight in armor should be set up, isolated there. If one were to lift his visor, the helmet would be found void.

The inner office of Mr. Perkins was soon to be literally, rather than metaphorically, empty. Perkins did not survive a crisis even then rumbling underfoot. This lover of peace, even purported peace, and of plenty, as though the sartorial splendor of the campus stood surrogate for a prospering universe—he was shortly to be dethroned. He was judged and found less than useful to his corporate masters.

His offense was his inability to preserve the status quo in a house owned, lock, stock, and laboratory, by absentee landlords.

The peace of Cornell, which to any open eye would appear a false peace, exploded. And Perkins vanished, as though by a conjurer's trick.

The faculty were a phenomenon notably different from the bureaucrats. These latter came as hirelings and, often as not, shortly departed, a promiscuous gleam in their eye. The faculty, on the contrary, had local leverage, permanent status. They could regard the administrators with a kind of established contempt; planted, watered, cosseted as they were.

They were a curious guild indeed, quite out of consonance with the times. Many of them confused the structure of self-interest, known as the tenure track, with a valid tradition. They guarded their turf as though it were an untouchable hereditary priesthood, beyond the ambition of younger mortals. Under fire as they shortly were to be, self-interest was working well for them.

But only for a time: the times were soon to become their enemy.

Betimes they prospered, discreetly. They published and taught gifted students, in an ideal setting; and retired thence to elegant homes. Under the great, invisible dome, they seemed a species of fabled anachronism, living a privileged nineteenth-century existence. Their diversions were leisurely, pedantic, or mildly scandalous: they traded gossip and malice and, at times, spouses. The liberal consensus, operating as a surrogate for conscience, governed both sexual conduct and political attitudes.

The consensus was delightfully flexible: no harm intended, none could be adduced.

How fragile their world was, and how apt for invasion of reality, would shortly be revealed, as the campus exploded under the double blow of black rage and antiwar passion.

When the bolt struck, a few of the faculty fled in the night, never to return. Images of terror possessed them; they disappeared in the mirror of their minds.

Other, hardier souls, stood firm. One could hardly maintain that they stood firm on principle. Rather, they had a more durable sense of the power of the daemon that had set them in place. The god whispered reassurance. America, the America they knew, would survive Vietnam. America had already proven impregnable for two centuries, against the successive fury of domestic slaves and Indians; and abroad, the threat of Britons, Spaniards, Filipinos, Germans. Racism, property, the dollar—these were mighty, and would endure. And so, ringed about with power, and rained upon with favor, would academe.

In the clamor and turmoil of '68, Annabel Taylor Hall sailed the churning waters like a galleon. Its lights were ablaze at midnight; it dared the eye of the storm.

In the view of many, we were anathema. We had created the storm we rode. We purportedly stirred it up; we even choreographed it. We were, at the least, aiding and abetting the intransigents in their declared task of politicizing social questions. Thus we were guilty, along with lesser crazies, of placing an intolerable strain on the campus life.

Civil disobedience, fasts and vigils, picketing, sit-ins, political drama and music and poetry, the hearing we granted to the inflammatory and outrageous, the animosity we fostered toward authority—thus went the charges.

And if we suffered the anger of the administrators, we received a comparable contempt from the faculty. The ministers and priests of Taylor Hall were offering little or nothing of intellectual substance to the students who crowded their gatherings. Their courses lacked accreditation, were in no wise subject to university scrutiny or control.

The students judged otherwise. What they sought, what many chose to pursue under our aegis, was simply none of the university's affair. There were large areas of concern untouched by the conventional course offerings; this was a matter of passionate concern on our part, and a matter never seriously denied by authorities. A bias against religious faith, and the intellectual pursuit of that faith, could hardly be denied, illustrated as it was by the lack of a university religious department.

It might further be adduced that the majority of the faculty favored a vigorous dusting off of certain hoary prejudices, immortalized in the marmoreal tomb of Mr. Cornell and his testamental instructions that no religious studies intrude on his fervent theism. Or on his campus. So be it.

So it was not to be. I remember offering courses at that time in the religious history and practice of nonviolence, in the drama of Pirandello, in the symbols of the Gospel of John. The courses were solidly attended; more, we enjoyed one another, our subjects, our freedom from the paper chase.

But the war, the war went on. It was the longest war in American history. How long it must have seemed to the enemy, to that tormented, remote land, on which rained a tonnage of bombs exceeding the total of bombs deployed in World War II! The war went on and on, this was our sense of it; an event that would not die, an event kept obscenely alive; like a monstrous corpse, pulse fluttering on a machine, miming life.

A decade-long war is a horrific thing, even for those who impose it on others. The resources available even to the most powerful, it comes to pass, are limited after all. And most limited of all is patience, the willingness of a nation to witness the suffering and death of its own, in great numbers, without issue, without rationale.

The demented decision that a given war must not be lost—this must confront, as a demented brain a sound one, the knowledge that the conflict cannot, in any understandable terms, be won. To say, as the president said, that "the duration of the war shall in no way inhibit our will to win"—this says nothing of sanity or sense, and everything of despair.

Rage tore the country apart, in ways unrepaired to this day. It tore the campus apart, in ways that also remain unhealed, if one is prepared to observe the pandemic illness of one-track careerism and political disaffection.

On campus, the war was like an underground fire in combustible earth. The choices available to salvage a semblance of right reason shrank to the vanishing point. One could do one's best to contain the fire of anger, alienation, purported lawlessness—but the fire gathered strength, and broke out elsewhere.

No method worked well. The dream of maintaining a normal campus in abnormal times faded, as such dreams will. By 1968, Cornell was a kind of watch and ward society, wakeful under the moon, threatened under the sun, dreading the next catastrophe, fatalistic about the morrow.

The fires burned away fitfully, moodily. They brought down, in those few years, reputation, fortune, the foil of ego so notably on display in its noble setting.

Willy-nilly, the university was offering me an extraordinary education.

One element of the strength of my position was a refusal to covet a place of honor. I cared not a whit for the usual emoluments: my work, and my affection, were focused elsewhere. So I was not easily catalogued or disposed of—though there were many eager to perform the first task in view of the second.

In any case, I could be accounted only an indirect threat to the faculty, as I had no desire to jostle them on their perches.

On the score of attainments, I stood strongly. Books were published and well received, my office was crowded each day with students in serious quest. I offered fringe benefits: poetry in the campus coffeehouses, meals for friends. Faculty members, usually younger ones, sought me out. We made common cause on the question of the war, and our part in campus resistance.

Thus my first year at Cornell passed, and a fateful year dawned, a year that was to mark me with the stigmata of the tumultuous times; neither victim nor executioner. Something else; the times themselves must reveal it.

Indeed, there were hints and shadows that went before, portending something momentous. Around Thanksgiving of 1967, I traveled to Washington, to support a vast gathering at the Pentagon, against the war.

The word *support* has almost a canonical ring: it expresses, all unintentionally, the moral limits of my generation at the time. Thus far and no further: support, but little or no initiative, little or no setting out on our own.

We elders were groping for a moral place in what we knew to be an immoral order of things. We were not subject to the bondage of the draft. Some among us were withholding taxes. But in the main, we saw our work in rather a pale light; we were counseling the young, marching and leafleting and raising what outcry we could muster.

My brother Philip visited the campus; as usual, he had more than socializing in mind. After years of intense pastoral work in Washington and Baltimore, after being unceremoniously ousted from his work in Newburgh, after the immense physical and spiritual gifts he had put out in those years, his life could never be thought to unfold a conventional future.

How unconventional those ways were, how brilliant and unsettling to conventional priests and conventional Christianity, how Philip was to open for me and many others new tactics emerging from a very old discipline; what leads he offered, what promises he forged and kept in sweat and tears, what a straight, unerring, and luminous path he walked, how he drew others by the light of his personal charm, his integrity, the fire of his eloquence—all these time would reveal. But his gifts were already there, in sight of superiors and peers and friends, in sight also of the fearful and disaffected.

I set down these lines two astonishing decades after the events I dredge out of memory. Philip is married, three children have been born to himself and Elizabeth McAlister. More than a decade has passed since their little community, Jonah House, was undertaken in Baltimore.

In the eighties, Elizabeth passed two years in prison for an antinuclear action in upstate New York. Philip has also been imprisoned frequently since the Vietnam war. Theirs is a history of conscience almost unbearably concentrated, all but unique in our lifetime. Trouble, as the Irish say, following on trouble; and to those capable of insight, glory upon glory.

Philip arrived at Cornell sometime in the late summer of 1967. There was a plan afoot; he wanted me informed of it, not precisely to induct me into the action. I think he sensed how far I was from being a ready candidate for something so audacious as he purposed.

The plan came to this. He and a few cohorts would enter a draft board in downtown Baltimore, and pour their own blood on the files contained in the building. They would then wait quietly, abiding by their act and its consequence.

It was all quite simple. It was also unprecedented, calculated to set the head spinning.

But the head on my shoulders was not so much set spinning as further stuck in place. I was shaken to the core by the venture. I was by no means convinced on the spot, or won over, even as a friend in court; much less as a participant.

Where was I then? I saw myself as walking one bit of turf, he another. But our paths were by no means crossing, nor were he and I walking parallel lines. I wrote him after his visit and its revelation, to the tune that I continued to see my work as standing by the students in their travail; nothing more.

He responded with considerable impatience. It developed that he had no approval to spare for the Boston defendants, whose trial had recently finished. The four celebrated defendants, he thought, were merely reacting to the government, rather than confronting it. Their conduct during the trial was consistent with reaction: they were bound to knuckle under by dint of legal stratagems. Philip's instinct, on the other hand, was to seek out an occasion, at his own time and place, to take the offensive and force the government to respond.

He had come on a way to do this: a moral assault on purportedly sacrosanct territory. An act, he insisted, very much in the spirit of King and Gandhi; but as tactic, something utterly new. Something, as he must have known, bound to raise towering waves, to erupt in controversy, denunciation, passionate pros and cons, even spite and scorn.

The proposed act was entirely in line with his temperament. His life had been a steady rhythm of improvisation and discipline. He was a surprising spirit; he dug deep and came up with directions, modes, arguments, lights in dark places. And equally of import, he had a capacity to beckon others along; he made virtue attractive. In his presence, as I saw time and again, less hardy spirits such as myself breathed deep, stopped out.

That action of the Baltimore Four, as things evolved, proved not only a watershed moment in the antiwar community. It was also a reshuffling of the Catholic cards, that holy tarot deck, stacked to the elbows with assured salvation and no losers. Did not every one of us hold a winning hand?

For many reasons, the Catholics were the least equipped to grasp the import of that audacious action. A raid on a draft board, carried out with scrupulous care for the safety of all concerned, including the women who worked there! It was part of the moral grandeur of the act that it claimed to draw on a tradition, one nearly suppressed by second- and third-generation American Catholics, as they busily went about getting assimilated in this country. Who were we, anyway? And was the old just-war morality of any point in the hideous Asian carnage?

The Catholics who ran the church said it was the only point. A cardinal said it constantly; other bishops said it by saying nothing. Then along came these upstarts, the so-called Baltimore Four. They tossed blood on the credentials of legitimate killing, the entrance cards into adulthood—if the truth were told, entrance into state and church alike.

Those draft files! They were, of course, more than they purported to be. They had an aura, they were secular-sacred documents of the highest import.

But who owned the tradition, anyway; and who was worthy to speak on its behalf? Was it the cardinal of New York, and his chauvinism? Was it the silent bishops and their uninstructed flocks, playing follow-the-leader, paying up, sent off to war?

Indeed, the issue was not simply that a tradition was traduced daily by those responsible for its purity and truth. The issue was a far more serious one. A tradition was something more than a moral fashion, to be laid aside when out of vogue, taken up again when the times dictated.

The tradition was a precious voice, a presence, a Person. The war had silenced the voice, outlawed the Person. Church and state had agreed, as they inevitably did in time of war, that the Person was out of fashion, "for the duration." He had nothing to offer in face of the guns. What indeed could He be thought to offer, with His utterly bizarre command—to lay down the guns?

He was a prisoner of war, this Jesus. He was in a species of protective custody. It was all done quietly, discreetly; out of sight and mind. Indeed, though the Embarrassment was removed, any hardheaded Christian could see that a veritable triumph had been achieved.

The subsequent game went something like this. It was as though He was still present: the church churned on, its wares were offered as usual, from font and table and pulpit. It all worked quite well; it was remarkable (no offense to Him intended), how His absence was scarcely noticed, or the derogation of the intent of His words, His healing, His reconciliation of enemies.

Priests spoke feelingly of this and that, His birth, public life, death, and resurrection were celebrated as usual. But these were rites held for the dead. They summoned nostalgia, not the hard force of presence. They touched on everything except the shame, the absence, the silence. So the sermons brought a mere ghost to bear, weightless, on every question but the real one. The faithful were exhorted to be moral, husbands to cherish wives, children to respect parents: it was all as usual. But the church had become a holy morgue, the dead were preaching morality to the dead.

Then, in the midst of this sorry charade, something happened. It was as though someone of infinite daring and courage, armed only with a rumor, a suspicion, had penetrated a castle keep, and found there alive, a fabled, beloved prisoner, long presumed dead.

He returned, this daring invader; he had a message. He could not free the Prisoner; but he brought back incontrovertible evidence: Jesus existed, His word held firm, He recanted nothing. The war was criminal; the guns were to be laid down. Likewise the bombers were to be grounded, and so on. Tell the people so, tell the bishops so, tell the pope so.

And further: blessed were the peacemakers, now as before; they were to be accounted true sisters and brothers of the Prisoner.

I suppose for the moment that a group of Mennonites or Quakers had performed the Baltimore draft action. In such communities, the act would touch on a history. It could be categorized, it would arise out of a morally consistent history. Each of these communities has endured much trouble from the law, both in Europe and in the American Revolutionary period. Each has borne extraordinary spirits who risked their lives in quest of moral stance and statement; each has a history of martyrs and prisoners of conscience on our own soil.

I am not waxing romantic. Such an action as the Baltimore Four dared might indeed erupt in controversy within pacifist communities. But the argument would be contained by the tradition; it would revolve around tactic rather than principle. And on that score, it might be thought relatively easy of acceptance; or at the least, of tolerance.

Not so among Catholics. For a thousand years, the peacemaking Jesus had been out of fashion. In the matter of war, as war became modernized and thereby totalized, the Catholics were at sea; without leadership, at least among those ordained to such office. And when, here and there, Catholics of courage arose and risked repute and life itself, as happened during the Hitler years, such would find themselves without sanction, friendship, support.

In consequence, no real debate ensued. Whether, for instance, it was right or wrong, morally expedient or morally outrageous, to enter a draft board and cast one's blood about: such questions were long ago answered. Or not so much answered as superseded. So long ago had such questions been dealt with, that it was unknown whether they had ever been raised at all. The moral questions, concerning government property and its inviolability in time of war, the attitude of Christians toward war itself—the American Catholic experience rendered the questions void.

There remained only an assumption that cried to heaven for redress; instead of the declared criminality of all wars, Catholics were to assume the normalcy of war. The objectors against war were thereby reduced to a suspect, isolated minority.

As a result, the war atmosphere among Catholics exhibited, in the main, the same fear, hatred, ignorance, as were ravaging the national community. The same and, for lagniappe, the example of Cardinal Spellman, and a blessing once more traced over just-war theory and practice.

In sum, the church also declared war against Vietman. A massive cultural weight was brought to bear, shored up, rendered unassailable by a summons to loyalty and obedience, by that molding of the common mind that Catholic practice brings to pass.

The war signaled the end of the questioning of war. What emerged from audiences of Catholics after the Baltimore action in 1967 were not questions at all, but accusations, indignation, anger, moral conclusions cut and dried. The war was moral, it was wrong to impede it, especially in such undignified, indeed hooligan, tactics, lawless, unclergylike. Priests belonged where priests had always been: in church sanctuaries and rectories; certainly not in draft boards and courts and jails, places where the faith could be held only in ridicule and scorn.

If indeed there were questions, they were not of the inquiring kind. They were rather in the nature of outcries concerning the unknown spaces where priests were venturing, slipping from moral foothold, freewheeling in the void.

No wonder. We Catholics were without landmarks in uncharted times. Our history had been narrowed, our heritage swamped. A nascent truth with regard to violence may have been clearly stated in Scripture; but what leverage the origins could exert, given the long history of justified intervention and the rampageous present— the scriptural light was indeed meager. That light had been quenched, or nearly so.

As a community we were somewhat in the predicament of the seeker whose story is so movingly told in the Acts of the Apostles. A courtier of Queen Candace, alone, reads the book of Isaiah, and is lost in perplexity. What might it all mean, this story of a suffering Servant of the Lord? Luckily, the seeker encounters the disciple Philip, who questions him: Has he understood the reading? The man answers, a perennial plaint: "And how am I to understand, with no one to aid me?"

No one to aid. We opened our Scripture, on those formal occasions when it was read at all, in a way entirely American. For all liturgical solemnity and reverence, we read as though the book were opened only to be closed again. We read stories about Jesus and his friends, one among them the undoubted Son of God. We read exhortations to love enemies, to do good to those who assail us, to walk another mile with the opponent, to turn the other cheek to the persecutor.

But our country was at war! And the bloody matter of war, like the bloody hands of Mars, closed the book in our hands.

We were taught, not by Jesus and the apostles, but by churchmen, a circumstance that many would be inclined to call a different matter indeed.

The pope and bishops taught, up to the Vietnam war and its horrid course, that a given war could be called just, and therefore in degree godly, under certain conditions. By such teaching, and under the enormous pressure of wartime hegemony and propaganda, the Vietnam war too was rendered just, and to a degree godly. Thus went the bare bones of the case, the teaching. (Also the silence.)

What put flesh on the bones, and a gun in the hand, and a blessing on the gun, was something more mysterious and influential by far than mere doctrine. It was the enormous weight and import of a culture—being American. Being at war.

There was no place, no appropriateness, for argument. The argument was the war, and the war was just. The argument was flesh and blood: young lives displaced, armed, sent off. And then, inevitably, the argument took another, final form: the bodies, the ritual of return. And finally, the stern rhetoric of the survivors, who, it was presumed, spoke for the dead, demanding an ever greater expense of the living.

The war was an old story, refurbished. It was the sin named original—once more rendered original. There were new weapons in the hands of a new generation; there was a new enemy, whom distance and ignorance rendered a blank; and to a degree known only to ignorance and isolation, rendered expendable, hateful.

I recall this history, my own and my brother's, perhaps at too great length, in order to put the Baltimore action into its place. It was not only a *défi* cast in the face of government. It reverberated also within the church: a moral explosion, a reaction, a casting off; or, in the words of one of the defendants at trial, "an exorcism, an anointing."

For the Catholics involved, it was in the nature of an adult baptism. A national history must be renounced, as the garments of adults were once discarded, before entering the waters. "A way of thinking" is a mild way of putting it. Philip entered the draft board that November day, decent in clerical black, surrounded by the respect due "the cloth," his status and education and good looks and record of service to church and military—all intact. He might have been paying a routine pastoral call on one of the board employees, themselves untroubled Catholics keeping the licenses in good order. Was he there to reassure them, to indulge in the easy camaraderie typical between clerics and the flock? He entered the building a priest. He could rejoice in "good standing," as the expression goes—in the estimate of his community, his superiors, the law.

He departed in handcuffs: a prisoner, a felon, displaced and disgraced.

A friend said to me at the time, a modest man, not given to aphorism or prophecy, "You know, they'll have to kill your brother someday: he'll never change."

It was in an atmosphere charged with ominous event that I drove toward Washington that November day. I knew the draft board action was imminent. Legally, I suppose, I could be called an accessory: a demeaning phrase, denoting, as it does to me, the status of an appendage, a bystander more or less guilty—and this not by reason of foreknowledge or silence, as the law would have it. But as conscience would have it, an accessory by reason of moral inertness.

Let me be charitable toward myself. I was not ready, and Philip was. He had, of course, marked advantages, having worked and lived for several years among the urban poor. While I had rusticated at Cornell and, to a degree, been stymied there.

I traveled to Washington to support friends from the university and elsewhere, who were planning to surround the Pentagon. Support was all I was ready for; or so I thought. Misjudging, in my ignorance, the shove of moral pressure, more especially the pressure engendered by perils descending on my friends.

It was my first such demonstration. Indeed, nothing had prepared me for the spectacle of the Pentagon: the awesome pile of utterly characterless masonry, pretentious as a pharaoh's tomb and as morally void. It was also the first mesmerizing sight of a great throng, pressing against the river entrance, sitting, standing, singing, praying, exhorting, spilling upward like water defying gravity, up the lawn, up the steps, in face of the massed soldiery.

It was almost as though one species of creation were confronting another. On the other hand, improvisation, color, variety of clothing and hair and bodily gesture. And on the other, the human remolded, set in place, predefined, all but predigested. The uniforms not only clothed the frames, they veiled the eyes, silenced the tongues.

The young soldiers were, by Pentagonal definition, the complete humans, born from Holy Mother State. Complete, they confronted the incomplete, the gunless hordes of the unviolent. Those who could not, or worse, would not, discharge a gun.

Evening approached, the massed floodlights were lit. We stood or sat or knelt in the glare of public knowledge and legal jeopardy. Eventually, it was announced with a great blare that "At midnight, the law will take effect: all who remain in place are liable then to arrest."

My friends, of course, chose to remain. And so, by force of example, did I. Again and again, in the heady Cornell days, we had applied to one another the word friend. It seemed fitting that the word be tested here, in a place where, presumably, only weapons were to be tested—or humans, it might be, but only insofar as these were useful appendages to the weapons; accessory, and after the fact, so to speak.

Buses were at hand, out there in the rim of darkness. It was no great task for the military to move in and carry or lead us away.

We were brought to a disused military camp in Virginia. There, for a matter of some days, we were treated somewhat like wayward children in summer camp, temporarily restrained because of minor infractions.

Then one day, out of the blue, a squad of legal skulls descended on us. It was the first time, but by no means the last time, that a fairly close community was disrupted by lawyers, dangling before the eyes of innocents the fast food of the culture: quick in, quick out, no questions asked.

The purveyors were wreckers of community, which in this case was tentative indeed, in its first stages, and extremely vulnerable to the dangling carrot: walking free.

Most of the formerly fervent seized the bait and departed on the instant. The remaining, who might be judged arbitrary spirits, requested a trial. They were thereupon judged apt to benefit from "a lesson."

We had begun an improvised fast, a way, we thought, drawn from civil rights experience, of gaining a modicum of mental clarity. There came a moment of clarity indeed: the moment when the children's camp days were over. We survivors of the legal eagles were placed in holding cells, to await transport to the D.C. jail.

There, during a waiting period, I was visited by a young priest, a chaplain. He had been flown in from Fort Benning, along with transport guards, part of standard government equipment. He leaned negligently against the bars of my cell and grinned into my face, for all the world like a delighted child at a zoo. And all the while, he was copiously refreshing himself from a container of orange juice.

Hardly worth attention, the episode was yet instructive. I remember the priest, the moment; I saw, perhaps for the first time, hilarious symbols: the priest in concert, the priest in contest. The strange crossings-over that occur: priests of the state, priests against the state.

We were taken off to Washington in cuffs and chains, and there segregated from the prison populace in our own dormitory. From thence we were led three times daily, after regular meal service, to a cafeteria area. A great rumble arose about our daring a fast: such deviations would not be allowed, we were risking being force fed, etcetera—none of which dire contingencies occurred. The fast continued. And within a week or so, we were released.

A friend in the Washington area was waiting to transport me to a Catholic Worker house nearby, where I was fortified by a bowl of soup, and so in short order regained my land legs.

But it was in the car en route that we heard the news. The derring-do of the Baltimore Four! The draft board raid, the successful pouring of blood on the files, and the summary arrests.

It was a curious juxtaposition. I had taken part in a low-intensity act, together with those who, shortly thereafter, would vanish once more, into the tunnels and byways of college routine.

But when Philip and his friends walked through the door of the draft board, there was no exit; not for years. They were seized by the great Seizer. They were trespassers on his turf, had dared muck up the exquisite order of his necrophilic files, where the names of the soon to be killed, or the soon to kill, or both, were preserved against the Day of Great Summons.

The files stood for all sorts of things, things best left in shadowy dossiers rather than brought into the light. For all the world (as we were later to see in Catonsville), the files in their drawers reminded one of a vast morgue, the corpses of lives not quite interred.

There a young person could legally enter, open the file, read his fate before the fact. The files legalized his own death, legalized also the deaths of others who might fall prey to his rifle.

First and foremost, the files bore witness to the absolute inviolability of legalized violence. The files were, as we were to describe them later, hunting licenses against humans. They declared an open season against the living, by the living—or as long a season as might be of advantage, in view of experimentation with use of new weaponry on unarmed populations, bombing of civilian centers, and so on.

The files were open to their subjects: they were open because no threat was to be construed by the young hands who would come seeking their status. A harmless legal privilege indeed, together with its fiction of open files, open society.

The young would presumably have nothing more in mind than a glance; a glance that implied an agreement. If they came, the supposition was that they would be at peace with their fate. But let no agitating outsider enter, with his load of moral scruple and troublemaking! The files were, in fact, off limits to moral scrutiny. They were an immoral fact masked, in the manner of Auschwitz, as an objective "fact in nature"; a fact, more accurately, in culture. For what, in the modern sensibility, is more opaquely innocent than a file cabinet? And who would be so fond as to claim that a file cabinet, lying dusty and inconspicuous in an out of the way office, was of the order of, say, Dr. Caligari's secret?

But now behold, on a November morning, the cabinet, a veritable sanctuary, stood void, violated. A photo shows Philip, his white poll and black overcoat: he is intently pouring blood into the dark maw. Tom Lewis stands by, calmly reading, presumably aloud, from the Bible. One of the employees, her face sulfurous with anger, presses forward. Her eyes and mouth are bulging, enlarged to a living O; she has a nightmarish look, like a figure out of Bosch.

Arrived at the Catholic Worker, I phoned home. My mother's

calm touched me. This was by no means the first test of her equanimity, nor would it be the last. I explained things, as best I might. "You mean," she responded, "that you are out of jail, and your brother is in?"

She was somewhat confused by radio reports, and wanted our whereabouts straightened out: that was all. No great matter; no emoting or wailing. She was past mistress of the art of conservation of soul. More, the years had built into our love tier on tier of supposition. Her sons could trust and be trusted, even when understanding was at short supply, or the cruel novelty of a situation toppled older, long-held verities. This was the woman, after all, who had placed a star in the window for each of four sons during the last war, whose prayers had been fervent for their safety during those terrible years. And now, and now? With her, a thousand difficulties did not create a single doubt.

The Baltimore Four were held in jail for some months, then released in view of a trial. The supposition was that being sufficiently chastened by their enforced stay, they could now be trusted to behave themselves. From henceforth, the war would cease to trouble their minds. Common sense would take over. What should now occupy them, indeed vex them, was their precarious legal situation: the charges against them were sufficiently severe to deter all but the most foolhardy.

Indeed, in the view of the court, which was one with the view of the prosecutors of the war, the four had done their utmost. Misguided or otherwise, the trial would reveal.

So went the fond presumption: their wings and talons were clipped. And because two of the four were clerics, and all four first offenders, there were heavy implications of comparative leniency.

It would be difficult to conjure up a greater illusion than this: that the law, which was protecting the horrid war, would effectively put Philip to silence. Indeed, the law would hear more of him, for years and years; and so would I.

Meantime, a group of Christians, including several Quakers, came up with a plan to dramatize the toll the air war was exacting against Vietnamese civilians. We would travel to that country, bearing a symbolic gift of medical supplies.

As is usual in wartime, the American government had devised a law forbidding any species of what it was pleased to call trading with the enemy. The law, as applied, was enacted to thwart just such an effort as we were planning. A group of us therefore called at the State Department to demand relief from the inhuman decree. We were met by an employee, icy of mood, bearing a Medusa look. She heard us out, our plea and exposition concerning the plight of Vietnamese wounded. Then she delivered the verdict: the law, in effect, stood. Any attempt to so "trade" would incur the penalties stated.

Our resolution stiffened, we resolved to defy the law.

It thereupon devolved on me to inform my Jesuit superior and seek approval for going to Hanoi.

Travel to Hanoi in wartime? One might better seek approval to swim in the sea toward the moon. The superior at the moment was a sterling upholder of law. He was also singularly disapproving of my tacky course toward salvation. It was he who later coined the marvelous distinction that, for the sake of puzzled or disclaiming Jesuits, resolved the Berrigan dilemma: to the effect that I was "in the order, but not of it."

In any case, I sought an interview. As expected, he refused approval on the instant. There was an evident impasse. I was proceeding under the assumption that in view of the imbroglio of 1965, my abrupt and unexplained exiling to South America, I had won a measure of credit with the order; a storehouse, so to speak, of merit, upon which I could draw from time to time. As, for example, this time.

By no means: the metaphor held no water. We were stuck. Then, in his prevenient way, he saw a method of disposing of the case, and at the same time dispersing the responsibility among several other Jesuits. He proposed that, in accord with common practice, a panel be assembled, that my case be exposed, together with his objections, and a common decision reached.

I agreed. Some days later, in a charged atmosphere, the group assembled. I told my story, objections were heard, questions raised. These latter revolved mainly around the vexed matters of conscience and law—matters about which, if truth were told, none of us knew a whit; but in which we abstractly presumed ourselves quite expert.

The scene had about it an aura both charming and bizarre. We were like children playing adults in Wonderland. We were untried and true, ignorant and confident: we were Americans.

If we had ears to hear, we were under a double indemnity of distance and immunity. We were clerics. How might the war, or the plight of the wounded, burned, poisoned civilians of Vietnam be thought to affect us? For all the weight they cast on our consciences, the victims might have been endangered fauna residing on the moon. And ourselves swimming toward their planet, now and again catching a glimpse of what might (or might not) be one (or another) living being. . . .

It was moral theology in action, with a vengeance. Which is to say, abstract and clean of hand and eye. We are unvisited by tears of compassion. Our governing images were of well-being, good order, convenience, normalcy—all those tried and tested ways by which Christians live safely and at seemly distance from Christ.

I was asked at one point whether "if I were not to go to Hanoi under such circumstances, I would judge myself guilty of mortal sin." Boggling of mind, I thought. But responded, "Yes, I would."

Another image occurred to me. We were like a team of jugglers, working in tandem. Now and then, we might dare an unexpected move, as the balls rose in a blur in the air, and we traded movement and gesture; never maladroit, never missing a cue. There was but one fault in the spectacle: the balls, sent aloft with perfection of timing, interplay, speed—they floated off like motes, they never came down.

I eventually won approval. But the project dissolved, in favor of a far different, more daring, one.

At Cornell one morning, my phone rang. It was a young antiwar activist, Tom Hayden, later to become notorious as a member of the Chicago Seven.

An invitation had come from Hanoi, offering to release three American pilots on occasion of the Buddhist Tet holiday in January of 1968. Two Americans were invited to come to Hanoi and receive the prisoners, conducting them back to the United States under auspices of the peace movement.

Hanoi once more: that haunt of a city. Howard Zinn of Boston University had already agreed to go; would I accompany him?

I would, with all my heart. And thereupon, within the day, assembled whatever meager belongings, and boarded a bus from Ithaca to New York.

The long trip through the winter night was light headed with unreality. I sat with a young soldier returning from a furlough with his family, back to his Washington assignment. He was a member of the honor guard attached to Arlington cemetery, assigned to accompany the remains of slain soldiers to their graves. I listened numbly to his description of such ceremonies. God help me, was I at the start of some unknowable adventure, or had I come full circle?

We plunged on into the night, the darkness wove its enigma about us. He talked on and on: the volleys, the folding of the flag, the emotion and dread of accompanying the families to the grave site, the small talk, the inadequate, stumbling phrases, as though learned by rote from a foreign language handbook. . . . He burst out: "It's horrible! I'd rather be in Vietnam taking my own chances! . . ."

We embarked the next day, Zinn and I. We had refused all formalities, courtesies, easements offered us by Washington. We traveled without visas, whether of exit or reentry. Our errand was our own business; and because the beneficiaries of our effort included the American military, the government had agreed not to hamper us. We were resolved to voyage strictly on our own.

We could hardly be thought of as government emissaries, even in the remotest sense. Yet we were risking our skins to bring home combatants who had wreaked considerable havoc against civilians and others. Altogether, ours was a curious enterprise; only two such quixotic characters, I thought, could possibly bring it off.

I treat the matter shortly, because it has been dealt with in some detail elsewhere. We landed eventually, against all likelihood, in Hanoi, in midwinter. The city was darkened, chill under the moon, digging in for the brutal, exterminating air war.

We passed an increasingly energetic and nerve-racking week, uncertain as to whether and when the purpose of our voyage might be accomplished. Our hosts were enraged at the continued bombings, uninterrupted as they were, even by such an errand of mercy as ours.

For me, being under American bombs was an education without parallel. It was as though the heavens had erupted and poured out the contempt of the gods. Neither we, nor our prize, the pilots, those choice wards of government, were exempt from the thunder and lightning. No one was exempt. We and the pilots were as expendable as the Vietnamese peasants or their children. The Vietnamese, the American airmen, and ourselves were trussed and bundled into a single inert package of misery and death. Night and day, the fiery contempt poured down.

The airmen were released, we started home with them, were interrupted in Vientiane, Laos, by the American ambassador, who boarded the plane and made his announcement: the airmen were ordered to complete their journey home in an Air Force plane. They departed with him after a heated exchange between the ambassador and ourselves.

We came back alone, Zinn and I. My education was proceeding apace. I must add to the curriculum, recently so enlarged, a new subject: that of betrayal.

My unlikely teacher was the ambassador to Laos, William Sullivan, overseer, as the world learned only later, of the extermination bombing of the Plain of Jars. Ambassador afterward to the Philippines, aider and abettor to Marcos. Ambassador finally to Iran, amicable adviser to the unspeakable shah. Sullivan, stony of face, impeccably turned out, meticulous of mind and habit, devious and earnest of manner, devoid of conscientious second thoughts—the perfect chattel, in sum, of imperial criminality. And to complete the iron portrait—practicing Catholic. In the circles I move in, one seldom encounters so astonishing a figure.

Years later, on a California campus, I was questioned about the episode. I told the story of the theft of the pilots and the betrayal of the prior agreement that Zinn and myself would be free to conduct the prisoners home. I, perhaps intemperately, in the heat of the narration referred to the ambassador as Killer Sullivan. After the talk a young woman approached me and identified herself as Sullivan's daughter. She recounted her memories of the episode: how, as a child in Laos, her father brought to their home one night two flyers; how the three departed for the States the following day. "But," she concluded, "we never heard the story you told here."

I could only advise her to repeat my version to her father, with my compliments, and ask his reaction.

CHAPTER 9

Catonsville: The Fires of Pentecost

Peacemaking is hard
hard almost as war.

The difference being one
we can stake life upon
and limb and thought and love.

I stake this poem out
dead man to a dead stick
to tempt an Easter chance—
if faith may be
truth, our evil chance
penultimate at last,

not last. We are not lost.

When these lines gathered
of no resource at all
serenity and strength,
it dawned on me

a man stood on his nails.

an ash like dew, a sweat
smelling of death and life.
Our evil Friday fled,
the blind face gently turned
another way. Toward life.

A man walks in his shroud.

The spring of '68 dawned over Cornell. No lovelier change of season could be imagined. I must have been one of very few mortals who walked to work of mornings, through a woodland, the sound of birds and released waters gushing in the early sunshine. I was, for a time, an early bird in more senses than one: the first campus member to visit North Vietnam, and much in demand to recount and reflect, not only locally, but across the nation.

More serious events were gathering steam. I was working to complete a diary I had sketched out in the course of my unprecedented voyage. But there were difficulties: too much happening, too quickly. The recent past, with present realities pressing hard, was receding into a kind of pluperfect. Only two months previous and I "had been" in Hanoi. But now was now; and a new question arose, jostling and tumbling the past. Where might such an experience lead, and when?

Where and when. The question was not to remain unanswered for long. Philip came to campus for a quiet visit, overnight. He was again free, in no sense quelled, either by months in jail, or by the prospect of an impending trial and sentence. He came with a proffer.

His visits, rare as they were, were invariably a joy: occasions of grace. He, his visits and letters, were slowly extricating me from an impasse.

My "Cornell conclusion" for what it was worth (not much), stood firm. It stood, hardly weakened by the exemplary action of the Baltimore Four. To wit: We, the good antiwar clergy, had gone as far as could be. We had counseled the young in their quest for a peaceable kingdom. We had even approached lawbreaking and conspiracy, in our support of the campus ministers who renounced their draft cards.

We had not yet come on the moral equivalent of the resisters: we were far removed from their legal risks.

How is an impasse broken? Only a startling discovery, epiphany, dawning, could reveal my ignorance for what it was. Short of that, in the Socratic sense, I did not know that I knew next to nothing.

Into our sublime, serene island, our El Dorado, came Philip. He is not to be thought of as a portent: nothing so pretentious. He was a friend, and he came bearing a gift.

Such a gift as stops the heart short. He and others, he stated simply, were not content that the action at the Baltimore draft center should rest there, a flash in the pan, a gesture. For it was more than that; and government leniency or sternness in the coming trial must not steal the thunder of the peaceable.

The action, in short, must be repeated elsewhere; and he, for one, and Tom Lewis, for another, were prepared to repeat it, in Catonsville, Maryland.

Would I join them?

Well, would I? The idea was immensely attractive; it was also a shocker. But it was less frightening than it would have been months before. I was freshly returned from Hanoi, where I had cowered under American bombings. That helped wonderfully to clear the mind. I told Philip I would give the proposal twenty-four hours, monitoring meantime the course of emotion and mood. And if my purpose held for that period, I was in.

Which in due time I was, up to my chin.

A sense, as I recall, of immense freedom. As though in choosing, I could now breathe deep, and call my life my own.

A sense, also, of the end of a road, or a fork, or a sudden turn; and no telling what lay beyond. At the same time, a certainty deeper than logic: what lay behind was best placed behind, once and for all, and no looking back.

Who was to tell me all this? There was no telling. There was only the force of a friendship, and an offer. And suddenly, my hands and heart lifted, and I knew. What had stood at center stage, the focus and heart of things (Cornell, and all I loved there, perhaps intemperately)—this receded quietly, in an hour, to the wings. At the center stood—darkness, myself, my friends. And what would come of it all, no one of us could tell.

There was shortly to be a spotlight on us: it was thin as a pencil slate, and would pierce us through and through; a testing light that touched on the very soul, and illumined and burned. The light of the adversary, light of the church, light of the eye of God? Light, perhaps, of self-knowledge: of all these together. But for a start, there was that opposite element, that darkness. I was in it, body and soul, blind, feeling my way, humiliated; but strangely exalted, freed.

The foregoing could now be called hindsight. At the time, there was no such thing; something closer to hindsightlessness, if the term can be credited. In place of eyes, or sight, I had only faith to go on, or trust, which perhaps comes to the same thing. I knew my brother, I knew his testing and his coming through, and the travail he was inviting on his own head. I knew also his love for me. So there was no such element as pure darkness. How could there be? Instead of sight, or evidence, or logic, there was something better to go by—a hand in mine, someone to walk with. Enough, and more.

Weeks later, I sat one day in the sun, at a little country airport in Maine, where I had gone to lecture on the Hanoi episode. While awaiting the plane homeward, I composed the words we were to release in May at Catonsville, Maryland; they began, "Our apologies, good friends, for the fracture of good order. . . ."

I was becalmed for a brief time. The new calm was different indeed from a metaphysical stalemate, a resigned self-satisfaction in the Cornell manner. It was a kind of clearing in the jungle. I had reached it at considerable labor. I knew the image for what it was: a sign of respite, after which I must move on once more.

My reading of the times was both tragic and energetic: the war; and something to be done. Mine, I knew, was a most unacademic sense. On campus, the ruling metaphor was tenure. Some had tenure, others set their timepieces by that clock of privilege, and trailed along behind the pack, picking up the scant largesse.

The metaphor went further: presumably the very stars of the heavens were tenured; firm, set in place. It followed that mortals and their lesser motions took their lead from the fixed nature of things above.

I was fixed nowhere, except in the lives of those I loved. I had determined to move on, out of the Platonic state of Cornellian beatitude. In view of the war, its cost, its call—to linger would be to lose.

Indeed, it might be argued that my decision was presumptuous in the extreme. Philip was well tested as to physical deprivation, living as he did. And more: he had been tried in lockup, and survived. In comparison with him, I was a coddled egg indeed: an academic who only of late proposed shedding his shell.

Would I survive? Was my purpose sound? Or was I indicated in the Gospel parable: the king who went out to wage war, with vastly inferior numbers of troops—a peculiar metaphor of war, but apt in raising the question—good sense versus nonsense.

Also touching me was the mysterious story of the man who would rid himself of demons—and did so. Only to find that behind his back, and mocking his careless mind, a very squad of evil has entered, multiplying the first wave: possession, so to speak, by inadvertence.

There was nothing for it, but to chance it.

Indeed, it has often been so, when everything of instinct leads me in a given direction—and everything rational says to me Nay.

It was only after the Catonsville action that I came on a precious insight. The knowledge thus came hardly, as perhaps real knowledge does. Something like this: presupposing integrity and discipline, one is justified in entering upon a large risk; not indeed because the outcome is assured, but because the integrity and value of the act have spoken loud.

When such has occurred, matters of success or efficiency are placed where they belong: in the background. They are not irrelevant, but they are far from central.

I was in need of such reflections as we faced the public after our crime. The revulsion could only be called ecumenical. All sides agreed—we were fools or renegades or plain crazy.

The supporting arguments were wonderfully diverse and inventive. The action was useless: it "spoke to no one." It was violent: it involved an assault on property, which the government had made sacrosanct. It was scandalous, including, as it did, two priests, who should have known better. And so on, and so on.

I tried, in response, to put matters biblically. That there was a history of such acts as ours. In such biblical acts, results, outcome, benefits, are unknown, totally obscure. The acts are at variance with good manners and behavior. Worse, they are plainly illegal. More yet: everything of prudence and good sense points to the uselessness, ineffectiveness of such acts. And finally, immediate and perhaps plenary punishment is bound to follow.

And yet, and yet, it is also said: The poor mortal is ordered to go ahead; in spite of all. To go ahead, in faith; which is to say, because so commanded.

One had very little to go on; and went ahead nonetheless.

Still, the "little," I reflected ruefully, had at least one advantage.

One was free to concentrate on the act itself, without regard to its reception in the world. Free also to concentrate on moral preparation, consistency, conscience. Looked at in this light, the "little" appeared irreducible, a treasure.

So, despite all, a history of sorts was launched on a May morning in 1968. Also, a tradition was vindicated, at least to a degree. Or so I believe to this day.

Some twenty years after Catonsville, the play I wrote, based on the trial record, is still being produced. In Germany, in 1983 and 1984, *The Trial of the Catonsville Nine* was staged in some forty West German cities; it was adopted as the official voice of the resistance against nuclear missiles.

Over the years, the play has been presented in Japanese, Chinese, and all European tongues. It was the first play to open in Athens in 1976 after the defeat of the junta. It was presented by a group of actors who had been underground for years.

And what delight it was, to be part of a Berlin audience in 1983, as the play was launched in its second birth. Up to that night, the protagonist and prophet of it all, Philip, had never seen the *Catonsville* play. He had always been in prison during its U.S. heyday. . . .

The night before that fateful May morning, we assembled at a friend's house, and made a rite, preparing the napalm. Kerosene and soap chips. A simple formula, out of a Green Beret handbook, ignited the hell.

Next morning, with fast-beating hearts, we drove to Catonsville. The draft board was on the second floor of a tacky frame building, above an office of the Knights of Columbus.

On Catholic ground! We entered, armed with our resolve and symbol: the container of home-brewed napalm.

We reassured, as best we might, the transfixed employees, withdrew the A-1 files, carried them outside to a parking lot.

And shortly a fire flared.

The act was pitiful, a tiny flare amid the consuming fires of war. But Catonsville was like a firebreak, a small fire lit, to contain and conquer a greater. The time, the place, were weirdly right. They spoke for passion, symbol, reprisal. Catonsville seemed to light up the dark places of the heart, where courage and risk and hope were awaiting a signal, a dawn.

For the remainder of our lives, the fires would burn and burn, in hearts and minds, in draft boards, in prisons and courts. A new fire, new as a Pentecost, flared up in eyes deadened and hopeless, the noble powers of soul given over to the "powers of the upper air."

"Nothing can be done!" How often we had heard that gasp: the last of the human, of soul, of freedom. Indeed, something could be done; and was. And would be.

We had removed an abomination from the Earth. It was as though, across the land, a series of signal fires had been lighted. The first was no larger than a gleam of an eye. But hill to hill, slowly at first, then like a wildfire, leaping interstices and valleys, the fires flared. As though by instinct, fire found its combustibles, beyond and beyond.

In the following years, some seventy draft boards were entered across the land. Their contents variously shredded, sacked, hidden out of sight, burned, scattered to the winds. In one case, the files were mailed back to their owners, with a note urging that the inductee refuse to serve.

That morning! We stood in the breach of birth. We could know nothing. Would something follow, would our act speak to others, awaken their resolve? We knew only the bare bones of consequence.

Consequence indeed. It was shortly made clear that our action was taken with utmost seriousness. There was, first of all, the unbelievable matter of Tom Lewis and Philip. Had they actually the effrontery to commit a second crime in the teeth of the first?

The act was done. We sat in custody in the back room of the Catonsville Post Office, weak with relief, grinning like virtuous gargoyles. Three or four FBI honchos entered portentously. Their leader, a jut-jawed paradigm, surveyed us from the doorway. His eagle eye lit on Philip. He roared out: "Him again! Good God, I'm changing my religion!"

I could think of no greater tribute to my brother.

Faith brought us to Catonsville, and a vagrant hope. In my case, it was faith seeking understanding. I went ahead on the basis of intuition and instinct, a smell, a sense of things, a rightness. But intuitions, as I knew (I was, after all, a Jesuit), are notoriously unreliable, all but incommunicable. I must set out to tell our story; first of all to myself.

And in public interplay and critique, I would also learn that "other side" of the action. What did it mean to others? Did they see it as blessing or curse? Only time would tell; meantime, we must tell the story.

After the action, in the county jail for a matter of eight or ten days, we undertook a fast. The warden of the place, an admirable Christian, was intrigued by our conduct, and came to our cells to talk. We asked leave to celebrate a Eucharist; he agreed, on condition that he be allowed to attend. And when Sunday came round, we joined the other prisoners and their families, and the warden and his family, for worship. Afterward, coffee and cookies were served.

Only later did I come to realize how unprecedented was this treatment of prisoners. And even at the time, I rejoiced in our friendship with Warden Foster, and accounted us lucky indeed.

I was released, and returned to Cornell to await trial. Philip and Tom Lewis, now considered recidivists and virtually unrehabilitatable, were, of course, kept fast.

Shortly, standing before audiences, I discovered something unexpected. The closer my explanation drew upon biblical instruction and source, the less palatable it became; and this to Catholics. It was as though in so speaking, one was by no means building bridges of understanding. One was putting up a wall, stone by stone, and mortising it tight.

It was quite acceptable to talk "politics." There was at least a nascent sense that the war was intolerable, granted the American system and its "normal" workings. One gained this small leverage. But the fact that the war might be inconsistent with the words and example of Christ, that killing others was repugnant to the letter and spirit of the Sermon on the Mount—this was too much: it turned living ears to stone.

And not only the ears of lay Christians. The layfolk followed the lead of experts: theorists and ideologues and moral theologians. The vast majority of these eminences had backed up wars and armies, for centuries. It was they who had built up a common mentality

among Christians: suppositions, solidarity of conscience, justifica-
tions, lesser evils, proclaimed limits. (Always the "lesser evils.")

In proclaiming that, under certain conditions, some wars were
immoral, they had salvaged a great deal; or so it was said. They
had saved humanity (and the church?) from the awful assumption
that all wars were good. So we were told.

My ears itched at these sounds. A sense that something deeper,
something unspoken, was implied here. A basis, a supposition: a
somber view of the human, entirely at variance with Christ's view.
What was a human being, anyway, or acceptable human conduct?
According to a number of theologians, as far as I could understand,
Christians and others were created so frail in decency and so prone
to evil that it was continually necessary to allow violence, greed,
license, some measure and movement. Thus salvaging (at least par-
tially, at least now and then) some hint of a less than worst case.

The theory implied something else: a quite minimal faith in the
Christ of the Testament. Was He to be taken literally, in this sorry,
stressful business of loving one's enemies? The church and the emperor (better, the church of the emperor) and the church's experts
decided, in effect, that He could not. He could not have meant His
moral statements, commands of undeniable rigor and clarity, to apply, here and now, everywhere and at all times. Apply moreover,
to public and political conflict.

Thus, one thinks, the morality of a "me too" church was early
born. Impeccable personal and sexual life, the family praying together and staying together. And born in the baptismal waters was
the emperor into the church—and the church of the empire. And
thus, at a stroke, was added a quality to the church; one hardly
envisioned by our crucified Lord: the church compatible.

In consequence of these events, or in cause (it is almost impossible to disentangle), a certain critical light is cast on the moral
teachings of popes, in my lifetime and formerly—teaching concerning the self-defense of nations; teachings that, willy-nilly, justify
the guns, simultaneously discharged as they often are, in the frenzy
of mutual murder.

One is led to think of actual war, any war, between "Christian
nations." Each side grasps the holy doctrine, and mounts a charge.
The war is manifestly just, "on our side." The universal pope has

set the norms, the national bishops have applied them, each to its own case, like a powerful magical unguent, guaranteeing a healing victory. Each side proclaims: We are wounded or dishonored or invaded; our cause is just, and shall prevail.

It must all be enormously puzzling to thoughtful folk. Which side is in the right?

In such wise also, the universal church is broken in bits, like a body fallen on a grenade. The church is held up to shame among the nations, including the warmaking nations, who contemn her even as they enlist her blessing. She is held to mockery before true history—which is the evidence not of self-contradicting teachings, contradicted in the act; but a history (her own, in spite of herself) of those who withstood, of the great, humiliated refusers.

What was to be done, what could be done? If the Nine of Catonsville had waited on the bishops or pope, our wait would have been long, and our consciences cooled. Until the hell of the war froze over.

In American chanceries during the terrible decade, if rumor of the war reached their occupants, it sounded as only a distant reverberation, a slight boom on the eardrum, no earthquake. Was the war beating at the door, like a despairing refugee? Did the war portend a kind of creeping catastrophe, a hair's crack in the flagstones of the floor? Nothing of the kind; or if something of the kind, unapprehended. As far as one could judge, all was business as usual. In more than a few dioceses, at the highest levels, there was political mutuality and stroking. And a supposition, suave on the air: the business of the American church is business.

One asked his soul, in near despair with such a church: What of the children of Vietnam, what of the victims of the merciless air raids, what of the Buddhist monks driven to self-immolation, what of the destruction of peasants and land and streams? And equally to the point, what was one to make of a church that could live, in a kind of spurious peace, with such crimes? Did we deserve the name Christian?

In the strange twilight "meantime" of our appeal, the defendants not in jail traveled the land, speaking of our crime, its meaning and consequence. It shortly became clear: the scandal attending our action in both church and state, was, quite simply—nonviolence.

The discovery was capital in my mind, and bears scrunity. State violence, when now and again it is found scandalous in the church, is commonly considered bearable, a matter of toleration, if not of lightheartedness. Almost any level of official violence is sanctioned. The gears hum and turn: how much violence, how tolerable. The answers emerge: in effect, almost any level. Or, at very least, the present level. Tolerable. Prosit.

The seven (or nine, or twelve) rules of justification of war lurch forth, for all the world like the classic figures of a steeple clock. The law, the law! It will tell the hour right!

Only let someone contradict the clock, dare cry "Murder!"

Alas, the scandal is the denial of violence, the interference with violence, the interruption: the shocking symbols, the untidiness, the blood, the fire—of nonviolence.

The violence, on the other hand, is inherent, normal, bearable: indeed, it owns and oils the very engine of reality. The meaning of the times, the meaning of the hour, are told, accurate to the moment, and vindicated in the tolling, by the clock in the cathedral tower. And who is to say Nay?

Alarms and rumors were sweeping the Cornell campus when school resumed in September.

There had been a period of high rejoicing and congratulation after the burning of the Catonsville files. Then a different mood set in. By the autumn of '68, the older antiwar organization, SDS, was dissolving, with a view toward a new incarnation, the Weathermen. And these new warriors did not, to say the least, stand in our corner.

I met old friends, a new look in their eyes. It was not that they expected me to change stance, or take up a gun, or to justify such. They knew me too well for that. But their lives had spun about: they had entered deep waters, and were drifting toward terrifying shoals. They were playing, in fact, an old game in a fresh costume. Willy-nilly, they were fast becoming highly secular, fervent enthusiasts of the old just-war theory; a theory of which they were, by and large, in wondrous ignorance. They were embracing a new form of the old impasse.

For centuries we had been plagued by just war of the right: colonial wars, wars of domination and settlement and economic control. Now wondrously, unveiled before us, was a new realization of the ancient theory. We had just wars of the left.

It was notable that the new twist on the old theology was not developed in a vacuum, but in the course of actual war. So, inevitably, the theory became self-justifying. One breathed the passion around! The peace movement was becoming a crowd of veritable fire-eaters. If ever there was a just cause, it was that of the Vietnamese people. And, by clear implication, the cause of those who supported the just cause—must itself be considered just.

And further: if those under immediate assault, the Vietnamese, were armed, and justly so—then, according to sane opinion, why not their supporters?

It is not often one is allowed to see a theory coalesce before his eyes, and set people marching about face, to an entirely new drumbeat. Prior to these events, my young friends on campus and I had been obliged to stir our imaginations, to improvise tactics as we went. Of infinitely more import: we had been gifted with a common assumption of trust and the rejection of violence. Our meetings were open, spontaneous, rowdy at times, in the will to give everyone a hearing. Decisions were arrived at in freedom. Friendship, standing by one another, flourished: it was the heart of our lives.

Now all was changed. And with heartbreaking abruptness.

One thing was clear to me, in a general confusion of spirit: I had a great deal to learn about human epiphanies and mutations under stress. Certainly my background left me unprepared for the drama, pain, uprooted morality, as I was then witnessing, and with much distress of heart, among the students.

I had come of age in a church that, for all its shortcomings, honored vows and promises. In important matters (always excepting the vexed question of war)—in matters that touched on life and death and innocence and marriage and the vindication of the poor—in these, at least, Christians were blessed with coherent moral guidance.

I had examples before me in the people of the church, especially in laypeople and nuns, of those who lived to the hilt the life commended by the Gospel. Such were my people. And some among them were of my immediate family.

I was thus hardly prepared for what met my eyes in the course of that autumn of '68. I had absorbed a far different conception of human nature, its conduct in crisis. Perhaps I had been a gull? Had presumed that a definition of the human was held in common in the religious and the secular communities?

There was yet another block to my understanding. I had little sense of how difficult it was to construct an ethical life, whole cloth. The students were obliged to do this, with little help, and often many a hindrance, from family, professors, peers. The construction was a task so nearly impossible as to be accounted a dream: my own. Even that handful of teachers who might offer light on a philosophy of human nature, or the history of religion, or biblical literature, or faiths of the world (and these were the closest anyone dared approach the forbidden topic in the deist stronghold)—even these, in practice, failed.

The students, those who inclined to religious inquiry, were offered courses that amounted to a kind of smorgasbord of the spirit. The SDS leaders, in their passage from chrysalis to Weathermen, were, in any case, totally disinterested.

Few of the students, and none of the leadership, had known a sacramental moment, a Passover or Eucharist. They were secular children of a ruinous culture, armed only with desperation and their own wits. They were the best and brightest; well schooled in problematics and politics. Some of them were also to become fairly skilled in the use of explosives and guns.

But of a tradition, mystery, prayer, sacrament, Bible, they were the unborn. It was a loss that explains much in the events that followed.

Their professors were another matter. Few or none of them had any perceptible trust in political action. They believed in something they were pleased to call the life of the mind. What they taught was, in consequence, deeply schizophrenic; an illness of which they were the first victims, but by no means the only ones.

I have an image of these eminences. They lead the eager and youthful along a certain path named Wisdom or Tradition. Teacher and neophyte arrive hand in hand, to a point where the path grows obscure. The place is known simply as The Present or Now or, perhaps, Finisterre.

A choice must be made. They part the undergrowth, and a chasm opens just ahead. Shall they, both together, construct a rude bridge? Or risk the leap? Or will each choose a direction, and take the long way round, in hopes of meeting eventually on the other side?

The professor does none of these things. His responsibility is something known as the life of the mind. By definition (his definition), the mind's life lies in broad savannas of theory, paradigm, the past; and whatever light these might cast on the dark thicket. His task ends; here and now, at Finisterre. He goes back.

Of mentors truthful, of priests or shamans, of those of my generation who might have healed the breach—by constructing a bridge, by a leap, even by taking the alternate way toward a common goal—of these there were very few. And all of them but one resided in Annabel Taylor Hall.

I remember that one, and his fate. He was a youthful professor of sociology. His lectures were accounted magical, a mixed tribute, I thought. But they were brilliantly presented, a river of wisdom leading to the sea. The students flocked to hear the wonder worker, who held forth in a hall so large that his voice must be amplified.

No elder professor could hold a candle to him; let alone a microphone, which, even among the tottering and tenured, was seldom required. But, as it transpired, the power and the glory, the future, even the future of the magic man, were not in the microphone, or its magical wielder. These were in the tenured; who, for reasons that can be imagined, were not amused by the magic show. They, after all, were holding sessions of their own; less magical and, at least according to their claim, more nearly joined to the river of wisdom.

Our magician, to put matters shortly, was the subject of two notorious events toward the end of that year. In the first of these, he was voted Outstanding Professor of the University, by an overwhelming student vote. And shortly thereafter, he was denied tenure, and departed the campus for parts unknown.

It was a lesson of note, an exercise in the sovereignty of pure contempt, laced with malice. The tenured faculty were under no obligation to attend to student opinions. They were the original imperialists, they grew inflamed at any challenge to their custody of the sacred shrine. Was there an interloper on their terrain? They had merely to frown, and all was accomplished. The frown was Jovian, thunderous: it set loose a storm.

Thus the breaking of one icon. But there were others, and the young revolutionaries invoked them passionately: Che, Ho Chi Minh especially, then Marx and Lenin, Fanon and Bakunin.

A pantheon, however mixed, ought, I imagined, to be reasonably durable. This one began in communal veneration, proceeded thence, and was transformed into the semblance of a fashion show. It all ended in broken statuary and disarray in the temple.

It was asking an exorbitant outlay that one topple the images in one season, and create new ones in the next. Something is lost to the brain or soul. We had urged students to slow down, even to become votaries of lives and experiences close to home, to study and perhaps arrive at respect for American heroes. The more unlikely, the more removed from current frenzies, the better. We looked about for secular or Christian saints, and found them aplenty on our own landscape: Thoreau, Emerson, Sojourner Truth, Martin Luther King, Jr., Dorothy Day.

The students listened intently, for perhaps a year. Then they changed gods. Ironically, they took on the habits of their professors: they adopted heroes from totally distant cultures. Now we heard much of Guevara, and more of Ho. But what light either of these might cast on the burden, the war, the warmakers and trustees, was not easily grasped.

It was October 1968, and the time of our trial approached. The defendants, and especially myself, were suddenly in an anomalous position. We were adversaries, not only of the government and its war, but of the Cornell Weathermen, who now presumed to speak for the activist students.

To their credit, these newborn romanticists in mufti did not boycott our trial or declare open season on us. For all our stubbornly held nonviolence, we were not placed in the sights of their as yet hypothetical guns. Indeed, the Weather contingent united with others on campus to organize on our behalf a great rally, the largest since the death of Dr. King. Moreover, officials announced no academic penalties against those who missed class to travel to Baltimore. Thus hundreds of students were free to attend their first wartime trial. It seems arguable that their education was in no wise interrupted.

The trial opened. Except for Tom Lewis and Philip, we defendants were green sprouts before the law. It showed at every turn. Our innocence, ironically, proved a strength; perhaps our only one. We were naive before the press, and spontaneous before Judge Thompson, who took on an avuncular air and tut-tutted us mildly, with a view toward more propriety in court.

Before Sachs, the prosecutor, we could only be patient, when his every move, infused heavily with scorn and ego, tempted us to angry contempt. His assistant, a black hireling of no note, has since sunk into merciful oblivion; but Sachs, burdened with no discernible conscience, has risen and risen in public service and servitude.

Thus a Jew and a black prosecuted us. The government had chosen well, for our arguments constantly drew on the extermination policies of the Germans against Jews. And several of the defendants had worked for years among the black urban poor.

We had rounded up a formidable team of defense lawyers, all but one of whom remain our friends to this day. The exception was a Jesuit, who broke with us in a particularly painful and abrupt way. He had agreed, as my friend from seminary days, to join our team at the trial. The trial opened; without explanation, he was absent. When I inquired later, with considerable indignation, as to his reasons, I was treated to a lame response. The tenor being that he was unused to trial practice, and could be of little use to us. Sic transit amicitia.

The trial lasted for one week. We were allowed, under the equable gaze of Judge Thompson, to deliver rather lengthy evidence: the stories of our lives, as these had led each of us to our malfeasance.

These were biographies that were both moving and durable in impact, across the world. On the stand, each defendant told a story, in tones confident or quavering, not without tears. Memories, anecdotes, spanned the continents, from our own country through Latin America, Africa, and Asia. They ranged from the ghettos of American cities to university campuses, from South to North, civil rights, writing, teaching, nursing, carpentering, preaching, building community. In faith and hope, the stories converged.

I resolved within myself that the stories, hanging like a perfume on the stale air of the court, and sending the spectators away in tears—that these must be told again. As they were.

The strategy of the defense was simple to the point of naivete.

Or so we were informed by the solicitous judge. He, after all, would claim the last word; and it would not be in our favor. So he could well afford to advise us gravely: a careful screening of jurors would ensure something referred to as a fair verdict.

We chose the first twelve jurors who presented themselves. We were certain that interviewing ten times that number would not reveal a group less contaminated in attitude or in connection with things military.

The passion of the defendants, the dispassion of the judge, the icy drumbeat set in motion by Sachs, the noisy and crowded evening sessions at the Jesuit church, the street marches, the feverish camaraderie! It seemd, at least for a moment, that all differences were dissolved, in tears, in anger, in common resolve. And then it was over. We had sought a quick trial: we did not wish our consciences sent down a slow legal drain, with many a vapid gurgle. Judge Thompson reminded us with ominous inference: we got what we wanted.

The jurors, if their state of mind were made visible, might have entered the court accoutred in military uniforms. They bore out an earlier insight. There were no civilians in modern war: there were only those suffering one or another degree of the infection of violence. The only relief from the plague was the course we had chosen: injure no one, burn the files, and pay up.

The jury announced their verdict: guilty. Our peers had judged the cure far more reprehensible than the illness. Thus were the choices of each and all narrowed: it was wartime. The court was one with the battlefield, the Pentagon, the Oval Office. One also with the New York chancery.

The war was a total war: civilians also bore arms. Those who impeded were to be tried; to be tried was to be convicted.

The war, those who waged it, were never to stand trial; in Baltimore, or elsewhere. We were to stand trial. It was a reminder, and the times verified it, in the stern drumbeat of Sachs.

Still, the verdict could by no means be construed as our doom, or a final word on our effort. This had been our hope, and the hope was sustained; not immediately, by any means, as hope seldom is. But in the longer haul of months and years. In the course of which two things became clear.

In the first place, warmaking or war preparation would never be tried in an American court.

Still, this or that court, no matter what its crimes against justice, its stacked cards, its vindictive blindness, would never succeed in closing the dossier on conscience. And this was exactly our hope. Time would work in its imperceptible way, mysterious, invisible; other lives would be touched as the stories of the courageous and nonviolent were heard, often by word of mouth only. Time taking its own sweet time, so to speak, the motion and motive of a larger soul.

In November we were sentenced: up to three years. Except for Philip and Tom, we were released on appeal. I returned to Cornell.

My father's health had worsened. He fell to the ground frequently and broke bones, almost as a matter of willfulness, attempting to draw attention to his unalleviated misery. Alas, he was displaced from his home and out of temper with the times. He was, moreover, the last leaf on the family tree. His sisters and brothers had all died; and they, not we, were his lifeline in the world.

In late autumn, I was summoned from Ithaca. His condition was desperate: he had been placed in a center of rehabilitation after a fall, but refused all therapy and food. There was no organic reason, the doctors said, why he should not heal; no reason except the primary one: he had no will to go on.

While there was breath in his body, it was incorrect to describe him as "having no will." His soul was in his will; to be neutral lay outside his powers.

His will was set in another direction, that was all. He lay there, emaciated, withdrawn, turned from life and the living. He turned his face to the wall. In the old days, cringing under his drama, we had summoned his brother the priest, who on occasion could cajole him back for a time to reasonableness. But his brother was long dead; and sons, even priest sons, could do nothing.

We tried. We stood about more or less helplessly, made small talk, offered whatever service came to mind: food, news, books, sweets, smokes. We were received, for the most part, with a stony stare; now and then there was a break in the mood, but never for long.

The situation could not go on. He weakened to a husk: his bones stood out, his face became a beaten mask.

The scene was, in its way, a kind of dark classic. The family, bemused, transfixed by the Irish patriarch who lives on and on, dictating things, exploding, humiliating, prodding, getting his way; and the rest of ye be damned.

But his hold was broken. He was tugging and twitching at the last strands, they were fast giving out. And we grew able, during those fruitless vigils, to judge things sensibly. We were doing all in our power, and that was that. He would be his old self until the end. The patience we were expending on his behalf, without a hint of response—this we owed one another, perhaps first of all.

Thus we kept our sanity. His tactics had hardly changed: they had only entered another phase. From time immemorial he had sought to keep the family in his clutch. The indignity of not measuring up! The standards set by himself and his ineffable sisters and brothers! And we, including the priests, forever falling short!

He was deprived now of his audience, the great ones of his generation, was forced to play in a blank theater his role of tragic hero. No matter if he had no audience: his stature mounted as those about him departed; or, in our case, diminished to a zero.

His old cat's eye looked out on us and past us.

He had sought to break spirits, as he had broken stones and clods on the old farm. My mother had refused to be broken; and, heartened by her courage, so had we. We had refused his measure—of ourselves, of the world, of politics, of the church.

In the old days, the older sons had been forced to fight him. But as time passed, there were other expedients, which my mother had first discovered.

We passed him by, like time's vessels. We found our own lives, and departed his presence. On visits home, we were patient with his monologues and diatribes. Ours was the patience of those who voted no contest, retired from the field. And left him without opponents.

His death thus failed in his calculation: it marked us with no least stain of guilt. We put our humanity to the test of those months, and found it not wanting, either in compassion or devotion. We stood by him, night and day. And we possessed our own souls.

That night in November I kept the watch. He was dying, they said. His breathing was labored, his big, hard hands twitched and started aimlessly. I did my best for him, which was not much: being his son had its inhibitions. He allowed me to hover about, which was something; to take his hand, to say a prayer aloud. And now and then, and unexpectedly, I won a response, an answering tightening of his hand in mine.

He had never been skilled in body language, having only a very small vocabulary of gesture to draw on. It was talk that served him, an enormous, salty range: wit and censure and pronouncement and derision and mimicry.

Indeed, his body was Irish, as was his tongue, and the tongue was nearly all the body's outreach. The body was in need only of such skills as might flog it through the world, safe and serviceable. Stooping for work, bending for religion, striding about, sleeping: all was grudging, minimal; love and affection most of all. It was said he had been a great dancer and one could well believe it: he had the body for it. But my memory is of a stiffened uprightness that allowed nothing supple or flowing or freely given: life was no drift downstream, no cavorting to a penny whistle.

Toward morning there came a gesture, when he was long past talk. The gesture was minimal, in the way of the dying. I recited the Lord's Prayer, he held my hand, who had never done so.

It had always been that unbearable man-to-man handshake, quick and hard. But there, for a minute or so, his hand lingered in mine. It was a touch, a lingering that redeemed. A faint hint of tenderness, and he was gone.

My brother Jerry was summoned; we gathered the small effects in a brown paper sack, kissed him solemnly on the brow, and departed.

My mother wept quietly. She was much comforted, she declared, that "someone in the family, especially yourself" was with him. Then she perked up. She had no mourning to don for the wake; and would someone please see to this?

We waked him in our style, not his. The Irish remnant tottered in from city and countryside to pay respects. Few were extant from the vaunted old days when, as we had so often been told, they would arrive at the house of the dead in great numbers, their "Democrat wagons" loaded with food and drink for the three-day wake, and the mass, and the funeral feast. And because the Tipperary clan prospered, we heard marvelous tales of the carriages and four, blocking Matson Avenue at my grandmother's funeral.

Ours was an unconventional rite: to the vast disappointment of the ancient Irish mourners, there was no viewing at all, but a plain, closed box, the cheapest available. After the mass, we hauled his bones, in the rear of a station wagon, into the hills above Syracuse. We buried him there, among his own, within a stone's throw from the farm where he had been born.

It was part of the high drama he could ignite that his friends, especially the nuns and priests, considered him an exemplary specimen, a very paragon of the sanctified. And this was no mere pious twaddle, doled out for the event of death. I watched my mother, as the Irish approached her with condolences: how privileged she had been in her marriage, how tragically deprived she must feel. And her lips never twitched.

Such self-control had been years in the testing. We had heard the like encomiums over the years, concerning a person totally other than the one we dwelt with. He was an ideal gentleman, by implication an ideal spouse and father. He moved in the world bathed in an aura of virtue radiating outward, presumably reflected back on us. It must be so. There we stood, his family, struck blind in the midst of a supernal light.

Were we missing something? It could not be doubted we were. With that admission, and the added codicil that those who so exalted him also missed something; with that one closes the book, as a grave is closed against the last day, its merciful judgment.

Our Catonsville appeal dragged on for two years, 1968 to 1970, but I heard little of it; and to all purposes, cared less. There was the usual round of campus duties, there was the war, like a fixed state of nature, there was travel and speaking out. The rumor, all unexpected, reached us that Nixon was amenable to a deal. Philip and Tom might be released from jail if Jimmy Hoffa, like Phil a prisoner in Lewisburg, were also let go. And so, without any effort on our part, it transpired toward Christmas of '68. A celebration indeed.

On campus, events hottened up. Opposition was growing against the Taylor Hall community and its unkempt crowd of pacifists and poets. The reaction centered on the fraternities, whose mansions lay in a circle about the campus. This was a segment of the community with which we were utterly out of touch: sons of Cornell alumni, scions of the business world.

That numbers of these students were indifferent to us, we could easily conclude. But that they hated what we stood for, and felt ignored and silenced on campus: this we took little account of.

In hindsight, the event should not have issued in shock; but it did. We might have been better prepared, were our ears attentive to the winds. But we were overbusy, preoccupied with the rush of event; and beyond doubt naive. In any case, it came to pass with the absolute crash of a falling sky. On a spring midnight in 1969, the chapel of Taylor Hall was firebombed and gutted to a shell.

We had misread a message; or perhaps the message was never delivered. In any case, there the ruin lay, a million dollars in damage; damage wreaked not against any random building, but against our place of worship, the scene of much prayer, of midnight vigils and fasts against the war, of weddings and baptisms and funerals, a place sacred to generations of students and faculty and graduates.

The following morning, the interior of the chapel would remind many of Coventry Cathedral after the terrible night of bombing in 1945. Few missed the analogy. In Taylor Chapel, moreover, a charred cross lay, trashed there. We propped it up against the broken altar.

Violence had come home. We had swallowed too easily the presumption of the university that something fondly referred to as "civilized discourse" could be relied on to resolve, or at least to mitigate, serious differences. We viewed the wreckage and shook our heads in disbelief: nothing of the sort. There were beyond doubt elements on campus for whom such genteel assumptions were a front, behind which they could make their move in ways appallingly direct..

Then another shattering event. The Student Union was occupied by armed blacks; they made their exit eventually from the building, armed and arrogant, amid a throng of watchers, and a great silence. The photo of the armed warriors and their bandoliers went like a shot around the world.

And finally, to cap the onslaught of the irrational, toward spring of 1970, as the campus essayed a first deep breath of relief, the Black Studies building was destroyed by fire.

There are ghettos and ghettos. The religious occupants of Taylor Hall had lived too long in the vortex of peaceable intent, relatively unopposed. We had concluded, perhaps inevitably, that our great adversary was indifference, an attitude never in short supply. But we underestimated the fury of a wave even then gathering force in secret. It was a tidal wave, it sought a larger prey than Cornell.

That year, the wave washed over the continent and its institutions, brief, shattering—a reminder of something in the culture not taken properly in account. Domestic violence, envy, a sense of being unmoored, being relegated early in one's life to the sidelines, cast into merciless winds—in one way or another, excluded.

We had opposed the war, but we had failed to make peace. That was the plain truth; it was set down in letters of fire on the chapel wall. Bitter and violent spirits detested our brand of religion, as well as our politics. And to demonstrate their contempt for both, they sent fiery vessels crashing through the chapel windows, and reduced the noble space to a shambles.

It was a lesson so conceived as to speed one's literacy in reading the signs of the times, the frenzies the times were unleashing. Cornell, I reflected, was producing three types. There were those who saw the war as a horror to be opposed with all one's might; those who went their appointed rounds, thinking few serious thoughts; and those others (and of their disposition I knew nothing) who might presumably oppose us. But in any case, these latter were beside the point, because they did not collide with our orbit. Or so we had fondly thought.

Collide they had; and the collision set us wobbling for weeks.

It was greatly to the credit of the community so assaulted that its work was in no way broken off, or even seriously interrupted. Other quarters were found in which worship was held, the building continued to hum away, day and night.

The early spring of 1970 brought a crisis of another sort. The carnage of the war was expanding, as was the reckless rhetoric that sought to justify the event. The Catonsville appeal was running out.

Then the date was set; we were ordered to turn ourselves in and begin serving our prison terms.

One of the nine evaded the summons. He was David Darst, youngest of our group, member of the Christian Brothers community—a Christian and a brother indeed. David had perished in 1969, victim of a highway tragedy in the Midwest. En route with others to visit a prisoner, the car had unaccountably collided, in a rainstorm, with a trailer carrying a load of combustible fuel. All in the car had died on the spot.

For many of us, it was as though a hole had opened in the universe, and someone dear beyond words had fallen out of life. David was a rare spirit; his life of twenty-four years was a concentrate of love and compassion. He had taught in the St. Louis ghetto and lived among the poor, had renounced carrying a draft card and been convicted for the act.

In the midst of such trials, he had joined us at Catonsville, in a way that seems, even at this remove, little short of miraculous. He had read of the Baltimore action; had written, expressing his willingness to join whatever the future might open.

Until we were locked up in the county jail, I hardly was acquainted with David. But the close quarters of jail are nothing if not a precipitate—whether toward anger or amiability. I grew quickly to love David, as did we all, for his candor and good humor under stress, his stature of intellect and spirit.

For my part, his decision to join us at Catonsville helped relieve me of a gnawing suspicion. Alone as I was among Jesuits, I must be crazy under the moon. I reminded myself; I was not alone, Philip had chosen before me. Then David, also a member of a religious order, made a like choice, and so blessed my own.

That spring, the eight Catonsville survivors met to discuss the immediate future. There was a sense that we were facing both a great opportunity and a great danger.

On the one hand, it was a strict canon of nonviolence that one took the consequences of illegal activity and paid up. On the other, there was the war. When would it end, what had we accomplished, if anything, toward its ending?

We had to admit it. Our action at Catonsville, and all the draft board actions since then, had failed even to mitigate the war. And the question arose: must we submit to the punishing arm of the same powers that were pursuing the war?

It was a harsh dilemma, an utterly new field of moral decision. The alternative to turning ourselves in was also narrow. It meant that we must disappear underground, become fugitives, involve others in a netwrok of conspiracy, risk further charges and longer sentences.

No one of us had ever lived in the underground: its demands, its loneliness, its cutoff from friendship and work. These were daunting realities, even in prospect.

There was also the question of public understanding, and our responsibility. Consistency and moral coherence were much on our minds. We surmised we had helped the Catholic community to make of the war a matter of debate, then of unease, even of scorn. We had helped raise questions never before argued in the church. And our conduct in the two years since Catonsville, whether during trial or public appearances or time in jail, had left little room for sound criticism.

These were solid achievements; their undoing would be a tragedy for all concerned. We knew it, and the knowledge hurt.

But if there was hurt, there was also a strange and fierce elation. A choice before us: to delay the unwarrantedly high price exacted for an act of conscience! And more: a chance to underscore once more, in a highly imaginative way, our opposition to the war.

Hours of reflection and prayer followed. We sensed, from the moment the discussion opened, that we would come to different decisions: some would choose to go to jail, some would not. I marvel to recall that different choices lessened not a whit our affection for one another. We were tasting the rewards of endurance; and the fruit was sweet indeed.

My own decision was fairly easy; but I feared for Philip, who already faced a long sentence, six years. Further interference with the gears of law would bring on a storm of retaliation. But I knew at heart that he would not submit: the truth was the only burden he chose to carry.

I remember an airline flight back to Cornell after one such session with the Eight. The plane left the great urban clot, shortly entered the dreamlike verdant Lake Country of the Southern Tier, approaching my El Dorado. I could sense the intoxicating breath of spring renewing the earth once again, in spite of all. The land of singing waters was unlocked, green, innocent. In spite of all our folly, and the war that would not end.

It was so easy to come once more to earth—then to come to terms, not with war, which, after all, left Cornell acres immune, innocent, unspoiled (the innocence of prestige and pride of place).

Harder to come to terms with Cornell itself—that seductive fiction—fantasy masked as reality, as one's due, as the gift of God to sedulous servants, furthering the holy will. And so on.

The facts of life stopped short at the gates: one entered a climate of mind, a supreme fiction. And once one walked those acres, the fictions of privilege and plenty took on the straightfaced look of fact, even the truth of things.

CHAPTER 10

Unless the Seed Falls: Underground

QUERY: Shall one then return
to the womb of his mother, reborn?

JESUS: As you said. Earth, old basket-born
hard-beaked hen
wants you for egg.

I hereby (he scrawled
inside his shell)
attest to my first

Will & Testament.
I shall go forth
bare assed as a new moon,
stellar as baby Jesus.
Everyone's sight and scandal.
Yes & No &
the vast milky Perhaps between.

I returned to the land of persuasive dream, but I kept my head. My decision was taken, once for all. The future, and its practical forms, was obscure: I could do no better than commend the virtue of hope to my soul—hope, a virtue like a single hair of head; by which, we are told, angels are wont to transport the endangered to safety.

I made known my decision to go underground. Cornell friends took the news well, to their honor and my delight. Quickly they formed a first circumference of this new circle of danger. They saw, without undue palaver, the reason for my decision. And in helping me, they put their own futures on the line. Consolations were burgeoning, along with losses.

It was the same with my family; at least with those we gave the news to. They may have quaked, and swallowed hard, absorbing yet another episode of derring-do. But they allowed us the presumption that love grants: in this case, that Philip and I had sweated through all pros and cons; that our decision had a long-belabored history, over which there was no point in lingering. They stood by our decisions, as we could see in their eyes, their embrace, their unfailing love.

The brother Jerry, his wife, Carol! Their story merits, in the annals of goodness and even of heroism, a longer telling than is possible in these pages. They had suffered the loss of a child, had adopted, in succession, four infants. Jerry is a respected college teacher; Carol in due time finished her degree, and proceeded to become a powerful advocate for the disabled, as well as a teacher of teachers.

I set down these clumsy notes, impossibly syncopating the years during which they stood with one another, with our aging parents, with all of us. Jerry is a professor burdened and blessed with a conscience: an all but extinct breed in the age of failsafe. Together with his daughter Carla, he has been sentenced repeatedly to federal jails for his antinuclear actions.

Inaccurate then to say that my brother and his family entered our conspiracy: they had always stood within it. The news we brought them was new only as a tactic. In a deeper sense, it was no news at all, but another phase of life, theirs and ours, lived accountably; and with what consequences, we knew beforehand.

The appointed time was near. On a mild April night, as the hour of the locust approached, my own hour struck, and I vanished under the new moon, into a realm of invisibility.

There were metaphors aplenty awaiting me in shadow and moonlight; and solitude to explore them; and, for a great change, time aplenty to search out the meaning of my new state of being.

I thought of the Chinese proverb placing certain times somewhere between a blessing and a curse: the time ahead was to be, in that special, ironic sense, interesting.

There was the image of death; and this my minor rehearsal or preamble. I was dying to the last turbulent tears. And the rub was not that I was departing an easeful existence or a soft job at Cornell. I had walked uneasily there, with a weather eye out for the flourishing of my soul, and a sidelong eye wary of the threats and incursions of dolce vita.

No, the death was—the end of friendship and access and the faces I loved. This was indeed closing the lid of a tomb.

Then there occurred a monastic, a cenobitic, image: one more nearly to the point of twilit attic rooms and hidden gardens, a hermetic image. I would know much solitude in the times ahead; and considerable loneliness.

In any case. I took along, in my baggage, a manuscript biography of Bonhoeffer, in preparation for writing an essay review. In the solitude of the back country, I meditated on the volume, and set down preliminary notes, a work of some two weeks.

My disappearance was not as yet a matter of public note, though word reached me that the FBI was on the prowl in my apartment and about the campus.

Then the news came of preparations for an immense antiwar rally at Cornell. And an urgent invitation: Would I be willing to attend and, under those circumstances, to make a public surrender to the law?

By this time, the disappearance of four of the Eight was beginning to attract notice. Here was something new and bizarre in the record of the Catholic left. Speculation was vivid: might the Eight be joining the Weather Underground, who had already vanished, after a series of bombings? Might the similarity of outrage and tactic signal an agreement: that violence was now the order of the day, for both groups?

The wires were fairly buzzing with speculation. The media, whose addiction to violence is matched only by its contemptuous indifference to nonviolence, were poised for the pounce: to announce the grand, hypothetical leap in the void of those grown witless and disenchanted.

The media were, alas, to be grievously disappointed.

Out of my rural solitude, on a faultless spring night, I duly made a sudden descent at Cornell, into the lights and noise and electric air of Barton Hall. Disorienting! I arrived on campus with an apocalyptic roar, a dazed passenger on a gargantuan, smoky motorbike. I was disguised, head to toe, as appropriate to sharp April weather, in the helmet, goggles, and coverall of a cyclist fresh from the open road.

The prior arrangement was a simple one. In the course of the music, mime, and speeches, I would deliver a statement, explaining the weeks of disappearance, relating the decision to the expansion of Nixon's war. Then I would submit to the FBI.

A flock of agents was visible in the crowd. Presumably disguised, they were dressed incongruously in hippie garb, radio antennae sprouting about their heads like the feelers of insects.

Then came a strange turnaround of event. The Bread and Puppet Theater had finished their splendid mime of the Last Supper. The lights went down. A rock band was assembling onstage. In the darkness, a whisper reached my ear: Why not disappear once more? We can help. . . .

If I agreed, it must be done quickly.

I agreed. The band was taking its place. In the disarray and noise and darkness, I was given hasty instructions. Something large and encompassing went over my head; a pole was thrust into my hand; I was instructed sotto voce to grasp an unknown hand, and follow, follow.

Thus concealed under the immense papier-mâché head of an apostle, I made my escape; into the night once more, blind as a midnight bat.

A spot decision. It was the way we get born, I reflected later; or the way we would do so, given a choice. But how would we choose?

The choices come before us like blind suppliants; the very substance of life. And oftener than we would admit, they are ignored or renounced, and depart like rejected lovers. Too much, their implication of blindness and trust and the yawn of the unknown. . . .

I went out. Is this also the way we die, I thought, assuming enormous good luck—the hand of a friend to lead the way and see us through?

In any case; in a moment, my life spun around once more.

It would be easy to make of the event a mere romantic caper, or quash its meaning in a welter of sentiment. I hope I was beyond all that. What fun! I grinned in the double dark: the sack over my head, the night beyond. And I both serious and lighthearted.

I had ample time, in the months following, to consider that

night, that choice, its rightness or folly. It came to me that something extremely simple was implied. I was trying, in a bad time rapidly worsening, to walk a consistent path.

Consistency was the difficulty, for myself and the others of Catonsville who, like myself, were vanishing, holding out. We wanted to say that because the war had worsened (Nixon had invaded Cambodia in April, the air war in Vietnam was more brutal than ever), we had decided to step up our resistance. Not in taking up weapons, a venture we considered foolhardy and fruitless, but by dramatizing our noncompliance.

In the months that followed, I was never granted the luxury of catching breath or settling for long in one place. The time of family and friends and a settled existence was over, for the duration. I read a line from Dante, mourning his exile: "Eating another's salt, walking another's stair." It fitted, with a bitter aptness.

I took stock of my resources. If I had let go of much, in the way of amenities and predictabilities, not all was lost by any means.

First of all, and precious beyond calculus, I had good friends; to convey me about discreetly, to house and feed me; in sum, to take their chances, along with myself. I discovered once more—the truest friendship meant far more than a mere convergence of interest. We were not so much pursuing a tactic together (though that was certainly implied). We were exploring our humanity, uncovering lost resources, meriting new graces, even summoning new skills.

Such realization sometimes brought me to tears, lodged as I was like a ghostly ancestor in someone's attic, or pacing outdoors in a secluded yard. Meantime, beyond doubt, my name festered away in the files (extremely active files, as it turned out) of the Punishment Brigade of the FBI. And this my friends and I took in account, as mandating prudence.

But the thought of pursuit lay somewhere at the back of my mind, and the minds of those who were of truest and deepest account to me. In the forefront, in the heart, love and respect flourished; and the intriguing thought of the advantage we might gain for the peace movement from my situation.

Friendship; and other necessary strengths. These must lie in myself, as I knew. I was a writer of sorts, and out there lay a public, increasingly uneasy in face of the wastrel war. How reach them, from where I dwelt, how continue to batter away at the truth?

I was like one of those crustaceans that, losing a limb by mishap, grows another in its place. If I must rove, anonymous, pseudonymous, displaced—still other ways opened, other tasks beckoned. Under guise and disguise, plotting and planning, old and useful things could be pursued: writing, meeting quietly with friends, even speaking in public.

We shortly set about such matters.

There was ill news to swallow: one after another, the undergrounders were run to ground; I was the sole survivor.

The capture of one of the Eight, George Mischi, roused me to a fury. The hounds of justice had burst into his aerie, their fangs bared—with drawn guns.

I resolved to issue in response a kind of *défi*. To this effect: it was a matter of public knowledge that my friends and I had disallowed, all our lives, the possession or use of arms. The fact must be known, even to the minions of law. It was therefore a disgrace that such people as ourselves were apprehended by gunmen, breaking and entering and brandishing their lethal hardware.

Further: in the event that they ran me to ground also, they had best do so without arms; or the world would hear of their violence.

The word got about. There was a note of cold comfort in the outcome. When, some months later, I was taken, it was by a whole coven of agents. But not a firearm was in sight; or, as far as could be learned, out of sight either.

I recall a few examples of what might be called, in a more normal setting, works in progress.

I was informed that a television interview could be arranged. I respected the work of the reporter suggested; and was assured that he would be sensitive to the issue of my safety.

We rendezvoused finally in a remote country motel. The preparations for the event were somewhat breathless and, in retrospect, hilarious. It was like a comic strip episode of Hairbreadth Harry: every installment a crisis.

Split-second timing! Thirdhand, secondhand, firsthand preparations! Testing! Dry run! Assembling the crew! Swearing to secrecy!

Everything went without a hitch. The media were capable of a measure of courage. After all, the war was hanging about everyone's neck, a stinking albatross; and what had CBS to lose?

So the reasoning went, a reasoning that, however slavish to market or mood, was still to my advantage.

My interlocutor, Edwin Newman, proved charming and intelligent, quite equal to the occasion. The camera crew were unexpectedly moved by the event. One of them motioned me aside after the filming: he offered to contribute his earnings of the day. Further, he offered refuge in his home, did need arise. It was all quite extraordinary.

Thus there were consolations in Gideon; sudden and unexpected.

A message arrived from the Weather Underground. Would I agree to an exchange of views; if not in person, perhaps by cassette? Could we discuss violent tactics of resistance, and nonviolent?

My reflections were duly recorded and dispatched. I learned years later, from one of those addressed, that the message had been received; had, in fact, a large impact on reassessing their position.

Especially helpful, I was told, was my insistence that the loss of a single life could never be justified by ideology, however noble.

I had an eerie sense that such messages as these were almost literally sealed in bottles and cast to the tides. Would they be lost at sea? Or, against all odds, would they arrive in someone's hands, be read and pondered? I could not know.

The not knowing became a parable of existence itself; and, in a darksome way, underscored the need of integrity. And even acted as its guarantee. One was in the dark—as to the worth, result, impact, political wisdom, of what one was about. Indeed, the tags and credentials of right action were of no account in my circumstance. I felt at times like the last survivor of human folly, scrawling on a blank wall some half-remembered emblem or word, whose meaning evaded my own mind.

What was I accomplishing? What was the effect of this blind pilgrimage—on the war, on the future, on others? I simply did what seemed right at the time, deprived of all normal means of judging the outcome. I moved in darkness and desolation. From time to time, through the good offices of a friend, a gesture, an unexpected kindness, a flare was struck. But only enough light to allow me next immediate step. Then the flare went out, and darkness descended once more.

Now and again came a sense of a providential, caring God. The inkling was seldom consoling, most often dark, a God of Job, an argument and questioning on my part; not invariably good tempered. A faith that did its sorry best, sweating out the times.

Still, a quite Buddhist concentration of mind. I knew nothing of the future. Only the next move—a move invariably taken in trepidation; but still with all my might, concretely and simply.

And then—the act was let go, its truth and goodness were entrusted to the four winds. Indeed, good consequences were a small matter to me, compared with the integrity of the action, the need responded to, the spirits (as I was reassured on occasion) lifted.

I was learning. It seems just to add that my learning never stopped. Some fifteen years after the events discussed, it gives me joy to report that I still seek out the Mystery, that One whose name is Shepherd or Invited or Friend at the Door or Jesus the Obscure or Holy Mother or The Poor One or The Distant Neighbor—or perhaps The Wounded Love, who wears a nimbus of thorn about a magisterial head.

The spring of '70 broke early; it was the most beautiful in my memory, deeply charged with the perfume of event, friendship, loss and gain, loneliness, and the soul's unmistakable voices. A strange, lightheaded sense overtook me: too much, too quickly, a very onslaught of reality.

The war worsened, the campuses were a flare of outrage. Jackson State and Kent State became bywords of shame. And in May, my play, The Trial of the Catonsville Nine opened in Los Angeles.

The director, Gordon Davidson, had asked me to prepare a taped message for the opening night audience. The news of the opening had reached me, of course, in rustication. The tape was prepared and sent. It was reported that when my voice sounded through the theater, a number of otherwise nondescript ticketholders leapt to their feet. They were FBI agents hoping, evidently, that ego or revolutionary fervor or some such nonsense would draw me into their net.

It quickly became clear that though the voice might be mine, the quarry was nowhere in sight. The agents sank back, crestfallen,

The Public Years

The Catonsville Nine issue from court after sentencing in October 1968. We were convicted of burning draft files in Maryland. The sentencing I named "the greatest day of our lives" up to that point. *Bob Fitch/Black Star.*

The moment of felonious truth. The draft files, carried to a parking lot, are burned with homemade napalm. Baltimore, Maryland, 1968. *UPI/Bettmann Newsphotos.*

I was captured by FBI agents on Block Island, Rhode Island. They were unpersuasively decked out in yellow slickers, posing as bird-watchers—in the course of a hurricane—on August 12, 1970. No birds were visible for miles. *UPI/Bettmann Newsphotos.*

On December 14, 1970, Philip and I were taken to court from Danbury federal prison. Our (hardly) chic getup is standard prison issue—so are the chains. *UPI/Bettmann Newsphotos.*

Friends arrive in snowy weather to welcome me out of Danbury prison on February 24, 1972.
UPI/Bettmann Newsphotos.

Father Ned Murphy, S.J., and I hold a banner outside of St. Patrick's Cathedral in New York during Nixon's Christmas bombing of Hanoi in 1972. *UPI/Bettmann Newsphotos.*

A decade after Vietnam, Philip and I are in no wise rehabilitated. In Morristown, Pennsylvania, on February 23, 1981, we are in court again. Our crime: bashing unarmed nuclear warheads and pouring our blood. Verdict: guilty. Sentence: three to ten years. Appeal: continuing. *AP/Wide World Photos.*

April 18, 1981, I speak at a New York rally, "U.S. Out of El Salvador." ©*Bettye Lane*.

to the amusement of the audience. One can only hope that, in one way or another, the hounds of Hoover received sound moneys' worth of the evening.

Another episode concerned my family. My mother's health was worsening; no doubt her illness was due in measure to the worry and uncertainty of the time. She was hospitalized in late spring, conveyed once more to St. Joseph's Hospital, where, in our childhood, she had been a TB patient.

The FBI were, of course, interested in her whereabouts, as a clue to my own. Was it not logical, according to their ethos, that a dutiful son would appear at his mother's bedside, she being aged and frail, and he a priest?

They enlisted the hospital nuns to monitor her and her visitors; to report, because she was afflicted with fever and nightmares, any word that might offer a clue.

The nuns, of a local Franciscan order, were happy to oblige. More, on their own initiative, they made clear their disapproval of my family and its misdeeds, through a contemptuous neglect of my mother, helpless as she was.

She had always been indifferent to comfort. But this was a matter of maltreatment. She broke down before my brother: she was "dying in this place"; and must be removed to another hospital, sooner the better. And that same day, an ambulance conveyed her out of the precincts of the implacable virgins.

I reflected on the many ways in which, willy-nilly, the Jesuits had prepared me for that time. During the seminary years our rule allowed only infrequent visits from family; visits home were rare indeed, and invested with the excitement of a state occasion.

Such discipline, enforced for so long a time, made my separation in '70, if not easily borne, at least bearable; and on my mother's part, sure of concurrence.

Thus spring passed into summer. My arrival in this or that household was prepared by "those in charge." I was invariably welcomed, marveling at the courage such a welcome, offered a fugitive, implied in the hosts.

In one house, I came on an edition of St. John of the Cross: *The Dark Night of the Soul*. For me too, I thought ruefully, dawn was long in coming. I meditated on the travail of the saint, celebrated so grandly in his great poem. It occurred to me that a clue to the seemingly opaque and useless days and nights lay in the imagery he explored. I too was walking a tunnel of night, in which there seemed neither middle nor end, rhyme nor reason. In the dark, I stumbled about amid intricate turns and twists. The tunnel was eerily silent, but for my own breathing. I could carry nothing with me; I had a sense of accomplishing nothing. Life was void: an unrelieved present without prospect or outcome.

The voices that spoke in me seemed to issue only from the aroused dead, stirred at my passing, and I all but one of them. Of the living, among whom I moved like one disembodied, a ghost, none underwent my passage, or could pretend to with any veracity. Under the tigerish eye of the law I saw, as though with a third eye, normal life proceeding without me: people moving about their business and pleasure, children at play, commerce, families intact. But I, was I one of the living or the dead?

There were beckoning hands: other hands held out bowls of food for the beggar. Then the hands withdrew, they knew the limits of their estate—and mine.

To speak of God—I remember only an ache, a void, as though of a breath indrawn and held, until it hurt. God was absence. Not nothing, but Someone who had withdrawn for the duration, where, I knew not. I heard only the voice of a messenger, angel or tempter: "You're on your own."

I began work on a manuscript, *The Dark Night of Resistance*, modeled on St. John of the Cross.

I learned later how a great stir was growing, both in public sympathy for me and in the covens of law and order. But of these developments I could know very little at the time.

Philip, now captive once more, wrote from prison to a friend. He observed that my dance through the underground was "the only thing of note going on, by way of an imaginative and valuable resistance."

And as for Mr. Hoover, exasperation grew, as I continued to provoke arrest with outrageous sallies into the eye of the storm.

The Catonsville Nine drama was flourishing in California, and shortly was to open in New York. My "Letter from the Underground," addressed to the Weather Underground, was also published, amid considerable comment.

There was one singular disappointment. It was by no means cat-astrophic, and I leave the moral of it to others.

Such activities as I undertook, both at Catonsville and after, often fall like a blade: they prove, in one way or another, divisive. Friends wave a farewell, and one sees them no more. And at the same time, mere acquaintances or even strangers move to one's side, all un-expectedly. Thus new friends are born, old friends fall away.

So it happened that a renowned university chaplain, in whose sanctuary I had preached in more tranquil times, was approached. Would he approve my appearing from underground, offering a Sun-day congregation a biblical reflection, and vanishing?

He turned the proposal down without explanation; though the refusal implied its reason clearly enough.

Still, work opened up in unexpected directions. The days were so occupied that they mocked any temptation to boredom or de-pression of spirit.

And there was also time, time to do nothing. Everything beautiful my eyes lit on in the burgeoning summer had about it a shadow, a plaint—as of something held, and then let go before its time. High summer in the air—and yet an autumnal mood. Letting go was at least half the having.

And compared with holding or grasping, letting go offered twice the discipline and many times the reward.

A death image again. I was to learn many years after, in my work of solacing the dying, the meaning of that letting go. I would see hands loosen their hold on the world, grow lax, abandon what I can only clumsily call a death grip—on illusion, untruth, posses-sions—a grip that makes for bad living and worse dying.

It was mid-August. We embarked on the most outrageous project of all. The proffer came through a pastor in suburban Philadelphia. Would I preach at his church, at the regular Sunday service?

Subterranean tremors! Everything must be taken in account, weighed, discussed heatedly. Was it an idea of substance, or a grandstand play? Was it worth the risks? Would it further exasperate the hunters, intensify the chase?

It seemed, after all, worth trying. Through a sermon, a message could be conveyed to Christians, in specifically religious surround-ings: namely, that being wanted in such times should be considered normal by peacemakers. This should be stated with peculiar force, in such a place. And for once, media and message could be startlingly one—a drama, the perils of peacemaking, a reminder, moreover, of its evangelical blessing.

And so it transpired. All necessary precaution was taken. The episode was filmed, and appeared later as a moment in the documentary *The Holy Outlaw*.

(And toward that autumn, the film was shown in Danbury prison. I recall the delight of the prisoners, their spontaneous applause, as the heinous career of one in their midst was set forth.)

My appearance at the church, and the subsequent safe exit, were in the nature of a last straw laid on a broad dromedary back. From that day, Mr. Hoover would spare nothing to bring me to ground. Sensing something of this, we resolved on a quick move to a new safe house.

News of the decision was transmitted, secretly (as we fondly thought) to Philip in prison. In so passing the word we were naive indeed, and the outcome was calamitous; as wiser heads than ours might have foretold. The letter into Lewisburg prison was intercepted and handed over to authorities by a prisoner who was also an informer.

For me it was to be the end of the road; and for many others, the start of a ruinous conspiracy roundup. Mr. Hoover would presumably have the last word on our fate; or so nearly the last as to make little difference. The end fell of a grand and daring adventure. There lay ahead the breakup of the so-called Catholic resistance, and the first ominous rumblings of the Harrisburg trial.

We made mistakes aplenty, if it is required to say so yet again. As our fortunes turned, there were no lack of friends or strangers to call us fervently to account. Philip, for trusting so evident a loser as the informant, so limp and canny an underdog and betrayer, his eye alert only for the main chance. And I was rounded on for repairing, at so dangerous a juncture, to Block Island, a geography of no exit. Thereby, so the theory went, I assured my capture.

Psychology was resorted to in explanation of my delict. I was evidently afflicted, according to instant experts, with world-weariness or fatalism or despair. And so invited capture, or even longed for it.

There was little doubt in my mind, given the clamor that arose in otherwise liberal throats, that my sojourn in the nether regions had offered a vicarious life to many—observing, as they did, and from safe distance, the moves, epiphanies, and vanishings. Much emotion, even a measure of borrowed integrity, had been invested in my "success."

With the cuffs on my wrists, I would have ample time, at government expense, to reflect on my lapses, from mere peccadilloes to the mortal sin that had led straight to capture.

But in a sane universe, I asked my soul, would I be called to accounts for this?

The trouble was that our world, including the world of peacemakers, was not notably sane. It was strange: the further one was distanced from acts of resistance, the louder the outcry raised against such as ourselves—who, all faults confessed, had simply done our best. And the contrary held true: no clamor of reproach arose, no bitter, journalistic jeremiads, from those given to the chancy work that made the underground possible, and even profitable. These latter, trusted and true, kept silent, and mourned my capture in secret; and continued to show their undeviating love in a thousand ways, after the blow fell.

I was captured at Bill Stringfellow's house on Block Island. The story of the birdwatchers and the snaring of their rara avis is part of island, and even mainland, folklore: no need to review it here. But my jailing was the first in a series of reverses that were to rain on us; blow after blow throughout the next year—such blows as rendered many insensible, frantic, or permanently embittered.

I suppose my roundup will appear in literary annals somewhere between epic and farce. I had journeyed to Block Island in a jaunty mood and disguise, and had arrived in presumed safety; though later events indicated something quite different. In reality the law was already hot at my heels.

I looked with longing toward a few paradisiacal days, after the long chase of months past. We settled in, Bill Stringfellow and Anthony Towne and I, supposedly to days and nights of friendship renewed, a period both relaxed and restoring.

A word of tribute is fitting here, regarding these two friends, both deceased and sorely missed. Friends such as are granted but once in a lifetime.

Anthony was an urbanite transmogrified by the times into a desert father. A long-time New Yorker like his friend, he moved to Block Island with a great shrug of relief. There he became an unofficial writer in residence: he wrote poetry and at least one splendidly barefaced and understated spoof, *The Diary of the Late God*. He also collaborated with his friend Stringfellow in literary and theological projects, most notably the biography of their friend, Bishop Pike.

In the long wintry season of his life, Anthony was caretaker of the property: he cared for the household dogs and cats, and welcomed the frequent guests to their home. He was a great, brooding bear of a man with a high-pitched, rasping laugh and a large capacity for affection, hard work, and storytelling.

As the lunacy of the world grew, Anthony appeared more and more an anomaly, a seeing creature in the kingdom of the blind. According to the debased criteria of production and efficiency, he was simply a puzzle: he could not be slotted.

Cast as I am into the mad machinery of airports and aircraft and city streets, of the manifestly mad Pentagon and the scarcely more bearable idiocy of campus and church, I appreciate all the more, and honor more gladly, the rotund, unexpectedly ascetic Anthony. Alas, I am cursed or blessed to live in mainline America. I often must travel amid affluent parasites, whose clothing and credit cards and briefcases and vocabulary of money and comfort and security— all are a converging sign, in the biblical sense, of a dying fall.

Anthony, even in memory, gives me hope. He turned his back on the witless folderol. He became, in consequence, a kind of landmark or sea mark, to many on and off the island: a precursor and interpreter of signs.

Standing solitary on the deck of the cottage on a starry night, with the winds freshening, Anthony would prognosticate: a stormy dawn, a nor'easter rising. He spoke before the foghorn blew or the lighthouse warned; and he spoke true, in this, as in matters of greater moment. When he died, we lost our keeper of times and places, our interpreter of signs. Our only comfort is that he has arrived where Signature and Sign are one.

Bill was sun to Anthony's full moon. A public man, an intellectual, theologian, lawyer, author, impresario, stern arbiter of world folly, summoner of church and state to accountability, cook and housekeeper and guest master, politico par excellence! And first and foremost, a Christian of conscience, who spoke with an altogether embarrassing directness, of what he knew—that the Bible can be honored only when it is set against life itself, measure to measured, life's judgment and conscience and teller of unwelcome truths.

Starting his law career among the neglected and excluded of Harlem, Stringfellow never ceased probing areas skirted by the experts. He was the first to urge impeachment proceedings against Nixon. He defended women seeking ordination in his church, and the clergy who approved, and in turn were threatened with punishment. He was the friend and later the biographer of the embattled Bishop Pike.

Stringfellow ran for public office on Block Island, on a ticket he wrote: it defended the voiceless, the indentured and aged and poor, and sought to restore an exploited ecology. He won office, but on a second try, was defeated in the Reagan debacle.

If the times ran strongly counter to Towne, it must be said that they were hardly kinder to Stringfellow. For the intense moral contrariety of their lives, they are precious in our sight, and their memory a benediction. For years, friends of every stripe and color and persuasion (and a few persuaded of not much of anything) gathered at their home, took counsel there, and returned to mainland America less hoodwinked, less quelled and defeated. Something of life and hope and renewal invariably came through.

Stringfellow could be short of temper, even querulous. He was not noted for suffering foolishness with grace. As the purveyors of public folly and violence cloned, and magnified the scope of their folly, and demonstrated their contempt for tradition and compassion, Stringfellow became the all but unique advocate of the embattled.

Power vested in the foolish drove him wild. I well remember one occasion: there arrived at his door a medical personage who had bought property on the island, and sought to retain Stringfellow as his lawyer. At one point, this character began to explain the source of his considerable fortune. He hymned the glories and profits accruing to a series of nursing homes he owned. "A great business," he exulted, "an enormous turnover."

At this point he was unceremoniously shown the door.

How much more prudent it seems, in such times, to trim sails in the name of "normalcy," to resign one's self to folly without and helplessness within. And thus to collaborate, not in celebrating the human, but in diminishing and degrading it.

Primary to Stringfellow's humanism was a very Protestant confession. Child of the Reformation, spiritual heir of Karl Barth, he was an apostle of modesty, of the little that can be done in face of the overwhelming encroachments of political and ecclesiastical powers.

That precious little! In his case, as in so many others, it made all the difference.

Thus he declared the human, in an inhuman time. In season and out, he defended the victims, raised his voice on behalf of the poor, denied to the dark principalities their assault and battery against the helpless.

And above all, day after day, he returned to the Testament; truer to say, he never closed it. The icon of Christ, he knew, must hearten those in the struggle.

His was a noble vocation, and an austere one, consistent with the lives of the saints.

Stringfellow lived for many years with death: in prospect, in periodic illness. The sheer poetry of it, his courage and good humor and patience, leads almost to an image of jealousy. At times, it seemed uncertain whether death was a closer friend than those who stood at his bedside, urging and hoping for his recovery. He would turn feverishly from side to side, as though to the one and the other, as though weighing arguments, lawyer as he was. And but for the end, he judged his friends the winners.

How we marveled and mourned, as though his chills and fevers were our own! And held our breath, and hoped against hope.

Crisis upon crisis, weakness succeeding pain, hospital episodes without end, the medicos and their nostrums descending on him like a very plague. Between episodes, he wrote his books, voyaged to campuses and pulpits, conferences and retreats. He never stopped: he was keeping death at bay.

And death idling, hanging around, bland, acute, forensic, oily of tongue and frosty of eye—how well Stringfellow knew him, how skillfully warded him off, exorcised him, erected shrines and invoked the saints against that principality.

When Towne died, Stringfellow determined that the burial of his ashes must await my return from Berkeley, where I had been teaching. The delay was a gracious thought, and typical.

We assembled on the Island; it was late autumn, one of the seasonal storms that scour the land was gathering. The ashes were to be buried on a hillock overlooking the sea; the only marker was a great four-foot iron anchor from a whaling ship.

Under the lash of wind and rain, some fifty friends huddled and endured. According to Stringfellonian decree, liturgies were not interrupted by a triviality such as a nor'easter.

The rains turned the book of devotions in my hands to a sopping porridge. It became next to impossible to decode a text fast vanishing. But we all mumbled our best. And when the psalms were completed and the ashes laid to rest, we turned with longing toward the shelter of the house, soaked as we were, and shivering with cold.

Not yet. Stringfellow announced in level tones: "Now we shall pause, face the house, and rebuke the principality of death, who has claimed this dwelling."

So instructed, so we did. There followed an exorcism, in the course of which demon death was, to all intents, banished from the premises. On our watery entrance into the house, there remained no trace of a fiery comet, or so much as a blackened hoofprint.

It was all in character. Stringfellow's biblical carefulness allowed for no trivializing of evil, and its secular counterpart, the gnostic psychologizing. And because he took the demonic as seriously as did Christ, we are perhaps justified in concluding that Stringfellow also took Christ seriously. In such matters as exorcism, it was evident to him that the integrity of the Gospel was at stake. And that consideration must constrain Christians to linger in inclement weather to perform rituals of moment.

He and I worked together, and prayed together, and sat at one another's table, for years. We suffered the death of friends; losses far deeper than the prospect of our own death. In the company of friends, we made joy of lighter hours, glorying in the jeweled wonders of the Island, that astonishing refuge of sinners and saints.

And then in the winter of 1985, after atrocious suffering, he died. It was five years after the death of his friend Anthony.

Eventually, we gathered to set their ashes side by side in a pine grove, on the spectacular cliffs over the sea. Mary Donnelly, faithful friend and tireless Island nurse, placed a plaque on the wall of the house. *Near this cottage, the remains of William Stringfellow and Anthony Towne await the Resurrection. Amen, alleluia.*

CHAPTER 11

Prison: Lights on in the House of the Dead

My generation was still born.
I saw them in prison,
con men with priest faces,
airbrushed skin, souls ground to salt—

no savor!
Everyone missed the boat—
Irish crooks, Irish priests
I saw them melt in fiery juices
mewing in sleep—
Vietnam! Vietnam!

No one had a clue,
retarded as fence posts
keeping the flocks & and herds of empire.

the winds went by
the wars went by

we were born to the bucks
we were worlds apart.

When we burned away
they kicked the ash—
turned up
face up
our bad luck. No heart.

On my entrance into Danbury prison, it was suggested that I, a priest, writer, teacher, dwelling for a time in this tender school of the spirit, might benefit from a change of profession. By no means, of course, in denial of my indubitably first vocation; so stubbornly adhered to over years fat and thin. But as a kind of buttress, so to speak, a secondary avocation and skill.

Would I therefore be agreeable to an assignment at the dental clinic—adjutant, mopper-upper, tool handler, x-ray technician, houseboy to all needs—would I agree that such an arrangement would prove of mutual benefit?

The choice was austere. Indeed, one might judge, were one inclined to jaundice of eye, that there existed no choice at all. To put matters shortly, I was assigned to that post.

I donned the white pants and shirt and proceeded to what the Esalen culture describes as a second career.

It was a matter of pincers and forceps, the hiss and whine of power drills, the to and fro arc of the relentless dentist, as the root of a molar, set as an oak root, saw the light of day, and the blood gushed forth.

I viewed, with fine dispassion, the oral cavities of rich and poor. The mouths of rich crooks, swung wide at the Open Sesame of the dentist, were like a Mafia strongbox, gleaming intemperately with gold, an emperor's sunrise.

And then the poor, and prisoners to boot: their dental needs had never, or seldom, or only clumsily, been met. It was a mercy to serve them, though the service was attended with much pain and bloodshed.

There was yet a further advantage here. The dental clinic lay immediately adjacent to the prison hospital. The two areas were, in principle, shut off one from the other. But the security was desultory, and the impending door often swung wide, with no guard in sight. So I was able, from time to time, to prowl the corridors of the hospital; even to enter the cell of this or that ill prisoner, greet him, offer whatever help I could, and learn something of his condition and prospect.

This was a great consolation to me. I thought of it as a kind of lagniappe, offered me by keepers who, on occasion, turned an eye aside, that I might move humanely through that inhuman house of the dead—and the dying.

The philosophy of the keepers, as I learned, required that the diagnosis of any and all ill, puzzling or simple, be settled on the basis of drug or knife, with dispatch. In this wise, I thought, prison medical practice differed not at all from the common methods in vogue outside. No one knew anything about natural supplements, proper diet, vitamins. No one cared to know. There was a simple medical fix for every ill, a shortcut to a relief of sorts.

The medicos cut corners, the drugs proliferated. Any prisoner who found his term unbearable could seek the zombie way out. Three times each day, the drug call was sounded, and the line formed.

One time a young prisoner had quite flaked out. He was a drug dealer, immensely talented in songwriting and singing. He was also witless and errant and utterly unprepared for the rigors of prison. He collapsed in the yard, was borne to the hospital and sedated out of this world.

Our young friend lay there inert, day after day, looking for all the world like a Renaissance cherub with its wings clipped. He had fallen out of the heavens, he had fallen out of America, whose heaven is an uncertain domain, apt for almost any fall from grace, parasitic or angelic. He fell to the prison hospital, he lay there on exhibit, marked Ruin: Too Bad, or perhaps Specimen: Nearly Extinct.

Could he be brought back to life, I wondered, could his feet be planted again on the earth? I assumed so, made my way to his side, proceeded, without politesse or prelude, to shake him out of his deadly torpor.

"Come back!" I cried; and "What the hell are you doing? Your friends want to know what's happened!" And "Get up, you drone!"

It could be thought of as a species of shock therapy.

We were well advised to distrust the prison chaplains, those sad purveyors of dead worship and conformity. Also the social workers, the medical staff, most guards, all lieutenants, certainly captains. Also the prison shrink, prowling the yard amid the brutes and briefcases, one drug pusher among many.

Our little band of survivors had other, different resources: a relentless confidence in the power of our beleaguered community of the incarcerated. We could care for our own, even in such a place. Further, and practically, our members had no need of drugs, of whatever brand; whether offered by psychiatrists or medicos or officers or those stupendous bribe and drug pushers, the parole board.

So my cry: "Come back, Johnny!"

Come back he did. And to what and whom, something might be said.

Shortly after my arrival in Danbury, Philip was transferred from Lewisburg, a gesture, perhaps of mitigation.

In Danbury, Philip and I presented our keepers with a conundrum of substance. We were priests; we were also convicted felons and, for the present, federal prisoners. A law stated that felons were prohibited, while in prison, from exercise of their profession. Lawyers could not lawyer, doctors could not doctor, teachers not teach. But here was a nifty dilemma: what should priests not do, which they normally did?

Ah, we have it. Priests offer the Mass. Therefore these priests, while in custody, shall be forbidden to offer Mass. It was all quite simple. And ironically and beautifully, it left Philip and me a very continent of territory in which to explore, ride rapids, go spelunking, try the Himalayan face, cross Gobi deserts—in sum, discover work to the benefit of the prisoners.

Priests who were prisoners could not offer the Mass for other prisoners. Very well, we would seek another opening. Priests, according to the law, were not teachers!

Therefore we would become teachers. We would organize classes, encourage reading, invite discussion. Indeed, we had wide access to friends in publishing houses in New York and elsewhere, and they to vast quantities of books.

The books poured in, a very Niagara. Word got around. After much dickering and puzzlement as to what we might be up to, the authorities assigned a room for our evening assemblies. The prisoners began reading: serious stuff, many for the first time. In subsequent weeks, we read and chewed to digestible pieces the following: sections of the Bible; Greek tragedies, a few substantial novels, including *Gulliver's Travels*, Marx; modern poetry; feminist works.

Prisoners came and went: they entered prison and left—for other prisons, for release. We were a large island in an archipelago of misery, in a sea whose tides moved in and out, aimlessly, witlessly, bearing its wreckage to and fro.

Still these little colonies of survivors, books in hand, were a sign of sorts. One need not be desperate or resigned or cynical or bored, as the prison decreed. And other prisoners could take soundings from us. They could hear, read, utter, ponder a word that went beyond the vengeful, the trivial, the wasted and wanton and boastful and brutal—the common coinage of the prison yard, the cells, the dreary human warehouse, its defeats and discards.

So, in their course, went the days and months. We encountered stupendous characters, we came on reasons for hilarity and tears, were rebuffed and remanded and summoned to petty judgment by petty minds. They declared, from time to time, suspicion that seditious goings-on were threatening the good order of bedlam. But why care, as long as the good work went on?

It was a Third Circle they were in charge of. Let everyone therefore walk the circle. Let no one dream of a straight line, or a zigzag; or wander or waver or weave a fresh path, apart from the ancient rut. . . .

Undoubtedly, there existed in the prison a rigid class system, adhered to by prisoners and keepers alike. It held firm in the big lineup, indistinguishable as to clothing or food; but nonetheless racist—and, close up, reflective of life outside.

The system flourished chiefly with regard to jobs and perks. It affected also the prospects and tactics of parole, the preparations leading thereto, agreements reached in the visitors room, access to legal aid—through the greening of outstretched official palms.

One could also arrange to receive drugs, one could arrange days off—even days out. Liquor was available, as were the services of women in town.

Indeed, it was not only from the dentist chair, and the Open Sesame, that one learned who was who and who nobody, who had what and who not. Money purred elegantly into the visitors parking lot, dismounted in furs and furbelows. The molls announced themselves at the gates like silly chatelaines of a castle long gone to ruin.

The lords and masters swaggered out to meet their queens. The big boys were humiliated, temporarily ruined—but their skulls, for all that, were bursting with a very springtime of Big Deals: entrepreneurs on ice.

The guards knew who was who, there was a sullen, gruff recognition—here the swing of a club, there the tight easement of a smile. Some prisoners were born zeros, smalltimers, niggers, spics, druggies, queers. No prelude, flat feet were wiped in their faces. The faces were mum, the feet walked away.

Others, ah, the others! This was a different species. They licked boots and wore creased pants, smiled till their faces creaked. Even in prison they had the look of a debased, beatific vision; not denied, only delayed. A look of jowels and jewels and deals and lawyers at one's beckoning; of orders summarily obeyed, routine money orders. Even bloody orders.

Their dreams pitched backward. Life had once been perfect: a well, a lake of avarice and appetite; perfect as a good brain, plenty of brawn, squads of dumb henchmen, a beautiful broad or three, could make it. In prison they talked and talked; but only to their own kind. It was impossible, I judged, inside their circle or out, to ravel out fantasy from fact. Fantasy, nostalgia, mirage, was their staple. They stooped to drink waters of illusion, and crawled on. They were pitiful and dangerous and one would be a fool to trust them an inch.

Then there were the blacks and Hispanics, among whom we found a few friends in spite of all. Most were illiterate or semiliterate. Here we had the seasonal roundup of expendables, the thinning of the herd. Such were dealt with en masse: seen one, you'd seen them all; dump on them; the worst clothing, the lowest jobs.

Driven to the wall, put down, despised, they would break out in bootless violence, importunities, obscenities. They howled in the long night of the North: for justice, for relief, for a furlough. They went on the hunt: for the social workers, those pariahs of scant solace, who cowered and hid out in their cubicles, or yelled for the guards.

In the Third Circle, there was no mediation, no shortcut, no parole. No one gave a damn. You stole a car, you did three years. And next to you in the dorm was a dour, overweight slob from Wall Street or the DA's office somewhere, or a contract maker and breaker from the Boston Mafia, a very godfather. Take your choice. This one had a fat hand in a fat till or he fixed cases or he had someone iced in the East River. He came in, worked a payoff or gave someone up or plea bargained; he did three months or so, they hardly laid a hand on him.

Danbury was also a place to finish your time in, after a long stretch elsewhere; in max, as was said. Close to the finish, prisoners were deposited here for the final six months; it was closer to the home folks, or more relaxed than "the wall."

In this wise there arrived one day in the prison, and subsequently in the dental clinic, a pair of poor southern whites. Not to finish their sentences. Rather to be put on hold, until the system might assign them; safely, as the rumor went, because their lives were endangered in the Deep South. They were the murderers of three young civil rights workers in Mississippi.

They were properly hangdog by now: far from Klan and mother and the good ol' guns that made corpses out of them outside agitatin' Commie Jews. . . .

The dentist was ready. I adjusted the bib around the neck of the first. I remember my horror: these were spectaculars unknown in our cages, largely given over to the humdrum and petty, the small fry. Under my gaze was a pair of sadistic torturers, murderers, racists gone berserk.

Thin of lip, weasely of visage, they settled back in the dental chair, as in the everlasting arms. Their eyes closed in beatitude. They had the souls of squid, floated on deep waters, their tentacles barely moving. They had devoured their prey, time digested all things.

In a few days they were moved out, whereabouts unknown, presumably somewhere in the North. Even for America, these two had gone too far: in a southern prison they might end up murdered.

America was teetering crazily: the war was proving, to all but its perpetrators, unwinnable; and to a growing number, morally repugnant. The country was in a morass, up to the bombers, down to a pavement of corpses.

It was the corpses that called the shots, so to speak. Not the Vietnamese corpses, but the American dead, arriving home in great mountains of boxes, closed against the horrified, grieving gaze of families and friends. Home at length, dead as cordwood.

And yet, to political intent, the dead were living indeed, on their feet, and vociferous as Dantean souls in purgatory. Intents and purposes! The dead manifestly had a purpose: to multiply their number. So many had died, should we now conclude that they had died in vain? And how were we to stifle the outcry of the protestors and troublemakers, except by multiplying our dead, manufacturing more dead, making of them the indisputable proof of our resolve?

In such an atmosphere, civil rights do not flourish. They go by the board. They become subject to the resolve that builds up the hecatomb of corpses: a good thing multiplied to a better thing.

To do this, the objectors must be silenced. And this is where we, Philip and our friends and I, came in.

Wartime: no such thing as too much of a good thing. Undeniably, we were prisoners, and might be judged harmless to the common weal. That was a good thing. But what of the repute of such prisoners as we: what of their appeal, which threatened, as the war became more obviously absurd, to become mass appeal?

Such prisoners might be judged to have very little going for them, lost as we were among misfits and expendables. But damnably, our plight seemed only to increase our visibility. The very silence and isolation cried out. Our story, *The Trial of the Catonsville Nine*, having flourished in California, was opening in New York. Our prison letters were being read widely; we were fast becoming freakish heroes in absentia. And what was to be done?

Mr. Hoover of the FBI was at the time redundantly extant. More: he sat in the saddle of a steed presumably fit for the course. The renowned jockey, somewhat overweight by now, somewhat muzzy in the head, still rankled greatly within. But the fact was, he no longer rode a winning horse. The priests had led him a merry chase, over hill and dale, ditch and paling—one of them for months at a time. The same priest had held him, Hoover, up to a species of public scorn. He had hinted that the reins were slackly held, the horse ill controlled. And he had dared dramatize his scorn, and for months, to considerable public joy. Was all this to be borne?

It was not. Hoover slapped together a public statement, denouncing conspirators, would-be saboteurs and kidnappers; something known here and there as The East Coast Consipracy to Save Lives. He ordered an indictment prepared.

The Justice Department, not at all on the side of unruly peacemakers, could still, with the nostrils peculiar to its kind, smell the rot in Denmark. They objected to a bootless project, doomed to go nowhere.

Nonetheless, Hoover's fury carried the day. The indictment came down.

CHAPTER 12

Harrisburg: Trial and Error

TO PHILIP

Compassionate, casual as a good face
(a good heart goes without saying)
someone seen in the street; or
infinitely rare, once, twice in a lifetime

that conjunction we call brother or friend.
Biology, mythology cast up clues.
We grew together, stars made men
by cold design; instructed

sternly (no variance, not by a hairsbreadth) in course and recourse. In the heavens
in our mother's body, by moon and month
were whole men made.

We obeyed then, and were born.

Those were terrible days. I have learned since, but was unaware
then, of a favored way of disposing of dissidents. It is to level a kind
of legal first strike, a killing blow. The aim is to traumatize, to raise
a public noise of such volume that the spirit of the accused is
crushed, friends demoralized. It is the shock that kills; or is meant
to.

That the shock did not kill, that it shortly wore off, that friends
came together, strengthened, sturdier of purpose, this is something
the powers were unable to take in account. But this is what occurred. Our friends, multiplied beyond imagining, girded for the
trial.

Then, amid great public clamor, a second indictment, more
tightly woven than the first, was announced. Several of us were
removed from the dossier of defendants, reduced to the largely symbolic status of co-conspirators: a stain on our repute, but no more.

Steam was gathering, under considerable pressure. There were unprecedented elements in the case; one could imagine the media licking their chops. There were nuns and priests, their mutualities and friendships—and who knew what more. There was this new-born, largely Catholic, resistance against the war; and who had seen the like before, in the generation of the redoubtable Spellman and his ecclesiastical lackeys? There were young and old, black and white, the newly converted and the old pacifists. Folklore, fantasy, rumor: the recipe would sell.

The trial opened in the spring of 1972. Every presumed connection and "covert act," together with the locale of the defendants, would have dictated a New York or Philadelphia or Washington setting. All this was ignored: the trial was arbitrarily set in Harrisburg, Pennsylvania. A predominantly Protestant populace, a moribund political atmosphere, far removed from the passions of war and peace: therefore a malleable jury—so went the government reasoning. And as usual, how wrong they were!

The departure of Philip and Elizabeth McAlister from their religious orders was public knowledge by now. So was their marriage. Justice and the war were by no means the issue as the media viewed the trial: scandal and rumormongering were.

What these two endured as their letters were read aloud in court and huckstered abroad, I leave to merciful imagination. Philip sat impassive. He came and went, jail to court and back, in prisoner's shackles. He was the center of it all, the eye of the storm. If the government had its way, he must be sunk in a deeper circle of hell; once and for all.

The other defendants might or might not be convicted; if convicted their sentences might well be short, and no harm done. Even their vindication could be tolerated. But Philip must be destroyed. The purpose shone in the fury of the prosecutor, barely under control, his face like an underground fire. It shone in the judge's gimlet eye, as it roved about the court taking the measure, taking soundings; but always coming to rest on Philip. It was as though Philip's answering glance, calm and at peace as he was, burned holes in the official black. This existence was an affront, this calm was insulting.

Something in the soul of this defendant, disgraced and imprisoned by collusion of church and state—something of resource or mystery seemed to be in charge. Could it be that Philip was disposing of matters, signaling the actors, arranging the outcome? Everything revolved around a seemingly helpless captive. They had never seen the like, this astonishing reversal of roles, these ironies.

I was fresh out of prison, on parole. I had been allowed by the parole system to travel to Harrisburg. And each evening, with the defendants and lawyers, I entered Philip's cell, and was party to the intense, sometimes hilarious, review of the day, and the forging of a strategy for the morrow.

I could not then, and am helpless now, to describe, let alone to evaluate, such strength as my brother showed in those days and nights.

His danger was very great: it was all but mortal. We knew (and our hearts sank at the thought) that if he testified, he would lie open to the prosecutor's line of questioning. The government was poised for the pounce. That was the befouled purpose of the trial: to prove Philip the brain of a conspiracy of "crime" that spanned the country. And to the crime they would fit the punishment, like a hood on the condemned.

The vote of the defendants, and my urging, was against his testifying. He must not testify. Indeed, as Ramsey Clark insisted, none of the defendants must do so. We must shock the court: even a kangaroo court was susceptible to shock. We must call a halt to the absurd charade that, like a stalking nightmare, pretended to substance and legitimacy. If substance or legitimacy were granted, the trial would seize on sane minds, and drive us mad.

Time ticked away like a concealed bomb. The prosecution, that shabby exercise in venom, hung on the word of a single witness: it came down to that. Boyd Douglass, longtime prisoner, loser, informant, detained in some secret lair by the FBI for an entire year, was now produced.

We in the courtroom had never seen so sorry a spectacle, this shambles clutching at straws of freedom, all ties frayed, the betrayer.

It was sad. He took the stand for days on end, a monotonous clone repeating his rote and rot. Alas for this crashing stereotype, a rag doll of a human, a victim deftly transformed into a victimizer. Prisoners, driven mad by prison, breaking their skull against the wall, anything, anything, to get out!

The keepers knew. With Douglass, a few bucks would turn the

trick, no great outlay. Such a one had no loyalties; time ticked away, on his wrist, in his heart; life was doing time, the only continuity, conscience was long gone.

I remember only a permeating sadness, the sadness he spread about the court, like a fog machine making fog. Sunk so low, used and then used up, degraded by scoundrels worse than himself, flung aside.

I thought: I should reach out to such a one, show a human feeling, a refusal to strike back. And then, even in imagination, my hand recoiled. I had touched something neither hot nor repugnant: a stench of—betrayer; the one Dante puts in the lowest circle. There he sat: a bone, a shock of hair, an incongruous suit of clothes, courtesy of the FBI, like the shroud they put on a corpse, all front, no back.

Only Christ, I thought, could love such a one. And coward and half a Christian as I was, I left him to Christ.

They built their case on this pillar of sand, and it collapsed. Indeed, carefully coached as he was, complicit as he was, and morally retarded, such patches and scraps of testimony as he offered would hardly convict a worm of turning.

Items: a few intercepted letters between Philip and Elizabeth. The tone was one of longing and love: they missed one another, their separation was borne for the sake of their peace work. In the manner of those in love, who the same time are resolved to act responsibly, they had discussed certain strategies of mitigation. Such discussions, one assumes, were going on all over the country, as citizens beat against the wall of the war, and wept: try this, try that, no, yes, maybe.

In a peaceable time, such flights of fancy would be disregarded, did they occur at all. But America in the seventies was carrying its wounds of anomie and vengefulness; and desperately sought relief in domestic victims. Someone must pay, and pay dearly, for a war that years before had gone sour, had gone against us.

The trial beat on. They did their worst. But Douglass was so obviously a loser and liar, his testimony by turns laughable in its frivolity and damaging in its contradictions. Where it should have been impregnable, it simply fell apart.

The jury listened patiently, impassively, as is the way of juries. They were presumably anti-Catholic, unpolitical, deaf and dumb to events in the great world. That was the mistake of the government, its contempt for its own citizens, country people, small town people, working people. And the mistake was the government's undoing.

It proved, in fact, next to impossible to hoodwink the jury. That was the one hopeful lesson of the long, wearing weeks. There was no one else to intervene, to save a just cause, the cause of justice itself. The prosecutor had a personal score to settle. A disappointed, embittered Catholic, he aired his grievances at social gatherings, and the word got around Harrisburg. Back and back the betrayal went, he fumed. Back to the Vatican Council, to Pope John, to upstart nuns and priests, to a church he could no longer recognize as his own tight little precinct.

And the judge made his animus clear from the first hour. He was like others of his kind: an empty soul, echoing and amplifying the dire bombast of the prosecutor, as the two wove their tawdry web.

The cables slipped, the web fell apart. The verdict was all but unanimous for acquittal: only one juror held out, day after day.

But the judge was unyielding. He wanted a verdict: no less than the prosecutor, he wanted a guilty verdict. No loose ends, finis to this troublesome and drawn-out affair. Day after day, week after week, he sent the jury back to its tedium and rancor. The deliberations were the longest in the history of the federal system. And still, no verdict.

And finally, to the relief of almost everyone concerned, the judge gave in. The case was stymied. A trial that had brought honor to few (and they the embattled defendants), and dishonor to many, stopped there.

The Harrisburg case, a stinking red herring from the start, proved also the undoing of Hoover. He died of its poison. He had given instructions, during the weeks of jury deliberation, that night or day, he was to be informed of the outcome. He learned it: equivalent acquittal. And the news shot him into another world.

News of Hoover's demise reached me in New York. I was approached by the media for a statement. I stated, as simply as I could, my hope: that Hoover had been granted the merciful judgment he had long and often denied to others.

The statement, need I add, was never broadcast.

CHAPTER 13

The Healer

I stood, a sick man
on feeble knees
peering at walls and weather,
the strange outdoors, the house of strangers—
there, there was a beginning.

The world peeled away
usual upon usual
like foil in a fire. . . .

In my boyhood, doctors were quite mysterious figures who were,
like God, presumed to be available on call. Their mystery was thus
rendered, so to speak, matter of fact. Today, looking back, my boyhood image of our family doctor is charged with a kind of internal
aura—the small town doctor has passed from fact to folklore, like
a forged iron weather vane or a Shaker chair.

Has my memory aided sound judgment, or inhibited it? Has
medical practice gotten better, or worse? A hopelessly tangled argument to wage on the basis of memory, which, like a clear sunset
after wretched weather, tends to turn all grays rosy.

In medicine, as in most walks of life, one notes, over fifty years,
many complexities, balled and rolling: a kind of internal momentum
furiously at work, driving all before it. The principle of motion is
random and clear; the destination of things hardly so.

One sound dollar, Cal Coolidge reminded us, begets another: a
depressingly conventional wisdom, implying both Yankee virtue and
inflation; inflation in the Good Green Stuff and in the soul as well.
Cal's internal inflation might indeed be deplored as avarice.

But what to name this powerful adhesive-in-motion, sometimes
named history, or change, or ego on the rampage? It gathers its
material, raw and chancy, worthless and valued, as it rolls along,

ego and ambition and professional savvy, sets them careening off in ever new untried arcs, some predictable, some vagrant. Or it makes common cause with avarice; for some adhesive sticks only to Cal's green stuff.

Our village doctor in Liverpool, New York, in 1927, charged one dollar for an office visit, two dollars for a home visit. He could be summoned for any imaginable emergency, from birth through death. Often as not, when made aware of the poverty of a given household, he charged nothing. Or serving a farm family, he took his fee in barter.

He had book learning and Yankee canniness both. We looked on him with the awe and affection reserved for few others: the parish priest perhaps. And like an old-fashioned priest, the doctor could sum up a situation with an adage, or lend an ear for an hour of sympathetic grief or silent listening. He had a crude, apt word as well for the unwise: the alcoholic, the irresponsible, the violent.

He was a religious man, and made no bones about it. I remember his calm in the midst of a crisis, a farm injury or a long, hopeless illness, when little alleviation was possible. Something was better than nothing: warmth and skill made the elixir, and when it could not cure, it calmed.

My brother Philip was stricken at age ten with strep throat: the illness fell like a thunderbolt in a clear sky. There were no antibiotics, and given the penury of the household, and dearth of anything resembling medical insurance, hospital was out of the question. (As far as I recall, it was never even considered: the poor did not go to hospital; they were born, and died, at home.)

My mother did what she could, and it was a magnificent great deal. There were months of day and night vigils, baths, poultices, special foods.

Daily she put on a mysterious armor of the soul—she never gave up. Nor did my father, hovering more or less clumsily in the background, keeping his grief and confusion much to himself. The will to heal my brother was like a voltage passing from parents to doctor and back. It burned in their eyes, a fuel of life and lifegiving: no wind of mischance or tragedy could snuff it.

Fever and chills, chills and fever, the illness raced on its course. The boy's weight and will slipped from us. The doctor was there, a third in that trinity Never Give Up, on call at any hour. Ever so gradually, tugging the lifeline, those three brought the boy back.

Perhaps most families, years after the fact, could recall a like episode. But such lonely triumphs of will and affection, I suspect, would be recounted almost as tales of lost art, all but buried in folklore. One's medical experience, to put matters in neutral, tends to summon different, far more somber, stories today.

I was released from prison in 1970, suffering from a spinal condition, variously attributed by prison doctors to arthritis, a faulty disc, or a combination of the two. In any case, the condition persisted in quite excruciating fashion. In quest of relief, I was eventually granted an appointment with a renowned internist at a New York medical center.

Prior to the encounter, I had, of course, been wheeled through x-rays and other occult rites. Ultimately I was granted audience with this personage for the first (and luckily for me, the only) time.

He entered the diagnostic room portentously, greeted me, and set himself to studying the film for a few minutes. Then without further ado came the decision: surgery was indicated; a fusion of the affected spinal discs. No discussion, no explanation. Divinity, so to speak, shuffling the cards: it is thus decreed.

I made bold to inquire what my chances of normal functioning might be after such an operation. The question seemed of little interest and less moment: his response could not have been more offhand. I was granted something in the realm of a thirty to seventy percent chance against a normal life.

Beyond doubt, I was in presence of the stern schoolmaster referred to in old-fashioned texts as life. The medical mandarin was a shattering contrast with the country doctor of my boyhood. A rather brutal remoteness, a god descended on wires. No mortal nonsense, no comeback. Choices? Interlocutors? Alternatives? None of these: Take It Or Leave.

He reached for pen and pad. "And until we can schedule the surgery, I'll prescribe something for pain."

He glanced up, for the first time: my wrathful expression must have met his eye. "But you wouldn't take the drug anyway, would you?" He dropped the pen. End of interview.

Anger, the soul of energy! I had scarcely been able to endure the cab ride to the hospital. Then I heard the verdict, its effrontery and heartlessness. I lurched out of the office; raging pain, no drugs, no knives, anger, and all. And somehow or other, hissing like a blast furnace, got my bones in motion, survived the forty-block trek, on foot, back to my dwelling.

Knives and drugs. Behind the big name and bigger bucks, the hush-hush atmosphere, the noiseless nurses and fluting phones and mellow wainscoting, the Gothic diplomas and stale air, the dispirited, affluent patients awaiting their fate, final and flat—behind the decor and staging—nothing.

Or at most, not much.

The demigod reigned over some debatable kingdom known as Health Industry. As to money, big time; as to healing, no great evidence.

Drugs and knives. Your common variety of witch doctor could probably have summoned a wider list of nostrums, a more ample apothecary.

I was plunged in misery. Adamant as to what I would not submit to, a tormented will, a sense of wrong, of being had. But where to go with such a sense? I was ignorant as the unborn.

It was like a prelude to love. Love is heightened, perhaps, by such improbables as dismay, chagrin, anger. I knew well, perhaps too well, of gruesome invasions. Cant and omnipotence and self-deception and pride of place. Further instruction as to hype and ego would be profitless. I had seen all these; further, as a convicted felon, I had witnessed the havoc wrought by prison doctors on the helpless. Enough was too much.

I knew what I hated, but I had no alternative, the alternative we name choice, or hope, or love.

The week following my walkout was like the darkness that precedes conversion. A ghostly fog, no direction, no outcome. Not yet. Wander about, believe, hope as best you can. Certain only of one thing, and that no great consolation: I must respect my sense of smell. The smell in that office was of death.

My own death? Perhaps—if I did not reject, with all my strength, the presumption and ignorance that would claim me.

Then through the urging of a friend and an act of God, a healer.

In those days the doctor rented a rather shabby storefront in the improbable town of Bogota, New Jersey.

You came in off the street, and took your place in a bare front room; the ambience was of a converted neighborhood store, formerly, perhaps, a display of fruit and vegetables, notions and candy, schoolchildren trooping in and out.

My boyhood country doctor redivivus? The heart positively leapt.

He heard my tale of woe, my meeting with Saw, Bones & Drugs, my fury and frustration. He examined me with care. Then it was his turn to explode.

What a strange relief it was to hear one's instincts justified! There was, Dr. Rose declared, spicing his judgment with expletives, no need of surgery. A spinal operation, with all its attendant risks, could only be termed medically irresponsible. What I required was simple enough: natural supplements, careful diet, periodic chiropractic.

He gave me a first spinal adjustment. He took his time, his hands walked my poor spine and read its ills right. His hands were like those of a blind man gifted with second sight. Sight and healing, one, all but preternatural; as became clear in the outcome—some fifteen years of good health, extending to this day.

The technology of medical practice exemplifies, with truly wondrous naivete, both folly and irony: a faster way of going backward. Dr. Rose's dependence on machinery is minimal; the most sophisticated of his appurtenances is a rather old-time x-ray machine, which he makes use of rarely. There is also a table that goes vertical on command to receive a patient, then hydraulically floats one horizontal, a pleasant waft. He uses an optometrist's fine beam to examine eyes, and a rubber and bandage attachment to take blood pressure. And that is just about all.

Each of these tools, I understand, has been "improved" or replaced of recent years: any self-respecting practitioner is advised to run, not walk, to the nearest high-tech merchant to take advantage of the latest in such. Dr. Rose is indifferent to this glittering flea market; he keeps out back a Model T Ford jitney, it chugs along quite well.

A congress of afflicted mortals assembles each day in Dr. Rose's unprepossessing office. One frequently meets one's friends there. If there exists a common sociological note, the patients are lower middle and working class, together with a smattering of nuns and priests engaged in the peace movement or work among the poor. Blacks and whites together, similarly in need of a refurbishing of the frame. The treatment they receive is wonderfully varied, improvised, informal: advice, encouragement, talk straight from the Rose shoulder, a good story or two given or taken.

He does his homework. What seems spontaneous, even inspired, in diagnosis or treatment, an uncanny skill of getting, without preamble, to the nub of a trouble—what labor, what thought this implies!

You are given as much time as you require. Scheduling is erratic at best. One arrives at 9:10 as specified (appointments are both meticulous and spurious, like announcements of airline takeoffs). You may still be cooling heels and ardor an hour or two later. No one leaves, no high or low dudgeon. Friends chat, the wise bring reading material. Healing is worth hanging around for.

The gods are big on promise, short on delivery. The true God and the truly godlike fail now and again.

Thus the healer. Some truly sorrowful cases, mostly of cancer, he cannot alleviate. "They come to me always as a last resort, after the knives and drugs," he mourns and rages.

There was a last resort case, of truly Jobian proportions. William Stringfellow has described his medical travails exhaustively in his books. We who were his friends knew far more of his sufferings and setbacks than readers or audiences ever could. We lived his dying. I was his friend through nearly two decades of illnesses, the variety and scope of which would fill a quarto volume of medical mischance. At the hands of doctors, like the woman in the Gospel, he had "suffered much."

It began with a surgical removal of most of his pancreas, in 1967. The operation saved his life, but left him with radical diabetes. Predictions were glum: he would be, from henceforth, a near invalid.

He was able to turn predictions around. If he could not be well, he would nonetheless be heard from. And who knew, even his disability might be put to harness, a metaphor of holy overcoming.

So it happened, as we his friends, are witnesses.

His life became quite literally and simply Christlike. Which is to say, all pieties aside, he became an icon of Incarnation, a harmony of apparent irreconcilables. He lived intensely in the Spirit; and in public he was a force to be reckoned with. With his friends, he was prodigally loving, hospitable, witty. On fools and folly (no one, he knew, was more desperately foolish than the worldly wise), he came down hard, a very demon of judgment. He loved the church, loved his layman's vocation. (He once confided to me that an Episcopal bishop had urged him to accept ordination without further theological delay.) But he passionately reserved to himself the harsh privileges of love: which is to say, pen and tongue.

On Block Island, where he lived his two last decades, the medicos, one after another, inherited Stringfellow as one inherits a piece of unclassifiable property, a house rumored to be haunted, perhaps: a valuable property, to be sure, but taxing to the nerves.

Each in turn looked him over, hemmed and hawed, looked wise, foolish, plain stumped. Generally they got nowhere. He was an unfit subject for the skills of this world, or at least the usual skills. He was too sharp, had suffered too long to be easily, or even skillfully, hoodwinked. Indeed, his best medical work was done, for years, by himself, on himself. It was both exorcism and purification: he kept death at bay—with hard work, meditation, Scripture reading, lecturing abroad ("in America," as he would say wryly, departing the Island; "I'm going to America").

And perhaps most typically of all, with waiting.

His dwelling was indeed the abode of spirits, as the Easter hymn has it: "life and death contending." The contention, together with the wager he placed solidly on the outcome—these he discussed, analyzed, interpreted biblically. He became one of the healthiest ill Christians in America: in the words of T. S. Eliot, a "wounded surgeon."

This was a rare illness indeed. It was as though he were being providentially kept alive, for years and years, in a kind of suspended animation, for the sake of the church. He was never well and seldom without pain. Yet he was hardly ever incapacitated, rarely missed an engagement, kept writing his books. The medicos shook their addled pates. They were puzzled that he evaded their nets and snares, nostrums and nuggets—and went on living and working.

It was quite a game. He traveled, lectured, conducted retreats, kept the waters troubled with analysis of public ills: in the church, in the society. Racism, sexism, warmaking, consumerism. His tones were now measured and forensic, now ragged with passion and fury.

The risks mounted. By 1982, diabetes was inhibiting his circulation to an alarming degree: he was threatened with the amputation of both feet. There was a sense among us of nothing to lose: I prevailed on him to see Dr. Rose.

As usual, a complete medical file was prepared in anticipation of our visit. The doctor was ready for us: the file had been carefully studied. Rose was convinced that talk of amputation was a quick fix that would serve only to wreak further havoc.

He urged Bill to undertake something known as chelation: a process of slowly purifying the blood and clearing arteries with transfusions of natural ingredients, over a period of months. A clinic existed in New York, equipped for the procedure.

Bill agreed, transferred necessary possessions to New York for six months (including two intractable, loud-mouthed canines), and appeared at the clinic in lower Manhattan several times each week. The treatment succeeded beyond our fondest hope. He was granted life and integral limbs for two more years.

This was the best anyone could hope for: a sorry best. His poor frame, stuffed with pills like an apothecary's jar, ferried about, injected, hospitalized, experimented on, kept in useful motion, against all expectation, for years and years—was, at length, shutting down.

He returned to his beloved Block Island and managed to plow through his last book, a study of biblical spirituality. In it, he speaks of his condition, but austerely, from a kind of lawyerly distance. His mind was lucid and his pen, that instrument of public weal and woe, unblunted.

He was never one to dwell on himself, even in prayer of petition. His prayer through the years was implicit in his fastidious and disciplined life: he sought a perduring good use of his intelligence, in service to truth. And we, irreparable loss at hand, could but agree: the prayer was granted; the grant was the style. He rests in peace.

I ventured to tell Dr. Rose, a few months after Bill's death, that it was surely due to his solicitude and skill that this so precious life had been granted two more years of breathing space. He responded in typical fashion. Nearly in tears, he brushed my thanks aside and confessed his deep love and respect for our friend.

CHAPTER 14

Israel: Ground of Contention

My life goes like this.
The Christians decided to make a Jew of me.
I ended up around someone's neck,
an albatross or crucifix—
anyway, a "saving metaphor."
Never a glimpse of the Author's sour sweet face,
though his heart
hammered away;
"Providence, you're providential!"
That way I hung in there, hanged.

And the Jews?
When I came round, they laid it down hard;
"Love us, love yeretz Israel!"
When I stammered out
distinctions, distinctions;
(the blood stained faces/the blood stained earth)—
they'd have none of it, fists came down.

So
my destiny (big deal)
is marginal as a cockroach or a crucifix. . . .

I'll add this; if you sought me
you'd see me
cross hatch in the narrow strip
Broadway,
between cross draughts of hell,
cross legged on a filthy bench
forever, next to nothing. . . .

It was in 1973 the storm broke, such a storm as exceeded all previous tornadoes, hurricanes, landslides, tidal waves. In my world, the like had never been seen on land or sea.

The date was October 19, 1973. I was invited to speak before an organization previously unknown to me, The Association of Arab University Graduates. I was teaching in Canada at the time; the travel to Washington would involve considerable inconvenience. But I was weighted with an obscure sense: something important was at hand. I accepted the invitation.

It was a considerable mercy that I knew nothing of the outcome.

A week or so after the event, an antiwar periodical in New York published the speech. And the skies fell in.

According to my critics, I had been guilty of every conceivable delict in "that speech." My tone was abrasive, my criticism of Israel was insufferably presumptuous. The audience of Arab students was ill chosen; the timing, if not malicious, was at least maladroit. I was, in fact, either a dimwit or an anti-Semite. I had followed the irresponsible drift of the American left into a morass. I was toying dangerously with neofascism. I was cloning the worst historical stereotypes of my church vis-à-vis the Jews, from Torquemada to Coughlin.

And so on, and so on.

I began to feel like Joanne Little. She recounts that after escape from a southern jail, she was hidden in a remote shack. A sheriff appeared at the door and she hid under a feather mattress. The hefty cop insisted on questioning the householder; and in the course of his inquisition, he settled his considerable behind on the aforesaid bed, for a long, long session. And Joanne, feathered but not tarred, wondered warmly if she would survive.

So I, tarred but not feathered, wondered about survival, as the most unlikely bedfellows came to rest—on me. B'nai B'rith had me on their wanted list that year. My crimes were castigated in the pages of *Commentary, World View, Commonweal, Village Voice,* the *New York Times.* I displaced God for a while in prime pulpit time. I was denounced as "insane" by a high official of the National Council of Churches. An Episcopal priest, visiting Jerusalem as guest of the Israeli government, improved the occasion by ranting at me. I was offered an unlikely peace prize; then the prize was disoffered, at the indignant behest of a liberal minister of midtown Manhattan.

Hate mail arrived; from, among other unlikely sources, the Jewish Theological Seminary.

Someone made a count. Nearly one hundred articles were written over the following year, topic: That Speech. It was variously denounced, debated, refuted, name called, expanded, contracted, demythologized. In some few cases, agreed with.

So it went. As the Orphic myths told so long ago, a hero is only a sandwich: up for grabs, down for good.

My reaction to all this, more than a decade later, is perhaps strange: it is simply gratitude. I am grateful for having spoken the truth, as I saw it, as it was given to me to understand. And this from three vantage points. From my religious belief. More proximately, from my tendency to speak up and let the chips fly. And closest of all, from the Vietnam decade, its chills and fevers and nightmares and bloodletting and courts and jails. Having endured a few of these makeshift delights, one is apt to pay small tribute to shibboleths.

For at least a year, the debate raged, fruitbearing and fruitless. At least this could be said (I became an addict of minimal returns)— that the skeletons were abroad, in daylight. It could never again be said that on this topic, Israel, nothing of criticism could be uttered by "outsiders."

Several years later, I found that tempers had by no means cooled. A distinguished Jew professed himself enraged because I had dared say in print what I dare repeat here: that I saw nothing of substance to repent of in my original words. He wrote that I must indeed be what less temperate souls had long named me—an anti-Semite.

So be it. I confess his words went off in my brain like a delayed mine. Now I was guilty (over and above the original crime) of the delict of nonrecantation. I asked my bewildered soul: how double can jeopardy get?

Subsequently, I was invited, by a Quaker group, to a small gathering of Christians and Jews in Boston. It was described as an off-the-record effort at reconciliation. I was invited to state my position: as I judged it, a remote hope was in the air that I had come to a better mind.

Nothing of the sort. I summoned the effrontery to venture an old conviction: that "the state of Israel, as presently constituted, has no future." I fully intended to explain my words, each word separately and in context, because I had chosen each with extraordinary care.

By the words "as presently constituted," I wished to criticize the law of return, the colonization of the Golan Heights, the military occupation of the West Bank, the seizure of land and building of Arab quarters in West Jerusalem: the attempts, in fine, to assimilate or subdue the Palestinian peoples within Israel.

In so speaking, I wished to separate out two realities. The first, a given web of assumptions; an accepted ideology; laws; economic, political, and military conduct; methods of exercising civil authority—all of which (with other elements) constitute "the state." To separate these from the consciousness of people, their ethical sense and expression, their customs, history, memory (an especially painful element here), their literature—in sum, how a people present their lives, hopes, culture, before the world. I wanted to distinguish Israel "as presently constituted," from Israel as "constituting herself."

The two, I believe, are quite different realities: in Israel, in America, or elsewhere. (Given practically every political arrangement in force on the globe, they had best be understood as separate realities, I thought, or it is all up with us.)

One thinks, for example, of the religious resistance today against American policies in Nicaragua, contrasted with Reagan's Contra war. In the former, the religious community is offering a quite persuasive example of Catholics "constituting themselves" as a separate moral force; in the latter, we have American policy, "as presently constituted"—God help us.

Alas, there was little chance in Boston to dwell on such matters. Those who greeted me warmly before I spoke could hardly allow a first sentence to leave my tongue. The meeting ended abruptly, in pain and disarray.

Talk about education! Here was history, coming to bear with a thump: history speaking far more abruptly, not to say brutally, than I.

Its terms are at times far less generous than I would allow to humans and their structures, even their follies—Israelis and Palestinians included. In the decade since I dared raise unmentionable matters in Washington, violating taboos of right, left, and center—in the years since, events have dealt with Israel in a fashion that

makes me the tenderest of Jewish mothers. Military, diplomatic, and
economic events are cutting Israel off from her friends, from her
ideals, from her past. Israel is moving toward the consummation of
her tragedy.

The connections she once formed, the sympathies she evoked
among the nations, especially the struggling peoples of the Third
World, are largely broken; connections that many believed, in light
of the tragic Hitler era, were symbiotic.

And there is the matter of Israel and the United States; and the
imperial adventure being played out, here and there.

Nicaraguans and Palestinians: two peoples, each denied a destiny of its own choice. The one victimized by military incursion,
the other by shameful political repression, the one resorting to last-
ditch domestic militarization, the other to terror.

The Nicaraguans are not alone in constructing, by force of brutal
necessity, a fortress state. What a cruel necessity, a forensic nightmare, self-fulfilling! Israel is caught in the same cruel web. Inevitably, one might think: because insecurity, danger, and the
imminence of terror are hardly conducive to political generosity, an
open society.

If there may exist here and there in Israel, a certain leniency, a
tendency to regard Palestinians outside Israel as human beings, raising legitimate grievances—this says nothing of the worsening fate
of the Palestinians within Israel's borders, whether on the Left Bank,
in Jerusalem, in Ramallah or Galilee. The noose is drawn. And this
too has about it the hideous quality of the inevitable.

The enemy outside the borders, if he is astute, resolute and
cruel, must be taken in account. He may be hated and hateful; but
he is hardly alone. His outcry is magnified a thousandfold in the
first, second and third worlds. He is heard from; sometimes to the
roar of bombs and carbines and the fall of innocent blood. Ever so
gradually, at such enormous cost, his demands strike on unwilling
ears.

But the Palestinians in Israel are something else again. In a nation under perpetual trauma, domestic Palestinians are regarded as
a kind of third column, Viceyites, potential traitors. So they are
denied civil rights, their lands are expropriated, political assembly
is denied, villages burned, prisoners held without trial, even tor-

tured. It is a sad and shameful litany. It turns the dream of a democratic homeland, to the nightmare of a garrison state. And this despite all tradition, rhetoric, heroism, skills of survival, liberal initiative and law, a history of martyrdoms even. Everything goes by the board. An admirable history, a hope, is wiped out by the expunging hand of taliation, retaliation.

I am impelled to say what I have said before. But my grounds for so speaking have shifted. Once I was angry with Israel, and overwhelmed by the Palestinian tragedy. I am no longer angry. Better, my anger has found a different object: the mythmakers and kingmakers, both Israelis and Americans. I am angry at the American Jewish establishment, who inflate the political and religious myths of divine choice and immunity from criticism, stoke the fires, make accommodation into a pipe dream, keep foolish Christians prating, in the name of repairing crimes against Jews, the oldest sophism of history: "To make peace, prepare for war."

This is indeed a baleful ecumenism, this ersatz "Jewish–Christian dialogue." It demeans both sides, blind as both are to the ghost in the shadows. Its victims will be, among many others, the Israelis themselves.

Toward them, I have no anger today; and only the briefest of arguments. It goes something like this: because you in Israel and I in America must exist under abominable political leadership, deprived of even residual intelligence and sense of humanity; and because our salvation lies in resisting political lunacy, militarization, neglect of the poor in our midst—why then do you not resist? In larger numbers, with a clearer voice, by symbolic acts of reconciling, by violating iniquitous laws, by preventing land seizures, by protecting the stranger in your midst (who is, in fact, no stranger, but an immemorial dweller in the same land).

So runs my argument. I consider it a matter between friends, at home and in Israel, an argument stemming from a common friendship and respect: respect for the Israeli people; for the farmers and workers and students and rabbis; for the children, above all; for the young mothers and fathers; for the aged, who issued once from one nightmare, only to be pushed into another. For these, I have utmost compassion. It is an emotion that, in 1973, I felt in large measure toward their opposite number, the Palestinian people.

Surely it ought to be clear by now that their American masters have no deep attachment to Israel. There is no common vocation in the world: no common vision of redress and political renewal. To the Americans, Israel is a useful outpost, a paramilitary base. And even her political and military usefulness, once taken for granted, is now being weightily reassessed. Certain pundits are convinced that the American hegemony in the Mideast can be maintained otherwise than through her.

Her fate thus is reduced to a matter of expediency, a reassigning now in progress, of once-favored colonial satraps. Israel has lost special status: along with other strategic colonies, she is subject, in a quite unprecedented way, to "reappraisal," she "comes up for review."

Thus a tragedy that once shadowed the Palestinian camps has shifted in the rude winds of the world. A dark Shekinah hovers over Jerusalem and the Galilee, over the kamikaze-style kibbutzim on the Golan Heights.

Israelis have long memories; but memory has a way of being shortened or even expunged, in the rush to war preparation, a quick fix. Yet another war? But what war, in the long haul of history, has Israel not lost? How many wars can she afford to win?

Every military buildup has sown dragons teeth at her borders. She sowed, she proclaimed victory before a wondering world. And in every instance, the wars settled nothing: the enemy was reborn, within a few years armed warriors sprang up once more.

There is no sane reason to believe that a nuclear force will bring a more benign harvest.

Alas for this highly sophisticated, intellectually alert European transplant, this sublime experiment gone wrong! The Israelis, increasingly isolated in the world community despite (or because of) a bristling arms trade, deaf to revolutionary aspirations, whether on their own behalf or others', urged to a hapless heroism by American compatriots (who dwell, need one add, at safe distance from the effects of their bellicosity), taxed to exhaustion, under permanent state of seige, forced to witness the outrages once inflicted on themselves inflicted time and again on a people helpless and homeless as they once were—

As if this were not enough! The threat of another war lies heavy on the land: it is simply taken for granted by politicians and generals, by advisers and patrons, there and here. And where is the promise, the covenant; and what is the fate of the chosen?

Gandhi, for once, met his match: in Martin Buber. Gandhi had said that Palestine belonged to the Arab people, and that it was "wrong and inhuman to impose the Jews on the Arabs." Most uncharacteristic; and by no means a fortunate choice of words. Buber responded in an open letter to Gandhi:

> I belong to a group of people who from the time when Britain conquered Palestine, have not ceased to strive for the concluding of a genuine peace between Jew and Arab.
> By a genuine peace we inferred and still infer that both peoples should together develop the land without the one imposing its will on the other. . . .
> We considered it a fundamental point that in this case two vital claims are opposed to each other, two claims of a different nature and a different origin, which cannot be pitted one against the other, and between which no objective decision can be made as to which is just or unjust.
> We considered and still consider it our duty to understand and to honor the claim which is opposed to ours, and to endeavor to reconcile both claims.

What a noble Zionist!

Call this, in conclusion, an imagined exchange between an Israeli and myself. (Actually not imaginary at all, but a pastiche of conversations held at length, in Israel and at home.)

ISRAELI: Where do you go when there's nowhere to go? This, it seems to me, is a question you've never had to face.

BERRIGAN: Yes, I have. In life at least. You don't go anywhere.

ISRAELI: What do you mean, you don't go anywhere?

BERRIGAN: I mean just that. You stay put. I believe the term is *sit in*. Which doesn't mean, by the way, that you sit there like a sitting duck.

ISRAELI: Then what do you do?

BERRIGAN: You start all sorts of things. You start making peace where you are. You start listening. You start, as the prophets say, doing the works of justice. You start resisting governments—mine and yours. A government that, in both cases, is not only anti-Palestinian, but anti-you as well. You seize to yourself the right to survival, a right that is threatened not primarily by Palestinians at all—but by your own leaders. You start putting interventionist diplomats, of whatever stripe, to the door; and slamming the door shut.

And you start granting to others the rights you demand for yourselves. You start creating safe borders by creating friendships across the borders.

ISRAELI: You're full of advice for those on the front lines. While you're at it, do you have some morsel of wisdom for American Jews as well?

BERRIGAN: My word to Israelis is, "Start something." My word to American Jews is, "Stop everything." Stop brokering war and urging the peddling of arms. Stop urging Israelis to be heroic on behalf of a homeland you keep your distance from. Stop being quintessential Americans first (all bombs in one basket), and Jews somewhere down the line.

ISRAELI: And how about the Christians? Will you grant they're part of the problem?

BERRIGAN: In many ways the worst part of all. They work off their guilt toward the dead by irresponsibility toward the living. Their ethical life reminds me of a misguided tour through Hades. That loud support for whatever Israeli policies!—policies, in fact, of the unenlightened and overmilitarized: they're entitled to respect or contempt on the same basis as any other nation's; no more, no less.

Misguided Christians: they're like misguided missiles; they do great harm, purportedly by chance, along the way to their goals. They kill—by indirection, it's said. I say killing is immoral, whether by indirection or folly.

ISRAELI: You don't allow, then, that Israel, for a hundred reasons, is a special case, entitled to special treatment and help?

BERRIGAN: No nation state is entitled today to anything more than skepticism. On the other hand, every people, considered just as people, is a very special case. Including Palestinians, stuck in camps where wanton murder must surely recall other camps, other deaths.

Speaking of Israelis, there's no need to invoke the past to arrive at a very special feeling. Their present situation would bring tears to a stonier heart than mine. Israelis are entitled to more compassion with every day that passes.

Their leadership, on the other hand—religious, military, political—is entitled to ever more contempt. So are their American masters. We must, in short, help save the Israeli people, as well as the Palestinian remnant—by making it impossible for present policies, benighted and ruinous as they are, to continue.

CHAPTER 15

Swords into Plowshares

Everything enhances, everything
gives glory—everything!

Between bark and bite
Judge Salus's undermined soul
betrays him, mutters
very alleluias.

The iron cells—
row on row of rose trellised
mansions, bridal chambers!

Curses, vans, keys, guards—behold
the imperial lions of our vast acres!

And when hammers come down
and our years are tossed to four winds—

why, flowers blind the eye, the saints
pelt us with flowers!

For every hour
scant with discomfort
(the mastiff's baleful eye,
the bailiff's mastery)—

see, the Lord's hands heap
eon upon eon,
like fruit bowls at a feast.

In September 1980, eight of us entered the secret nuclear factory
of General Electric in King of Prussia, Pennsylvania. To no good
intent, as could be surmised by those who know something of our
felonious history. We entered easily, we damaged two unarmed nuclear warheads and threw our blood over them.

The story is told in detail elsewhere, and will require only the barest review here. Worth stressing is the spiritual preparation we agreed on, as required for so chancy an event. We passed several months in reflection and prayer and discussion: a wearying but, as we judged, absolutely crucial process.

I remember facing my fears and doubts, finding my heart strangely lifted by like revelations from the others. Everyone stood to lose—nearly everything except our lives. The biggest loss, the one that loomed most fearsomely, was the prospect of years in prison, consequent family ruptures. And other losses: our good name and, as we saw it, our good work in the world.

Strange that so much should be unknown as to benefit or outcome of such activity; but that the worst befallings should be so certain of occurrence. Would the Plowshares act stand in solitary witness? Or would it perhaps set in motion a series of awakenings, other actions like ours? We could not know at the time; in six years since we entered that nuclear Auschwitz, some twenty other groups would so act: in the United States and even in Europe.

We acted, and stood by the act; and were apprehended, and finally, in 1981, were tried in Norristown, Pennsylvania, and duly convicted. Several of us were subsequently sentenced to three to ten years; the others to lesser time.

Our judge was the redoubtable Samuel Salus III, a phenomenon of note, even for that dark profession.

Truly, Salus was someone to reckon with. An instance of power perfectly meshed with the forces that fuel the times: corporate ego and greed. In Salus, the law's majesty sat ludicrously on a spiritual straw man. Malice, anger, racism, a flailing ego—and a family man to boot. Imperfect perfection of homo Americanus!

Those of our group, including my brother Philip, passed considerable time after our trial in Salus's lockup. We were moved to wonderment at sight of his many victims. Less than ten percent blacks in Montgomery County; but the jailhouse was overwhelmingly black. Such sentences meted out, in duration and scorn of spirit, as to make the angels tremble.

And the judge is, as far as can be judged, by no means moved to repentance for his crimes. He goes on passing judgment. The delayed thunderbolts of God are truly more awesome than their befalling: the delay sets one trembling.

During our trial, Salus struck me as a kind of contemporary Caiphas. The latter eminence, we are told, was "high priest that year." As such, he was inclined to upbraid less hardy souls of the establishment: they were dilatory in disposing of the troublesome defendant. "How ignorant you are! Can you not realize how needful it is, that one man die for the nation, lest everyone perish!" A weighty argument indeed, and by no means gone to rust.

But outspoken wickedness by no means exhausts the import of Judge Caiphas. In the gathering tragedy, John sees something of infinitely greater import than a corrupt ecclesiastic, faithful to the usual interests. He confers on this inflamed spirit a dignity beyond the ordinary. The blindness of Caiphas, the weightlessness of his moral capacity, become the instrument of God.

Talk about turnabout and fair play! "Caiphas said this not out of native insight, but because he was high priest that year (John underscores this twice, a capital point); and so he prophesied that Jesus must die; and not only for one people, but to gather in one, all the scattered people of God."

The words are written, of course, from the advantage of considerable hindsight. In the breach, the game of the high priest looked like the usual hype of power—foul means for purportedly noble ends. A bore, a stereotype, an authority beyond accounting. Caiphas, a prophet? It took much time for John to see that those crooked lines did indeed straighten out; that a crooked life, despite itself, served a goodness toward which it offered only ignorance and contempt.

Intriguing. Probably the matter furthest from the mind of Judge Salus, as he set about in pursuit of the Plowshares, was the following: doing his level judicial best to call a halt to the arms race.

And yet I was reminded of the point of John: it is precisely officially sanctioned wickedness that brings about a purpose infinitely above and beyond. If one may paraphrase without danger: "This the judge did, sending the Plowshares to prison, to safeguard law and order. He did this, not only because he was irascible and impatient of any challenge, but because he was a judge; and so exercised a mysterious influence of which he was quite unconscious, in the world of God's providence.

"Thus even the judge bespoke something of the divine; and

while he did evil, served to arouse and unite the scattered will of the people, previously resigned to a nuclear fate."

Or something of this sort.

It will require time, hard time or good—but in any case what looks more and more like prison time—until we are granted that biblical wisdom that came to John. To know what the wickedness of power, in spite of itself, brings to pass. Until then, full speed ahead, in the dark!

As of this writing, summer of 1987, there is no word from the appeals court. We continue with our work: teaching, writing, demonstrating. There is little hope offered, either in the political or judicial process, of mitigation of official folly. An old story, perennially new.

CHAPTER 16

The Foundering of Academe

Love, great love, who is the heart's
daystar and oracle,
whose teasing oracle is
"touch me and be,"
who walks the bestiary mind
lion and lamb, man and woman, one—

great love forbidden utterance.

This tears me, as wild horses
in a mad dream ran wrecking.
Or worse—in a dream of waking, stood
horrible, rampageous, real in the world.

In the early '80s I taught in New Orleans, at the Jesuit university,
for three successive summers. The stint seemed to me, landlocked
as I was in New York, a "treat" in the old-fashioned sense conveyed
by my mother. Something old, something new; certainly something
undeserved; a bonus.

The classes were unmitigated joy. We dredged the Scriptures
together, the students were responsive and serious: mainly older
people, experienced in the works of belief and living. Little nonsense, no time lost; a number of characters in attendance also; salt
and savory.

The Jesuits welcomed me. There were endearing eccentrics
among them also: there seemed ample place for such in the South-
land, in contrast with our northern academic skulls and skills.

So I was content, and walked to heart's content in the nearby
park, a wonder of past made present, with its great, old brooding
oaks trailing their Spanish moss, its zoo, ponds, inevitable joggers
disporting in the steaming heat. And taught and rapped with stu-

dents and others and studied and read and was available to peace groups in the city. And generally speaking, held my soul at peace.

There was, however, a fly in this paradisiacal ointment. To wit: the military was flourishing on campus.

I had best make a confession of sorts. It is undeniably a peculiarity of temperament or background or some such, that this fact, which most would call a fact of life, namely, the military on Christian turf, would rub me wrong. Rub me, in fact, raw. In the ordinary way, as I am frequently given to understand, conjunction of soldiers and priests, the Red and the Black, is no greater moral inconvenience than, say, the marriage of sociologists and classicists (or engineers or lawyers). So what (I am queried by academic brows) is my problem?

Moral unease in the matter is thus commonly met with the barely suppressed amusement reserved for the opinions of the retarded; or at very least, the intemperate.

And if the subject is pressed, among those who might, by supposition, as they say, "see my problem," namely theologians or campus ministers, I must report that the reaction does not greatly differ. Perhaps, just perhaps, there is a modicum more comprehension, a dawning light in the eyes, as of the indistinct outline of a matter newly apprehended, a matter of some possible, though remote, merit. A granting that "Yes, here you may have a point."

That is the moment, alas, when in the mortal mind, knowledge is infected with bad faith. Yes, you may have a point. Implying that the point, conceded as possibly serious, yet were best, if you please, dropped. Too hot to handle.

"You have a point. It may even be a serious one."

We have here, in the classical sense, an incipient act of faith— of sorts. The new faith is as yet lax, boneless.

"About that serious point of yours, I regret to report that nothing will be done. At least by me."

Where is it written that faith without works is bad faith?

At the university, the buck stopped with the theologians. They saw my point. Indeed, as fixtures on campus, some of them for years, they could not but have felt some inkling of unease as the squads marched by, all spit and polish; and the wars marched by, all blood and horror.

As for myself, I took my time, three summers, to size things up. Perhaps too much time in that garden of forgetting.

Indeed, every garden needs a serpent. And such a charming one as we had in residence! Besides, this one was a far older resident than myself. He was "integrated in the community," he and his commanding officers and cadets. More: the benison of a great, nameless sponsor hovered over, periodically pouring largesse—student aid, scholarships, notice from on high. A very rain of gold; O that coil and smile!

Should this wondrous creature, then, not be held in esteem? Was he not beyond the critique of an interloper?

Nearly everyone, it was clear, objected to my objection; at least by silence: the sociologists, classicists, engineers—yes, and the theologians.

"All this will I give you, if falling down"—? It was impolitic to refer to so disquieting a text: it went contrary to the rules of the club.

Thus my dilemma. The theologians would concede my point (to a point). Then their hands would drop. They were bereft of resource, helpless as everyone else.

It must be added, as a matter of truthfulness, they were helpless by choice. They chose to be impeded, in the way of most of us, when unpleasant demands arise, like a cry in the night or a puff of smoke and a flare in a dwelling. What can it mean to the passerby? Must I risk, break, enter, save someone? Come now, let's not be precipitous!

Sometimes, in such circumstance, a heated debate gets underway, conscience on the one hand (a simple matter, really, walking toward the flare, the cry). But then those special interests (jobs, repute, the tenure track, prudence, keeping the peace)—they also cry out; interests that, truth told, are in the nature of long-time squatters in that garden known as Soul.

Religion, military, what to do, what not to do? The debate need have no outcome: it need only churn on and on, a smoke machine. It need only be swept up in the usual fiddle-faddle of the campus minuet. Frivolous? Mischievous? *Ne nominetur inter nos!*—dodge, delay, cowardice. The minuet goes on.

I eventually saw it. The trouble in our garden was not due to the serpent: one must be just, even to crawling creatures.

The serpent had rights too, accruing to an old resident. Besides, the professors and officials were sound environmentalists. You could see it in their clear eyeballs and trim waists: they were joggers, golfers, careful eaters. Daily, at monastic dawn, they bent over health foods, as above a Eucharist.

More: they attended "relevant" liturgies.

They also knew their Bible: for example, the serpent belonged where he was, the Lord had placed him there.

Indeed, to remove him would reduce the scope and variety of the garden; weaken the Lord's intention: "Each living thing, according to its kind."

No, the implication was clear: the serpent wasn't the problem. I was. And if someone should go, I was well advised to know who. Talk about handwriting on hallowed walls! I was getting looks on campus, sociological looks and theological, and certainly presidential, looks that spoke a volume.

Three summers, emoluments, good quarters, good southern board. I too was onto a good thing.

You understand, the gifts and grants fell short of a really first-class tickle of forbidden parts. It was sedate and formal, that garden. It lacked the head-on quality, that blow to the solar plexus, the neon strike, straight for the eyeballs, of New York avarice, pride, lust.

This was southern comfort. It was a reeking, perfumed atmosphere, the ghostly beckoning of Spanish moss from the cork oaks, the somnolent breezes off the levee, those ample porticos along St. Charles Avenue, their snooty look of forever and a day, the antique streetcars chugging and swaying their tin hips and clanging by, Come aboard, come aboard! And the tourists from the hinterlands gaping at all the goodies.

Why indeed rock this sublime, so to speak, houseboat, moored securely to the Mississippi bank? New Orleans, showpiece of Catholicism, the Jesuits purring happily along, puttering, prognosticating, prospering, purveying the faith: what has been from the beginning, what is, what shall be. . . .

Call it ecological anxiety, I couldn't go on indefinitely prospering, et cetera. The serpent was gaping at the classroom window, curled around the cork oak outside. He wouldn't come in, he knew it all anyway. But he pressed things, he signed through the windowpane: "It says here you can't serve two."

HE'S A GOOD JOE, BUT THERE ISN'T ANY PROBLEM, CAN'T
HE GET THAT INTO HIS HEAD?

I resigned. Not much of a gesture, but something.

The event, it can be imagined, was something short of a catastrophe in Eden. I'm told things on campus hum along handily: the
sociologists sociologize, the engineers tinker, the classicists wax eloquent on Cicero and Horace and Caesar's wars and Pax Romana.
The theologians are in perpetual high gear: Christ and sacraments
and prayer, sensitivity and counseling and oh-so-relevant liturgies,
and a course called something like Conflict and Resolution: The
Prophetic and the Pastoral.

And my glittering opposite number hardly winks an eye. He
teaches too, in his own way, the original medium and message in
one great coil and smile. Hip, hip, the ROTC boys march by, Catholics on the move, imbibing from this original source, the one holy
catholic apostolic lesser evil.

1987. Let it be known that a minor miracle has occurred in New
Orleans. A letter from the religion department chair informs me that
ROTC has been quietly removed from campus. And would I, in
virtue of this, consider returning to New Orleans to teach in the
summer session of 1988?

Somewhere between bewilderment and joy, I would.

I dwell in New York with a community of Jesuits, in an old,
shabby pre-World War I building on West 98th Street. And as the
years go on, we have been joined by other hardy souls, for whom
life on upper Broadway presents no terrors.

I have adopted, willy-nilly, the life of a gyrovague, lecturing and
teaching in Europe, Canada, Detroit, Berkeley, commuting for three
months to Yale, venturing also for several semesters into the South
Bronx, to offer courses at a unique college of, for, and by the poor
people of the city.

It was at the College of New Resources that I learned something
of the wit and courage that produce survivors. New Resources indeed!

Our students were all poor, mostly black, intensely given to "getting somewhere" in a sense that was both touching and persevering.

We first undertook the experiment in a church basement: no
partitions between classrooms, the noises and voices and shuffling

of chairs and the children's prattle! All these echoing through the place made one wish at times, clasping his temples, that he was skilled in lip reading!

After three years, we graduated to a vacant Catholic high school building whose clientele had fled to safer ground. There, night and day, our marvelously adapted "learnery" hummed and roared away; and eventually grew to a four-year college, the only one of its kind in the South Bronx. Its continued existence must be accounted a miracle of sorts in the penurious Reagan years.

Our deepest trouble in the first years involved the teachers. We came only gradually, in the way of such matters, to a sense of what qualities were required, if one were not to play the bull in the china closet. The South Bronx, devastated by drugs, prisons, dearth of health services, decent housing, and so on, had produced few teachers. The vicious circle spins fast. So we must scout about the city for candidates.

We came up with a mixed bag indeed; including a number of Ivy League graduates willing, in more or less condescending fashion, to play domestic Peace Corps, and "go down to the poor."

This was the mental cast; though, of course, politesse forbade such words. Nonetheless, the classroom language, whether of mouth or body, gave the game away. We shortly began to realize, to our chagrin, that an old cycle was being renewed under our sponsorship. We were perpetuating, despite all intention to the contrary, an education of contempt.

Our teachers were the miscreants. They came to us, trailing clouds of glory—or of ivy. But no ivy flourished in the South Bronx, only macadam, broken sidewalks, stalled cars, the burnout and staggers and muggings—inferno on the hoof. That and the winter winds to scald the soul.

And then, as one also came to know, something else: some few, the noble-souled survivors. Lives of surpassing hope and wisdom and surprise, of humor and endurance and an eye out for one another. "The poor go to the poor for help." In my experience, the saying was verified time after time.

To say that I was astonished at the spectacle of a people who not only scraped along, but actually, now and then, flourished, exulted, celebrated, in such killing circumstances—the astonishment was simply the measure of my own ignorance, my need of instruction.

At least I was teachable. Practically speaking, it meant a measure of saving humility. I could be attentive to my betters; and so learn from them.

What I heard was the story, told again and again in stunning variation, of those who had made a new life for themselves in the Bronx. Many had come from the Deep South, in childhood: there were veterans of the civil rights days, of southern and northern jails, dogs, sheriffs; many had marched with Dr. King. A number also were skilled in writing, storytelling, poetry, drawing, dance, music.

It was all there, that cauldron of passionate soul, waiting just beneath the subdued look, the years of contempt, the neglectful and tragic schooling—and then drugs, prisons, the violence that created such an unlikely setting for "what mine eyes have seen."

Thus, knowing at least how little I knew, I learned.

But this was by no means the common story. Those teachers of ours, the first and second years! The credentials of several, if truth were told, were a mingling of the ignorance and arrogance endemic to academe. They had come to the South Bronx, in the manner of colonialists, to enlighten the natives. They were, so to speak, overdeveloped as to tongue, and mightily underdeveloped as to capacity of learning.

Thus, in all sorts of overt and subtle ways, they perpetuated our problem, the sorrowful story of most of our students: failure, discouragement, cynicism, dropout. Something, to indulge in understatement, none of us needed.

It was also, as we discovered to our chagrin, much easier to hire such specimens than to rid ourselves of them.

Rid ourselves we did. And things went better.

I had sworn a vow to my soul on emerging from prison, that I would never again set roots down on any campus; for I liked less and less what I saw there. I would come and go, for a semester at the most, teaching in a way that freed me and the students from the paper chase; and then would depart, no strings, no tenure track, nothing lost.

What I disliked, and wanted to remain at distance from, is perhaps best told in a story. On one occasion, visiting the University of Bradford in northern England, I walked the hills for an afternoon with the school's president. He was a scholar and, as it developed, of a vintage not only rare, but extinct in the States. He was a Marxist, and for some years had been a member of the Communist Party in Britain.

We trod and talked. We paused at the crest of a noble hill, and saw in the valley beneath us, the superb ruins of a monastery dismembered centuries before by Cromwell. My host pointed with his walking stick, and reflected: "I sometimes have a feeling that the university as we know it has outlived its time, like the monasteries. And that they too will vanish in somewhat the same way."

His was a thoughtfulness and candor unknown to me. More: he summed up my own impression; that the Vietnam years, as I had undergone them at Cornell, had sealed the fate of the universities as we knew them. They had reneged on even the pretense of a critique of public folly. Their gears, so to speak, had been retooled. (The metaphor, failing in elegance, is borrowed from Cornell President Perkins.) The universities had become, for all their flights of rhetoric and fancy, apt tools of the warmaking state. To all intent, they meshed with a greater and more powerful engine: that of government, the military, multicorporate gigantism.

I thought my part in such arrangements ought, in the name of conscience, be minimal. I would certainly appear on this or that campus, as invitations occurred. But I must stand apart from the center of privilege and perquisite. I might, in consequence, preserve a measure of moral clarity.

I lived for a semester in the neighborhood of the University of Detroit, and taught there. It was a lively three months indeed. Nixon was, as horridly usual, bombing North Vietnam. I traveled to Washington, of set purpose: to be arrested in protest at the Pentagon. Subsequently, I dismayed the university as well as the courts by refusing to return to Washington for trial and sentencing. Instead, I wrote the judge as to my whereabouts, informing him that I was sending the equivalent of my air fare to a Vietnam relief organization.

For three months I also joined the Jesuit seminary in Berkeley. The prestigious ecumenical complex was seated grandly on the sunlit hills over the city. The weather matched the manner: both were beyond reproach. I said to my soul: we have here an anomaly of note.

The Jesuits, who for reasons best known to God and themselves, had invited me to join them for a semester, held pride of place in this place of manifest pride.

I had the impression that hiring me had gone distinctly against the grain. My credentials, by their standards, were wobbly, to speak charitably. And the fact that one course I devised, on the history and practice of nonviolence, attracted several hundred hearers, both of town and gown—this unseemly crowding was of small help in integrating me with the pros. Was this theology or show biz? At times I wondered too.

The episode seems worth lingering over, if only because it marked a deep dissatisfaction with "the faith as taught" at Berkeley. Too easy, too remote, too elite. Too many of "one's own," too little variety and verve. And perhaps above all, too many purportedly clean hands, washing one another.

The class and I prospered. The evening sessions challenged both decor and decorum; they had all the pizzazz of a tumultuous town meeting. At the start of each session, the peaceable and peace-making, among others, lined up at an open microphone: ten minutes were given over to announcements of events in the Bay Area. It shortly became apparent that much skill and experience were present; more, that the hunger for community and study was being fed by these, scarcely licit, goings-on.

After the flood of announcements, I offered a forty-five minute reflection on some aspect of our subject. Theologically speaking, my method was scarcely tolerable: I strove to be practical and earth-bound, dredged up examples drawn from my own questionable past.

This part of the evening was followed by an hour or so of questions, reactions, manifestos (frequently), declamations; and (now and then, a relief of sorts) a hearty condemnation of myself, my ancestry, my misdeeds, my ethos, my prospectively dour destiny.

Following all this, we took a breather, a kind of medicinal recovery period, or a mill-in of sorts. Dogs, books, paraphernalia, cushions, implements, posters, leaflets, food and liquids and their containers, were cleared. The crowd dispersed about the premises, to pursue their inquiries in smaller groups.

And finally, in a state somewhere between exhilaration and exhaustion, the survivors met in a lounge.

The total proceeding commonly perdured from seven thirty in the evening to after eleven. Perhaps a dozen irrepressible souls survived to the finish line. Sometime around midnight, we sought out a pub or sandwich shop for a delayed supper.

It was certainly offbeat, and just as certainly memorable. It might even be classifiable as education.

I could not easily forget the arrangement that held the seminary, and inevitably ourselves, in thrall. Status and degrees were granted by the University of California. And at the same time, the university provided cover for the malignant Livermore Laboratories, a vast nuclear weapons research center some thirty miles distant from Berkeley.

It was a state of affairs I had seen before. Most universities and think tanks played a like game; in this one, the religious community was providing a cover for other, less publicly advertised, enterprises.

Among the resident Jesuits, I seemed the only one troubled by this gentleman's agreement. Seminary, nuclear bombs? There seemed to be no trouble of mind integrating—or forgetting: it was all but impossible to say which.

Still, others in the seminary complex, less burdened by special interests or theological amnesia, were indeed troubled. And in our class, happily and haphazardly ecumenical, toward spring of that year, trouble of mind coalesced. On Ash Wednesday, after long pondering and considerable perplexity, we made our move.

It was all quite simple. We proposed that a service of ashes be arranged. The day arrived, the service proceeded—with a difference. Hundreds of worshipers streamed out of the chapel, bound for the university headquarters across the way. There, while most held vigil, some thirty of us entered the president's office, requesting a meeting concerning the university and its lethal spawn, Livermore.

We were, of course, denied audience. And equally, of course, we sat down.

Our vigil went on and on. Meantime, we held another Ash Wednesday service. We had brought with us photos of the Livermore weaponry. These we fastened to the walls of the reception room. Then we poured ashes on the floor in form of a cross: prophetic dust. As we hoped and prayed, a symbol never to be realized, in spite of all: the future in a handful of dust.

Our symbols were ill received. The photos were judged intolerable and torn from the immaculate walls. We were heartily reproved, by the personnel, for our vagrancy and messiness and disrespect for august surroundings.

And then toward midnight, the campus police cleared us out; and later, in Berkeley court, charges were dropped.

But the Livermore action by no means died aborning. Our ashes of Wednesday were multiplied, and continue to be poured, along with other vital signs, in a campaign that persists to this day.

I dwell on our action in Berkeley as a paradigm. Often, indeed interminably, repeated, East Coast and West.

And yet, when I pause over the word repeated, I wince, sensing the inadequacy. Does conscience ever repeat itself? Certainly there is a pattern in my past and that of so many others. We go on, we go on: it is, oftener than not, a contest of sheer endurance. We see nothing happening (indeed we see only worsening of the ills we dare object to).

To see nothing happening; this makes no difference: so we are told by our sternfaced tradition, our Scripture, the voice of prayer, the voices of the great dead. The end is in the means: this is the message, it and the medium are one. Little difference that the end is delayed, even beyond our lifetime (if indeed we are so fortunate as to survive the immediate years ahead). Keep at it, keep at it. The skies are adamant, the ears of the powerful turn to stone. No matter: keep at it.

Then I see the prospect: the same actions stretch ahead, wearying and energizing at once, at times like the tics in the machinery of time itself; at others, like the beat of a heart. Nothing else for it, keep at it.

And immediately I am brought up short. Time is no engine, making dumb moments, cloning routine, boredom. Time is all heart: it beats steadily, it conjures up images of hope and resolve. It has its own body language; it thrusts out, now the open hand of a beggar: Give this! And again the index finger of a passionate rabbi: Go there!

If this is true, and every act on behalf of life has it own resonance and aura, there can be no talk of repeating acts of conscience. Each wears a face, each countenance is its own.

Time thus takes on the face of the living: the unborn, the departed, walk the earth. To tell the times right is to read the faces, to beckon the dead and the unborn to one's side. It is to take them to very heart—which might also be named, taking them seriously.

And then to walk with them, the cloud of witnesses.

Indeed, apart from such events as Ash Wednesday, I was simply stalemated in Berkeley. Ought I perhaps never have come? I remember on arrival the drowning sense that took me. It was not so much that I was out of my depth intellectually—rather I could find no place for myself, I was at a loss for what was expected of me.

It must be confessed, I had no confidence in the seminary proceedings. Perhaps that was it. The year charged ahead with such confidence! Young and old, teachers and taught, exhaled a sense of knowing their errand and direction, north, south, straight as arrows—discipline, books on books, discourse, exams, all the paraphernalia.

And then, the dark side of this luminous side. The isolation, the pride of place, the assured future, the security.

I knew, of course (who did not?), the high repute in which the Jesuits were held, that they rode the catbird seat, that their classes were respected and largely attended. My satisfaction in this was all but rubbed out in my perplexities. What could it all mean? What sort of future were we offering our students? And perhaps more to the point, were our lives making sense—to ourselves?

I could get nowhere with such questions: the more I puzzled and fretted, the clearer I saw my situation, its impossibility. With the exception of a small number of students, no one was troubled at Berkeley; whether by the university connection, the arms race, or the impermeable good life. It was all fair weather, a good voyage, the gods puffing the sails.

Few among the Jesuits, as far as I could judge, were prepared to welcome me as a peer; which indeed in that Himalayan height, in the thin air of professionalism, I was not. No difficulty in admitting it. But still a question: why this narrow, cozy spirit? The dean, thinking perhaps to ameliorate things, and offer occasion for the faculty to view the phenomenon at close quarters, announced an evening with Berrigan. And two women, and not one Jesuit, came.

At that point, feeling something like a litterbug in the garden of experience, I thought to sack up my questions like a dumb holiday debris, and depart. And almost did.

If only it were that easy, or if it could be called responsible toward my students (or even, despite all, toward the Jesuits), so to settle things in my mind! I could not. The questions might be my own peculiar load (I suspected that in the classy clothing they lurked in others' pockets as well)—but even if they were mine alone, that did not disqualify their claim to validity.

Another image occurred. I felt as though I was walking in a storm that had weirdly broken over the seminary, a snowfall in the torrid Berkeley summer. It was a senseless onslaught, out of season, out of right reason. It was a snowfall in the sun. It was all that storm of theology evaporating. And the sun shone on and on, the intoxicating soporific days and nights, and Scripture and liturgy without end.

And out there a red dawn, Livermore Labs and the apocalyptic light that could evaporate everything in the hour of its rising.

Degrees of sense, degrees of senselessness. I would never be so fond as to name New York a celebration of the mind, a city where logic shines. And still, for a variety of reasons, the lunacy of the place is at least assailable, a mad throat in one's grasp. And that tactile, visible, audible feel of things makes the city, at least for me, bearable. There is something to strike up against; there are also those to strike with.

The snow, of this writing, falls in plenty, and lies there on the bare ground, palpable, frozen, gritty. Here and there in the sprawling incomprehensibility of things, theology, like northern snow, falls and is grounded. Under the wintry sky, one's sense of God and one another becomes—one hardly knows how to describe it (one must not glory in that sense, it barely survives)—perhaps urban? In any case, one welcomes it gingerly, strangely grateful for the heft, weight, pressure.

There is no ignoring it. No one in our New York summer, short, sharp as the flash of a blade, no one rots in the sun. The faces, the shapes and misshapes! The homeless; the beaten; the displaced; the beggars displaying their wounds and stumps, on the street, in the subway; the mutterers and mad—those lowering looks, like a chorus of vengeances—all forbid the easy entrance, the soft-shoe exit.

Each to his own lunacy. I returned from Berkeley to New York with a great susurration of relief. And certain, to no great satisfaction, that a like relief was expressed at my going.

Life was, so to speak, a double negative. One could not not do something.

Thus the world. Double, negative. One could, if one so chose, conjure up a better world, one less woebegone and wounded. One could even enlist others to join the game and construct fabulous mansions in the sand. Indeed, they were all around us, these unsolid demesnes, raised by fantastics.

Alas, the next tide would take them away, imaginative or hopeful as the children might be. The times took them away; for the times were a riptide. Pride of place was of no avail: the world was a neighborhood; and the neighborhood was going to very hell.

CHAPTER 17

AIDS: The Dream, the Awakening

For them, clocks race, and
midnight goes off, a
publican's bark;
GENTLEMEN, TIME!

O the achievers
O the go getters
O the young lovers

Beautiful people
look, at the end
like skid row smouldering

The mothers totter
pillars of salt

The church stalks off
righteous and wrong

sunsets whisper
Get out of town!

Faces on dollars,
works & pomps,
grow arms and legs and
run like a million
lottery winners
away away

Here comes a sorrowful
priest, his cry—
Let go! let go!

Nevertheless

the world clings

and earth blows hot
and flesh ignites

Nevertheless

Take hope! take hope!

at a leper's touch
the oxymoronic
world grows sane
at the lepers' bell
the kingdom comes

In the mideighties, at St. Vincent's Hospital in Greenwich Village, I am surrounded with those dying of AIDS. Connections seem somewhat elusive. Still, an image recurs: the dying are falling out of the Dream.

The Dream image. A dream of immortality. Youth as immortality. And, more especially, youth in a dream setting: achievement, money, sensuality, a jewel in its precious setting. The ego, and its pavane.

Certain quite privileged lives must (in their own estimation) be ensconced in a fitting decor: clothing, setting, entourage. Starved faces may appear wraithlike at the window, hands beat at the door. Cries are heard; myths and slogans, vociferous, alert; life and death and politics and ethics and economics. The voices, and their owners, outsiders all, are furious at the spectacle of the "haves"; they attach inelegant names to our Dream and its Dreamers. Selfish, un-Christian, inhuman, parasitic. And worse: the economic inequities, the appetite, the arrogance of those in possession, hardly allow adequate expression, emotional or cultural discharge.

In fact, reaction to gays outside the "safe borders" of our culture tends in many respect to run with an adverse domestic current. Third World and First: Down With Them! Perennial envies, fears, hatreds, excoriations, religious dreads, biblical denunciations, form an all but universal chorus. Sodom, corruption, sin, contrariety to nature, and so on. In this matter, it scarcely matters the culture or time.

Perhaps we have a clue here to the mauling of gays by many revolutionary governments. Their leaders, loud in condemning nearly every aspect of capitalistic life, strangely echo the images of gays held by the right in America and Europe—gays as the pampered darlings of economic injustice. And in consequence (in the Third World), no room for gays, in presumably "virile," young, revolutionary societies.

The point, I take it, is a serious one. And it is at just this point of revolutionary exclusion, when old hatreds jazz up in chic new fatigues—at this point one would think, the church is called to intervene, to translate, object. Raising, for instance, a question: what revolution can claim credence or respect, when it drags ancient hatreds in its wake, under whatever plausibility?

Alas, the church does no such thing. It joins, in fact, the worst sentiment and politics; whether of First, Second, Third Worlds. Gays are the universal political solvent. Solve their existence, solve it all!

Shall we call them gypsies, Jews?

But I was discussing parallels, meeting points where understanding might blaze out anew. The nukes "protect" gays as well as straights; so we are told. A truer evaluation, one which very few come to, especially in light of a fairly comfortable existence, is that the nukes enslave us all—gays as well as straights.

The content of the Dream is decreed, all said, by the nukes. If one can imagine it, penetrating the decor of the culture ("We're making it, even making it big; and to hell with the hindmost")—the Dream hovers between sweetness and light on the one hand, and febrile nightmare on the other. The Dream is simply a Star Wars scenario playing indefinitely in a theater of the absurd—the fantasies of its directors, producers, actors, audience.

According to its confabulators, the scenario will supply the determining images for centuries to come: dreams of dominant technique, of imperial control, of freedoms honored in theory and progressively ridiculed and scorned in practice. The future will be the present, intensified, concentrated: legitimatized regimes of terror.

Present images, increasingly plausible and enslaving, will rule our children and children's children. (Presuming the blessing of progeny: the scenario both presupposes this, and simultaneously endangers it beyond words. Like the monster in Dante's *Inferno*, it both begets and eats offspring.)

This mess of mythological pottage, this self-contradicting Dream, makes slaves of us, keeps most of us inert and victimized, makes hostages of our children as well as ourselves. And yet we are instructed by the highly placed Smilers to keep smiling through, as though the dollars in our pockets or the brains in our heads were still workable, negotiable, a sound tender. As though, in plain fact, our world were not raving mad in its chief parts. And driving us mad, as the admission price to its Fun House.

Another, related matter occurred to me. In a peculiar and spurious visitation, the Dream arrives. It is an image of the past, presenting itself as present. It validates notions as disparate as the just-war theory, sacred nationalism, war as liberator, myths and modes of loyalty, patriotism, religious–civic fealty. It freezes these, focuses reverential attentiveness, sets in mind a consensus of hopes and myths, achievements, possibilities, visions of normalcy—all of them dead dinosaurs.

Fixation and distraction, both together. The Dream denies and suppresses utterly, certain truthful, even crucial, aspects of present day life and its tasks: aspects of danger, resources of moral courage, necessity of risk. And perhaps most important of all, it suppresses a history of moral sensitivity regarding civil and criminal law—sensitivity that, time and again in our American past, trespassed on forbidden ground—and so saved the day. Such events, convictions, taken seriously and followed through, are of enormous import, offering as they do a slim chance of human survival.

I reflect on a dolorous fact. Many gays, among many others, spent their days drifting through the Dream, enacting it, embodying it.

In its embrace, one was reasonably sure of an unimpeded appetitive life: dolce vita, as the culture defines it. Conspicuous consumption, gratification: this is living. And indeed it is, if one is inclined to entrust a sweet skin to such mentors as presume to speak for us today, in politics and education and the commercial world, as well as in most churches.

This is how I came to see my work among the AIDS ill: a great chance opening before me, surrounded as I was by ruin and early death.

Most of us, I suspect, undergo something similar to this, the birth pangs of a "terrible beauty" (though far short of what I have seen)—if we come to much of anything: whether of adulthood, moral coherence, a religious sense of things.

In roiling waters, one must not launch a frail boat without serious forethought. No unconsidered word must be uttered. Indeed, the word, when truthful and unimpeded, is likely to be entirely opposite: disconsolate, abandoned. . . .

Who was it, anyway, who first told of the terror of the world? And how are we to comprehend a God who not only allows such tragedies as daily pummel our souls—a God who actually underwent like things in his own flesh?

And worse: who can this God be who refuses, after all the centuries and their repetitious outrage, to renounce these shameful origins?

In the early winter of 1984, I undertook this work: one that, despite all its air of improvisation, had about it a tease of the familiar.

Familiar indeed: I had, after all, spent some three years as a hospice volunteer among the dying on the Lower East Side of New York. So what else, in the parlance, was new?

New York is a very necromancer's cave of the new. Especially, some might be inclined to say, of the newly horrible. New York had become, in the space of a few years, a concentrated center of AIDS. I would investigate all this, firsthand, as a volunteer. Nothing dramatic, no great thing. But I had a sixth sense, residing somewhere in the bones, that I could be of help.

A bit of history may be in order. I first encountered the gay community at Cornell, where I was teaching and working in the late sixties.

My position was, in a sense, both anomalous and enviable. Certain pieties, certified at its founding by Ezra Cornell, still clung to the ivy of the place. Thus I was hired and designated, without anyone knowing quite what the term might mean, as a religious employee. As far as might be judged, that placed me somewhere on a rung above a hewer of wood and drawer of water, and several rungs below the faculty. All to the good, I thought.

I arrived during the Vietnam war, against which I had sworn what resistance I could muster.

We were gifted on campus with a first-rate team of chaplains, most of whom would prove supportive in the breach; and at least two of whom would themselves challenge the law of war.

Entirely to my advantage also was the heady freedom in the air of our Gothic bastion, Annabel Taylor Hall. In the inelegant phrase, I grabbed my freedom and ran.

My "office," (a closet located somewhat off the beaten track) shortly became a haven of sorts. There, day after day, gathered the motley sons and daughters of the late Ezra's Great Learnery. They were a hybrid flock, much inclined toward intellectual unruliness, inordinately talented, antiwarlike, innocent of the world, and in senses both startlingly lucid and vaguely mystical, quite religious and gentle in spirit.

They sought a measure of solace of spirit in the uncomfortable circumstances of My Place—squatting on the floor, strumming their instruments, listening, speaking loud or low, passionately, redundantly excoriating the war and its makers.

And now and again, a solitary arrived: someone on a serious quest of conscience; personal resistance against the war; Canadian exile or prison for refusal of the military; forks in the road, violence or nonviolence; coping with parents and family. Shifts of mood, hope and horror, the heavens a crazy fallout, the media, gods of dust, casting dust in the eye.

So they came to my door. I did my best, one to one, one to many.

And then one day someone appeared on a different quest. A young man whose bearing suggested a burden above the "ordinary" of those extraordinary days.

He was, he informed me, a member of a small nascent group of gays on campus. His friends and he had recently applied for university status and privileges. And had been, in due course, refused.

They were presently occupied in appealing the decision, which they judged arbitrary in the extreme. Would I support their petition, and lend my name to the appeal?

It seemed to me, after no great palaver, that a simple matter of justice was laid before me. Of course: use my name.

The group was instated in due time. And to all appearances the matter ended there.

But it did not. Some weeks later, my Cornell superior, notable for plain speech and uncluttered conscience, approached me. His manner was distraught. As to this campus matter of the gays, had I not been imprudent? Was I unaware that my endorsement of such a group would be construed as an admission of personal gayness, I being the sole celibate member of the religious team?

He was serious as a face on a gravestone. His mood, which might be characterized as modified mortician, was apt to induce a measure of trauma. I reacted, however, with calm. If I had judged aright, and the matter of gay status on campus (as the status of any other special interest group)—if this was a question of justice two cents plain, then the famous chips might fall—wherever wind, tide, or malice deposited them.

Sic solvitur. The winds blew over. Whatever allegations it pleased the malicious to sow, dispersed. And to this day, I am inordinately grateful for that beginning.

My education along the preceding lines continued, even in prison. Danbury Federal Pen, whence I repaired in 1970, contained, among its resident ornaments a contingent of urban gays.

Their reserved section of our federal housing could best be described as a kind of *cage aux folles,* crowded with veritable birds of paradise, the flock neither in moult nor (at least for the instant) in migration.

They were, like every endangered species, skilled in the wiles of survival. Chief among these was an instinct for flocking together in the storm. The prison authorities unwittingly cooperated in this, judging our imprisoned masses of crooks, druggies, car thieves, politicians, extortionists, et al.—less apt to be drawn into unmentionable conduct if the gays were strictly segregated.

The decision, to judge by their reaction, was strictly fine with the gays. They were, in any case, great flockers. Nightlong, after lockup, they would regale one another, and perforce ourselves, cell to cell, with their inimitable, wondrously vulgar cacophony, an auditory farrago, mockery and mime. It was a marvel, it was outrageous. It went on in defiance of all rules (and all possible inclination toward sleep) until the small hours.

I reflected on the meaning of this unaccustomed scene, and only much later came on a clue. The clue went roughly like this: the gays were staging a drama of absurdity and redemption, for the benefit of some, the fury of others.

We were, after all, consigned by the law to a species of secular hell: such went the presumption of our judges and keepers. Abandon hope, all you who enter.

They abandoned nothing of the kind, our aviary. They were under lockup indeed, like all of us; but they were there under protest. Therefore, in a spirit of celebration and rage, they would make their protest visible and audible and public. Take it or leave it.

In this project, sedulously pursued, it goes without saying that they differed greatly from the mass of prisoners, defeated and housebroken. Many of the latter reacted in ways both shameful and predictable: derision, the fear that strikes out in fury. Thus, more or less blindly (but not entirely by any means) missing the point of the comico-serio-tragico drama; the plumage, the swish, the contralto tones. The costumes and decor of pure revolt.

They mimed and mirrored, according to the sound advice of Shakespeare, the "manners of the time." Why were we locked up, they and we? And what might be expected to transpire in such a place, by way of improvement of our mores? And who, in any case, was equipped to judge us in such obscure matters, say, as crime, sexual or political conduct, rehabilitation?

There was no answer that might make even a modicum of sense. There was only an amoral, doughy, "That's my job" copout of all and sundry, top to bottom of the dead prison tree of command.

That being the case—and equally to the point, the world outside being the large image of the small madnesses and puny brutalities of prison—it followed that this skilled mockery, this reduction and distillation of prison absurdities, this celebration of unimpeded wild freedom, touched also on a larger plight and horizon: the culture, America.

America, for most of the gay inmates of Danbury, meant New York and, more precisely, Broadway. It was uncanny. In 1972, on release from durance vile, I settled in with Jesuits, on the Upper West Side of Manhattan. It shortly appeared that several of the "old boys" of Danbury occupied an aviary close by.

On Broadway, one is daily tempted to a conclusion that is constantly challenged and frequently proven false. The conclusion goes somewhat like this: one has been exposed, on that unlikely thoroughfare, to every possibility and improbability of the human condition. Nothing more, in the area of the bizarre, could possibly be concocted by the Lord of the Dance.

Wrong. Each day on Broadway, one is proven wrong, by evidence of his own astonished eyes. One makes his way innocently along. Comes—something else, some astonishing, altogether unique specimen. The boundaries of the probable are once more pierced.

Thus my education, proceeding apace.

One day, immersed in the usual crowd, I was ambling southward on my street, some errand or other in view. Suddenly there rushed toward me, uttering a piercing, somehow familiar and birdlike cry, an exhorbitant figure.

It was indeed one of our prison avifauna, resplendent in female costume. Approaching precipitously, the apparition flung himself into my arms.

Daniel, don't you remember me? he shrieked.

Indeed I did.

He proceeded, no need of urging, to recount a spate of names and news concerning old jailmate friends. And to inquire with fervor as to my well-being. And by what happy chance was I found, as he expressed it, walking "on his street"?

Meantime, the crowd of Broadway denizens, cynical as they might be as to further possible variations and habiliments of the human condition—these were stopped dead in their tracks. Those who thought they had seen everything, saw something unreckonable. An undoubted male, vivid in female getup and makeup, had affectionately accosted a rather nondescript passerby, notable for neither getup nor makeup. For all my chagrin at suddenly being thus thrust into a lurid limelight, I was forced to a rueful grin: my friend was a crowdstopper.

But there was more to come: some would say worse.

There could be glimpsed on Broadway, from time to time, one or another member of an extravagant gay commune. My friend dwelt in their company; many among them repaired irregularly by subway to Times Square, where they were, so to speak, part of a mysterious workforce. Thus did my education, as to the human, its wondrous absurdities and illimitabilities, continue.

Speaking of my education, there was the matter of John McNeill, Jesuit psychologist and philosopher; a matter that continues to harass his spirit and mine. In the midseventies, he had been a prime mover in founding a group of Catholic gays. Members of Dignity, as it came to be known, came together to offer solidarity and solace, and to press for a measure of rights within the church. That their rights were violated and ignored was no great secret: it was, in fact, a millennial disgrace.

Shortly, Dignity began to attract public attention: it became a matter of note that the disgrace was in process of being uncloseted; and this largely through McNeill, a priest of integrity and substance.

He was becoming a public figure to reckon with, writing and speaking throughout the land on the touchy topic. Then he assembled a book, *The Homosexual and the Church*: it was acknowledged as a solid biblical study whose thesis vindicated the rights of gay Catholics to a place and voice in the church. The book was published to considerable praise and was widely circulated.

But trouble was not far distant. Within the year, McNeill was informed that church authorities disapproved of his writings. More, the formal approval of the book, which he had scrupulously sought and obtained, was summarily withdrawn. Finally, the hammer fell. He was ordered to cease and desist all writing and public speaking on the topic of homosexuality.

Many in McNeill's Jesuit community were appalled. Dignity had been holding its meetings on our Jesuit premises for some time. Several priests of the community, moreover, were involved in Dignity, in counseling its members and attending its meetings. For good or ill, John's plight was undoubtedly our own.

I pondered the matter. One galling feature of the episode was the secrecy with which it had proceeded; a method that bore a familiar Torquemadan odor.

I proposed to my friend that we break the seal and submit matters to public scrutiny. If this appeared a good move, McNeill must agree to something, a painful concession indeed: my access to correspondence between himself and superiors of our order. If he agreed, I would write and publish an article on the whole matter.

After some hesitation, he handed over the material. The article was published. Many, including McNeill, expressed gratitude for the move.

Almost a decade later, one would be indeed fond to report that the ecclesiastical atmosphere has lightened. The restrictions on John McNeill hold firm: indeed, if anything, they have tightened. John appears as yet another courageous victim of the attempt underway to ravel the seamless robe of the Second Vatican Council. Precious gains must be set back, the personal and social freedom of Catholics reduced to tatters.

McNeill's predicament was my own, it was simple as that. My own freedom was assailed when McNeill's was. My life could never be construed, even after many years and many conflicts, as a matter of just entitlements or emoluments—were these so simple a matter as a quiet place in the sun where an old dog might doze.

Alas (another image), there were no free rides on the planet: one paid, willy-nilly, as one went. And as often as not, the coin was stained with blood and tears. Thus went McNeill's and my trip through time, a careening express ride, unsteady tracks.

In the spring of 1987, the ordeal of John McNeill ended. He was dismissed from the Jesuit order.

End of the seventies, and a Berkeley episode.

In the course of my sojourn, I was invited to address the gay fellowship of the Unitarian-Universalist church. I improved the occasion, as Dickens would say, by inviting my congregation to consider the implications of gay socialization, East Coast and West.

Which is to say. Among the upwardly mobile, positively leaping the jagged waterways of America, must surely be accounted the gay urbanites of New York and the Bay Area. And then the ramifications—of buying into America with such fervor. Indeed, the gays underscored, for all to see, the rewards and aura attendant on professional achievement. Also to the point, I thought, was a patina of *haute couture* consumerism, whether in San Francisco or the appetitive Upper East Side of Manhattan.

Were such achievements, I questioned aloud, matter for unmixed rejoicing? I allowed myself to doubt it, pointedly.

A further doubt: that the gay rights movement deserved to be taken seriously—as long as a unifocal vision ignored the larger suffering of the world. As long as it neglected as well the forming of necessary connections with that world. Did I need remind the congregation of the nuclear arms race, epitomized a few miles from Berkeley, in the notorious Livermore Laboratories? In those secret precincts and outside, it was hardly a matter of ignorance that every nuclear weapon since Hiroshima had been developed.

And were those present aware of the plight of the poor of their city, of crimes against the powerless, of officially sanctioned, or at least tolerated, homelessness—many of these offenses occurring in so-called inviolate neighborhoods, with the approval, or even urging, of gay dwellers?

As I recall, my remarks were received with only a modicum of resistance.

He was to emerge in my mind as a symbol, even while he lay there in the hospital bed at St. Vincent's, very much himself; but stricken too.

A symbol of that procession of the young and doomed, their class, elegance, verve, money, wit, New York edge and polish. All this—and then, the Interruptive Shove.

It was inelegant, a bum's rush.

Something akin to the shove and jolt of subway voyaging, put up with, in the seldom dull journey from here to somewhere. Half the pain is getting there.

But the subway crush and batter is one thing; the chic apartment, the summer lair in the Hamptons or Connecticut, quite another. No swaying, ill-tempered multitudes of the IRT express tarnish the allure, the ambience: friends, evenings over wine, gently spiteful gossip, vacations, all the perks of all the trades. The good life and then some: the best.

And then, something else, something terrifying. The Interloper. Defying, with an utterly inviolable arrogance, the conventions, the secure symbols, status, good looks, money, credentials, the evidence of "making it."

I am meeting Douglas for the first time. And in a hospital, a place hardly designed for easeful intercourse of spirit. Friendship does not flourish here: alienation does, and fear and trembling. People enter under duress, hell-bent for release, prompter better. Who indeed has wit to praise this sterile overnight caravansary, no hiding places, the staff often abrupt and grudging?

He was young, as are nearly all. Rangy, over six feet, unconventionally good-looking, alert of eye: the eye of a storm.

There was the matter of the sterile mask, a symbol commonly denounced by the ill. A sign of anonymity: yours, the patient's. Sign of distancing and fear. One sufferer described the surreal goings-on: a flock of marveling medicos would shuffle in and surround his bed, masked, for all the world like a Night of the Klan. They muttered their polysyllabic incantations ("like butchers around hung meat"), they scrawled mysteriously in their books and departed.

It was bizarre, he said bleakly: one hardly knew, especially if one was in fever, whether he had dreamed the episode or undergone it.

I put on the mask that first time; it was practically the only time. And only under gentle duress; because my young friend was flushed with pneumonia, and requested that I don the thing. He dreaded infections from the outside, quite enough invasive crawlers were occupying his person.

There was touch of the sardonic I found quite comforting. It covered the shock nicely, a clean bandage over a suture. That he was in shock could hardly be concealed for long; he had been diagnosed that morning: it was AIDS.

I was in a species of shock myself. It was my first venture into the AIDS world. I had dreamed perhaps that the transition could be managed gently, gradually. Hadn't I worked with dying cancer patients for some three years? I had even conjured an image: a child being led, step by step, days passing in course, into an adult world. Does death invade that world? Tell the child so, by all means; but ever so gradually, with due regard for the bewilderment, the gradual awakening.

Then the image dissolves, another forms. There is a face before you, a suffering face and young. Its wearer is being pushed violently out of custom and orbit.

Another image. A child is assigned, without prelude, in midterm, to a different schoolroom. No friends, no familiar books, the geography of the room fairly bristling with the unknown. Students an impenetrable phalanx, their glances halfway between cruelty and curiosity.

Take the image further. Now the child is transported to another school altogether: it lies in a distant part of town. The world that appears from the bus window—where am I, why am I here? Totally, terrifyingly unfamiliar. No landmarks. The child is set down, with a thump, on a different planet. And how will one be received there, wearing, as one does, a different skin?

Death calling the shots. The mask, the gloves, the white robes, the accoutrements of a butcher's warehouse, a walk-in freezer, a city morgue. The scene, know it or not, is a revving-up for the end. Get ready, take off.

Douglas and I make small talk. Did I know he is an artist? And would I care to see his portfolio?

I turn the pages, astonished, delighted, the achievement blazes out.

A running commentary begins. He had returned within the year from Australia and New Zealand. There were honors and perks: a year in residence, a major showing in the Australian capital. At last he was earning income from his art sales.

I had no adequate words, the photos of his work were enchanting. He was of the true artificer tribe, a weaver of reeds and palm and hemp, into quasi-human shapes, some on stilt legs, impenetrable, dynastic, ancestral. They were garbed in natural browns, grays, muted rusts. Their limbs curved gently or were twisted in menace, their great height was now protective or fierce, angelic or demonic.

There were large photos of his museum show in Melbourne. I saw a long gallery, some sixty by twenty feet, shapes recumbent and standing, a mysterious procession, masks, majesties. Found objects, an assembly of demigods, recognizably (but barely) human. An exodus of sorts; or perhaps an entrance rite.

He called the assembly *Floating Forest*. In the midst was suspended a hammock or portable cot: on it rested a figure, wrapped in silence, like an ear of corn in its husks. It was regal and timeless, hieratic, an imperial mummy attended by the living.

Before and after the mysterious corpse, other figures stood, walked, threatened.

Was the artist miming the fate of all, or his own?

I ventured: "The dead figure walks again, in spite of all. You seem to have come on a Resurrection theme."

Then, "I wonder if your intuition got ahead of events, and you knew in some way, years ago, what was coming."

He nodded agreement. And in a piece he wrote two years later, shortly before his death, I came on this:

> What was gnawing at the most basic level of my physical being began to express itself in "Floating Forest." Three large figures constructed of handmade cast papers emerged. I was surprised at myself, feeling I had bitten off more than I could chew. . . .
>
> One piece was a sleeping figure covered with paperbark I'd collected in Arubem Land. It was resting in a dream canoe and was very peaceful and gentle.
>
> Next came a nightmare tableau comprised of three elements; a flying sled impaled with sharpened sticks, a bound figure covered with bottle-brush pods and pierced with twigs. And finally a huge, menacing cockroach that hung over the other two. . . .
>
> The last piece was "Survival," a hollow, winged creature with its innards totally exposed. Layers of fiber unwound from its head as it flew—illusions lost in flight.
>
> The environment was exhibited in Adelaide, Melbourne and Sydney. It was very well received and thousands wandered through it. I couldn't believe I'd done it.
>
> For me the meaning became very clear two years later, in October of 1982, when I was diagnosed as having AIDS. . . .

I was absent, in Latin America, for several months. Douglas had had rough going during my absence. In and out, out and in the hospital. Between bouts, he functioned at home, but only with help. One day there was a call from him: welcome home, and would I stop by?

The change in him was a shutter coming down on the day. He dragged himself to the door and greeted me with a smile like a cheerful skeleton's. Thinned down now, thin as a walking bone. And those telltale splotches on the face, deep brown on pallor: the mold of death.

We talked and talked, making the best of things; he offered, and was able to steep, a cup of tea. The effort was incongruously huge.

"I sleep until near noon, and it's three in the afternoon, and I'm exhausted," he said.

I asked about his work. Some half-done things, he dismissed it with a shrug. "But one thing's to the good. My doctor's favorite sport is dunning me for money. I've offered him a few things in lieu of cash; and he's agreed. So that's an ape off my back."

It was one thing to be dying, I thought—enough burden for anyone; but then to be plagued for payment, in return for services that, truth told, alleviated little or nothing?

It was all loony.

He was to last a while longer, that was all. There would be no "prosperity and long life," as the Bible describes the sojourn of the patriarchs. At thirty-five, his biography was entitled *Decline and Fall*.

So Douglas wove beforehand the drama of sin—death—life.

Still, the original intuition made his terrible illness at least relatively bearable. Whereas, taken alone, borne alone, without that penumbra of mystery and meaning—catastrophe might well have pitched him into the pits. Where so many, not so favored or enlightened, have landed.

Maybe, I surmise, something, a coming together of insights, symbols, hunches verified—something like this might describe a way of coping with disaster: events touching all, not just the AIDS-stricken.

After a month's absence, I phone him. He is very weak, has had another terrible episode in hospital. Will I come over, he longs to read me a few pages out of his biography.

It sounds like the first notes of a swan song.

This occurs to me, and offers a measure of light. Those stricken are under a mysterious summons. They are "going on ahead." Something like our artist, who wove his rushes, more or less unconsciously, by a law blind to his eyes and clear only to his fingers—wove his own future: for encouragement and warning and a dire sign.

A few years later, the artist would face death. But something else happened: he had woven his own healing and return; as he came, slowly and with terror and much trouble of spirit, to realize.

To put matters shortly, statistics instead of tears, during my Latin American sojourn, every AIDS patient I had visited in St. Vincent's died. One exception only, my friend the artist. The bell tolled for every one but him. Perhaps he had a stronger will to survive, or dietary mitigations helped. In any case, he wasn't winning, he was bartering time.

I was like a stunned calf, hearing the news: name after name, all gone. It was as though all normal sense of time had flown the coop. Time and its sane clocks had gone mad. What time was it in the real world? Had I been away fifty years or five months? Everyone had died.

In Argentina I had read *One Hundred Years of Solitude*, that straightfaced mockery of time. For me, the cosmic clock had indeed gone cuckoo. I moved in dream. The people I loved were moving about the business of living, sedate, sensate, on their feet; but in the wavering slow motion of underwater trolls walking in sleep. You could not talk, you could only gesture feebly, witlessly, reading lips as though they were lips of fish.

And every gesture was of farewell. This was how I felt, on my return to New York; only one left, of all who had been ill, in and out of hospital.

In those early ventures of mine among the sick, almost everything was in the nature of a first, clumsy try: would one be welcome, would one be shown the door? How would one be received? How would a greeting, even an innocuous statement, be taken? It was all quite chancy. So much had to be a matter of faith, on both sides.

They land in the hospital, it's like the aftermath of a riptide. The sailing was sweet at first; a cruise in the gentlest of seas. Then the wind and the wreck.

Pardon the inextricable metaphors, it's like a tangled net cast ashore after a storm. Like the knotted nets I come on along the beaches of Block Island. Salted and sandy and cold: the sea waters, like hands of Triton, knot the cords about and around interminably. Combustive complication, I fret to myself.

First to the complication. Most of the ill at St. Vincent's are Catholics.

Gay and Catholic. No news to anyone, the official church atmosphere in New York toward their kind is a very whiff of brimstone. So the following is predictable when I venture into a hospital room. Alarm flags are hoisted—by patient, family, lover. Panic, anger, war. In sum, and at very least, who needs you?

Another complication: the matter of family. A considerable matter indeed, when the chips are down. And, as is probably common knowledge, Catholic families, at least as far as elders are concerned, are not great homophiles.

A subject such as gayness, frowned on by the ecclesiastical mighty, is not likely to flourish in the front parlors of Queensborough. Not likely. Especially when the church, again and again, traces a blessing (powerful big medicine this) on the ingrained phobias of Irish or Italian or Polish or German (or anything) Catholicism.

They gather about the bedsides of their stricken ones: parents, sons, daughters, brothers and sisters, lovers, wives. Sorrow, disorientation, anger, fear, dread of the unknown. The lovers have it hardest of all, making their unsteady way through the gauntlet of church, state, family, neighborhood, job, housing, life in sum; including the feral looks laid on them from the corner deli.

And then, as if this weren't enough, in comes this priest—about whom, if one has ear to the ground, one has heard a few things. So what good can come of this?

As to the good, or what remote part I might have in its making, I wouldn't sweat a bet on an inflated nickel. Who could waste a thought on an abstract good? The only good I could understand lay there, a life ill unto death, the human interrupted, normalcy and expectation gone awry.

AIDS; and the mysterious immunity system breaks apart.

Meantime, I wonder; about everyone. There are enough learned tomes at our disposal to blot out the sun. They tell us, in one way or another, that the immunity system of an entire civilization is collapsing.

Indeed, we are so enchanted with death, that masked charlatan who boasts a curative for any and all ills—so won by his wheedling and dealing, as to summon his services on behalf of all the living! Including ourselves. Come, unholy spirit of nukes and nightmares!

In such a hypothesis, of course, the God who showed another way, who, eternally immune, rendered himself vulnerable to death—he is necessarily declared passé. There are newer, more rational and persuasive, less inflictive and exigent gods in the world. At our disposal, it goes without saying.

The gods of death. Their tactic is the breaking down of the promise of immunity from death, the immunity that we name faith, or grace, or love of God or one another. Let no one be immune! Let hearts be hardened. Let compassion be obliterated. Let all be persuaded, by hook and crook, by bomb and brutality, that death is, in effect, a good way of life.

Various priests come and go in the hospital. A bare nod back and forth. Walkie-talkie, mortician black, dog collar, a look that can bring on the dire conniptions.

Then there's a young priest, a Jesuit, much given to this difficult work. In his nervous, darting way, he knows what he's about, lets his imagination run free, comes up with wonderful gifts—for the ill, for me.

I think at times: we don't deserve him. And we don't. But that's hardly the whole story. He's an artist, ekes out a living (earning his keep is a stipulation of continuance in New York—bed and board under the new dispensation being strictly one's own responsibility). And like so many of the freewheeling talented, he is fiercely exploited by the book Brahmins, for whom he does stunning illustrations; mainly for children's books.

He's currently planning a day of prayer with the AIDS ill. His art and art history help him uncover all kinds of helpful parallels— looking back, for instance, to the days of Jesuit beginnings, when Ignatius cared for prostitutes in Rome, and commended the same work to the Jesuits. And then another tradition: when a plague broke out in the city, Jesuits risked their lives caring for the dying. In those days of no inoculants, and with contagion a risky probability, many lost their lives—including the young saint, Aloysius Gonzaga.

My friend draws on such episodes for his art, and so sheds light in dark corners—where, because of the present atmosphere of panic, many prefer to cower.

He's also produced a sublime and compassionate rendition of our Lady of Guadalupe, for the hospice headquarters. Virgin and child are seated between St. Francis and St. Aloysius. Each saint is supporting and offering to the Healing Pair, a dying man, obviously stricken with AIDS. Thus several provocative and disturbing parallels are drawn taut. For instance, that AIDS is our current plague, and Jesuits are called to a service first undertaken by Aloysius. And further: AIDS people are being regarded as lepers. To round off the dreadful farce, a leper's bell would be quite in order.

We had a birthday party for Douglas. Friends came, including his favorite nurse. There was a scrumptious meal, and a gift and singing of Happy Birthday!—all those beloved, kitschy details that delight the heart of the very ill.

He came in bravely from the cold, bearing a few crocuses. I thought the gesture said very nearly everything: especially about bravery.

We had a good time over many hours. It occurred to me, glancing from time to time at our guest: this is bound to be his last birthday, let's live it up! Indeed, he looked like a walking death's head: skin drawn, flesh fallen away. When he smiled, his jaw was drawn wide like a dog's. He was kept alive on large transfusions of blood, but that game, as he and we surely knew, can be played only so long: he was caving in.

Meantime, with a great measure of help, he kept going in his little apartment, within walking distance, just south of mine.

Months later, winter gone, there was a call from him; his voice rasping and wispy at once, as though he were intoning his plight from the Bridge of Sighs. As indeed he was.

Would I come visit him, this afternoon, the sooner the better?

I brought him purple tulips, on a spring day that surpassed all temperate records.

He could scarcely summon the strength to look up when I entered. Something lurked in the half-darkened room: a menacing, shadowy presence hovered there, an unspoken claim, a bill overdue. It was as though a bailiff or landlord were lounging in the corner, biding his time.

The long and short of it: my friend was about to be hauled away to the hospital. Yet once more. This time, he explained wearily, to be carved open for insertion of something known as a chest catheter. "If I'm going for a bit longer on Earth, I guess it'll have to be endured." He was rueful and resigned, stretched there on the crooked wheel of misfortune.

Then he changed the subject, shy and eager at once. Could he read to me from a series of vignettes he was writing? Would I be interested?

He took up the book. His hands, in just a few months, had grown old and weathered as a superannuated monkey's. His voice, steady as he began reading, broke, and he shook his head, as though casting off a cloud of grief and despair.

The writing? He was an inspired weaver, and the gift touched on words too. He wrote of crisis and surprise and courtesy, of youth and its rude awakening, of love's tumble and turnabout, of that fortune or misfortune we name family. He told of the peculiar Catholic horror—parents who came to know his delicts, his fault in nature; to fear it, and, for a long, desperate time, to refuse credence or support.

There we sat, young Lazarus and I, in a communion of grief. The afternoon sun fingered the room, the artifacts scattered about like a noble flea market, all created by the dying man and his spasmodic, doomed genius, all up for the cruel dispersion time wreaks. Ars longa, vita brevis. Indeed. Time was scattering us. He to the four winds; and I—I must find reason (or abandon reason) to hope on, walk on, go through those motions that signify or simulate life. And which was the harder summons I could not tell.

His art shone down at us from the walls, on tables and chairs and floor. Baskets, weavings, watercolors; and then standing free, standing guard, those noble columns of rush and rope, tall as warriors or angels.

He paused in his reading, I pointed to an unfamiliar piece. When had he done that? "Just recently; it's one of a series. I've been trying to make sense of this damn illness. This one I call *aids in hell*. There's another, *aids and beatitude*; and a third, *aids purified*. I thought first of a crucified figure in hell, but didn't want the thing too explicit."

What followed might be entitled *Heavenly Harassment; or You'd Better Come Quick Into Our Corner, Or Else*.

His mother, a distrait Catholic, had sought counsel concerning his "spiritual plight." Then she had launched the arrow of salvation, known as The Parish Priest.

Douglas: "I finally said, OK, I'd see him, just to keep the peace. An intelligent man, things went well for a while, we talked art, theology. Then all of a sudden, his eyes flashed, he shot straight from the hip. 'What's the most important thing in life to you?' I stuttered, taken aback: 'Why, love, I guess.' He barked: 'And who confers love?'

"'Maybe someone known as God?' (I decided by then my only hope was to go his route, outplay him maybe with a bit of footwork. Then get rid of him somehow, before he set me climbing the walls.)

" 'Correct!!! And who is God's emissary in such matters? Jesus Christ!!!' (By now he was answering his own shouts.)

" 'And what does J.C. give us? Seven sacraments!!! Channels of grace!!! Forgiveness!!! New start!!! YOU'RE INVITED TO REPENT AND START OVER.'

"I thought it about time I poked my head up. I said something about the hard time I had with Catholic doctrine, having tried and been faulted for living as a homosexual by the church.

"He was shockproof.

" 'Homo, hetero, whatever, whichever! he bayed. All bound by the same law: no sex premaritally, postmaritally only for purposes of procreation!'

"He had salvation down pat.

"My mother wants me to see him every week, I'll tell her, I couldn't bear it, not ever again."

I listen to my dying friend. Appalled and saddened. Should anyone, no matter with what delict weighted, lax and weak, the ghost all but given up—should he be punched about like an abused child, required, to endure this? And if so, in whose name?

And further, does it occur to these gentlemen of rectitude and remorse that this Jesus, of whom they fashion a great blunderbuss— might, just possibly, be a creation of their own distemper? And all to no avail, they being no longer the arbiters and judges of the tribes of Earth?

We embraced on parting, the artist to his torment, I to the street. He blurted: I want you to say my funeral mass, I've agreed to it for my parents' sake; and some friends will be there. Will you do it?

He died a month later. One sets down the news with exhaustion and relief. A race too long in the running, and no winner.

He had composed words to be read at the funeral:

This service is something I took pleasure in preparing. It is a sharing from me of certain readings and songs that have made a difference in my life. That have had an impact on who I am and continue to be. The voices of Judy Collins and Joan Baez will always comfort and inspire me. The writings of Suzanne Langer and Gaston Bachelard helped me figure out who I was in a real and tangible way.

As I write this, sitting in my bay windows, the sun is filtering through the shutters and my plants surround me. The sky is moving with dappled clouds, an ever changing panorama of movement, dispersal and new forms.

As sad as I am, I have a strong awareness of having had an extremely full, interesting and exciting life, one that I know is continuing in a new and remarkable way. I am thankful for all of the opportunities I have had to know the world. And I am especially amazed at the wonderful friends and family I am blessed with. And I am curious and mystified as to what awaits me, indeed us all.

He had asked that his ashes be scattered in the tide of the East River, along whose banks he had wandered in early years, this child of lucidity and torment. A changeling, one thinks, a very swan among cockerels. And what were the cluckers, naysayers, vigilantes, to make of the strange visitant in their midst? . . .

One day, he found his element, and sailed off with the tide, grandly as a galleon. And more: for there came back on the wind such a cry of victory as our landlocked mortal ears had never heard.

CHAPTER 18

Another Way: Toward Life

I had lost everything for a year,
a stick in a blind hand—
conundrums, fantasy.

The blind hand struck; the stick
stuck rotting in rich ground.
Four seasons come and gone.

Imagine a face? summon
sustenance, vision, from that ground?

My mind took no fire
from fiery truth; hands hung
like hanged necks, dead, dead as a show.

But the children of Birmingham
clairvoyant, compassionate among the dead—
I see you all night long.
Dawn winds freshen. The cock
makes children by the clock.
the trees lift up their dawn.

As the eighties careened onward, it was a small and smaller matter
who the president was. Any more than in former centuries of horrid
event and lowered spirit, it had greatly mattered who the king was,
or the general was, or the shah was, or the secretary of this or that.
It all went on: the wars went on, the military gorged itself, seized
lands, declared its works and pomps no one's business. It became
more and more difficult to say who was in charge of the country.
Perhaps no one was in charge: perhaps the machinery, the atoms,
the nukes, the computers, had themselves taken control, frictionless,
mad, malevolent, whirring along on their own momentum.

These were surely bad times, I assured my soul; but bad times passed, and were inevitably succeeded by good, and then "Demos," that infallible sphinx, would open his stone jaws. The people would thunder in the desert, sanity would be restored, the wastes would flower.

Well, maybe; and then again, maybe not.

If you looked only to the day, if your sights could not carry your soul higher and further, the news continued bad. It was as though a monstrous press, set in motion by demiurges, whirred away through the night, preparing the bad news of the next day. The demons were in charge: they created the bad events.

The president opened the morning news along with everyone else. But, one thought, he must read a special edition, a presidential one. The news, for him, had a different tone than for the citizens. It included instructions, anticipated decisions: bad news, buildups, invasions, incursions, amputations.

The Really Big News, the Headlines, contained something the Really Big Boys printed for him alone: the disinformation he was to utter that day; the Benign Line that sugared the recessions; the boyish ha-ha that stroked away wintry discontent, homelessness and hunger, Contra war, bloodletting, cruelty, contempt.

The Presidential News also appointed his cronies, shifted them about; just as it shifted the political cards up and down its papery sleeve.

Thus the president had available a genie, a mechanical guru, a perfect, uncontrollable machine, greased with self-interest, violence, blindness. It did his work, and called the work his own.

It is perhaps worth noting: the president had no more control over the workings of the machine than did the citizens. Indeed, if truth were told, he had far less, condemned as he was to his role: a powerless presence, smiling relentlessly, a spurious front of normalcy. He had to lie and lie, weave and feint, smile and smile. He lied even concerning the existence of the first lie: the machine did not exist; the president was in charge. It was a double helix of death.

Above all, the president must deal the stacked cards as though the game were fair, as though the poor had equal stakes with the wealthy, as though international law weighed for anything. As though indeed jargon about democracy or normalcy or tradition or freedom or security had meaning or resonance, as though such words were uttered with due care, restraint, thought: for the truth's sake.

His press conferences recalled the wondrous old-time mayor of New York, who used, on occasion, to improve Sunday morning by a radio reading of the comics. There was no pretense that the mayor had written the comic strips, or that he had seen them through the press, or, least of all, that he was taking what he read seriously. The subject might be *Buck Rogers* or *Gasoline Alley* or *The Gumps* or *Alley Oop*. The mayor read and commented, he had good humor and a rumpled, winning way. No one, strangely enough, listened as though he were announcing news from the real world. He was simply there as an inspired clown, to make us laugh, to dramatize someone else's words and drawings, pratfalls and foolishments, outrageous and hilarious by turn, to the delight of young and old.

Now we have something else. Star Wars, The Kingdom of Evil, Freedom Fighters, Rambo and the gang. With a difference, of course: the subject matter is distressingly belligerent, for one. And far more disturbing, the funnies are being taken literally. We are being asked to believe, and many are believing, that the TV presidential comics are a good, fair, sound version of the real world.

In fact, the words and images evoked in these sessions are not the president's at all, any more than in olden times, they were the creation of the mayor of New York. Indeed, in the present instance, it is hard to discover whose they are. The multicorporate giants, moonlighting as public officials, perhaps? Or the generals? Or the electronic religious preachers? Or Hollywood? Or perhaps a combination of all of these?

In any case, the president's words and images are arranged, not to convey sanity or reality (though in their straightfaced way, they are so offered)—but to mask reality, diffuse it, render it ambiguous or beside the point or simply beyond anyone's grasp.

The press rolls on, the news arrives. It is always bad news. It is invariably old news: sensible minds could predict it. They could also, did they so resolve (some do), do something of far more import. They could deny its sovereign pretension over them, could create a measure of good news of their own. One could so conduct one's life, that is to say, as though something new, something good, something human in the old-fashioned sense, were possible. Even on the day of the Malevolent Funnies.

I sought the name of the genius who ran the press and composed its message. I came up with the name: Lord Nuke. And in naming him, I came on a biblical secret. The name of the beast was the ultimate trade secret. Naming the beast, breaking the code, was also the prelude to any turnabout, any hope: to whatever good news one could create.

Once the beast was named, one noted with relief how the mind was cleansed of false names, those by which the Beast "deceived all." The masks came down: normalcy, security, national interest, family values, legitimate defense, just war, flag, mother, democracy, leadership, religion. The Beast stood there. He was naked and known. More: once named, he was also in chains.

Lord Nuke's ancestry was also revealed in the naming, for those who cared to know. The Beast had not newly appeared on Earth, as the press claimed in tones of wonderment and awe. He was old as the knife of Cain, and the wielder of the knife; older than that: old as the first sin. And the consequence: death.

This was a further truth, a dismemberment of an ancient power. One could make the connection, name the complicity; his aliases, the clues to his ancestry; names such as Deceit, Pride, Envy, Death.

Lord Nuke had been in the world from the beginning. That was a wisdom denied conventional politics; denied also, alas, conventional conscience.

I could not despise any conscience that chose to join us in the fray. Still, at question was our own conscience; as well as the discouragement and dismay that follow on the perennial denial of a good outcome. Things got worse; and where indeed was the Good News?

We had to persevere. Our adversary Death was so patient in pursuit of the Grand Design. We had to go beyond mere horror, which, in the circumstance, appeared as a forbidden luxury; beyond blunting and deadening helplessness, all those ways of falling between the paws of Death before the event.

Helplessness, statemate, fear, paralysis of will: these were, after all, conventional reactions. They were taken in account by Lord Nuke: indeed, he wore such a mask as could reduce any Hercules or Achilles to mush.

Conventional reactions: they led to conventional actions. They

perpetually suggested that conventional politics would lead us out
of our labyrinth, or clean the Augean stables of Congress or the
Pentagon, or roll the stone (the stone in the guts) up the hill of
impossibility—and lodge it there.

Some twenty years have gone by since a few of us, East Coast
and West, began to understand these few things, and to act on them,
in ways we inherited from Gandhi and King and, above all, from
Jesus. In ways also that we had to invent.

On the great Ferris wheel of the years, perpetually turning,
friends came up adversaries, adversaries friends. And each and all,
whatever the effect of the turning world on wit and thought, were
of aid. In raising questions as the wheel arose; then in bringing us
back to earth, as we landed, rubbing our eyes. We, having seen
the world from a distance, from above the fray. And astonished and
heartened and appalled at once.

And now, for our trouble, we have the first stages of Star Wars;
and for president, an unflappable applauder and smiler. The Leader
who gives us the comics straight, as reality; golden of tongue and
cheeky and cheery, the very daddy of denial. The leader. And then
those millions who look to him and desire him dearly, and applaud
him and find the cockles of the heart both numbed and warmed.
And to that degree, as Bonhoeffer stated in another circumstance—
become the Misled.

In a single year of the presidency, unprecedented tragedy struck
the poor of the land. Hundreds of thousands lost Medicaid, lost the
day's single meal, lost day care, lost diet supplements when ill or
pregnant, lost homes. A million of the poor were dropped from food
stamp programs. And at the same time, the very wealthy received
a great predestinatory boost: a substantial income tax cut.

Lord Nuke, of course, rides high, and prevails. The mathematics
of his power is impressive. Someone gifted with doomsday humor
estimated that if his 50,000 warheads, on which he sits enthroned
at this writing, were packaged as Hiroshima-sized bombs, and one
among them exploded each hour, the booms would continue for
almost two centuries. Quite a fireworks indeed.

But alas, fewer and fewer to clap hands. And then, of a certainty,
no one at all.

We did not know, and do not know to this day, what can be done about Lord Nuke; if "knowing what is to be done" is meant to include something commonly called efficiency or results or turnabout.

We knew, and have never doubted, that something must be done; and not anything at all, random or romantic or ill prepared for. Something of integrity and symbolic resonance: something that speaks for us, and perhaps even for all.

We had to improvise as we went, in a tactical sense. So we improvised, and went. There resulted an element of trial and error—and, on occasion, of hilarious lefthandedness. But in the deeper sources, where resolution is forged and blessed, where motives have their mysterious start, there was no improvising at all. One does not improvise a tradition (and tradition, in season and out, was our point): one receives it with open hands, all undeserving.

At depth, the bottomless depth of our predicament, there is, strangely enough, no doubt, though there is much darkness. We were touched by the God of life, we were called in dangerous and denying times, to cherish and convey life; in God's name. To know this was enough.

In such ways, in reflection and prayer and Bible study, we matured. Or so I thought, and was grateful. We were, beyond doubt, a different crew in the eighties than the one, freshly minted and green of mind, who resolved in the late sixties to impede the Vietnam war. We were, at that time, mere beginners in the bristling world.

But as of now, we could qualify, if ever we might, as seasoned veterans. I say it with fear and trembling, knowing that given what awaits, I may merely be prattling into a prevailing wind.

And then I reflect: if there is a God, and if nonviolent resistance is God's work, then the outcome is in other hands than ours. And not merely the outcome, but each step, which, with respect to the end, takes on the dignity of an end in itself; and must be carefully weighed and judged as such. A primary illusion, as we know, being the notion that sloppy or ambiguous means may slouch toward a pure end; and, all unworthily, be crowned by it. Illusion indeed.

Philip and Elizabeth can tell our story with far more detail and verisimilitude than I. On the East Coast, Jonah House has been, for all these years, the unthrottled throat from whence has issued the great No. It is this community that, against all odds, has persisted; given the tics and turnabouts of the acculturated, a near miracle.

A twelve-year presence at the Pentagon, the White House, the State Department, the Congress, the Department of Energy, the Air and Space Museum. The list of mighty fortresses reads like a later Pauline rendering of the principalities and powers. The community set its faces against Lord Nuke, his sponsors, creators, hucksters, emissaries, justifiers. I rejoice to recall those faces, faces of Alleluia, faces that speak for life.

And then the search for ways and means, the tactics and planning, the discipline, the Eucharist, the life together, the Bible study. All the good sustaining and supporting that keep feet on the ground, walking, standing, refusing, unfaltering, not giving up.

And let us never forget: the arrests, the courts, the jails and prisons; the hanging judges and voracious prosecutors, the inert juries, victimized, bored to their jawbones; the loneliness and separation; a constant presence, an argument forever denied, never quenched; that outcry.

The story is barely indicated here. It belongs to the secret annals of the poor; which, being our true history, is, in the nature of things (the nature of power and control, the fear and trembling of those in power and control)—sedulously ignored. The story is told almost nowhere; the silence being part of the great coverup of Lord Nuke. Indeed, he is aware that to ignore those who challenge and impede is to enforce his bad news, and so his empery.

With what a surge of gratitude and love I set down these inadequate words! For I long to be saved from Lord Nuke, his clutch and assault on the soul. From the silken persuasion of psychologists turned theologians (and vice versa) that he does not exist. Or that if he does, it is all to the good (or at least to the lesser evil); it is inevitable, it is the price we pay, he is part of the normal order of things.

So I am prodded to make my peace with Lord Nuke. He declares even that he will be the first signatory of that peace, as pledge of good faith. That there is room for both him and myself in the world. Indeed, that I have potentially much to offer: gifts of moment, which he would willingly honor.

He assures me that a nuclear landscape is no threat to me or anyone of my kind. Look, he suggests: peace once concluded between us two, then my "apostolate," my "mission," my "evangel-ism," can proceed on schedule, freed from these unmannerly, at times devastating, interruptions, court, jail. . . .

In making peace with him, I can, moreover, be of immense help to others, those who vaguely, or starkly, are troubled by his shadow. I can assure them, by force of example and good sense, that there is place in the world both for the Gospel of Christ and this other lord. That there are good works to be done, wounds to be bound up, traumas to be assuaged. In sum, and to the glory of God and ourselves, a new order.

He continues. There is such labor, if this achievement is to be, such large place for the likes of me, as to occupy, enthrall, perplex, awaken; enough for ten lifetimes. And look, I have only one—and why waste and misspend it? Impeding at the same time, as I do, the normal risks attendant on "freedom of scientific inquiry," as well as the normal enmities, hostilities, skirmishes, brushfires, as are con-sonant with the real world. . . .

That indeed (he goes on) throughout history, every nation and people has had its naysayers, its thrivers on doom and doomsday. Would I be one of these, to be abominated by sensible minds, deny-ing as I do (and must do no longer) that enmities among mortals are to be accounted normal (how he loves the word); and so is their working out, by means that "of course" must be continually ques-tioned (he is generosity itself, he bows to the doubters, allows slower minds their crawl).

I need to be saved. I must be saved, lest I be pounded into a shape of moral bafflement, the misshape of normalized abnormality. A shape that resembles no true history and tradition; but only vio-lence and its offspring, its purveyors, its yeasayers.

I cannot do this on my own, save myself. I have no capacity, even for a heresy. I was not born to become a great heterodox, or even a puny one. Pelagianism, even of the fractured kind, is beyond me: too puny of spirit even to play at the Promethean.

No, I must be salvaged, by others. By grace, by Christ. Saved, from "the times, which are evil." So it is said in Scripture, a news simply put, in terms one can take or leave. And despite all, as I believe, good news.

I sit in my room, this dusty autumn day, in my sixty-sixth year.

Uncertain, and yet certain of a few things, a few irreducibles. Among the few, certain of the existence of God. Among the few, of my need of prayer. A need, be it added (or subtracted, as necessary), not to be explained away; a need following on existence, on being in the world. In this world, which is a nuclear one, threatened almost beyond bearing. As most of us, in one fashion or another, from desultory to panicky, know.

Threatened, as only a few comprehend.

I write *comprehend*, and want immediately to modify it. I mean a vivid sense of the incompatible realms and claims staked out when Lord Nuke is granted room: when we inch over, make place; or worse, bend the knee.

For if he reigns (read; reigns supreme), how is the God of life to reign, or even so much as to be granted existence, the world gone altogether gnostic, its kingdom of light quenched, its kingdom of darkness lit by nuclear flares?

The raising of the question means something; at least an incipient truth is in the air, the terms of the conflict are at least granted. Cold comfort, better than none.

I look from my window, on the mix and muddle of my neighborhood, Upper Broadway. It is a world of feigned, fragile normalcy. One must peer closely, walk the street, to come on the truth of things. The poor are well concealed, they are pushed between the cracks. They once had homes; now they come from the cold, night after night, into an improvised parish shelter. They once had food and clothing. Such could be taken for granted. Life was not stuck in the mire of day-to-day survival, a filthy prospect at best.

Very few are aware that such things happen, that such people exist. Mostly the great heave-ho of the street is buying and selling, the stroking of appetite and fantasy. It is an appalling normalcy.

One can easily come to think that this "normal" beat, buying and selling, marrying and giving in marriage, this turning wheel of the world, this noiseless meshing of the gears of things—appetite and money, ego and power, pride of place—that the arrangement, being normal, expresses a very law of the universe.

Indeed, to push matters a little (the matter is always being pushed, first a little, finally a great distance)—that the way of the world is, in fact, the will of God. And finally: nukes are the will of God.

The world runs thus; and religion must go with what goes. The energy by which the great wheel turns is nuclear energy. The ballast and balance of the great wheel is the weight and counterweight of the weapons. They may indeed deter, threaten, and terrorize those who ride the wheel; these are the unpleasant words.

But there are more comforting aspects as well, to be taken gratefully. For without the nukes (without Lord Nuke attentive to the wheel and its gears; indeed, unless the nukes fueled the gears), who could mount the wheel and ride so pleasant a voyage above so fair an Earth? And the weapons are not only the fuel of our passage: they are the sleepless observers, the guardians, surveillants of the way we go and return—and eat and drink, and earn a living, and pay for it.

More: they regulate conscience, a far more delicate flywheel; telling the time for us, nicely adjusting our hope (not too high, not too low), our inner moods, our allowances and boundaries; our secret, finicky, slovenly episodes as well.

They dictate, in sterner moments, who shall live and who die, who be cherished and who thrown away, what is to arouse us, what lull. What capacities shall die in us: indignation, anger; and what flourish: fear, dread of life, cupidity. . . .

They also instruct us, like priests of a newer covenant, in the manner of our death and dying. As they will, in due time, bring these events to pass.

So we are instructed to see ourselves, our place in the world.

No government is capable of speaking for us. Of saying, for example, "We have had enough, the last war has already occurred. Now we will bend ourselves to create a human community, putting to that noble effort all the good things formerly laid out in tribute to war. We shall forthwith begin to take compassion seriously, and justice, and the right use of the Earth. We have become human at last."

What we are asking of one another is that Mars be transformed in Christ. That our species be so transformed: neither victims nor executioners. That conversion of heart lead to conversion of structures; as they inevitably do.

This at least the Christians have to offer, as the warmakers claim the political day, and the multicorporate ties strengthen and thicken like the cables of a gigantic noose and bind humanity in one bundle of terror.

We insist that the arms race and the imminence of war are not primarily matters of policy or economics gone wrong, or Cold War tensions, or the rest. The ferocity of the weapons, their hold on humans, is not to be explained by ideologies East and West, or wrong diplomacy, or avarice. Something else: something more mysterious, awesome, biblical is at work; the age-old claim of death in the world.

Yet the weapons are subject, like every weapon since the knife of Cain, to the judgment of God. God does not cower under the weapons. God is still God: the counterclaim is futile.

This is our secret. It has been freely dwelt on, for years and years, in print, before audiences secular and Christian, in the course of biblical retreats, in courtrooms, at nuclear plague spots. Indeed, for those who could hear, it offered a clue as to why the Christians remained both consistent and imaginative; why they lived and acted as though they believed.

It is quite wonderful, when you think about it. The counterclaim, that death rules the universe and speaks the last word about human destiny—this awakens no dismay or despair. It serves only to illuminate and press the claim of God, to isolate and heighten its splendor and tragedy, its clarity and persistent truth. The Christians have begun to believe. By that token, they are among the few who refuse to believe—in Lord Nuke.

Indeed, among Christians as among others in the land, there flourish all kinds and varieties of "faith." Most of the versions are so short of works as entirely to dissipate a sense of standing on any ground. Its votaries cultivate—ego, in the refined guise of psychology, esthetics, social refinement.

They assemble to clarify their game and assure the outcome. The supposition (everything not so bad, you stroke me, I'll stroke you) winds sinuously about the floors and pillows and hot tubs, like a rational serpent in a sleepy garden. The serpent offers them, Adam and Eve alike, the apple of time, that fruit of sweet forgetting. And has takers, by the thousands.

The Christians had other work in the world. Not many of them: indeed, there were never enough of them for the work to be done.

But some at least, refused to take part in a body count. Closer to the point of their calling, as well as their chagrin; they kept evacuating from their hearts the terror that was the climate of the times.

The disarmament had to start close at hand. We knew it, and we did not know it. Which is to say, we were part, not of the problem (the reality far surpassed such a word), but of the mystery. St. Paul had put it well, with a bluntness that was hardly more comforting now than then: death dwelt in us, the claim lay heavy on us too.

But we found a measure of freedom from the claim, found it in what we hoped might be called faithful works. All those impolitic, uncouth scenes; those tumultuous arrests; those fits and starts that, in the estimate of critics, got nowhere! Those trials, the talk, impassioned, spontaneous, patient, headlong, now mounting gently, now crashing against the Gibralter phizes of judges and juries! The tide fell short, fell back repulsed: the faces of stone yielded nothing.

There have occurred, since 1980, some twenty Plowshares antinuclear actions. And in their legal aftermath, not one acquittal, only a few hung juries. Prompt convictions in every instance, many of our friends in prison.

Most Christians, if they so much as know of our existence, are unaffected or overtly hostile. The bishops are silent or quizzical. The liberal Protestant pulpits that once welcomed me (the Catholic pulpits were never so venturesome) have closed their access. One is told that such activities as we intransigently sponsor are needlessly provocative, will bring down the skies, presumably on innocents or bystanders.

What remains a source of strength is that Christians who work and live among the poor understand our actions. Their faith is a call to the works of faith: the Sojourners, Jonah House, Catholic Worker, The Community for Creative Nonviolence, and so many others. They believe, they walk with us; and with them come the poor and homeless whom they serve.

This has been, for my part, the chief glory and joy of these years. In a wondrous twist of an old adage, the poor we have with us. We go with them, through the gates of hell. On the birthday of Dr. Martin Luther King, Jr., this year, as in years past, the homeless of Emmaus House in East Harlem vigiled and poured blood at the notorious Riverside Research Corporation in New York. Within, in utmost secrecy and isolation and moral unaccountability, scientists and engineers of note prepared for the final round of world violence: the Star Wars scenario.

Another scenario, a far different one, is played at their doors; it is by now familiar, predictable and public. We sit, we pour blood, we pray and sing. And are hauled away by the police.

I think of the gates of hell, of the poor of the city storming the gates. And I think too that we will enter the gates of heaven in their company; they undoubtedly preceding us. For of such as they is the kingdom of God.

So goes this year, the eighty-seventh of the century, the sixty-sixth of my life. Cursed or blessed or both, I live in interesting times. To say the least is to say Alleluia.

Epilogue

The phrase resonates. I hear it like the tolling of a passing bell; or the "Hear ye!" of a tired, pretentious, dusty courtroom, with the buzz of a half-dead fly at the windowpane like a mad recorder of nothing. Summing up proceedings.

In such a place, unlikely and familiar at once, the phrase is esteemed immoderately. One hears it invoked with a kind of last-ditch fervor appropriate to the setting—ignorance, Olympian inflation. The phrase: "Indifference of consequence is no excuse before the law."

Given the world's reasoning, the phrase is invested with considerable logic. The one who acts is presumably responsible; so the act is a form of promissory note. Indeed, a cloud of "expert testimony" is commonly called up by the prosecution, to that effect. The virtuous violators owe a debt, for all their virtue: it must be paid, and in full. Judges and prosecutors are bound to pursue the matter. There is a hangman, if required, to dispose of it.

This is the classic web; its black-robed artisans weave it fine and strong. If you are virtuously indifferent to consequences, you shall nonetheless suffer those consequences. And you had best be ready: dark eventualities await.

Perhaps I make of a simple matter a tedious one. But it has struck me, even haunted me, that in matters of moral accountability, year 30 or thereabouts, the Roman artificers of law and order launched arrows that missed the mark.

We latter-day Christian citizens are no less beset. In a later century, we inherit the baggage and rubble, the defacing and the altering and the superimposition upon, of the original vision.

We are—Americans. We swim in the common waters, altogether (or at least somewhat) at home in that perfumed and polluted tank.

Native element? I swam in it too, I had more than an inkling of appetite and inner schism. I knew the culture sought to draw me under, even as it appalled me. I suspected (probably another illusion) that my moral fog was less total than, say, the fog of the mainline culture. But that, on scrutiny, proved too easy an out. The moral fog was indivisible: all one. Some breathed shallow, others deep. But we were enveloped in the same miasma, a machine that was churning out moral impenetrability. The machine was made in America.

I knew it in the bone. Short of a powerful intervention, we were the people of the lost way.

And to find our way, as I came to sense, we must be attentive to a landmark: the cross. The conclusion held not only for me, but for all, of whatever way. We could interpret it as we might, summon equivalent images from whatever source. Or we could wave the matter huffily aside, as appetite or mood might incline. But there was a heart of the universe, suffering and redeeming at once, and we stilled its beat, or walked to a contrary drumbeat, at our peril.

The foregoing might seem a large treatment of a small episode. My excuse for dwelling on it is a simple one. I was learning, from working with the dying, as I had learned from the blacks in earlier times, and then from the war resisters (and as I would learn from the sanctuary movement and from the Plowshares prisoners—both in the eighties)—learning to ask and ask again, a quite simple question. In the nature of things, the question was destined to occupy me, not for a decade, but for a lifetime.

Indeed, it could be adduced that, were I not so slow a learner, the questions would have occupied me earlier, from my first years. What is a human being, anyway? Did I have the spiritual equipment (the matter must be deemed spiritual) to approach at least a hint of an answer?

Behold our Jesuit, then, among his Jesuit kind, seeking now answers, now something humbler—the right questions.

He knew that he occupied a privileged skin, could claim the perks of education, tradition, family. Could he grow thoughtful about such matters as his own humanity? Or would he accept unquestioningly the place in which, or on which, he had been set from birth—dwelling, as he did, aloft, on a kind of sanctified pylon? And if he stood there dumb, was he not reduced to the status of an immobilized icon of the culture? How then could he presume to be even a gentle shaker of the political and social (and religious) scene?

He could not. The supposition was ridiculous.

More: given the fate of the majority of humans, and given the Gospel directives concerning unselfishness and sacrifice, the supposition that faith could be unquestioning, that his good fortune implied no onus, was a matter of thoughtless enjoyment—this lay under a heavy judgment; it was morally offensive.

It was not that he lacked conviction. His lack was rather an imagination that would set conscience alight. He had a sense of abiding in darkness, swelling in the soil like a living thing, but mole-blind as to his own form.

What did he look like? It was not a question of searching out a mirror, but a metaphor: the "likeness" was his bridge to the world and creation and God; but in certain moods it appeared to him that the bridge was broken at the keystone.

For years, he was searching for a language, an image that would contain and convey certain passionate convictions. The convictions were firmly in place; but they had the limitation of being private, almost jealously so, and in consequence were spoken of only rarely and with reluctance.

He was in a strange position indeed. It came to this, that he was on only the most formal, distant terms with his own soul. He paid respects in passing, lifted his hat, so to speak, to that mysterious entity. A penetrating glance, body and soul; then they passed in the night.

Further, he knew how hard life would go if he was to continue on his path, pledged as he was to nonviolence and serviceability. Hence the barren tribute, which he knew well, and repeated as courtesy required. It went nowhere.

That distance, how he longed to bridge it! Yet it seemed difficult to the point of impossibility to give, or even to lend his heart—even into the tenderest hands; to declare that such convictions as he held in a very grip of death (or of life)—that these, like the shape of a heart or a hand, were meant to be held out, given or lent as required, blind, blank, commendable, heartwarming, handy.

O he knew the words!

Sometimes he was in another grip, a terrible one: the sense that he had broken in two, into the private and public halves of a person. Was it modesty, or cowardice, or a rift in nature? He did not know. It was as though in a nightmare a guillotine crashed down on him, not across his neck, but down the length of his being. And the dream did not dissolve in daylight; it only translated itself into the same waking sense. The sense was one of embarrassment and unease, inhibition and pain, and he scarcely knew how to bear it.

In the whole business of living; in dealings with the larger public, on all sorts of contentions and questions, he was a long time coming to the light; and then only in sparse measure. The light that finally flared in his soul took this form: a religious imagery of sacrifice.

It was a simple image; and given an almost totally secular and self-gratifying culture, it would remain puzzling to most.

Where did the two, the cross and the world, meet? Or perhaps more to the point, could they meet at all? Or were they inevitably two, not one (in the divided image of himself), circling one another, sparring, never at peace?

To push matters further, might this intractable opposition be the contemporary (as well as the perennial) translation of the cross symbol itself? Was he on the track of a clue, a very old story made new—the world and Christ and their essential incompatibility, the world being itself the primal opponent and crusher; and Christ, a consequential God indeed, the solitary and rejected One? Could the two ever meet otherwise than in conflict—a bloody cross-road, a crisis and cross-purpose of soul, of community, of history itself?

The Grand Inquisitor had laid out the terrain, drawn the line. The schema seemed, to the Jesuit, accurate to the bone. We lived in a world of sin; the Inquisitor, for all his icy "realism," was a cynical witness to the truth.

Sin was a matter of a "fallen world," of structures bent to inhuman purpose. This being so, Christ would enter such a world under a cloud. The cloud would envelop and blind the eminences and authorities, set them to hound and destroy.

Mad they went, self-driven under the cloud. But functional too, in that dreadful way of the sea creature who, in spasms of death, locks jaw and teeth on the living. Thus went the final pages of the Gospel, Pilate and Herod and the others. And thus too went those closest to Jesus, their minds grievously clouded with self-doubt and panic. And his executioners, creatures of that justice system of which the Jesuit also heard much.

He was sure of one thing; but in the light of its severe limits, it appeared to him as no great thing to be sure of. It was one thing to follow Christ; it was quite another so to live in the world that the world, however reluctantly, might turn its adamant face in a new direction. The world was like a mountain, he thought, with superhuman faces carved in its stone. Its turning about was the turning of a mountain, north to south, the altering of the axis and poles of existence itself.

He was a mere insect on that monstrous face. He avoided destruction only because such as he could be of no annoyance to the imperial brow. The best he could do: he whispered into ears of stone his riddle—Turn, turn, turn.

Such reflections were of considerable help in a bad time. They turned him, like a firm hand on a blind child, in a new direction.

His work with the dying swept him into deep, even drowning, waters. How convince the church that Christ found a place for everyone, except, ironically, those who denied place to all but themselves? Eventually, with great pain, seeing the pain of the excluded ill and dying, the Jesuit gave up on the bootless task of constructing an "acceptable" argument in favor of someone's rights, the place of this one or that in the church. Gradually and at some cost, he began to concentrate his thought on simpler and closer matters. What did a truly human life look like, in such times as we were enduring?

A certain freedom here. He walked free from the need of self-justifying or of debate, whether modish or rancorous. And at the same time, Christian symbols and images came to life. He approached, he reached a point, at once dazzling and darksome. The point being the political and social consequence of the cross of Jesus.

The point was one of sacrifice. I say it with many a tremble. In my own lifetime, I know how many have invoked the words: cross, sacrifice, gift of life; laid bare also, as they dug about, tributaries polluted and pure, blood and tears: patriotism, loyalty, blood kinship, and so on. What a horror is made of a good and holy thing! A suspect and obscure and even nefarious image.

And still, our central image. Linked to which, fastened to which, our Savior (despite the impurities and crimes of Christians) remains, as I know, as now and again I celebrate in some obscure corner of the heart—remains to all comers and seekers, true and firm and faithful.

I came to know a few things, and the knowledge has not since departed, but stands me in good stead. I learned a modest translation of the word *sacrifice* and its image, the cross. I know that in its pristine rigor and crude innocence—even in its imperialized grandeur, the cross (which is to say, the crucified One) invites the living to the heart of reality, in an embrace as guileless and self-giving as it is indifferent of consequence.

As I walk patiently through life
poems follow close—
blind, dumb, agile, my own shadow,
the mind's dark overflow, the spill of vein
we thought red once, but known now, no.

The poem called death
is unwritten yet. Some day will show
the last first line,
the shadow rise,
a bird of omen
snatch me for its ghost

and a hand somewhere, purposeful as God's
close like two eyes, this book.

Index

Abraham, and Isaac, 120
Action, political, 227–28
Acts of the Apostles, 204
Adams, Henry, 119, 193
Addis Ababa, 160
Affection, 2
Afghanistan, invasion of, 157
Africa, South, visit to, 158–60
AIDS (Acquired Immune Deficiency
  Syndrome), 308–30. See also Gay
  community; Homosexuality; St. Vincent's
  Hospital
Aloysius, Saint, 326
American: Jewish establishment, 285;
  policies, and Nicaragua, 283, 284
Amnesia, 192, 303
Ancestors, as warriors, 109
Angels, 241
Anger, 1, 67
Anselm, 121
Anti-Catholicism, 71
Anti-Semitism, 67, 68, 139, 281
Antithesis, the shadow of, 113
Anti-war sentiment, 187, 190
Apartheid, 159–60. See also Racism
Apocalypse, 90
Aquinas, Thomas, 105
Arab people. See Palestinian people
Arab quarters, in West Jerusalem, 283
Aristotle, 89, 97, 101
Art, sacred, 3
Association of Arab University Graduates,
  speech to, 281
Auschwitz, 209, 291. See also
  Extermination Camps
Authority, 145

Baltimore Four action, 201, 203, 205–6,
  208–10
Barth, Karl, 256
Beasts, 1, 2, 334
Beauty, "terrible," 312
Being, preternatural, 1
Berrigan, Agnes (aunt), 27
Berrigan, Elizabeth (aunt), 27
Berrigan, Freda (mother), 8–26, 30, 44,
  148, 234–35; equanimity of, 209–10;

gratitude towards, 72–73; hospitalization
  of, in 1970, 249; illness of, 75–76;
  moral clarity of, 51–52; and Philip's
  illness, 273–74; retirement of, 150; self-
  possession of, 14–17
Berrigan, James, 11–13, 52
Berrigan, Jerome, 12–13, 33, 54, 234;
  antinuclear actions of, 242
Berrigan, John, 11–13, 52
Berrigan, John (uncle), 29
Berrigan, Josephine, 25, 29
Berrigan, Louise (grandmother), 8–9, 13–
  14
Berrigan, Margaret (aunt), 27–28
Berrigan, Ned (uncle), 25, 28–29
Berrigan, Philip, 12–13, 33, 38, 144, 170;
  and the alliance of poverty and war,
  175–76; and the Baltimore Four action,
  199–201, 205–6, 208–10; and the
  Catonsville action, 216–18, 220–22,
  229–32, 235, 239; completion of his
  first book, 176; departure from his
  religious order, 268; exile of, 177; at the
  Harrisburg trial, 268–69; illness of, 273–
  74; and Jonah House, 336–37; marriage
  to Elizabeth McAlister, 199, 268; and the
  Plowshares act, 291; poem dedicated to,
  267; in prison, 250, 252, 262; visit to
  Woodstock, 105
Berrigan, Thomas (brother), 10–13, 52
Berrigan, Thomas (father), 21, 23–28, 40–
  44, 50, 147–48; characterization of, 7–
  8, 17–20; charm and warmth of, 64–65;
  fits of anger, 8, 11; last days of, 232–35;
  loyalties of, 24–25; pain of life with, 54;
  and Philip's illness, 273–74; poetic
  ambitions of, 62–64; and reading books,
  61–62; relationship with, 73; retirement
  of, 149–50; shadow of, 61
Bible, the, 164, 227, 255, 323
Blessed Virgin, 125
Block Island, 252–54, 257, 278, 279, 324
B'nai B'rith, 281
Bolsheviki, 95
Bomb, the, 105, 108
Bonhoeffer, Dietrich, 243, 335
Bread and Puppet Theater, 244

Breath, 81
Brooklyn Preparatory School, 138
Buber, Martin, 287
Buddhist: concentration of mind, 248;
  ecstasy, 173; monks, in Vietnam, 224;
  saying, regarding spirit, 140
Buh, Monsignor Joseph, 20

Cain, knife of, 334, 341
Caiphas, 120, 292
Cairo, 160
Cambodia, invasion of, 245
Camus, Albert, 95, 160
Cantonsville action, 136, 216–22, 224;
  and the play, *The Trial of the
  Cantonsville Nine,* 248, 250, 266;
  reaction to, 225; trial of, 229–32, 235,
  238–40
Cassandra, 99
Cataclysm, 5
Catholic: approval of the Vietnam war,
  170–71; church, 14–15, 66; gays, 317,
  324–25, 329
Catholicism: anti—, 71; and pacifism, 142
Catholic Peace Fellowship, 187
Catholic resistance, 252
Center: as a core or heart, 173; and the
  periphery, of events, 13; true, 163
Charity, and justice, 175–76
Charmot, Pere, 124, 125–30
Chesterton, G. K., 166, 181
Chicago Seven, the, 212
Christ, 81, 82, 108, 121, 257; and the
  believing community, 122; Body of, 99;
  to follow, 348; and freedom, 103; glance
  of, 144; icon of, 256; images of, 91,
  104; life of, 92; and love of one's
  enemies, 223; and Mars, 340; mind of,
  173; moral lucidity of, 123; moral
  statements of, 223; sacrifice of, 180,
  292; as a Surrogate of God, 129; of the
  Testament, 223; view of the human,
  223; visions of, 129; and war, 104, 222;
  and the world, 347
Christian Peace Conference, 161–63, 164
Christians: calling of, 121–22; in eastern
  Europe, 153–54, 156–58; and Jews,
  gathering of, 282; socialist, 157; tradition
  of nonviolence among, 167, 169, 197
Church, the: image of, 173; and the state,
  137, 145, 155, 268; and the Vietnam
  war, 177, 181–82
Cicero, 97
Civil disobedience, 160, 196
Civilian Conservation Corps, 12
Civil Rights Movement, 167, 266
Clark, Ramsey, 269
Clergy and Laity Concerned, 179, 187
Cold War, 89, 137, 154, 162, 341
College of New Resources, 298–99

Communion, 30, 33, 78
Communism, 171
Community, Jesuit commitment to, 120
Community for Creative Nonviolence, 342
Compassion, 2, 174, 183, 212, 289;
  attitude towards, 340; of Christ, 180
Confirmation, 30
Conflict, inner, 119–20, 121
Conrad, Joseph, 179
Conscience, 196, 206, 211, 255; acts of,
  239, 304–5; centrist, 172; conventional,
  334; freedom to concentrate on, 220;
  the gift of, 121; institution vs., 146; and
  nuclear weapons, 340; and
  professionalism, 151, 305; public, 137,
  174; quest of, 313; untroubled, amidst
  great crimes, 178
Consistency, 245
Consumerism, 278
Contra war, 283
Coolidge, Calvin, 271–72
Cornell, Ezra, 312, 313
Cornell University, 136, 186–214; antiwar
  rally at, 243; gay community at, 312–14
Cosmology, 25, 101
Coughlin, Charles E., Father, 66–71
Courage, 1, 5, 134, 202, 220
Creation, 4, 138, 187
Cross, the, 349
Cushing, Richard (archbishop), 116–17
Czechoslovakia, Christians of, 156–58

Danbury prison, 259–66, 314–16
Dante, 245, 270, 311
Darst, David, 237–38
Davidson, Gordon, 248
Day, Dorothy, 69–72, 141, 144, 229; and
  opposition to the Vietnam War, 171–73
D-day, 105
Death, 21, 50, 127–28, 257, 275; calling
  the shots, 321; claim of, in the world,
  341; gods of, 325; and the hunter and
  the hunted, 6; image of, 242–43, 251;
  immunity from, 326; and Lord Nuke,
  334; and nuclear weapons, 340; and
  rebirth, 131, 322
De Chardin, Teilhard, 114
Declaration on the Jews, 178
Defarge, Madame, 133–35
De Gaulle, Charles, 128
Deicide, 5
De la Colombiere, Claude, 129
De Lubac, Henri, 114, 125
Depression, the, 12, 65
Dissidents, disposing of, 267
Divine, the mind's search for the, 121
Dixon, Frances, 32
Dominicans, 124
Donnelly, Mary, 257–58
Douglass, Boyd, 269–70

Dream, the, 309–11
Dresden, 157

Earth, 49, 50, 90, 221, 241; mother, 21;
  right use of the, 340
Education, 59
Ego, 3, 122, 127, 159
Eliot, T. S., 96, 278
Emerson, Ralph Waldo, 193, 229
Empathy, 101
Ethics, 101
Ethiopia, 160
Eucharist, 58, 222, 227, 297, 337
Eumenidies, 53
Europe, Eastern, visits to, 153–58, 161
Evil, 2, 4
Exodus, book of, 84
Extermination Camps, under Hitler, 164,
  178

Fabric, of life, 44, 152
Factionalism, 67
Faith, 3, 14, 101, 117, 217; and bad faith,
  295; and the church, 108; communality
  of, 151; and immunity from death, 326;
  and natural truths, 127; searching mind
  of, 113, 221
Fall, the, 49
Fanaticism, 124
Fate, 12, 53
FBI (Federal Bureau of Investigation), 243–
  45, 248–49, 266, 269–70
Fear, 2
Finisterre, 227–28
Finn, Francis, 76
Folklore, 2, 14
Foster, Warden, 222
Fox and Geese (game), 12–13
Francis of Assisi, Saint, 1–3, 326
Francois de Sales, Saint, 128
Franklin, Benjamin, 189
Freedom, 157, 221, 348; American, 158;
  attainment of, 103–4; denial of, 48; and
  fate, 53; Fighters, 333; human, and
  Christ, 103–4; personal, 104; sense of,
  47, 48; in theory and practice, 310;
  through choosing, 217
Friendship, 79, 138, 152, 179, 243; as the
  heart of life, 226; as strength, 245; tests
  of, 178, 207; value of, 218
Fromhart, Louise (grandmother), 9–10, 22,
  66
Frost, Robert, 96

Gaffney, Marcella, 32–33, 73–74
Galilee, 284, 286
Game: of Creation, 4; rules of the, 13
Gandhi, Mahatma, 200, 287, 335
Gay community, 310–11; at Cornell, 312–
  14. See also Homosexuality

Générale, Madame, 152–53
General Electric, nuclear factory of, 290
Genesis, 183
God, 107, 122, 292, 306; absence of,
  250; and creation, 138, 346; existence
  of, 48, 101, 105, 339; faith in, 48–49;
  glory of, 102; goodness of, 58; of
  heterodoxy, 162; of Ironies, 171; of Job,
  248; judgment of, 127, 341; Kingdom
  of, 158; love of, 326; mercy of, 127;
  and nonviolent resistance, 336; and the
  outcast, 159; and the problem of evil,
  312; providence of, 49, 292; service of,
  127; spirit of, 103; Surrogate of, 129;
  will of. See Will of God
Golan Heights, 283, 286
Goodman, Paul, 107
Goodness, 2
Gospel, 70, 110, 174, 181, 277;
  directives, 346; freedom of the, 103;
  integrity of the, 257
Grail, quest for the, 79

Hamlet, 138
Hanoi, 136; trip to, 211–14, 216
Harrisburg trial, 252, 268–71
Hate, 47
Hatred, 96
Hayden, Tom, 212
Healer, 275–77
Heart, 21, 119, 186, 294; change of, in
  the legend of Saint Francis and the wolf,
  1–2; of reality, 349; Sacred, Feast of the,
  129; of things, 4, 173; time as, 304
Heaven, 89; and Hell, 50, 127
Heschel, Abraham, 178–79
Hint, and Breath and Pulse, 81
Hiroshima, 89, 105, 107–8, 157, 319
History, 3, 283; significance of, in war,
  109
Hitler, Adolph, 164, 203. See also
  Auschwitz
Hoffa, Jimmy, 235
Hollywood, 62
Holy Communion, 48, 53
Holy Outlaw, The (documentary), 252
Holy Spirit. See Spirit
Holy Trinity, 58
Homer, 97
Homicide, 5
Homosexuality, 317, 329. See also Gay
  community
Hoover, J. Edgar, 249, 266, 271
Hope, 2, 275, 304, 309
Howlett, Miss., 31
Humanism, 99, 102, 129
Hunter, and the hunted, 6
Hurley, Dennis (archbishop), 158

Identity, 109

Ignatius, Father, 89, 93, 102, 127; as a child of his times, 128; and the passion for the perfect, 103; sons of, 110
Images: of hope and resolve, 304; and the One, 81–82; poetic, creation of, 96; of sacrifice, 349
Imagination, 2, 62, 134, 139, 145; poetic, 96; renewal of, 69; works of, rejection of, 101–2
Immortality, 309
Indians, Chippewa, 20
Innocence, 157, 183, 230
Integrity, 157, 183, 219; of the action, 248; of the Gospel, 257; need for, 247
International House, 150
Intuition, and rightness, 221–22
Iron Range, 21
Irons, Jeremy, 82
Iroquois nations, 141
Isaiah, book of, 204
Israel, 280–89

Jackson State, 248
Jehovah, 189
Jerusalem, 281, 283, 284
Jesuits, 19, 61, 72, 83; commitment to community among, 120; as an enigma, 122; entry into the order of, 85–88
Jesus, 58, 204–5, 241, 292, 329; cross of, 348; as a prisoner of war, 202. See also Christ
Jews, 280; and Christians, gathering of, 282. See also Anti-Semitism
Joan of Arc, 77, 137
John, Gospel of, 197, 292–93
John of the Cross, Saint, 249–50
John XXIII (pope), 89, 111, 125, 178, 271; election of, 147
Jonah House, 342
Jones, Mother, 58
Joy, 3
Judgment, 50, 127; moral, 99, 137, 203
Jupiter, 18
Justice, 46, 100, 183, 268; and peace, 184; quest for, 69, 340; works of, 175
Juvenal, 97

Kennedy, John F., 165, 166
Kent State, 248
Kierkegaard, Søren, 121
King, Martin Luther, Jr., 164, 200, 300, 335, 342
Kingdom, the, 128
King of Prussia, Pennsylvania, 290
Knox, Ronald, 107
Korea, 89

Language: command of, 101; of the dead, 96
Laos, 214

Laporte, Roger, 179–80
Latin America, 136, 147, 322; exile to, 182–83
Law, of the Universe, 102
Lawgiver, 102
Left Bank, in Jerusalem, 284
LeMoyne College, 136, 146, 150–51
Letter of Paul to the Romans, 157
Lewis, Tom, 209, 221–22, 227, 232, 235
Little, Joanne, 281
Livermore action, 303–4
Livermore Laboratories, 303, 306, 319
Liverpool, 273
Lord Nuke, 334–6, 337, 340, 341
Love, 2, 23, 275, 294; harsh privileges of, 278; of humankind, 129; power of, and Death, 6
Lua, Sister Mary, 57–60
Luther, 113

McAllister, Elizabeth, 199–200, 268, 336
McNeill, John, 317–18
Maison des Étudiants, 152–53
Margaret Mary, Sister, 129
Mars, 340
Martyrology, 102
Mary, Virgin, 58
Marx, Karl, 229
Members of Dignity, 317. See also Catholic, gays; Gay community
Memory, 8
Mennonites, 202
Merton, Thomas, 107, 136, 144, 160
Metaphors, 242, 346; drawn from nature, 153; of warmaking, 164
Methuselah, 86
Metro-Goldwyn-Mayer, 62
Meyer, Karl, 141–42
Miasma, 122, 181, 345
Mind, life of the, 227–28
Miracles, 2, 5
Miriam, 134
Mischi, George, 246
Montgomery County, blacks in, 291. See also Apartheid; Racism
Moore, Marianne, 140
Moral: coherence, 239, 312; judgment, and war, 99, 137, 203; lucidity of Christ, 123; statements of Christ, 223; teachings of popes, 223; understanding, 139; war as, 204, 205, 223
Morality, 138, 174; of a "me to" church, 223. See also Charity; Justice; Nonviolence
Moses, 171
Mystery, the, 159, 227, 248

National Council of Churches, 281
National Recovery Act, 65
Nativity Center, 138

Nature, 5. See also Earth
Navarro, Ramon, 135, 136
Neuhaus, Richard, 178, 179
Newman, Edwin, 247
Newman, John Henry (cardinal), 89
New Orleans, 294
Nicaragua, and American policies, 283, 284
Niebuhr, Reinhold, 100
Nine of Catonsville. See Cantonsville action
Nixon, Richard M., 235, 245, 255
Nonviolence, 69, 109, 174, 302, 346; Christian tradition of, 167, 169, 197; as God's work, 336. See also Violence; War
Norm, war as the, 166, 203
Normalcy, 212, 256, 311, 339; and the media, 243; and social action, 224–25
North, true, 102
Nostalgia, 96
Nuclear: fate, 293; freeze, 164; threat, 339; weapons, 137, 220, 303, 319, 340–42

Obedience, 144, 180; as a church matter, 15; of the Jesuits, 103
O'Briens, the, 74
Occam's razor, 102
Olympus, 15
One, the, 81, 127, 248; crucified, 349; symbol of, 108
Onondaga, Lake, 22–23, 30, 79
Order: cosmic, 103; disorderly, passion for, 173; divine, 143; at the heart of things, 173; of Visitation, 129
Orphic myths, 282
Orthodoxy, 71, 113, 161–62
Orwell, George, 107

Pacelli, Eugenio Maria Giovanni (cardinal), 68. See also Pius XII (pope)
Pacifism, 142. See also Nonviolence
Paine, Tom, 189
Palestinian people, 283–85, 287–89
Pape, Honor, 10
Pascal, 1, 122, 186
Passion: antiwar, 196; for justice, 121; for orderly disorder, 173; for survival, 139
Passover, 227
Paul, Saint, 94, 110, 342
Peace, 109, 164, 245. See also Peacemaking
Peace Corps, 147, 299
Peacemaking, 163–65, 173, 183–84, 215
Peguy, poem of, 137
Pelagianism, 338
Pentagon, protest at the, 206–7, 301
Perkins, James, 192–95
Person, outlawing of the, 201–2
Philosophy, 117

Phu, Dien Bien, 124
Pike, James (bishop), 254, 255
Pirandello, drama of, 197
Pius XII (pope), 124, 142. See also Pacelli, Eugenio Maria Giovanni
Plane of Jars, 214
Plowshares act, 290–93
Plowshares antinuclear actions, 342
Poetry, 14, 62–64, 96, 139–40
Politics, superpower, 104
Pontifex Maximus, 81
Pound, Ezra, 96
Powell, Mamie, 55–56
Power: disease of, 143, 145; lust for, 122
Prague, 155, 161
Prayer, 119, 127, 227, 339
Pretoria, 158
Priesthood, 119, 138
Promise, the, 138
Psychology, 101, 252
Pulse, 81

Quakers, 202, 210, 282

Racism, 139, 159–60, 161, 278, 291. See also Apartheid
Ramallah, 284
Reagan, Ronald, 283, 299
Reality, 49, 79
Religion: at Cornell, 190; and crime, commingling of, 178; and the military, 295–98; as a symbolic vehicle, 188; and the world, 340
Remembrance, 192
Ressurection, 322
Revelation, and science, 114
Romanticism, 96
Roosevelt, Franklin Delano, recovery program of, 67
Rose, Angelo, 276–77, 279
Russia, visit to, 161

Sacrament, 227
Sacre Coeur, nuns of, 135
Sacred, the, and the profane, 108
Sacrifice, 348–49
Saint John the Baptist Grammar School, 33–36, 46, 76
St. Vincent's Hospital, 309, 319, 323
Salus III, Samuel, 291–92
Savior, blood of the, 179
Science, "value free," 193–94
SDS leaders, 225, 227
Sermon on the Mount, 72, 128, 222
Sexism, 278
Shakespeare, William, 63, 76
Shekinah, 84, 179, 286
Silence, 159, 190, 205

Sin, 49, 53, 127; drama of, 323; original, war as, 165–66; of silence, 190; world of, 347
Sinai, 15
Sinead, son of, 82
Smith, Al, 68, 71
Socrates, 58
Sojourner Truth, 229
Solomon, 81
Sophocles, 97
Soul, 49, 134, 139, 221, 296; conflict in the, 119; of peacemaking, 163–65; relation to, 346; and the world, 140
Source, hunger for the, 4
Spellman, Francis (cardinal), 137, 172, 203, 268
Spinal condition, onset of, 274–75
Spirit, 46, 49, 81, 90, 277; and a plan of life, 92
Spiritual Exercises, 104, 127
Star Wars, 333, 335, 343
State, the, 283; and the church, 137, 145, 155, 268
Stringfellow, William, 253–58, 277–79
Sullivan, William, 214
Supermen, men as, 14
Survival, human, 311

Taylor Chapel, firebombing of, 236
Technology, 104
Tenderness, 41
Teresa of Avila, 50, 69
Tertianship, 133
Theology, 111–12, 117–18, 120; anti-Barthian, 127; creativity in, 124; Jesuit, 113; natural, 101, 127; Protestant, 113
Theory, and practice, 71
Thompson, Marion (judge), 230–31
Thoreau, Henry David, 193
Time, 45, 49, 94; and hope, 304–5; as kind, 55
Time Without Number (book), publication of, 140
Towne, Anthony, 253–56
Townsend, Dr., 67
Trial of the Cantonsville Nine, The (play), 248, 250, 266. See also Cantonsville action
Trinity, 34
Trust, sublime, 3
Truth, 3, 110, 127, 255; Buddhist, 3–4; order of, 173

Universe, law of, 102
University: of Bradford, 300–301; of California, 303; Cornell, 136, 186–214, 243, 312–14; of Detroit, 301

Van Gogh, Vincent, 87
Vatican II (Second Vatican Council), 89, 118, 125, 178, 318
Vietnamese civilians, 210–12, 214, 226
Vietnam War, 89, 157, 161, 167; attitude towards, at Cornell, 189–214, 243; bombings of, 301; and the church, 177, 181–82; and the invasion of Cambodia, 245; opposition to, 170–71; protest against, by Buddhist monks, 224. See also War
Violence, 109, 122, 166, 204; and cruelty, 159; and the firebombing of Taylor Chapel, 236–37; legalized, 209; as normal, 8, 225. See also Nonviolence; War
Vision, 79, 104; —s, of Christ, 129

War: anti—, sentiment, 187, 190; and Christ, 104, 222; and Christianity, 108–9, 112; between "Christian nations," 224; the Cold, 89, 137, 154, 162, 341; of competing talent, 98; demonstrations against, at Cornell, 189–215; First World. See World War I; god of, 177; and history, 109; machine, 163, 165; and the media, 268; as moral, 204, 205, 223; and morality, 174; and moral judgment, 99, 137, 203; nature of, 109; as the norm, 166, 203; as original sin, 166, 205; and peace, 109; politics of, 154; and poverty, alliance of, 69, 175; question of, 137, 204; Second World. See World War II; soul of, 163–64; Vietnam. See Vietnam War
Warmaking, 99, 163–65, 278. See also Peacemaking
Weapons, nuclear, 137, 220, 303, 319, 339–42
Weathermen, the, 225, 227, 229, 243
West Bank, occupation of the, 283
Weston, 111
White Rose group, 164
White School, the, 31–37
Will, divine, 101, 109–10
Will of God, 15, 77, 110, 143, 169; and nuclear weapons, 339; and poverty, 175; and the way of the world, 339
Winton, 5, 8
Wolf, figure of, 1–3
Word, and act, 121–22
World War I, 130
World War II, 98–100, 105, 126, 141

Yin, and Yang, 120
Young Christian Workers, 138

Zinn, Howard, 212, 213–14